The Global Divergence of Democracies

A *Journal of Democracy* Book

•

BOOKS IN THE SERIES

Edited by Larry Diamond and Marc F. Plattner

Globalization, Power, and Democracy (2000)
(Edited by Marc F. Plattner and Aleksander Smolar)

The Democratic Invention (2000)
(Edited by Marc F. Plattner and João Carlos Espada)

Democratization in Africa (1999)

Democracy in East Asia (1998)

Consolidating the Third Wave Democracies (1997)
(with Yun-han Chu and Hung-mao Tien)

Civil-Military Relations and Democracy (1996)

The Global Resurgence of Democracy, 2nd ed. (1996)

Economic Reform and Democracy (1995)

Nationalism, Ethnic Conflict, and Democracy (1994)

Capitalism, Socialism, and Democracy Revisited (1993)

Published under the auspices of

the International Forum for Democratic Studies

The Global Divergence of Democracies

Edited by Larry Diamond
and Marc F. Plattner

The Johns Hopkins University Press

Baltimore and London

9 8 7 6 5 4 3 2 1

Chapters in this volume appeared in the following issues of the *Journal of Democracy:* chapter 3, April 1995; chapter 5, July 1995; chapter 13, January 1996; chapters 8 and 9, April 1996; chapters 10 and 11, October 1996; chapter 6, January 1997; chapter 15, July 1997; chapter 20, October 1997; chapter 25, January 1998; chapter 12, April 1998; chapter 14, July 1998; chapter 18, October 1998; chapters 2 and 23, January 1999; chapters 1, 4, 7, and 19, July 1999; chapter 16, October 1999; chapters 21 and 22, April 2000; and chapters 17, 24, and 26, July 2000. Chapter 17 copyright © 2000 Charles Fried; for all reproduction rights, please contact the Johns Hopkins University Press.

The Johns Hopkins University Press
2715 North Charles Street
Baltimore, Maryland 21218-4363
The Johns Hopkins Press Ltd. London

Library of Congress Cataloging-in-Publication Data

The Global Divergence of Democracies / edited by Larry Diamond and Marc F. Plattner.
    p.   cm. — (A Journal of Democracy book)
  Includes bibliographical references and index.
  ISBN 0-8018-6842-4 (alk. paper)
    1. Democracy--Cross-cultural studies. I. Diamond, Larry Jay. II. Plattner, Marc F., 1945- III. Series.

JC423 .G59 2001
321.8--dc21

                                     2001029611

A catalog record for this book is available from the British Library.

CONTENTS

Acknowledgments vii

Introduction
Larry Diamond and Marc F. Plattner ix

I. Democracy and Liberty: Universal Values?

1. Democracy as a Universal Value
   Amartya Sen 3

2. Buddhism, Asian Values, and Democracy
   His Holiness the Dalai Lama 18

3. Confucianism and Democracy
   Francis Fukuyama 23

4. Muslims and Democracy
   Abdou Filali-Ansary 37

5. How Far Can Free Government Travel?
   Giovanni Sartori 52

6. Democracy and Liberty: The Cultural Connection
   Russell Bova 63

7. From Liberalism to Liberal Democracy
   Marc F. Plattner 78

II. Consolidating Democracy

8. Toward Consolidated Democracies
   Juan J. Linz and Alfred Stepan 93

9. Illusions about Consolidation
   Guillermo O'Donnell 113

10. O'Donnell's "Illusions": A Rejoinder
    Richard Gunther, P. Nikiforos Diamandouros, and Hans Jürgen Puhle 131

11. Illusions and Conceptual Flaws: A Response
    Guillermo O'Donnell 140

12. What Is Democratic Consolidation?
    Andreas Schedler 149

III. Foundations of Successful Democracy

13. What Makes Democracies Endure?
*Adam Przeworski, Michael E. Alvarez, José Antonio Cheibub,
and Fernando Limongi*   167

14. Party Systems in the Third Wave
Scott Mainwaring   185

15. What Makes Elections Free and Fair?
Jørgen Elklit and Palle Svensson   200

16. Federalism and Democracy: Beyond the U.S. Model
Alfred Stepan   215

17. Markets, Law, and Democracy
Charles Fried   231

18. Free Politics and Free Markets in Latin America
Jorge I. Domínguez   245

19. A New Jurisprudence for Africa
H. Kwasi Prempeh   260

20. How Democracies Control the Military
Richard H. Kohn   275

IV. Prospects and Challenges for Democracy in the New Century

21. A Quarter-Century of Declining Confidence
Susan J. Pharr, Robert D. Putnam, and Russell J. Dalton   291

22. Latin America at the Century's Turn
Abraham F. Lowenthal   312

23. The Postcommunist Divide
Jacques Rupnik   327

24. Putin's Russia: One Step Forward, Two Steps Back
Michael McFaul   333

25. Will China Democratize?
Michel Oksenberg   348

26. Is Pakistan the (Reverse) Wave of the Future?
Larry Diamond   355

Index   371

ACKNOWLEDGMENTS

Although this volume is the eleventh in the series of *Journal of Democracy* books to be published by the Johns Hopkins University Press (JHUP), it is only the second that attempts to cover a broad range of issues rather than focusing on a particular aspect of democracy. Our first general anthology, *The Global Resurgence of Democracy,* was also the very first book in the series, appearing in 1993. A few years later, we saw a clear need to update it, and a second, revised edition was published in 1996; about half the material in the revised edition was new, but we felt comfortable publishing it under the original title. When we began to think about whether to publish a third edition of *The Global Resurgence,* however, it seemed to us (and to our editor at the Johns Hopkins University Press and invaluable advisor Henry Tom) that it would make more sense to publish a wholly new volume instead.

This was by no means because we thought that all the material in our previous anthology was dated. Indeed, it contains numerous essays on such subjects as constitutional design and civil society that are of perennial interest, and we are sure that it will continue to be sought out by both teachers and students of democracy. Nonetheless, as we elaborate in the Introduction to this volume, the historical and international context changed so markedly between the mid-1990s and the beginning of the new century that a new focus and a new title seemed to be required. The global resurgence of democracy was the dominant trend of the earlier period; today it is the global *divergence* of democracies that commands attention. Fortunately, the *Journal* has published a wealth of new material in recent years addressing this theme.

As veteran editors, we have learned that the publication of a book is a collaborative enterprise, and that this is even more true of the publication of a quarterly journal, which is the equivalent of producing a book every three months. Our names appear on the cover of this volume, but the contributions of many others who do not receive such billing are indispensable, and we are pleased to have an opportunity to thank them here. We must begin with the staff of the *Journal.* Its current staff—Zerxes Spencer, Stephanie Lewis, Jordan Branch, and Kristin Helz—

have done a superb job of preparing this volume for press, without slackening in their efforts at producing the *Journal*. Stephanie Lewis, our production editor, has borne a particularly heavy responsibility, and she has discharged it magnificently. Alice Carter, Larry Diamond's assistant at the Hoover Institution, compiled the index with dedication and skill. The essays in this collection also reflect the editorial efforts of past *Journal* editors—notably Phil Costopoulos and Mark Eckert, as well as Miriam Kramer and Mahindan Kanakaratnam.

A critical contribution to our work is made by our colleagues at the Johns Hopkins University Press, which publishes the *Journal* as well as our book series. Carol Hamblen, our liaison at JHUP's Journals Division, has worked with us for many years now, and she has always been responsive, efficient, and agreeable. Henry Tom, our editor at JHUP's Books Division, has not only made sure that our books are published quickly and in handsome editions, he has been a wise counselor on more substantive matters as well.

Next, we want to thank the *Journal*'s parent organization, the National Endowment for Democracy, whose Board of Directors and president, Carl Gershman, have given us unstinting support from the outset. We have also benefited enormously from the help of many others at the Endowment, especially from the advice and contacts of its program staff. The *Journal* receives significant financial support from the Endowment, but it could not survive without contributions from private sources as well. We thank all those foundations that have assisted us in recent years, including the Carnegie Corporation of New York and the Donner Canadian Foundation. Our greatest debt of gratitude, however, is owed to the Lynde and Harry Bradley Foundation, which has steadily supported the *Journal* since its founding in 1989. Whatever success we have achieved would not have been possible without the Bradley Foundation's generous assistance.

Last, but certainly not least, we want to thank not only the authors whose essays appear in this volume but all those who have contributed to the pages of the *Journal*. Editors are wholly dependent upon the manuscripts that they receive, and we are delighted to be able to publish the work of so many distinguished scholars and insightful writers in the pages that follow.

INTRODUCTION

Larry Diamond and Marc F. Plattner

This book is the eleventh volume of essays that have been gathered together for publication by the *Journal of Democracy* over the past decade. When the *Journal* began publishing in January 1990, the "third wave" of democratization had only just reached Eastern Europe. The Soviet Union still existed and was still a dictatorship. There were only a handful of democracies in Africa. By the end of 1990, there were only 76 democracies in the world, less than half of all the independent states. Five years later, democracy had swept through every major region of the world except the Middle East. By the end of 1995, there were (in the judgment of Freedom House) 117 democracies, and these comprised about three-fifths of all the states in the world. The pattern has held more or less steady during the past five years. By the end of 2000, Freedom House classified 120 countries as electoral democracies (see Table 1 on the following page). One could quibble with a few of its judgments about particular countries, but the overall pattern is striking. A quarter-century after the inception of the third wave, and a decade after regional waves of democratization hit the postcommunist world and Africa, global democratic progress in the world seems to be holding steady.

To be sure, democracy is no longer in a state of "global resurgence" (the title we gave to our first *Journal of Democracy* anthology in 1993 and to the second, revised edition in 1996). The tremendous momentum of democratic expansion that characterized the 1980s and the first half of the 1990s has drawn to a halt. Significantly, this halt has not yet been followed by a "reverse wave" of democratic breakdowns, though as Larry Diamond observes in the concluding chapter of this volume, the October 1999 military coup in Pakistan highlights more general problems of governance that threaten many insecure democracies around the world.

For the time being, the discernible trend is the "global divergence of democracies"—the title we have given the present volume. Democracy remains unchallenged as a global model and ideal of governance. The values of freedom, human rights, and popular sovereignty have continued to gain in the world. The first section of this volume presents

TABLE I—NUMBER OF ELECTORAL DEMOCRACIES 1974, 1988–2000

YEAR	NO. OF DEMOCRACIES	NO. OF COUNTRIES	DEMOCRACIES AS A % OF ALL COUNTRIES	ANNUAL RATE OF INCREASE IN DEMOCRACIES (%)
1974	39	142	27.50	n/a
1988	66	167	39.50	n/a
1990	76	165	46.10	n/a
1991	91	183	49.70	19.70
1992	99	186	53.20	8.10
1993	108	190	56.80	8.30
1994	114	191	59.70	5.30
1995	117	191	61.30	2.60
1996	118	191	61.80	0.90
1997	117	191	61.30	-0.90
1998	117	191	61.30	0
1999	120	192	62.50	2.60
2000	120	192	62.50	0

Sources: Data from Freedom House, Freedom in the World: The Annual Survey of Political Rights and Civil Liberties, 1990–91, 1991–92, 1992–93, 1993–94, 1994–95, 1995–96, 1996–97, 1997–98, 1998–99, 1999–2000 (New York: Freedom House, 1991 and years following); and Aili Piano and Arch Puddington, "The 2000 Freedom House Survey: Gains Offset Losses," Journal of Democracy 12 (January 2001).
Note: Figures for 1990–2000 are for the end of the calendar year. Figures for 1974 estimate the number of democracies in the world in April 1974, at the inception of the third wave.

a few outstanding examples of the accumulating body of argument and evidence in favor of the universality of democratic principles and their basic compatibility with diverse religious and cultural traditions. At the same time, the impressive global resilience of democracy has been paralleled by a more subtle and less favorable trend. Even setting aside the long-established democracies of Europe, North America, Japan, and Australia, the remaining 90 or so democracies increasingly diverge among themselves, not only in the nature of their institutional structures, but in the quality and depth of their democracy, and hence in their progress toward consolidation.

This divergence is visible in terms of regional patterns, though there is significant variation within regions as well. Regions of the world vary quite dramatically in the distribution of both electoral democracy and liberal democracy. All democracies—in the minimal sense of electoral democracies—share at least one broad, essential requirement: The principal positions of political power are filled through regular, free, and fair elections among competing parties, and it is possible for an incumbent government to be turned out of office in those elections. The standard for electoral democracy—what constitutes "free and fair"— is more ambiguous than is often appreciated. It could be argued that, as a result of the dubious conduct of their recent national elections, such prominent multiparty states as Russia, Ukraine, Nigeria, and Indonesia fall into a gray area that is neither clearly democratic nor clearly undemocratic. One may also dispute whether some states classified by Freedom House as democracies, such as Liberia and Sierra Leone, really pass the test.

However we judge them, elections are only one dimension of democracy. The quality of a democracy also depends on its levels of freedom, pluralism, justice, and accountability. The deeper level of *liberal* democracy requires the following:

• Freedom of belief, expression, organization, protest, and other civil liberties, including protection from political terror and unjustified imprisonment.

• A rule of law under which all citizens are treated equally and due process is secure.

• The political independence and neutrality of the judiciary and of other institutions of "horizontal accountability" that check the abuse of power, such as electoral administration, the audit, and the central bank.

• An open, pluralistic civil society, including free mass media;

• Civilian control over the military.[1]

These various dimensions of democratic quality each constitute a continuum, and it is hard to say exactly when a regime has sufficient freedom, pluralism, lawfulness, accountability, and institutional strength to be considered a liberal democracy. Our classification of regions in Table 2 on the following page uses as an indicator of liberal democracy an average freedom score of 2.0 or lower (better) on the combined Freedom House 7-point scale of political rights and civil liberties.[2] A somewhat looser standard is Freedom House's "free" status (which requires an average freedom score of 2.5 or lower).

As we see in Table 2, electoral democracy stretches into every major region of the world, although it is much more widely present in some regions than others. With the transition to democracy in the former Yugoslavia at the end of 2000, all of Central and Eastern Europe (outside the former Soviet Union) is democratic. This means that today every European country is at least an electoral democracy, while most former Soviet states are nondemocracies. Latin America and the Caribbean are overwhelmingly democratic; only Cuba and now perhaps Haiti depart from the trend. In other regions of the developing world, however, the frequency of democracy falls off sharply. Fewer than half the states in Asia and only about a third of those in sub-Saharan Africa are democracies, but the latter proportion represents a dramatic increase from a decade ago. In the Middle East and North Africa, there are still only two democracies, Turkey and Israel. *Lebanon*

The distribution of liberal democracy in the world is even more skewed, as indicated by one summary statistic. Of the 75 liberal democracies in the world, 54 are found either in the advanced industrial democracies of Western Europe, North America, Australia, New Zealand, Japan, and Israel (which Diamond in the concluding chapter calls the "core" states) or in states with populations of less than one million. Of the other 129 Asian, African, Latin American, Middle Eastern, and

TABLE 2—REGIONAL DISTRIBUTION OF DEMOCRACIES,
LIBERAL DEMOCRACIES, AND "FREE" STATES, 2000–2001

REGION	NUMBER OF COUNTRIES	NUMBER OF DEMOCRACIES (% OF TOTAL)[1]	NUMBER (%) OF LIBERAL DEMOCRACIES FH score <2.5	NUMBER OF "FREE" STATES (% OF TOTAL) FH score <3.0
Western Europe & Anglophone states	28	28 (100%)	28 (100%)	28 (100%)
Latin American & Caribbean	33	31 (94%)	20 (61%)	22 (67%)
East Central Europe & Baltics	15	15 (100%)	9 (60%)	11 (73%)
Former Soviet Union (less Baltics)	12	4 (33%)	0	0
Asia (NE, SE, S)	25	11 (44%)	3 (12%)	7 (28%)
Pacific Island	12	10 (83%)	8 (67%)	9 (75%)
Africa (Sub-Sahara)	48	18 (35%)	6 (13%)	9 (19%)
Middle East/ North Africa	19	2 (11%)	1 (5%)	1 (5%)
Total	**192**	**119 (62%)**	**75 (39%)**	**86 (45%)**
Arab Countries	16	0	0	0
Predominantly Muslim Countries	41	6[2] (15%)	0	1 (2%)

Source: Aili Piano and Arch Puddington, "The 2000 Freedom House Survey: Gains
Offset Losses," Journal of Democracy 12 (January 2001): 87–92.
1. Djibouti, Liberia, Haiti, and Sierra Leone are not counted here as electoral democracies, even though they are rated as such by Freedom House. Peru is counted as a
democracy with the restoration of free and fair elections after the resignation of Fujimori.
Yugoslavia (Serbia & Montenegro) is also counted as a democracy with the electoral
downfall of Milosevic.
2. Counted among this group are Mali, Niger, Senegal, Indonesia, Turkey, and Albania.

postcommunist states with populations above one million, fewer than
one in five are liberal democracies.

There are also striking differences in the distribution of regimes within
major regions of the world. The 15 postcommunist states of Central and
Eastern Europe (including the Baltic states) are moving toward the
liberal democratic West in their levels of freedom; the majority of these
states are now liberal democracies. Of the remaining 12 states of the
former Soviet Union, none is a liberal democracy, and less than half are
electoral democracies.

Of the 25 states of Asia (East, Southeast, and South), only three are
liberal democracies (11 are democracies). We see the effect of size when
we compare Asia with the Pacific Island states. Of the latter 12 states,
ten are democracies and eight are liberal democracies. Similarly, while
half the states of Latin America and the Caribbean are liberal democracies,
these are mainly clustered in the Caribbean region. Only a third of the
12 South American states are liberal democracies. Liberal democracy is
scarcely present (10 percent) among the 48 states of sub-Saharan Africa
(and the liberal democracies of Africa are again disproportionately those
with fewer than one million people). By contrast, there is not a single

Arab democracy, nor is there a single majority-Muslim country that is a liberal democracy. Only 15 percent of the states with predominantly Muslim populations are even electoral democracies.

Democratic Consolidation

The divergence in the quality or depth of democracy is matched by a parallel divergence in progress toward the consolidation of democracy. As the contributions to Section II of this volume make clear, "consolidation" remains a contested if not controversial concept in the comparative study of democracy. Nevertheless, the trend among scholars has been toward accepting the utility of "consolidation" as a concept, and the type of definition presented in this volume by Juan Linz and Alfred Stepan has been particularly influential. In this view, democracies are "consolidated" when their institutions, rules, and incentives become "the only game in town" politically. Linz and Stepan posit overlapping behavioral, attitudinal, and constitutional dimensions of consolidation, through which "democracy becomes routinized and deeply internalized in social, institutional, and even psychological life, as well as in political calculations for achieving success." In consolidated democracies, there may be intense conflict, but no significant political or social actors attempt to achieve their objectives by illegal, unconstitutional, or anti-democratic means. Further, there may be severe problems of governance and widespread disapproval of the government of the day, but elites and the public at large overwhelmingly believe that "democratic procedures and institutions are the most appropriate way to govern collective life."

At bottom, then, the consolidation of democracy represents a kind of mirror image of the process of democratic breakdown that Linz and Stepan studied a generation ago.[3] Just as democratic breakdowns feature the erosion of democratic legitimacy and the rise of disloyal and semi-loyal political actors, so consolidation is buttressed by a deep and widely shared legitimation of democracy. And this legitimation—internalized, practiced, and transmitted across political generations—involves more than just a commitment to democracy in the abstract; it also entails adherence to the specific rules and constraints of the country's constitutional system.[4]

What is striking about the third wave of democratization that began in 1974 is how slow progress has been toward consolidation, defined in this way. Outside of the new democracies of Southern Europe (Spain, Portugal, and Greece) and a few scattered others, the third-wave democracies have generally not yet taken firm root. As is noted in the concluding chapter of this volume, only in Central and Eastern Europe is there evidence (from both elite behavior and mass public opinion surveys) of wide progress in entrenching democratic norms and practices.

Just as the post-Soviet states diverge from postcommunist Europe in the quality of democracy, so do they diverge in stability as well. In fact, democracy in Russia and Ukraine is further away from consolidation and more in danger of complete collapse today than it was in the mid-1990s. This regression is reflected in the title of Michael McFaul's chapter on Russia under Putin: "One Step Forward, Two Steps Back."

Public opinion data suggest that Uruguay has now joined Costa Rica as a consolidated democracy within Latin America, but significant pockets of skepticism, if not disillusionment, with democracy persist elsewhere in the region. In East Asia's most advanced third-wave democracies, Korea and Taiwan, the depth of mistrust and division among competing political parties renders their commitment to democratic institutions, procedures, and norms somewhat ambiguous. Opinion surveys show that the mass public is also ambivalent in its commitment to democracy. Public opinion appears surprisingly appreciative of democracy in Africa, but politicians and ruling elites have yet to compete and govern in a way that exhibits rigorous adherence to the constitutional rules and behavioral constraints of democracy.[5]

From an alternative perspective, however, the noteworthy point is not that so many third-wave democracies have yet to achieve consolidation but rather that they are still standing—and in no immediate danger of collapse—more than a decade after their founding. Throughout almost all of Latin America, Guillermo O'Donnell argues in chapter 9, elections are institutionalized and meet standards of fairness and competitiveness that roughly satisfy Robert Dahl's criteria for "polyarchy." These electoral democracies diverge from the older, more established ones of the "Northwest" (Europe and North America) in the extent to which the institutionalization of democratic practices is informal and riddled with clientelism, nepotism, and formally corrupt acts. As a result, the rule of law is weak, the constitution often bends to executive will, and democracy is less responsive, but this does not mean that democracy will not endure. For O'Donnell, the concept of consolidation adds little analytically: "All we can say at present is that, as long as elections are institutionalized, polyarchies are likely to endure." O'Donnell criticizes many theories of democratic consolidation for their inability to specify precisely when a democracy is consolidated. And he appeals to scholars to free themselves of the teleological illusion that emerging democracies elsewhere in the world must necessarily come to resemble those of the "Northwest" in order to survive.

O'Donnell's powerful critique has occasioned vigorous debate among scholars of democracy. In chapter 10, Richard Gunther, P. Nikiforos Diamandouros, and Hans-Jürgen Puhle (whose edited work on Southern Europe is a primary target of O'Donnell's criticism) reply with a defense of consolidation theory. They conceptualize consolidation in terms very similar to those of Linz and Stepan, but add a qualification that injects both precision and flexibility into the discussion. This is the notion of "politically significant" groups. Democracy is consolidated when "all politically significant groups regard its key political institutions as the only legitimate framework for political contestation, and adhere to democratic rules of the game." No democracy will ever command the loyalty and behavioral compliance of every citizen and group. What matters for Gunther, Diamandouros, and Puhle are the organized groups and movements (along with their leaders) whose resources and strategic location give them the ability to mobilize broad support for some challenge to the legitimacy of the democratic system. Which groups will be politically significant will vary from society to society, as will the speed with which a system may move toward consolidation (as they define it). Greece and Spain consolidated democracy within a few years of their transitions in the 1970s; other regimes remain unconsolidated (and vulnerable) well over a decade after transition. The three authors also rebut O'Donnell's criticism that the indicators of consolidation are vague, misleading, or contradictory. Public statements of political leaders and organizations, official documents and declarations, symbolic gestures, and patterns of behavior can all be used to identify whether a political actor supports or rejects the democratic rules of the game. Public opinion survey data are invaluable in assessing the extent of public support for democracy. Moreover, the three authors do not accept the criticism that consolidation theory is almost invariably teleological. Instead, they see the process as nonlinear and indeterminate, vulnerable to stagnation, reversal, and even failure. Finally, the pervasive clientelism of which O'Donnell writes—with its risks of generating deep resentment over power imbalances—is precisely, in their view, one of the sources of stagnation or potential reversal.

In his reply in chapter 11, O'Donnell criticizes another element of the Gunther, Diamandouros, and Puhle work, the conceptions of "partial" vs. "substantial" or "sufficient" consolidation. O'Donnell considers these to be confused and imprecise stages that do not admit of easy identification empirically. Further, he argues that when democracies are viewed in terms of their degree of consolidation, many regimes tend to be defined by the attributes that they are *lacking* in relation to a paradigmatic (and in his view, still teleological) endpoint, rather than in terms of their actual properties. This, he asserts, yields "analytically useless residual categories."

In the final contribution to Section II, Andreas Schedler parses the multiple meanings that have emerged for the term "democratic consolidation." For some authors, consolidation means simply avoiding authoritarian regression, achieving democratic permanence or sustainability; this naturally leads to a focus on neutralizing disloyal actors, real and potential. For others, consolidation involves preventing the erosion of key liberal elements of democracy, such as the rule of law and civilian control of the military. Alternatively, consolidation can mean deepening the quality of democracy (moving it from electoral to liberal or even "advanced" democracy). A variant of this perspective equates democratic consolidation with "completion" of the missing elements of democracy. This involves such key challenges as removing authoritarian enclaves, leveling the hegemony of a long-ruling party, and strengthening civil liberties and judicial independence. To the first two "negative" forms of consolidation and the latter two "positive" variants, Schedler adds a fifth, "neutral" usage—"organizing democracy." This involves establishing and institutionalizing the political parties, legislative bodies, state bureaucracy, judicial system, and other structures required for effective democratic functioning. All of these conceptual approaches have their value, according to Schedler, but the problem with the study of consolidation is that it lacks a conceptual core, "a meaningful common denominator." One way out of the confusion would be for each scholar to practice "transparent toleration," making clear how "consolidation" is used in a particular study, while remaining open to other understandings. For Schedler, however, a better approach is to "restore its classical meaning"—avoiding democratic breakdown and erosion. According to this understanding, a consolidated democracy is one that can be expected "to last well into the future."

Is Democracy Becoming a Universal Value?

While there has been a striking trend in recent years toward a "global divergence of democracies" in *practice,* the acceptance of democratic *principles* is still growing across cultures. In fact, international covenants increasingly recognize democracy itself as a basic human right. On 27 June 2000 in Warsaw, foreign ministers and other high-ranking representatives from 106 countries assembled at the inaugural meeting of the Community of Democracies and adopted a declaration pledging their governments "to respect and uphold" a wide range of "core democratic principles and practices." These included not only the types of individual rights enshrined in previous human rights accords but key elements of electoral and liberal democracy as well. Among these elements acknowledged more explicitly than ever before were the following:

• "The right and civic duties of citizens to choose their representatives through regular, free and fair elections with universal and equal suffrage, open to multiple parties, conducted by secret ballot, monitored by independent electoral authorities, and free of fraud and intimidation."

• "The right of those duly elected to form a government, assume office and fulfill the term of office as legally established."

• "The obligation of an elected government to refrain from extraconstitutional actions, to allow the holding of periodic elections and to respect their results, and to relinquish power when its legal mandate ends."

• "That the legislature be duly elected and transparent and account-able to the people."

• "That civilian, democratic control over the military be established and preserved."[6]

Many of the states present in Warsaw were not by any stretch democ-racies. These included a number of Arab states (Egypt, Algeria, Tunisia, Morocco, and Kuwait) and assorted other pseudodemocracies (Kenya, Azerbaijan, and, at that time, Peru). Even these nondemocratic states, however, committed themselves to "respect and uphold" these various democratic principles. No major cultural or geographic area of the world was unrepresented at the Warsaw meeting or in the signing of the declaration. This was one more manifestation of the increasingly global appeal of democratic values and practices.

Whether democracy and liberty are in fact universal values is the question that occupies the opening section of this volume. Writing from different geographic, cultural, and religious perspectives, the first four contributors all argue powerfully for the universality of democracy. In chapter 1, Nobel Prize–winning economist Amartya Sen identifies the rise of democracy as the preeminent development of the twentieth century. Sen's essay, which was initially presented as a keynote address to the inaugural assembly of the World Movement for Democracy in New Delhi, does not deny the existence of "challenges to democracy's claim to universality." But, Sen argues, "democratic governance has now achieved the status of being taken to be generally right," and the burden of justification is on those who seek to reject it. If democracy is not quite literally a universal value, it is now recognized "as a universally relevant system." Any country can become a democracy. In Sen's memorable phrase, "A country does have to be deemed fit *for* democracy; rather, it has to become fit *through* democracy." Even in poor countries such as India, democracy "has worked well enough"; in fact, highly pluralistic India "is held together by its working democracy," and India's poor have adhered to democracy, not rejected it. The argu-ment that authoritarian regimes do better in economic development is based on highly selective evidence. If one weighs all the statistical evidence, there seems to be no clear relationship between democracy and economic growth, and there is no theoretical reason to assume that democracy inhibits the economic and social policies that promote growth. In fact, democracy has some distinct advantages, such as preventing famine and fostering transparency. But "the merits of democracy and its claim as a universal value" stem from three other considerations: Political freedom and participation have intrinsic value for human well-being. Democracy also has instrumental value in enabling people to express their needs and claims. And democracy has

FALSE!

"constructive importance" in helping society "to form its values and priorities." In these respects, democracy is a universal value, in that "people anywhere may have reason to see it as valuable."

Sen explicitly takes issue with the "Asian values" school, which sees democracy as in conflict with such Asian religious and philosophical traditions as Confucianism and Buddhism. These religions, and Islam as well, have multiple political themes and implications; at a minimum, they are not monolithically hostile to democracy. The authors of our subsequent three chapters provide substantial evidence in support of this claim. In chapter 2, the Dalai Lama argues for the compatiblity of democracy and Buddhism. Both Buddhism and democracy are "based on the principle that all human beings are essentially equal, and that each of us has an equal right to life, liberty, and happiness." Each system recognizes the dignity and potential of the individual. And certainly the Buddhist belief that "the purpose of meaningful life is to serve others" is not in conflict with democracy. The Buddhist tradition also offers some recognition of the need for collective discourse and consensus in key decisions. Like Sen, the Dalai Lama explicitly rejects the "Asian values" thesis and maintains that civil and political rights are necessary for full development. The Dalai Lama sees democratic values spreading around the world "as more and more people gain awareness of their individual potential." What pains him is that his own Tibetan people in China do not have basic democratic rights. Among Tibetans in exile, however, democratic principles and institutional practices are becoming entrenched, with the active support of the Dalai Lama.

In chapter 3, Francis Fukuyama shows the compatibility of Confucianism and democracy. He stresses (as Abdou Filali-Ansary does with regard to Islam in chapter 4) that cultural and religious traditions are not fixed, but rather evolve as historical conditions change. At one point, experts thought Confucianism was incompatible with capitalist economic development, a notion that now appears absurd given East Asia's economic success. Citing the work of Tu Wei-ming, Fukuyama notes the distinction between "political Confucianism," which legitimated a very hierarchical authority structure that culminated in the emperor, and "the Confucian personal ethic" concerning family, work, education, and daily life. With the overthrow of China's Qing dyanasty in 1911, political Confucianism was ruptured and its cultural impact has faded. This has left the personal ethic as the more important legacy for contemporary culture, and this has more favorable implications for democracy. Fukuyama stresses in particular four elements of compatibility between Confucianism and democracy. First is the emphasis on merit-based institutions (as epitomized by the traditional Confucian examination system); these have promoted more egalitarian patterns of income distribution, which are conducive to democracy. Second is the Confucian emphasis on education, which has generated

levels of literacy, information, and prosperity that have fostered democracy in some Confucian countries and are likely to do so in others in the
coming generations. Third is the relative tolerance of Confucianism
with respect to other religions. And fourth is the emphasis on family
ties, which take precedence over obligations to political authorities.
Thus "Confucianism builds a well-ordered society from the ground up
rather than the top down." Fukuyama distinguishes as well between the
Confucian traditions of Japan and China. In the former, political
authority has remained relatively strong, while in the latter it has been
undermined by the strength of family ties. This cuts both ways, however.
The long-term cultural challenge for democracy in China, he speculates,
"will not be a culturally ingrained deference to state authority, but a
sense of citizenship too feeble to generate spontaneous coherence, or
call forth sacrifices for the sake of national unity."

   For Abdou Filali-Ansary, the key historical force in shaping the politics
of Muslim societies today was not the early centuries of Islamic history
but rather the nineteenth-century encounter of Muslims with the modernizing West. This led to an equation of secularism with atheism and "a
strict and irreducible opposition between two systems—Islam and non-
Islam." The resulting polarization "between Muslim and European,
between believer and secularist" came to dominate all approaches to
religion and politics. In its substantive principles, Filali-Ansary argues,
Islam can "easily accommodate secularization" and favors individual
freedoms and religious choice. But the conflicts of the nineteenth century
steered Muslim societies in a different direction, "toward the loss of
individual autonomy and total submission to the community and the
state." In the Middle Ages, Islamic civilization thrived precisely because
it adapted the norms of Islam to the conditions of the time. In the nineteenth
century, however, norms and conditions (including the implementation
of Islamic law) became confused, and some Muslims "elevated the actual
conditions and rules under which their medieval forefathers lived to the
status of a norm," a moral and religious imperative. This is what entrenched
the view of Islam as an immutable system "unalterably opposed to all
conceptions and systems associated with modernity," including secularism
and democracy. Nationalist state ideologies in some Muslim countries
deepened this trend toward establishing Islam not just as a religion but as
an identity and political system.

   For Filali-Ansary, the notion that Islam is intrinsically opposed to
the West, to modernity, or to democracy and human rights is thus false.
Rather, these tensions are products of historical developments, and they
can be muted by new historical developments. In fact, those
developments are underway. With the failures of nationalist, socialist,
and other authoritarian regimes, a growing number of contemporary
Islamic thinkers (even fundamentalists) are recognizing that Islam is
not opposed to democracy and are embracing democracy because "it

responds to the needs of contemporary societies." This positive trend
can be accelerated, Filali-Ansary believes, by avoiding discussion of a
reified and "utopianized" general concept of democracy and focusing
instead on its specific elements or benefits, such as transparency, freedom
of expression, and the rule of law. Religious conceptions must also be
updated by de-emphasizing the literal meaning of sacred texts while
maintaining "the overall ethical and moral teachings."

The Focus →

In chapter 5, Giovanni Sartori takes a somewhat more circumspect
view of how far "free government" can travel. To be sure, he decisively
rejects the notion that democracy cannot travel beyond the West. "That
democracy is a Western invention does not entail that it is a bad invention, or a product suitable only for Western consumption." Moreover,
he argues that the liberal constitutionalist aspect of democracy—what
he calls "demo-protection," or keeping a people free from tyranny—is
something that transcends cultures. For Sartori, the "universality and
exportability of democracy" rest on "the harm-avoidance rule," namely,
that nobody wants to be tortured, falsely imprisoned, or otherwise abused
by the state. Sartori is somewhat more skeptical, however, regarding
how far the other element of democracy—"demo-power," or the
implementation of popular rule through universal suffrage in competitive
elections—can travel. Successful democracy in the latter respect requires
"the taming" of politics so that it "no longer kills." This in turn requires
secularization and some degree of toleration for opponents. To the extent
that a system of "demo-power" becomes one of "demo-distributions," it
also requires some economic base that can sustain such distributions
and, ideally, some reassertion of "control of the purse." In fact, Sartori
worries that the pressure for "demo-benefits" threatens the fiscal health
of all democracies.

Human Liberty

The partial skepticism of Russell Bova in chapter 6 is in a sense the
inverse of Sartori's. Sartori argues that people in any society need the
protection of liberal constitutionalism but that not all societies can
sustain electoral democracy. By contrast, Bova finds that while electoral
democracy is present in almost every major region of the world, it is
only regularly accompanied by strong protections for individual liberty
in countries with a Western cultural heritage. To be sure, there is a
strong relationship between democracy and liberty. Using independent
empirical ratings of countries on each dimension, Bova finds that the
more closely a country adheres to the standard of multiparty elections
by secret and universal ballot, the higher is its human rights score, on
average. But this, he argues, is partly due to the fact that democracy
emerged in its modern form "in the Europe of the Enlightenment," with
its emphasis on natural rights and individual liberties. Outside the areas
of Western cultural heritage, this emphasis is less strongly rooted and
human rights are consequently less well-protected, even in democracies.
Bova's data show that even when the West is extended to include Latin

America and Eastern Europe Western democracies have much better human rights scores than non-Western democracies, though the latter protect human rights much better than authoritarian regimes in the same regions. In addition, he notes that while new democracies whose cultural heritage is broadly "Western" (in Central Europe and Latin America) have, on average, improved human rights performance relatively quickly after the transition, even older democracies outside the West have serious human rights problems. These findings lead Bova to conclude that "political culture is key to understanding the diffusion (or lack thereof) of human rights."

The relationship between democracy and freedom has been a major theme of intellectual debate about political regimes in recent years. Former Singaporean prime minister Lee Kuan Yew has led a school of thought that insists it is possible to have liberal "good government" without democracy. In chapter 7, Marc F. Plattner refutes this notion. Without question, many of the new democracies in the world are not liberal. But the idea that an enduring liberal autocracy is possible in the contemporary world is illusory. "Today," Plattner observes, "wherever one finds liberalism . . . it is almost invariably coupled with democracy." Moreover, all of the relatively liberal nondemocracies of nineteenth-century Europe have now become democratic. This common evolution is not coincidental, for "the philosophy of liberalism contains within itself the seeds of its own democratization." One of these seeds is the liberal doctrine of human equality. There is a close link between the principles of natural equality and natural liberty; "if all men are naturally free, then none can have a natural right to rule over others." Citing Locke's *Second Treatise,* Plattner shows the logical progression from the concepts of liberty and equality to the principle of the "consent of the governed," and from this, to the notion that the people "are ultimately sovereign." While in theory nondemocratic government could be legitimate if it obtained the consent of the governed, in practice this principle has led to democracy—government "of the people, by the people, and for the people." As Tocqueville showed, once electoral rights are extended, there is no natural stopping point short of universal suffrage. In contemporary times, "the principle of universal inclusion . . . has only become more sacrosanct." Yet today it is tempered by a growing readiness to restrain the power of electoral majorities with autonomous judiciaries and other independent agencies. The growing consensus on the importance of constitutionalism and the rule of law in democratic development "reflects a triumph of liberal ways of thinking."

Foundations of Successful Democracy

There is a vast empirical and theoretical literature on the economic, social, cultural, and political factors that sustain democracy and prevent

its erosion or breakdown.[7] New scholarly research and empirical experience continue to add to our understanding of this great diversity of
facilitating and inhibiting factors. Section III of this volume presents
eight recent articles on some of the key political and economic foundations of successful democracy.

In chapter 13, in a now celebrated article (which has recently been
expanded into a book),[8] Adam Przeworski, Michael Alvarez, José
Antonio Cheibub, and Fernando Limongi show the powerful impact on
democratic survival of economic development and economic
performance. Like O'Donnell, Przeworski and his colleagues doubt
whether consolidation is a discernible process and a useful concept.
Because the age of democracy does not confer any immunity against
democratic breakdown (when economic development is controlled for),
they conclude that consolidation is "an empty term" and that it is more
useful simply to examine what makes democracies endure.[9] What they
find is rather striking. Confirming the classic thesis first offered by
Seymour Martin Lipset, they demonstrate a strong positive relationship between the affluence of a nation and the likelihood of its sustaining democracy. During the time period of their study, 1950–90,
democracy (by which they mean simply electoral democracy) had a 12
percent chance of breakdown in any given year among the lowest-
income countries. With each level of increase in per-capita income, the
expected life of democracy increases, until the highest income level of
over $6,000 (in 1985 purchasing-power-parity dollars). At that level of
affluence—now exceeded not only by Spain, Portugal, and Greece but
by South Korea and Taiwan (and probably Argentina and Chile) as
well—"democracies are impregnable and can be expected to live
forever."

In less affluent countries, and especially in the poorest ones, annual
economic performance becomes critical. Democracies are significantly
more likely to persist when they experience real economic growth
(especially rapid growth, in excess of 5 percent annually). Rapid
inflation, above 30 percent annually, is also toxic to democracy (though
they find that moderate inflation somewhat improves prospects for
democratic survival). And despite the scantiness of data on inequality,
the authors find that democracy is much more likely to endure in
countries where income inequality declines over time than in those
where it increases. It appears that the ability to meet popular expectations for more equal income distribution improves the prospects for
democracy.

One of the most important institutional arenas assumed to affect
consolidation is the party system. In chapter 14, Scott Mainwaring
underscores the importance of a well-institutionalized party system for
democracy. Well-institutionalized systems have stable patterns of
interparty competition; electoral volatility is low and major parties

Argument for strong parties.

persist for decades, making politics more predictable, whereas in poorly institutionalized systems parties frequently enter and leave the political arena. In well-institutionalized systems, parties also have strong legitimacy and deep roots in society, with stable bases of individual as well as organizational support. Finally, parties in such systems have substantial material and human resources and strong, well-established internal organizations. One reason why most third-wave democracies have not become consolidated is that their party systems are weak and poorly institutionalized in these respects. For example, third-wave democracies in Latin America and the post-Soviet states have much higher electoral volatility and split-ticket voting than more established democracies do. These incline a system toward deadlock and ungovernability. Because parties are more weakly rooted, personalities tend to dominate politics, and populist leaders may undermine democratic accountability. Where party systems have developed or reasserted institutional strength—as in Spain, Portugal, Greece, Uruguay, and Chile—democracy has moved more briskly forward toward consolidation.

In terms of electoral competition and accountability, the quality of democracy depends not only on the strength and coherence of parties and the party system but also on the quality of elections themselves. In chapter 15, Jørgen Elklit and Palle Svensson, two Danish political scientists who have monitored and advised on numerous transitional elections, identify the elements that make up a free and fair election. Freedom, they note, implies the absence of coercion or unjustified restriction, while fairness requires reasonable, impartial, and equal treatment of all participants. For a free and fair election, these principles must apply not only on voting day but also in the preelection period and in the postelection process of counting and reporting the results and adjudicating complaints. These three time periods and two dimensions (of freedom and fairness) are then used to produce a checklist for assessing an election. Within this checklist, Elklit and Svensson place particular importance on the requirements for freedom—such as freedom of movement, speech, and assembly during the campaign, and the unfettered right to vote on election day. Within the fairness dimension, they suggest that it is very difficult to achieve a perfectly level playing field during the campaign, and they therefore stress the correct and impartial application of election law by an independent electoral commission. Assessing elections in democratic transitions requires more than a technical application of the items in the checklist. In the end, observers should evaluate "the degree to which the preferences of the electorate have been expressed," and they must also ask whether an election—even with shortcomings—will "stimulate further democratization" by strengthening political freedom and contestation and enhancing political participation and debate.

Political participation can become particularly problematic and

Importance of Federalism

unstable when multiple ethnic or nationality groups coexist within the same polity. As Alfred Stepan argues in chapter 16, federalism is an important, if not indispensable, institutional framework for making democracy viable in this context. But not all federal systems are the same, and analytic thinking about federalism has been excessively influenced by the U.S. model. The United States is an example of "coming-together federalism"—a bargain between previously sovereign polities to create a new federal state. More often, however, democratic federations (such as India, Belgium, and Spain) emerge through a "holding-together" process, in which political leaders judge that the only way to hold the country together as a democracy is to "devolve power constitutionally and turn their threatened polities into federations." The United States, like Brazil, has a heavily "*demos-constraining*" form of federalism, in that constitutional rules (such as the policy scope of the territorial chamber and inequality of represen-

and the U.S.

tation within it) severely limit what a popular majority can accomplish politically. This protects minority rights but also can entrench inequality and promote deadlock, as it has in Brazil. Federal systems range widely across a continuum in this regard, with Germany's and especially India's being much more "*demos*-enabling." Finally, not all federal systems treat their subunits in a symmetrical fashion, as the United States does. In fact, Stepan notes, symmetrical federations like the United States are generally composed of one broad nationality group (at least in linguistic terms), while most multinational federations—notably, India, Belgium, Canada, and Spain—are asymmetrical. Most multinational polities in the world are not democracies. Viable democracy in such countries (notably, Indonesia and Nigeria), Stepan argues, will require devolution of power, probably through some type of federal arrangement, and the United States may not be the most appropriate federal model for these countries to emulate.

rule of law

One of the central problems confronting all new democracies, whether multinational or not, is to construct a fair and effective rule of law. There is, Charles Fried asserts in chapter 17, an intimate relationship between the rule of law, the free market, and democracy. These, in turn, depend on trust. "Without trust there can be no freedom, no markets, and in the end, no prosperity." Trust and mutual respect between citizens of a society make possible the key institutions of a market economy: property rights, contracts, and transparent institutions to protect and enforce them. Relations of trust and respect are undermined, however, by gross inequality. In particular, "bandit capitalism" exaggerates inequality and inhibits trust. A true market must be based on freedom, honesty, and formal equality between the exchanging parties. Laws and courts uphold these key conditions for the market not so much by punishment as by generating the trust and respect that cultivate voluntary compliance and so relieve the need for enforcement and punishment in most cases. Laws provide "reasonable expectations" on the basis of which strangers can trust and respect one another and therefore do business with one another. By protecting property rights and facilitating exchange, the law fosters prosperity. "Yet the laws are only as good as the judges who interpret and apply them," and judges can only be good (impartial) when they are independent of political pressures and secure in their work.

The quest for a viable democracy and market economy has been long and troubled in Latin America. Yet as Jorge Domínguez notes in chapter 18, the 1990s have been a period of free politics and free markets without precedent in the region's history. For decades, the conventional wisdom in the region has been that democracies do not generate growth-friendly economic policies and that they are unable to undertake necessary structural reforms of the economy. Domínguez finds, however, that the performance of Latin American democracies since the 1980s does not bear out the pessimists on either count. To a considerable degree in recent years, democracy and market reforms have gone together in Latin America. It helped that statist, import-substituting policies fell into crisis under failing authoritarian regimes in the late 1970s and early 80s. Another key factor was the emergence of greater professional and political understanding of the need for market reforms, fostered in part by international training and assistance. Yet Domínguez shows that there are also compelling logical reasons why democracy should foster market reforms. Democratic regimes can involve the opposition in support of a market economy more than authoritarian regimes do. When all major parties share a basic commitment to the market, a democratic regime provides long-term assurances to capital that are often missing in the opaque and unpredictable circumstances of authoritarian rule. At the same time, markets can enhance democracy by reducing opportunities for corruption and rent-seeking and strengthening checks on the abuse of power. With evidence from several specific cases—Chile, Argentina, Brazil, El Salvador, and Nicaragua—Domínguez shows that democracies have been able to advance economic reforms, even by democratic means, in the new, more promising epoch in Latin America.

Kwasi Prempeh shows in chapter 19 that positive change is taking place in Africa as well. While Africa remains well behind Latin America and some other regions in the vigor of democracy and the market, the judiciary in Africa is gaining new power and autonomy. Particularly encouraging is the growth of judicial review, which at least generates the potential for judges to defend individual rights and contain the abuse of power. Also promising is the growth of the statutory independence of judges (in their jobs, salaries, jurisdiction, and judgments). The problem however, is that jurisprudence often lags behind formal constitutional provisions. In the years following the adoption of the democratic 1992 Constitution in Ghana, the courts tended to side with the state rather than defending freedom of expression and the press. This not only paved the way for criminal prosecution of journalists but also diminished public faith in the judiciary in Ghana. Formal provisions for judicial review and independence are therefore not sufficient. Prempeh maintains that Africa also needs "a new jurisprudence of constitutionalism" that rejects the past deference to the supremacy of the executive and of the state in general. This requires "more active judicial intermediation and interpretation," which in turn requires judges who understand "the overarching values and philosophical foundations of a liberal democracy." The risk of a resurgence of illiberal jurisprudence can also be contained by clarity in the constitutional text (particularly in identifying the legal departures from the illiberal old order); immediate repeal of repressive laws from the authoritarian era; the establishment of a constitutional court (still lacking in most of Africa's transitional democracies); judicious borrowing of constitutional precedents and doctrines from other democratic systems; and enhancement and reform of legal education.

A no less pressing problem for many new democracies is to establish civilian control over the military. This is the challenge that Richard Kohn examines in chapter 20. The highest form of civilian control is when civilians are supreme even in setting military and national security policy. The more immediate challenge for most new democracies, however, is "to establish a tradition of civilian control, to make the military establishment politically neutral, and to prevent or preclude any possibility of military intervention in political life." Looking mainly at Western experience, Kohn derives a number of lessons for fostering such control of the military by elected civilian officials. The first requirement, he stresses, "is democratic governance itself." Civilian control in a democracy requires a rule of law, civil liberties, and other aspects of legitimate and effective democratic functioning. The role of the military must be clearly specified by civilians, and essentially constrained to external defense (not internal security). Second, subordination to the civilian executive must be supplemented with parliamentary oversight and accountability. Executive and legislature must constitute a "divided but shared rule" over the military. Third, the military must judge (from experience) that violations of civilian control will be punished, and that revolt would likely be resisted, either by other armed elements of society (the police, the militia) or by the soldiers themselves because they are draftees rather than professionals. Fourth, the military establishment must itself be socialized and dedicated to an ethos of political neutrality. This is more likely to occur if the officer corps is reasonably representative of society. Finally, establishing civilian control requires political leadership that treats the military with firmness but also with knowledge, respect, and strict political neutrality.

Prospects and Challenges for Democracy

Although the essays in this volume focus mainly on regions of the world where democracy has only recently emerged or is still struggling to do so, this is not meant to imply the absence of any reason for concern about the state of democracy in the West. While all Western democracies are liberal and consolidated, and none faces any imminent danger of breakdown, this does not mean they are all in good health. In chapter 21, Susan Pharr, Robert Putnam, and Russell Dalton take the temperature of the "trilateral democracies" (in Western Europe, North America, and Japan), and they find reason for concern. These countries do not confront the "crisis of democracy" that was much talked about a generation ago. Since the early to mid-1970s, popular protest and political polarization have ebbed, and most of the industrial democracies have recovered economically. Yet public opinion surveys over the past two decades show a broad, consistent, and deepening trend of disaffection with the institutions of representative democracy throughout the trilateral democracies. While commitment to democratic values is higher than ever and no ideological challenge to democracy is even faintly visible in these countries, public confidence in and support for political parties, parliament, and the "political class" have steadily eroded. Trust in other political institutions, such as the judiciary, armed forces, and civil service, is also on the decline in most countries. The downward trend is starkest in the United States, where the percentage of the public trusting the government "to do what is right" has fallen from three-quarters in the late 1950s and early 1960s to 39 percent in 1998. Political alienation and disillusionment are spreading in most of Europe as well, and appear most persistent of all in Japan. In virtually all of these advanced democracies, the authors' voluminous data show, confidence in politicians is steadily declining, as is citizen attachment to and involvement with political parties. These trends, Pharr, Putnam, and Dalton argue, reflect "a growing disenchantment with partisan politics in general" that appears to be driven by a combination of factors: the diminishing capacity of national political leaders, in an era of globalization, to respond to citizens' interests and desires; specific failures of political leadership and judgment; and the impact of broad declines in social capital and social trust. Preserving the health of democracy in these countries will require the reversal or more creative management of these trends.

As Abraham Lowenthal shows in chapter 22, democracy is in still greater difficulty in Latin America. Most Latin American countries suffer these same trends of declining confidence in politicians and representative institutions, but without the deep entrenchment of democratic norms and practices that makes for consolidation. Thus growing democratic disillusionment is more likely to lead to political turbulence and even turmoil. Yet Latin America (including the Caribbean) is a large and diverse region, and Lowenthal stresses that its countries are not moving in a single direction. As is also true globally and within some other regions, there is a clear pattern of divergence among the democracies of Latin America. Mexico and the Southern Cone countries, particularly Chile, Argentina, and Uruguay, are doing much better than the Andean and Central American ones (save for Costa Rica).

Underlying Latin America's democratic troubles, in Lowenthal's assessment, are a number of intractable problems. On the social and economic side, these include inadequate and diminishing economic growth; serious difficulties in implementing the economic and state reforms that would accelerate growth; high levels of poverty; and levels of inequality that are, on average, the worst of any major region of the world. These aggravate, and are aggravated by, a host of persistent political problems: personalistic and erratic political leadership; the inability to construct durable and broad coalitions for economic reform; and judicial, bureaucratic, and regulatory institutions in crying need of greater professionalization and transparency. On the positive side, many Latin American countries have greater freedom and more vigorous civil societies than a decade ago. Nonetheless, if the region is to avoid serious democratic setbacks in coming years, economies must be reformed and invigorated, gross inequalities must be attenuated, and democratic institutions must be strengthened. The latter challenge requires not only institutional renewal and greater responsiveness on the part of political parties and legislatures but also dramatic reductions in crime, corruption, and tax evasion. Enhancing the rule of law is a general priority for the entire region and a particularly urgent one in the Andean countries, where democracy is under grave pressure from the drug trade and corruption.

Even more than in Latin America, "divergence" appears to characterize the paths of postcommunist democracies. In chapter 23, Jacques Rupnik goes so far as to argue that the differences among these countries, particularly between the consolidating democracies of Central Europe (notably Poland, Hungary, and the Czech Republic) and the democratically regressing post-Soviet states, are now so great that "the word 'postcommunism' has lost its relevance." The Central European democracies have made striking progress in meeting the main challenges of building democracy: establishing the legitimacy of democratic institutions and constructing a relatively stable party system, a market economy, and a pluralistic civil society. These achievements stand in stark contrast to the political stagnation and regression in the former

Soviet Union, save for the Baltic states. (Writing in late 1998, before the electoral breakthroughs in Croatia and then Serbia, Rupnik classifies the Balkans with the former Soviet Union.) Rupnik notes several factors that have favored more rapid democratic development in Central Europe. Well before 1989, these states faced political crises and dissident challenges that helped to revive civil society. After 1989, they embarked on much more aggressive market reforms than the Balkan and post-Soviet states, and these reforms accelerated the development both of new middle classes and of a variety of nongovernmental organizations. Moreover, partly owing to the historical impact of the Habsburg Empire on elite norms and practices, these Central European states made much more rapid progress in institutionalizing a rule of law. In addition, these states did not have to contend with the legacy of a collapsing multinational state that haunted the former Soviet and Yugoslav states. Finally, these countries were secure in their borders and preoccupied internationally with integration into NATO and the EU, for which democracy was an essential requirement.

Russia, by comparison, faces a much more uncertain future, as Michael McFaul explains in chapter 24. Russia conducted another peaceful, multiparty presidential election in March 2000, but it "was not contested on a level playing field." The democratic process was seriously tainted by the enormous advantages of incumbency enjoyed by former president Yeltsin's hand-picked successor, acting president Vladimir Putin. While Putin's first-ballot victory can be seen as a "vote for the future," symbolizing generational change and "the end of revolution" as well as a certain optimism, it was facilitated by growing state control over the mass media and the absence of an effective opposition. The liberal democratic forces in Russia "suffered a major setback" in the presidential election. Their standard-bearer, Grigory Yavlinsky, won only 6 percent of the vote despite an effective and well-funded campaign. Right-wing nationalist forces also lost ground politically, but that gain for democracy has been more than offset by Putin's gross indifference to the massive human rights violations that Russian forces have inflicted in Chechnya. These, McFaul writes, "reveal the low priority that Putin assigns to democratic principles." Also worrisome are some of the reforms Putin has proposed or considered, including the elimination of proportional representation to elect half the seats in parliament and a switch from elected to appointed regional governors. For now, Russian democracy still limps on, but it is "weak and unconsolidated." Democratic norms and expectations have yet to take firm root among the population, and "people clearly want a leader with a strong hand who promises to build a stronger state." It is not yet clear whether this will lead to a de facto one-party state, or just a more autocratic interlude in the longer-term quest to develop democracy in Russia.

In China, democratization has yet to begin, and many are skeptical that it will be on the political agenda at any point in the foreseeable future. The late Michel Oksenberg argues in chapter 25, however, that movement toward democracy in China may come more rapidly "than most analysts think likely." The Chinese Communist Party will be concerned to find a way to preserve its dominance, but its leaders "are likely to find introducing democracy at lower levels of the system and firmly committing themselves to the attainment of full democracy over a protracted period to be an increasingly attractive option." Several factors are pressing for a speedier transition. Rapid economic growth is beginning to transform the society, making it more autonomous vis-à-vis the state. China's political leaders are themselves feeding democratic expectations as they openly discuss political participation and "their country's eventual evolution into a democracy." Once debate begins on the methods for fostering this democratic evolution, "it will assume a life of its own and accelerate the process of change." Worker unrest associated with the reform of inefficient state-owned enterprises is likely to grow, and this may press Beijing to shift more political authority downward and increase the number of lower-level offices that are democratically elected. The democratic model of Taiwan, as well as the considerable political openness and competition in Hong Kong, are also likely increasingly to influence China's political thinking and evolution. "Finally, the involvement of China's leaders in world affairs will have a cumulative effect on their approach to governance at home." They will come under growing pressure to reduce the gap between their openness to political dialogue and questioning abroad and their unwillingness to countenance it at home. And their quest for international stature may impel them to demonstrate that they have some kind of democratic mandate from their people.

Well before China democratizes, however, many of the new democracies that have come into being during the third wave will have to confront deepening crises of governance that threaten their stability. In the concluding chapter, Larry Diamond argues that the October 1999 military coup in Pakistan could prove a harbinger of future democratic reversals in strategically significant "swing states" (such as Indonesia, Nigeria, Russia, Ukraine, Turkey, and the Philippines) if significant progress is not made to address three core challenges: First, corruption must be contained and the rule of law strengthened through vigorous efforts to build, reform, and strengthen various institutions of "horizontal accountability." Second, these countries must push forward reforms to liberalize the economy, enhancing openness and competition, while also rationalizing and strengthening ineffectual state bureaucracies. And third, they must find ways to manage their ethnic, regional, and religious differences peacefully through greater decentralization of power and resources and other innovations in the design of political institutions. If an agenda for political reform is to advance, both civil-society organizations and political parties must gain in institutional strength, effectiveness, and popular support.

In the past quarter-century, democracy has spread around the world to an unprecedented extent. Yet as we have argued, most third-wave democracies are still a long way from consolidation, and even many older ones—such as Venezuela, Colombia, and Sri Lanka—are increasingly endangered. To return to the theme implicit in our title, the global divergence in the *quality* of democracies must be stemmed, or those democracies that are functioning corruptly and abusively may, before long, not be functioning at all. In the coming decades, the global future of democracy will depend heavily on whether diverse democratic regimes can converge on a common pattern of more accountable, responsible, and effective governance. In many countries, the reform agenda is a long and daunting one, but it is not beyond the reach of committed and resourceful democrats.

NOTES

1. For a fuller description, see Larry Diamond, *Developing Democracy: Toward Consolidation* (Baltimore: Johns Hopkins University Press, 1999), 10–12.

2. For a justification of this empirical standard for liberal democracy, see Larry Diamond's essay in this volume, p. 359.

3. Juan J. Linz and Alfred Stepan, eds., *The Breakdown of Democratic Regimes* (Baltimore: Johns Hopkins University Press, 1978).

4. This theoretical perspective on consolidation is elaborated and applied in Juan J. Linz and Alfred Stepan, *Problems of Democratic Transition and Consolidation: Southern Europe, South America, and Post-Communist Europe* (Baltimore: Johns Hopkins University Press, 1996); and Richard Gunther, Hans-Jürgen Puhle, and P. Nikiforos Diamandouros, "Introduction," in Richard Gunther, P. Nikiforos Diamandouros, and Hans-Jürgen Puhle, eds., *The Politics of Democratic Consolidation: Southern Europe in Comparative Perspective* (Baltimore: Johns Hopkins University Press, 1995).

5. For assessments of "How People View Democracy" in postcommunist Europe, Africa, Korea and Taiwan, and Latin America, see the following collection of articles: Richard Rose, "A Diverging Europe"; Michael Bratton and Robert Mattes, "Africans' Surprising Universalism"; Yun-han Chu, Larry Diamond, and Doh Chull Shin, "Halting Progress in Korea and Taiwan"; and Marta Lagos, "Between Stability and Crisis in Latin America," *Journal of Democracy* 12 (January 2001): 93–145.

6. The full text of the declaration is available at *http://democracyconference.org/declaration.html*.

7. For an analytic overview of this literature, see Larry Diamond, Juan J. Linz, and Seymour Martin Lipset, "What Makes for Democracy?" in Larry Diamond, Juan J. Linz, and Seymour Martin Lipset, eds., *Politics in Developing Countries: Comparing Experiences with Democracy* (Boulder, Colo.: Lynne Rienner, 1995), 1–66.

8. Adam Przeworski, Michael E. Alvarez, José Antonio Cheibub, and Fernando Limongi, *Democracy and Development: Political Institutions and Well-Being in the World, 1950–1990* (Cambridge: Cambridge University Press, 2000).

9. As they acknowledge, however, consolidation is not "just a matter of time." Indeed, theorists of consolidation (in this volume and elsewhere) do not argue that consolidated democracies will last indefinitely. Rather, they maintain, as Linz and Stepan put it, that the breakdown of a consolidated democracy "would be related not to weakness or problems specific to the historic process of democratic consolidation, but to a new dynamic" of insoluble problems and shifts to disloyal or semiloyal norms and behavior on the part of key political actors. Nor do theorists of consolidation rule out the possibility that unconsolidated democracies may persist for some time.

I

Democracy and Liberty:
Universal Values?

1

DEMOCRACY AS
A UNIVERSAL VALUE

Amartya Sen

Amartya Sen, *winner of the 1998 Nobel Prize for Economics, is Master of Trinity College, Cambridge, and Lamont University Professor Emeritus at Harvard University. The following essay is based on a keynote address that he delivered at the inaugural assembly of the World Movement for Democracy, held in New Delhi in February 1999, and cosponsored by the National Endowment for Democracy, the Confederation of Indian Industry, and the Centre for Policy Research (New Delhi). This essay draws on work more fully presented in his book* Development as Freedom, *published by Alfred A. Knopf in 1999.*

In the summer of 1997, I was asked by a leading Japanese newspaper what I thought was the most important thing that had happened in the twentieth century. I found this to be an unusually thought-provoking question, since so many things of gravity have happened over the last hundred years. The European empires, especially the British and French ones that had so dominated the nineteenth century, came to an end. We witnessed two world wars. We saw the rise and fall of fascism and Nazism. The century witnessed the rise of communism, and its fall (as in the former Soviet bloc) or radical transformation (as in China). We also saw a shift from the economic dominance of the West to a new economic balance much more dominated by Japan and East and Southeast Asia. Even though that region is going through some financial and economic problems right now, this is not going to nullify the shift in the balance of the world economy that has occurred over many decades (in the case of Japan, through nearly the entire century). The past hundred years are not lacking in important events.

Nevertheless, among the great variety of developments that have occurred in the twentieth century, I did not, ultimately, have any difficulty in choosing one as the preeminent development of the period: the rise of democracy. This is not to deny that other occurrences have also been important, but I would argue that in the distant future, when people look back at what happened in this century, they will find it difficult not to accord primacy to the emergence of democracy as the preeminently acceptable form of governance.

The idea of democracy originated, of course, in ancient Greece, more than two millennia ago. Piecemeal efforts at democratization were attempted elsewhere as well, including in India.[1] But it is really in ancient Greece that the idea of democracy took shape and was seriously put into practice (albeit on a limited scale), before it collapsed and was replaced by more authoritarian and asymmetric forms of government. There were no other kinds anywhere else.

Thereafter, democracy as we know it took a long time to emerge. Its gradual—and ultimately triumphant—emergence as a working system of governance was bolstered by many developments, from the signing of the Magna Carta in 1215, to the French and the American Revolutions in the eighteenth century, to the widening of the franchise in Europe and North America in the nineteenth century. It was in the twentieth century, however, that the idea of democracy became established as the "normal" form of government to which any nation is entitled—whether in Europe, America, Asia, or Africa.

The idea of democracy as a universal commitment is quite new, and it is quintessentially a product of the twentieth century. The rebels who forced restraint on the king of England through the Magna Carta saw the need as an entirely local one. In contrast, the American fighters for independence and the revolutionaries in France contributed greatly to an understanding of the need for democracy as a general system. Yet the focus of their practical demands remained quite local—confined, in effect, to the two sides of the North Atlantic, and founded on the special economic, social, and political history of the region.

Throughout the nineteenth century, theorists of democracy found it quite natural to discuss whether one country or another was "fit for democracy." This thinking changed only in the twentieth century, with the recognition that the question itself was wrong: A country does not have to be deemed fit *for* democracy; rather, it has to become fit *through* democracy. This is indeed a momentous change, extending the potential reach of democracy to cover billions of people, with their varying histories and cultures and disparate levels of affluence.

It was also in this century that people finally accepted that "franchise for all adults" must mean *all*—not just men but also women. When in January of this year I had the opportunity to meet Ruth Dreyfuss, the president of Switzerland and a woman of remarkable distinction, it gave me occasion to recollect that only a quarter century ago Swiss women could not even vote. We have at last reached the point of recognizing that the coverage of universality, like the quality of mercy, is not strained.

I do not deny that there are challenges to democracy's claim to universality. These challenges come in many shapes and forms—and from different directions. Indeed, that is part of the subject of this essay. I have to examine the claim of democracy as a universal value and the disputes that surround that claim. Before I begin that exercise, however, it is necessary to grasp clearly the sense in which democracy has become a dominant belief in the contemporary world.

In any age and social climate, there are some sweeping beliefs that seem to command respect as a kind of general rule—like a "default" setting in a computer program; they are considered right *unless* their claim is somehow precisely negated. While democracy is not yet universally practiced, nor indeed uniformly accepted, in the general climate of world opinion, democratic governance has now achieved the status of being taken to be generally right. The ball is very much in the court of those who want to rubbish democracy to provide justification for that rejection.

This is a historic change from not very long ago, when the advocates of democracy for Asia or Africa had to argue for democracy with their backs to the wall. While we still have reason enough to dispute those who, implicitly or explicitly, reject the need for democracy, we must also note clearly how the general climate of opinion has shifted from what it was in previous centuries. We do not have to establish afresh, each time, whether such and such a country (South Africa, or Cambodia, or Chile) is "fit for democracy" (a question that was prominent in the discourse of the nineteenth century); we now take that for granted. This recognition of democracy as a universally relevant system, which moves in the direction of its acceptance as a universal value, is a major revolution in thinking, and one of the main contributions of the twentieth century. It is in this context that we have to examine the question of democracy as a universal value.

The Indian Experience

How well has democracy worked? While no one really questions the role of democracy in, say, the United States or Britain or France, it is still a matter of dispute for many of the poorer countries in the world. This is not the occasion for a detailed examination of the historical record, but I would argue that democracy has worked well enough.

India, of course, was one of the major battlegrounds of this debate. In denying Indians independence, the British expressed anxiety over the Indians' ability to govern themselves. India was indeed in some disarray in 1947, the year it became independent. It had an untried government, an undigested partition, and unclear political alignments, combined with widespread communal violence and social disorder. It was hard to have faith in the future of a united and democratic India.

And yet, half a century later, we find a democracy that has, taking the rough with the smooth, worked remarkably well. Political differences have been largely tackled within the constitutional guidelines, and governments have risen and fallen according to electoral and parliamentary rules. An ungainly, unlikely, inelegant combination of differences, India nonetheless survives and functions remarkably well as a political unit with a democratic system. Indeed, it is held together by its working democracy.

India has also survived the tremendous challenge of dealing with a variety of major languages and a spectrum of religions. Religious and communal differences are, of course, vulnerable to exploitation by sectarian politicians, and have indeed been so used on several occasions, causing massive consternation in the country. Yet the fact that consternation greets sectarian violence and that condemnation of such violence comes from all sections of the country ultimately provides the main democratic guarantee against the narrowly factional exploitation of sectarianism. This is, of course, essential for the survival and prosperity of a country as remarkably varied as India, which is home not only to a Hindu majority, but to the world's third largest Muslim population, to millions of Christians and Buddhists, and to most of the world's Sikhs, Parsis, and Jains.

Democracy and Economic Development

It is often claimed that nondemocratic systems are better at bringing about economic development. This belief sometimes goes by the name of "the Lee hypothesis," due to its advocacy by Lee Kuan Yew, the leader and former president of Singapore. He is certainly right that some disciplinarian states (such as South Korea, his own Singapore, and postreform China) have had faster rates of economic growth than many less authoritarian ones (including India, Jamaica, and Costa Rica). The "Lee hypothesis," however, is based on sporadic empiricism, drawing on very selective and limited information, rather than on any general statistical testing over the wide-ranging data that are available. A general relation of this kind cannot be established on the basis of very selective evidence. For example, we cannot really take the high economic growth of Singapore or China as "definitive proof" that authoritarianism does better in promoting economic growth, any more than we can draw the opposite conclusion from the fact that Botswana, the country with the best record of economic growth in Africa, indeed with one of the finest records of economic growth in the whole world, has been an oasis of democracy on that continent over the decades. We need more systematic empirical studies to sort out the claims and counterclaims.

There is, in fact, no convincing general evidence that authoritarian governance and the suppression of political and civil rights are really beneficial to economic development. Indeed, the general statistical picture does not permit any such induction. Systematic empirical studies (for example, by Robert Barro or by Adam Przeworski) give no real support to the claim that there is a general conflict between political rights and economic performance.[2] The directional linkage seems to depend on many other circumstances, and while some statistical investigations note a weakly negative relation, others find a strongly positive one. If all the comparative studies are viewed together, the hypothesis that there is no clear relation between economic growth and democracy in *either* direction remains extremely plausible. Since democracy and political liberty have importance in themselves, the case for them therefore remains untarnished.[3]

The question also involves a fundamental issue of methods of economic research. We must not only look at statistical connections, but also examine and scrutinize the *causal* processes that are involved in economic growth and development. The economic policies and circumstances that led to the economic success of countries in East Asia are by now reasonably well understood. While different empirical studies have varied in emphasis, there is by now broad consensus on a list of 'helpful policies' that includes openness to competition, the use of international markets, public provision of incentives for investment and export, a high level of literacy and schooling, successful land reforms, and other social opportunities that widen participation in the process of economic expansion. There is no reason at all to assume that any of these policies is inconsistent with greater democracy and had to be forcibly sustained by the elements of authoritarianism that happened to be present in South Korea or Singapore or China. Indeed, there is overwhelming evidence to show that what is needed for generating faster economic growth is a friendlier economic climate rather than a harsher political system.

To complete this examination, we must go beyond the narrow confines of economic growth and scrutinize the broader demands of economic development, including the need for economic and social security. In that context, we have to look at the connection between political and civil rights, on the one hand, and the prevention of major economic disasters, on the other. Political and civil rights give people the opportunity to draw attention forcefully to general needs and to demand appropriate public action. The response of a government to the acute suffering of its people often depends on the pressure that is put on it. The exercise of political rights (such as voting, criticizing, protesting, and the like) can make a real difference to the political incentives that operate on a government.

I have discussed elsewhere the remarkable fact that, in the terrible history of famines in the world, no substantial famine has ever occurred in any independent and democratic country with a relatively free press.[4]

We cannot find exceptions to this rule, no matter where we look: the recent famines of Ethiopia, Somalia, or other dictatorial regimes; famines in the Soviet Union in the 1930s; China's 1958–61 famine with the failure of the Great Leap Forward; or earlier still, the famines in Ireland or India under alien rule. China, although it was in many ways doing much better economically than India, still managed (unlike India) to have a famine, indeed the largest recorded famine in world history: Nearly 30 million people died in the famine of 1958–61, while faulty governmental policies remained uncorrected for three full years. The policies went uncriticized because there were no opposition parties in parliament, no free press, and no multiparty elections. Indeed, it is precisely this lack of challenge that allowed the deeply defective policies to continue even though they were killing millions each year. The same can be said about the world's two contemporary famines, which are occurring in North Korea and Sudan.

Famines are often associated with what look like natural disasters, and commentators often settle for the simplicity of explaining famines by pointing to these events: the floods in China during the failed Great Leap Forward, the droughts in Ethiopia, or crop failures in North Korea. Nevertheless, many countries with similar natural problems, or even worse ones, manage perfectly well, because a responsive government intervenes to help alleviate hunger. Since the primary victims of a famine are the indigent, deaths can be prevented by recreating incomes (for example, through employment programs), which makes food accessible to potential famine victims. Even the poorest democratic countries that have faced terrible droughts or floods or other natural disasters (such as India in 1973, or Zimbabwe and Botswana in the early 1980s) have been able to feed their people without experiencing a famine.

Famines are easy to prevent if there is a serious effort to do so, and a democratic government, facing elections and criticisms from opposition parties and independent newspapers, cannot help but make such an effort. Not surprisingly, while India continued to have famines under British rule right up to independence (the last famine, which I witnessed as a child, was in 1943, four years before independence), they disappeared suddenly with the establishment of a multiparty democracy and a free press.

I have discussed these issues elsewhere, particularly in my joint work with Jean Drèze, so I will not dwell further on them here.[5] Indeed, the issue of famine is only one example of the reach of democracy, though it is, in many ways, the easiest case to analyze. The positive role of political and civil rights applies to the prevention of economic and social disasters in general. When things go fine and everything is routinely good, this instrumental role of democracy may not be particularly missed. It is when things get fouled up, for one reason or another, that the political incentives provided by democratic governance acquire great practical value.

There is, I believe, an important lesson here. Many economic technocrats recommend the use of economic incentives (which the market system provides) while ignoring political incentives (which democratic systems could guarantee). This is to opt for a deeply unbalanced set of ground rules. The protective power of democracy may not be missed much when a country is lucky enough to be facing no serious calamity, when everything is going quite smoothly. Yet the danger of insecurity, arising from changed economic or other circumstances, or from uncorrected mistakes of policy, can lurk behind what looks like a healthy state.

The recent problems of East and Southeast Asia bring out, among other things, the penalties of undemocratic governance. This is so in two striking respects. First, the development of the financial crisis in some of these economies (including South Korea, Thailand, Indonesia) has been closely linked to the lack of transparency in business, in particular the lack of public participation in reviewing financial arrangements. The absence of an effective democratic forum has been central to this failing. Second, once the financial crisis led to a general economic recession, the protective power of democracy—not unlike that which prevents famines in democratic countries—was badly missed in a country like Indonesia. The newly dispossessed did not have the hearing they needed.

A fall in total gross national product of, say, 10 percent may not look like much if it follows in the wake of a growth rate of 5 or 10 percent every year over the past few decades, and yet that decline can decimate lives and create misery for millions if the burden of contraction is not widely shared but allowed to be heaped on those—the unemployed or the economically redundant—who can least bear it. The vulnerable in Indonesia may not have missed democracy when things went up and up, but that lacuna kept their voice low and muffled as the unequally shared crisis developed. The protective role of democracy is strongly missed when it is most needed.

The Functions of Democracy

I have so far allowed the agenda of this essay to be determined by the critics of democracy, especially the economic critics. I shall return to criticisms again, taking up the arguments of the cultural critics in particular, but the time has come for me to pursue further the positive analysis of what democracy does and what may lie at the base of its claim to be a universal value.

What exactly is democracy? We must not identify democracy with majority rule. Democracy has complex demands, which certainly include voting and respect for election results, but it also requires the protection of liberties and freedoms, respect for legal entitlements, and the guaranteeing of free discussion and uncensored distribution of news and fair comment. Even elections can be deeply defective if they occur without the different sides getting an adequate opportunity to present their respective cases, or without the electorate enjoying the freedom to obtain news and to consider the views of the competing protagonists. Democracy is a demanding system, and not just a mechanical condition (like majority rule) taken in isolation.

Viewed in this light, the merits of democracy and its claim as a universal value can be related to certain distinct virtues that go with its unfettered practice. Indeed, we can distinguish three different ways in which democracy enriches the lives of the citizens. First, political freedom is a part of human freedom in general, and exercising civil and political rights is a crucial part of good lives of individuals as social beings. Political and social participation has *intrinsic value* for human life and well-being. To be prevented from participation in the political life of the community is a major deprivation.

Second, as I have just discussed (in disputing the claim that democracy is in tension with economic development), democracy has an important *instrumental value* in enhancing the hearing that people get in expressing and supporting their claims to political attention (including claims of economic needs). Third—and this is a point to be explored further—the practice of democracy gives citizens an opportunity to learn from one another, and helps society to form its values and priorities. Even the idea of "needs," including the understanding of "economic needs," requires public discussion and exchange of information, views, and analyses. In this sense, democracy has *constructive importance,* in addition to its intrinsic value for the lives of the citizens and its instrumental importance in political decisions. The claims of democracy as a universal value have to take note of this diversity of considerations.

The conceptualization—even comprehension—of what are to count as "needs," including "economic needs," may itself require the exercise of political and civil rights. A proper understanding of what economic needs are—their content and their force—may require discussion and exchange. Political and civil rights, especially those related to the guaranteeing of open discussion, debate, criticism, and dissent, are central to the process of generating informed and considered choices. These processes are crucial to the formation of values and priorities, and we cannot, in general, take preferences as given independently of public discussion, that is, irrespective of whether open interchange and debate are permitted or not.

In fact, the reach and effectiveness of open dialogue are often underestimated in assessing social and political problems. For example, public discussion has an important role to play in reducing the high rates of fertility that characterize many developing countries. There is substantial evidence that the sharp decline in fertility rates in India's more literate states has been much influenced by public discussion of the bad effects of high fertility rates on the community at large, and especially on the lives of young women. If the view has emerged in, say, the Indian state of Kerala or of Tamil Nadu that a happy family in the modern age is a small family, much discussion and debate have gone into the formation of these perspectives. Kerala now has a fertility rate of 1.7 (similar to that of Britain and France, and well below China's 1.9), and this has been achieved with no coercion, but mainly through the emergence of new values—a process in which political and social dialogue has played a major part. Kerala's high literacy rate (it ranks higher in literacy than any province in China), especially among women, has greatly contributed to making such social and political dialogue possible.

Miseries and deprivations can be of various kinds, some more amenable to social remedies than others. The totality of the human predicament would be a gross basis for identifying our "needs." For example, there are many things that we might have good reason to value and thus could be taken as "needs" if they were feasible. We could even want immortality, as Maitreyee, that remarkable inquiring mind in the *Upanishads,* famously did in her 3,000-year-old conversation with Yajnvalkya. But we do not see immortality as a "need" because it is clearly unfeasible. Our conception of needs relates to our ideas of the preventable nature of some deprivations and to our understanding of what can be done about them. In the formation of understandings and beliefs about feasibility (particularly, *social* feasibility), public discussions play a crucial role. Political rights, including freedom of expression and discussion, are not only pivotal in inducing social responses to economic needs, they are also central to the conceptualization of economic needs themselves.

Universality of Values

If the above analysis is correct, then democracy's claim to be valuable does not rest on just one particular merit. There is a plurality of virtues here, including, first, the *intrinsic* importance of political participation and freedom in human life; second, the *instrumental* importance of political incentives in keeping governments responsible and accountable; and third, the *constructive* role of democracy in the formation of values and in the understanding of needs, rights, and duties. In the light of this diagnosis, we may now address the motivating question of this essay, namely the case for seeing democracy as a universal value.

In disputing this claim, it is sometimes argued that not everyone agrees on the decisive importance of democracy, particularly when it competes with other desirable things for our attention and loyalty. This is indeed so, and there is no unanimity here. This lack of unanimity is seen by some as sufficient evidence that democracy is not a universal value.

Clearly, we must begin by dealing with a methodological question: What is a universal value? For a value to be considered universal, must it have the consent of everyone? If that were indeed necessary, then the category of universal values might well be empty. I know of no value—not even motherhood (I think of *Mommie Dearest*)—to which no one has ever objected. I would argue that universal consent is not required for something to be a universal value. Rather, the claim of a universal value is that people anywhere may have reason to see it as valuable.

When Mahatma Gandhi argued for the universal value of nonviolence, he was not arguing that people everywhere already acted according to this value, but rather that they had good reason to see it as valuable. Similarly, when Rabindranath Tagore argued for "the freedom of the mind" as a universal value, he was not saying that this claim is accepted by all, but that all do have reason enough to accept it—a reason that he did much to explore, present, and propagate.[6] Understood in this way, any claim that something is a universal value involves some counterfactual analysis—in particular, whether people might see some value in a claim that they have not yet considered adequately. All claims to universal value—not just that of democracy—have this implicit presumption.

I would argue that it is with regard to this often *implicit* presumption that the biggest attitudinal shift toward democracy has occurred in the twentieth century. In considering democracy for a country that does not have it and where many people may not yet have had the opportunity to consider it for actual practice, it is now presumed that the people involved would approve of it once it becomes a reality in their lives. In the nineteenth century this assumption typically would have not been made, but the presumption that is taken to be natural (what I earlier called the "default" position) has changed radically during the twentieth century.

It must also be noted that this change is, to a great extent, based on observing the history of the twentieth century. As democracy has spread, its adherents have grown, not shrunk. Starting off from Europe and America, democracy as a system has reached very many distant shores, where it has been met with willing participation and acceptance. Moreover, when an existing democracy has been overthrown, there have been widespread protests, even though these protests have often been brutally suppressed. Many people have been willing to risk their lives in the fight to bring back democracy.

Some who dispute the status of democracy as a universal value base their argument not on the absence of unanimity, but on the presence of regional contrasts. These alleged contrasts are sometimes related to the poverty of some nations. According to this argument, poor people are interested, and have reason to be interested, in bread, not in democracy. This oft-repeated argument is fallacious at two different levels.

First, as discussed above, the protective role of democracy may be particularly important for the poor. This obviously applies to potential famine victims who face starvation. It also applies to the destitute thrown off the economic ladder in a financial crisis. People in economic need also need a political voice. Democracy is not a luxury that can await the arrival of general prosperity.

Second, there is very little evidence that poor people, given the choice, prefer to reject democracy. It is thus of some interest to note that when an erstwhile Indian government in the mid-1970s tried out a similar argument to justify the alleged "emergency" (and the suppression of various political and civil rights) that it had declared, an election was called that divided the voters precisely on this issue. In that fateful election, fought largely on this one overriding theme, the suppression of basic political and civil rights was firmly rejected, and the Indian electorate—one of the poorest in the world—showed itself to be no less keen on protesting against the denial of basic liberties and rights than on complaining about economic deprivation.

To the extent that there has been any testing of the proposition that the poor do not care about civil and political rights, the evidence is entirely against that claim. Similar points can be made by observing the struggle for democratic freedoms in South Korea, Thailand, Bangladesh, Pakistan, Burma, Indonesia, and elsewhere in Asia. Similarly, while political freedom is widely denied in Africa, there have been movements and protests against such repression whenever circumstances have permitted them.

The Argument from Cultural Differences

There is also another argument in defense of an allegedly fundamental regional contrast, one related not to economic circumstances but to cultural differences. Perhaps the most famous of these claims relates to what have been called "Asian values." It has been claimed that Asians traditionally value discipline, not political freedom, and thus the attitude to democracy must inevitably be much more skeptical in these countries. I have discussed this thesis in some detail in my Morganthau Memorial Lecture at the Carnegie Council on Ethics and International Affairs.[7]

It is very hard to find any real basis for this intellectual claim in the history of Asian cultures, especially if we look at the classical traditions of India, the Middle East, Iran, and other parts of Asia. For example, one of the earliest and most emphatic statements advocating the tolerance of pluralism and the duty of the state to protect minorities can be found in the inscriptions of the Indian emperor Ashoka in the third century B.C.

Asia is, of course, a very large area, containing 60 percent of the world's population, and generalizations about such a vast set of peoples is not easy. Sometimes the advocates of "Asian values" have tended to look primarily at East Asia as the region of particular applicability. The general thesis of a contrast between the West and Asia often concentrates on the lands to the east of Thailand, even though there is also a more ambitious claim that the rest of Asia is rather "similar." Lee Kuan Yew, to whom we must be grateful for being such a clear expositor (and for articulating fully what is often stated vaguely in this tangled literature), outlines "the fundamental difference between Western concepts of society and government and East Asian concepts" by explaining, "when I say East Asians, I mean Korea, Japan, China, Vietnam, as distinct from Southeast Asia, which is a mix between the Sinic and the Indian, though Indian culture itself emphasizes similar values."[8]

Even East Asia itself, however, is remarkably diverse, with many variations to be found not only among Japan, China, Korea, and other countries of the region, but also *within* each country. Confucius is the standard author quoted in interpreting Asian values, but he is not the only intellectual influence in these countries (in Japan, China, and Korea for example, there are very old and very widespread Buddhist traditions, powerful for over a millennium and a half, and there are also other influences, including a considerable Christian presence). There is no homogeneous worship of order over freedom in any of these cultures.

Furthermore, Confucius himself did not recommend blind allegiance to the state. When Zilu asks him "how to serve a prince," Confucius replies (in a statement that the censors of authoritarian regimes may want to ponder), "Tell him the truth even if it offends him."[9] Confucius is not averse to practical caution and tact, but does not forgo the recommendation to oppose a bad government (tactfully, if necessary): "When the [good] way prevails in the state, speak boldly and act boldly. When the state has lost the way, act boldly and speak softly."[10]

Indeed, Confucius provides a clear pointer to the fact that the two pillars of the imagined edifice of Asian values, loyalty to family and obedience to the state, can be in severe conflict with each other. Many advocates of the power of "Asian values" see the role of the state as an extension of the role of the family, but as Confucius noted, there can be tension between the two. The Governor of She told Confucius, "Among my people, there is a man of unbending integrity: When his father stole a sheep, he denounced him." To this Confucius replied, "Among my people, men of integrity do things differently: A father covers up for his son, a son covers up for his father—and there is integrity in what they do."[11]

The monolithic interpretation of Asian values as hostile to democracy and political rights does not bear critical scrutiny. I should not, I suppose, be too critical of the lack of scholarship supporting these beliefs, since those who have made these claims are not scholars but political leaders, often official or unofficial spokesmen for authoritarian governments. It is, however, interesting to see that while we academics can be impractical about practical politics, practical politicians can, in turn, be rather impractical about scholarship.

It is not hard, of course, to find authoritarian writings within the Asian traditions. But neither is it hard to find them in Western classics: One has only to reflect on the writings of Plato or Aquinas to see that devotion to discipline is not a special Asian taste. To dismiss the plausibility of democracy as a universal value because of the presence of some Asian writings on discipline and order would be similar to rejecting the plausibility of democracy as a natural form of government in Europe or America today on the basis of the writings of Plato or Aquinas (not to mention the substantial medieval literature in support of the Inquisitions).

Due to the experience of contemporary political battles, especially in the Middle East, Islam is often portrayed as fundamentally intolerant of and hostile to individual freedom. But the presence of diversity and variety *within* a tradition applies very much to Islam as well. In India, Akbar and most of the other Moghul emperors (with the notable exception of Aurangzeb) provide good examples of both the theory and practice of political and religious tolerance. The Turkish emperors were often more tolerant than their European contemporaries. Abundant examples can also be found among rulers in Cairo and Baghdad. Indeed, in the twelfth century, the great Jewish scholar Maimonides had to run away from an intolerant Europe (where he was born), and from its persecution of Jews, to the security of a tolerant and urbane Cairo and the patronage of Sultan Saladin.

Diversity is a feature of most cultures in the world. Western civilization is no exception. The practice of democracy that has won out in the *modern* West is largely a result of a consensus that has emerged since the Enlightenment and the Industrial Revolution, and particularly in the last century or so. To read in this a historical commitment of the West—over the millennia—to democracy, and then to contrast it with non-Western traditions (treating each as monolithic) would be a great mistake. This tendency toward oversimplification can be seen not only in the writings of some governmental spokesmen in Asia, but also in the theories of some of the finest Western scholars themselves.

As an example from the writings of a major scholar whose works, in many other ways, have been totally impressive, let me cite Samuel

Huntington's thesis on the clash of civilizations, where the hetero-geneities *within* each culture get quite inadequate recognition. His study comes to the clear conclusion that "a sense of individualism and a tradition of rights and liberties" can be found in the West that are "unique among civilized societies."[12] Huntington also argues that "the central characteristics of the West, those which distinguish it from other civilizations, antedate the modernization of the West." In his view, "The West was West long before it was modern."[13] It is this thesis that—I have argued—does not survive historical scrutiny.

For every attempt by an Asian government spokesman to contrast alleged "Asian values" with alleged Western ones, there is, it seems, an attempt by a Western intellectual to make a similar contrast from the other side. But even though every Asian pull may be matched by a Western push, the two together do not really manage to dent democ-racy's claim to be a universal value.

Where the Debate Belongs

I have tried to cover a number of issues related to the claim that democracy is a universal value. The value of democracy includes its *intrinsic importance* in human life, its *instrumental role* in generating political incentives, and its *constructive function* in the formation of values (and in understanding the force and feasibility of claims of needs, rights, and duties). These merits are not regional in character. Nor is the advocacy of discipline or order. Heterogeneity of values seems to characterize most, perhaps all, major cultures. The cultural argument does not foreclose, nor indeed deeply constrain, the choices we can make today.

Those choices have to be made here and now, taking note of the functional roles of democracy, on which the case for democracy in the contemporary world depends. I have argued that this case is indeed strong and not regionally contingent. The force of the claim that democ-racy is a universal value lies, ultimately, in that strength. That is where the debate belongs. It cannot be disposed of by imagined cultural taboos or assumed civilizational predispositions imposed by our various pasts.

NOTES

1. In Aldous Huxley's novel *Point Counter Point,* this was enough to give an adequate excuse to a cheating husband, who tells his wife that he must go to London to study democracy in ancient India in the library of the British Museum, while in reality he goes to see his mistress.

2. Adam Przeworski et al., *Sustainable Democracy* (Cambridge: Cambridge University Press, 1995); Robert J. Barro, *Getting It Right: Markets and Choices in a Free Society* (Cambridge, Mass.: MIT Press, 1996).

3. I have examined the empirical evidence and causal connections in some detail in my book *Development as Freedom* (New York: Alfred A. Knopf, 1999).

4. See my "Development: Which Way Now?" *Economic Journal* 93 (December 1983); *Resources, Values, and Development* (Cambridge, Mass.: Harvard University Press, 1984); and my "Rationality and Social Choice," presidential address to the American Economic Association, published in *American Economic Review* in March 1995. See also Jean Drèze and Amartya Sen, *Hunger and Public Action* (Oxford: Clarendon Press, 1987); Frances D'Souza, ed., *Starving in Silence: A Report on Famine and Censorship* (London: Article 19 International Centre on Censorship, 1990); Human Rights Watch, *Indivisible Human Rights: The Relationship between Political and Civil Rights to Survival, Subsistence and Poverty* (New York: Human Rights Watch, 1992); and International Federation of Red Cross and Red Crescent Societies, *World Disaster Report 1994* (Geneva: Red Cross, 1994).

5. Drèze and Sen, *Hunger and Public Action*.

6. See my "Tagore and His India," *New York Review of Books*, 26 June 1997.

7. Amartya Sen, "Human Rights and Asian Values," Morgenthau Memorial Lecture (New York: Carnegie Council on Ethics and International Affairs, 1997), published in a shortened form in *The New Republic*, 14–21 July 1997.

8. Fareed Zakaria, "Culture is Destiny: A Conversation with Lee Kuan Yew," *Foreign Affairs* 73 (March–April 1994): 113.

9. *The Analects of Confucius*, Simon Leys, trans. (New York: Norton, 1997), 14.22, 70.

10. *The Analects of Confucius*, 14.3, 66.

11. *The Analects of Confucius*, 13.18, 63.

12. Samuel P. Huntington, *The Clash of Civilizations and the Remaking of World Order* (New York: Simon and Schuster, 1996), 71.

13. Huntington, *The Clash of Civilizations*, 69.

2

BUDDHISM, ASIAN VALUES, AND DEMOCRACY

His Holiness the Dalai Lama

The Dalai Lama, the spiritual and temporal leader of the Tibetan people, fled Chinese-occupied Tibet into exile in India in 1959. One of the world's great exponents of nonviolence, His Holiness was awarded the Nobel Peace Prize in 1989. The following essay is based on a lecture that he delivered on 10 November 1998 at George Washington University in Washington, D.C. The lecture, one in a series entitled "The Democratic Invention," was cosponsored by the Mário Soares Foundation, the Luso-American Development Foundation, and the International Forum for Democratic Studies.

While democratic aspirations may be manifested in different ways, some universal principles lie at the heart of any democratic society— representative government (established through free and fair elections), the rule of law and accountability (as enforced by an independent judiciary), and freedom of speech (as exemplified by an uncensored press). Democracy, however, is about much more than these formal institutions; it is about genuine freedom and the empowerment of the individual. I am neither an expert in political science nor an authority on democracy and the rule of law. Rather, I am a simple Buddhist monk, educated and trained in our ancient, traditional ways. Nonetheless, my life-long study of Buddhism and my involvement in the Tibetan people's nonviolent struggle for freedom have given me some insights that I would like to discuss.

As a Buddhist monk, I do not find alien the concept and practice of democracy. At the heart of Buddhism lies the idea that the potential for awakening and perfection is present in every human being and that realizing this potential is a matter of personal effort. The Buddha proclaimed that each individual is a master of his or her own destiny, highlighting the capacity that each person has to attain enlightenment. In this sense, the Buddhist world view recognizes the fundamental sameness of all human beings. Like Buddhism, modern democracy is based on the principle that all human beings are essentially equal, and that each of us has an equal right to life, liberty, and happiness. Whether we are rich or poor, educated or uneducated, a follower of one religion or another, each of us is a human being. Not only do we desire happiness and seek to avoid suffering, but each of us also has an equal right to pursue these goals. Thus not only are Buddhism and democracy compatible, they are rooted in a common understanding of the equality and potential of every individual.

As for democracy as a procedure of decision making, we find again in the Buddhist tradition a certain recognition of the need for consensus. For example, the Buddhist monastic order has a long history of basing major decisions affecting the lives of individual monks on collective discourse. In fact, strictly speaking, every rite concerning the maintenance of monastic practice must be performed with a congregation of at least four monks. Thus one could say that the Vinaya rules of discipline that govern the behavior and life of the Buddhist monastic community are in keeping with democratic traditions. In theory at least, even the teachings of the Buddha can be altered under certain circumstances by a congregation of a certain number of ordained monks.

As human beings, we all seek to live in a society in which we can express ourselves freely and strive to be the best we can be. At the same time, pursuing one's own fulfillment at the expense of others would lead to chaos and anarchy. What is required, then, is a system whereby the interests of the individual are balanced with the wider well-being of the community at large. For this reason, I feel it is necessary to develop a sense of universal responsibility, a deep concern for all human beings, irrespective of religion, color, gender, or nationality. If we adopt a self-centered approach to life and constantly try to use others to advance our own interests, we may gain temporary benefits, but in the long run happiness will elude us. Instead, we must learn to work not just for our own individual selves, but for the benefit of all mankind.

While it is true that no system of government is perfect, democracy is the closest to our essential human nature and allows us the greatest opportunity to cultivate a sense of universal responsibility. As a Buddhist, I strongly believe in a humane approach to democracy, an approach that recognizes the importance of the individual without sacrificing a sense of responsibility toward all humanity. Buddhists emphasize the potential of the individual, but we also believe that the purpose of a meaningful life is to serve others.

Many nations consider respect for the individual's civil and political rights to be the most important aspect of democracy. Other countries, especially in the developing world, see the rights of the society—particularly the right to economic development—as overriding the rights of the individual. I believe that economic advancement and respect for individual rights are closely linked. A society cannot fully maximize its

economic advantage without granting its people individual civil and
political rights. At the same time, these freedoms are diminished if the
basic necessities of life are not met.

Some Asian leaders say that democracy and the freedoms that come
with it are exclusive products of Western civilization. Asian values,
they contend, are significantly different from, if not diametrically
opposed to, democracy. They argue that Asian cultures emphasize
order, duty, and stability, while the emphasis of Western democracies
on individual rights and liberties undermines those values. They
suggest that Asians have fundamentally different needs in terms of
personal and social fulfillment. I do not share this viewpoint.

It is my fundamental belief that all human beings share the same
basic aspirations: We all want happiness and we all experience suffering. Like Americans, Europeans, and the rest of the world, Asians wish
to live life to its fullest, to better themselves and the lives of their loved
ones. India, the birthplace of Mahatma Gandhi and of the concept of
ahimsa, or nonviolence, is an excellent example of an Asian country
devoted to a democratic form of government. India demonstrates that
democracy can sink strong roots outside the Western world. Similarly,
our brothers and sisters in Burma, Indonesia, and China are courage-
ously raising their voices together in the call for equality, freedom, and
democracy.

The fact that democratic reforms are on the rise around the globe,
from the Czech Republic to Mongolia, and from South Africa to
Taiwan, is testimony to the strength of the ideals that democracy
embodies. As more and more people gain awareness of their individual
potential, the number of people seeking to express themselves through
a democratic system grows. These global trends illustrate the universality of the desire for a form of government that respects human
rights and the rule of law.

The Case of Tibet

I am deeply committed to the political modernization and
democratization of my native Tibet and have made efforts to develop a
democratic system for Tibetans living in exile. In 1963, I promulgated
the democratic constitution of Tibet, and our exiled community has,
under difficult circumstances, responded well to the challenge of this
experiment with democracy. In 1969, I declared that whether the
institution of the Dalai Lama should continue to exist depended on the
wishes of the Tibetan people. And in 1991, our legislature, the
Assembly of Tibetan People's Deputies, adopted the Charter of
Tibetans in Exile, which expanded the Assembly's membership and
transferred from me to it the power to elect the Cabinet. While this
Charter was modeled on constitutions from established democracies, it

also reflects the unique nature of the Tibetan culture and system of values: It protects freedom of religion, upholds the principles of nonviolence, and emphasizes the promotion of the moral and material welfare of the Tibetan people.

Respect for basic human rights, freedom of speech, the equality of all human beings, and the rule of law must be seen not merely as aspirations but as necessary conditions of a civilized society.

In 1992, in order to guide our efforts to have an eventual impact on Tibetans living in Tibet, I announced the Guidelines for Future Tibet's Polity. This document is based on my hope that, before too long, we will achieve a negotiated settlement with the Chinese government granting full autonomy to the Tibetan people. I believe that, once such an agreement is reached, it is the Tibetans inside Tibet who will bear the major responsibility for determining Tibet's future governance and that the officials presently serving in positions of leadership in Tibet shall bear an even greater responsibility in the future.

Unfortunately, Tibetans living in Tibet have not shared in the democratic freedoms that we have implemented in exile. In fact, over the last several decades, our brothers and sisters in Tibet have suffered immeasurably. Through direct attacks on all things Tibetan, the very culture of Tibet has been threatened. I believe that the Tibetan people have a right to preserve their own unique and distinct cultural heritage. I also believe that they should be able to decide their future, their form of government, and their social system. No Tibetan is interested in restoring outdated political and social institutions, but we are a nation of six million people with the right to live as human beings.

As we Tibetans have begun moving toward democracy, we have learned that to empower our people we must give them a sufficient understanding of their rights and responsibilities as citizens of a democratic society. For this reason, I have focused considerable attention on education. The more the Tibetan people learn about their individual potential and their ability to play a role in their own governance, the stronger our society will become.

In some respects, I have been the unluckiest Dalai Lama, for I have spent more time as a refugee outside my country than I have spent inside Tibet. On the other hand, it has been very rewarding for me to live in a democracy and to learn about the world in a way that we Tibetans had never been able to do before. Had I continued to live in and govern Tibet, I would certainly have made efforts to bring about changes in our political system, but it is quite probable that I would still have been influenced by the conservative political environment that existed in my homeland. Living outside Tibet has given me an invaluable perspective. I know that our previous political system was outdated and ill-equipped to face the challenges of the contemporary world.

Today, the world has become increasingly interdependent. In this age of cross-border cooperation and exchange, it is very important for the United States and other democratic countries to help preserve and promote democratic trends around the world. For example, the dismantling of the Soviet Union was seen as a significant victory for democracy and human rights. In fact, many Western leaders, including those in the United States, took credit for the Soviet Union's demise. Today, however, conditions in Russia are dire and many of the former Soviet republics face the prospect of political and economic chaos. The failure of Russia's experiment in democracy would have adverse repercussions throughout the world and could give power and strength to democracy's detractors. I therefore believe it is the responsibility of the democratic free world to come to the aid of those countries who took the courageous step toward democracy and now are struggling to make it work.

I also understand that it is the right of all people to be concerned with the security of their nation. But it is surely more important to help create stability in troubled areas like the former Soviet Union, through economic and other means of support, than to invest in increasingly sophisticated weaponry and a soaring national defense budget. Furthermore, despite the fact that each nation has the right to determine its own security needs, I believe that a nonviolent approach is the most constructive path to securing peace in the long term.

In conclusion, I would like to stress once again the need for firm conviction on all our parts in acknowledging the universality of the key ethical and political values that underlie democracy. Recognition of and respect for basic human rights, freedom of speech, the equality of all human beings, and the rule of law must be seen not merely as aspirations but as necessary conditions of a civilized society.

3

CONFUCIANISM AND DEMOCRACY

Francis Fukuyama

Francis Fukuyama *is Bernard Schwartz Professor of International Political Economy at the Paul H. Nitze School of International Studies of the Johns Hopkins University, and author of* The End of History and the Last Man *(1992), and most recently,* The Great Disruption: Human Nature and the Reconstitution of Social Order *(1999). An earlier version of this essay was presented at a conference sponsored by the Institute for National Policy Research in Taipei, Taiwan, in June 1994.*

The caning for vandalism in 1993 of American high-school student Michael Fay by the Singaporean authorities underscored the challenge now being put forth by Asian societies to the United States and other Western democracies. The issue was not simply whether Singapore, as a sovereign state, had the right to subject an American expatriate to its laws and legal procedures, but a much more fundamental one. In effect, the Singaporeans used the case of Michael Fay to argue in favor of their brand of authoritarianism, charging that American democracy, with its rampant social problems and general disorder, could not be regarded as a model for an Asian society. This claim forms part of a larger argument that Singaporeans, beginning with former prime minister Lee Kuan Yew, have been making for some time now to the effect that Western-style democracy is incompatible with Confucianism, and that the latter constitutes a much more coherent ideological basis for a well-ordered Asian society than Western notions of individual liberty.[1] While Singaporeans have been the most outspoken proponents of this view, many people in other Asian societies, from Thailand to Japan, have come to share their beliefs. The standing of the United States in Asia has already been affected: On the issue of using trade policy to pressure China into bettering its human rights record, Washington had few allies in the region, and it was forced to back down on its threat of withdrawing China's most-favored-nation (MFN) status.

Are Confucianism and Western-style democracy fundamentally

incompatible? Will Asia formulate a new kind of political-economic order that is different in principle from Western capitalist democracy? The fact is that there are fewer points of incompatibility between Confucianism and democracy than many people in both Asia and the West believe. The essence of postwar "modernization theory" is correct: Economic development tends to be followed by political liberalization.[2] If the rapid economic development that Asia has experienced in recent years is sustained, the region's democratization will continue as well. In the end, however, the contours of Asian democracy may be very different from those of contemporary American democracy, which has experienced serious problems of its own in reconciling individual rights with the interests of the larger community.

Modernization Theory Confirmed

Although it is no longer considered "politically correct" to advocate modernization theory, it has actually stood the test of time relatively well. In a seminal article published in 1959, Seymour Martin Lipset noted the empirical correlation between a high level of economic development and stable democracy.[3] Although the thesis that economic development gives rise to political liberalization has been debated endlessly since then, it was strengthened considerably with the democratic transitions that began in the mid-1970s, and it is more valid today than it was when it was first enunciated.[4]

The correlation between development and democracy is nowhere better illustrated than in Asia. The states of the region have established stable democratic institutions roughly in the same order in which they began to develop economically, beginning with Japan and extending now to South Korea (which held its first completely free elections in 1992) and Taiwan (which held free legislative and presidential elections in the mid-1990s). There have been a number of failed prodemocracy movements in China, Thailand, and Burma, but even these cases reveal a link between development and democracy. In the Chinese and Thai cases, in particular, the leaders of the prodemocracy movements tended to be relatively well educated, "middle-class," and cosmopolitan citizens—the type of individual that began to emerge during earlier periods of rapid economic growth. The only anomaly in this picture is the Philippines, which, despite having the lowest per-capita income of all the noncommunist states in Southeast Asia, has been a democracy since the election of Corazon Aquino in 1986. Clearly, though, democracy would never have come to the Philippines had it not been for the direct influence of the United States; moreover, democratic practice is not well institutionalized there, and the country retains a semifeudal authority structure in the countryside and features one of Asia's few remaining communist insurgencies. It would not be surprising, in fact, if Philippine democracy were suddenly to collapse, a scenario that is difficult to imagine in South Korea or Japan.

Although modernization theory proposed a correlation between development and democracy, it was hazy on what the causal connections between the two phenomena were. Some proponents, such as Talcott Parsons, argued that democracy was more "functional" than authoritarianism in a modern industrialized society.[5] I have argued elsewhere that the linkage between the two cannot be understood in economic terms.[6] That is, the fundamental impulse toward liberal democracy springs from a noneconomic desire for "recognition." The relationship between economic modernization and democracy is therefore indirect: Economic modernization raises living and educational standards and liberates people from a certain kind of fear brought on by life close to the subsistence level. This permits people to pursue a broader range of goals, including those that remained latent in earlier stages of economic development. Among those latent urges is the desire to be recognized as an adult with a certain basic human dignity—a recognition that is achieved through participation in the political system. Poor peasants in the Philippines or El Salvador can be recruited by landlords to take up arms and form death squads, because they can be manipulated relatively easily on the basis of their immediate needs and are accustomed to obeying traditional sources of authority. It is much more difficult to persuade educated, middle-class professionals to obey the authority of a leader simply because he is wearing a uniform.

The case of Japan seems to provide further confirmation of the proposed link between development and democracy. Japan, of course, has been a formal democracy since General MacArthur imposed a democratic constitution on the country during the U.S. occupation. Nevertheless, many observers both within and outside of Japan have noted that Western-style democracy, with its emphasis on public contestation and individualism, did not seem to sit well with traditional Japanese culture. Some commentators even went so far as to argue that, despite its democratic legal structure, Japan was not a democracy in the Western sense at all, but rather a mildly authoritarian country run by an alliance of bureaucrats, Liberal Democratic Party (LDP) officials, and business leaders.[7]

The political upheaval that has occurred in Japan since the fall of the LDP government in July 1993, however, would seem to bear out some of the premises of modernization theory. The Japanese people deferred to the authority of the bureaucracy-LDP-business triangle for much of the postwar period because that alliance delivered a high rate of economic growth to a nation that had been devastated by the Pacific war. Like many an authoritarian leadership, however, it ultimately failed to hold up its end of the bargain: It presided over the creation and subsequent puncturing of a "bubble economy" in the 1980s, and suffered from creeping and pervasive corruption. There is no guarantee that such a system will be self-correcting in the absence of popular "feedback loops"; moreover, as the Japanese population grew wealthier and more able to take its prosperity for granted, its willingness to defer to the political leadership and overlook abuses diminished. Although it is very difficult to predict the outcome of Japan's current political struggle, it seems unlikely that the old ruling triangle will carry its power and authority intact into the next generation.

Modernization theory came under heavy attack in the 1960s and 1970s from two principal sources. First, Marxist critics argued that capitalist democracy was not the proper goal of political and economic develop-ment, and that modernization theorists were apologists for an unjust global economic order. Another group of critics, who might be labeled "cultural relativists," argued that modernization theory was Eurocentric and did not take account of the diversity of ends dictated by the world's different cultures. While the Marxist critique is less prominent today owing to the collapse of communism, the relativist critique remains very powerful, and has intimidated many people out of arguing for the existence of a universally valid development path whose ultimate out-come is free-market democracy.

Some of the criticisms to which modernization theory was subjected did have a certain amount of validity. Clearly, for the theory to retain its strength, it would have to be modified somewhat in light of subsequent experience. The developmental history of England or the United States cannot be held up as a standard against which subsequent experiences must be measured. It is evident that there is not a single path to modernity: The "late" modernizers have taken a very different route to development (with the state playing a more powerful role) than earlier ones. Indeed, it is difficult to come up with a universally valid rule for the sequencing of political and economic liberalization. Although many states, particularly in Asia, have succeeded in following the "authoritarian" transition to democracy, it would have been absurd to propose that the former communist regimes in Eastern Europe delay democratization until their economies were liberalized.[8] Moreover, there is considerable variation in the way that both capitalism and democracy are implemented: Japanese corporations and labor markets are structured very differently from those in the United States, and there is no reason to think that Japanese and American practices will converge any time soon. Finally, the time frame required for economic development to produce conditions favorable to stable democracy is longer than anyone anticipated 40 years ago: Sustained economic growth is difficult to achieve, and democratic institutions are even harder to create.

Nonetheless, a significant connection between development and democracy has been borne out over the past 50 years. Few of the original formulators of modernization theory are still around to defend it and willing to do so.[9] But they gave up too easily. If we define democracy and capitalism sufficiently broadly, and are not dogmatic about the means by which either one can be achieved, then the experience of the Asian nations can be seen as proof of the underlying hypothesis.

Asia's Confucian Traditions

Despite the positive relationship that has obtained between development and democracy in the past, many observers today would argue that Asia will not continue to democratize in the future, or that the form democracy takes there will be so specifically rooted in Asian traditions as to be unrecognizable to Westerners.

The most prominent proponent of an Asian alternative to democracy has been former Singaporean prime minister Lee Kuan Yew. Singapore under Lee developed a model of what might be called a "soft" or paternalistic form of authoritarianism, which combined capitalism with an authoritarian political system that suppressed freedom of speech and political dissent while intervening, often intrusively, in its citizens' personal lives. Lee has argued that this model is more appropriate to East Asia's Confucian cultural traditions than is the Western democratic model. In fact, he has said that Western-style democracy would have deleterious effects in a society like that of Singapore, encouraging permissiveness, social instability, and economically irrational decision making.

Many Western authorities on democracy would agree with this assessment of the relationship between Confucianism and democracy. Samuel P. Huntington, for example, has written that "Confucian democracy" is a contradiction in terms:

> Almost no scholarly disagreement exists regarding the proposition that traditional Confucianism was either undemocratic or antidemocratic. . . . Classic Chinese Confucianism and its derivatives in Korea, Vietnam, Singapore, Taiwan, and (in diluted fashion) Japan emphasized the group over the individual, authority over liberty, and responsibilities over rights. Confucian societies lacked a tradition of rights against the state; to the extent that individual rights did exist, they were created by the state. Harmony and cooperation were preferred over disagreement and competition. The maintenance of order and respect for hierarchy were central values. The conflict of ideas, groups, and parties was viewed as dangerous and illegitimate. Most important, Confucianism merged society and the state and provided no legitimacy for autonomous social institutions at the national level.[10]

According to Huntington, the only Asian countries to experience democracy prior to 1990 were Japan and the Philippines, and democratic transitions there were possible only because both countries were influenced directly by the United States and were less Confucian than other Asian societies.

In my view, the arguments of both Huntington and Lee greatly overstate the obstacles that Confucianism poses to the spread of a political system that is recognizably democratic in a Western sense. The most striking area of apparent incompatibility between democracy and Confucianism is the latter's lack of support for individualism or a transcendent law that would stand above existing social relationships and provide the ground for individual conscience as the ultimate source of authority. Despite this important difference, it is not clear that a Confucian society is incapable of creating workable democratic institutions that meet democracy's essential requirements.

Let us begin with the ways in which Confucianism is obviously compatible with democracy. First, the traditional Confucian examination system was a meritocratic institution with potentially egalitarian implications. In traditional China, the examination system was not—for various reasons—truly open to all who were qualified (neither, of course, are Harvard and Yale). In their modern form, however, the examination systems implemented in many Confucian societies as gateways into higher-educational systems and bureaucracies are significant paths to upward mobility that reinforce the relatively egalitarian income distributions that prevail throughout much of Asia. The second main area of compatibility is the Confucian emphasis on education itself. Although an educated populace is seldom noted as a formal requirement of democracy, in practice a society's general level of education has been an important underpinning of democratic institutions. Without a high level of literacy, people cannot know about and therefore participate in democratic debate; moreover, as indicated above, education tends to make people wealthier and more concerned with noneconomic issues such as recognition and political participation. Finally, like most Asian ethical systems, Confucianism is relatively tolerant. In the past, Confucianism has coexisted with other religions, notably Buddhism and Christianity; while Confucianism's record of tolerance is not perfect (witness the periodic persecutions of Buddhists in China), it is arguably better than that of either Islam or Christianity.

The compatibility of Confucianism with modern democracy goes even deeper than this, however, and in ways that are less often recognized. Huntington describes Confucianism as if it were comparable to Islam, being essentially a doctrine that unified the political and social spheres and legitimated the state's authority in all areas of life. Yet to say that Confucianism merely strengthens the group against the individual and the state against all subordinate organizations or institutions vastly oversimplifies the doctrine's real impact. The scholar of Confucianism Tu Wei-ming distinguishes between what he calls "political Confucianism," which legitimates a hierarchical political system culminating in the emperor, and what he calls the "Confucian personal ethic," which regulates day-to-day life.[11] In China, political Confucianism was very much tied to the imperial system and its supporting bureaucracy of gentlemen-scholars. This system was abolished with the overthrow of the Qing dynasty in 1911. Despite efforts by the Communists in Beijing and other Sinitic governments overseas (such as that of Singapore) to appropriate the legitimacy of the imperial system, the continuity of political Confucianism has been disrupted in a fundamental sense. Tu argues that in fact the more important legacy of traditional Confucianism is not its political teaching, but rather the personal ethic that regulates attitudes toward family, work, education, and other elements of daily life that are valued in Chinese society. It is these attitudes, rather than inherited ideas about political authority, that account for the economic success of the overseas Chinese.

One could go even further and argue that the essence of traditional Chinese Confucianism was never political Confucianism at all, but rather an intense familism that took precedence over all other social relations, including relations with political authorities. That is, Confucianism builds a well-ordered society from the ground up rather than the top down, stressing the moral obligations of family life as the basic building block of society. Beyond the traditional Chinese family, or *jia,* are lineages and larger kinship groups; the state and other political authorities are seen as a kind of family of families that unites all Chinese into a single social entity. But the bonds within the immediate family take precedence over higher sorts of ties, including obligations to the emperor. In classical Chinese Confucianism, one's obligation to one's father is greater than to the police; in a famous story related about Confucius, "The king boasted to Confucius that virtue in his land was such that if a father stole, his son would report the crime and the criminal to the state. Confucius replied that in his state virtue was far greater, for a son would never think of treating his father so."[12] (The Chinese Communists tried to change this state of affairs, but that is a different story.) Of course, in a perfectly ordered Confucian society, such conflicts between rival obligations should not occur. But occur they do, and while in classical Chinese dramas these conflicting obligations were often portrayed as a source of anguish, the superior authority of the family was made quite clear in the end.

In this respect, Chinese Confucianism is very different from the version that evolved in Japan when neo-Confucianism was imported into the country after the end of the Song dynasty (960–1279 A.D.). The Japanese modified Chinese Confucianism in certain strategic ways to make it compatible with their own imperial system. In China, even the emperor's authority was not absolute; it could be undermined altogether if his own immorality caused him to lose the "mandate of heaven." The succession of Chinese dynasties over the centuries is testimony to the impermanence of Chinese political authority. Japan, by contrast, has been characterized by a single, unbroken dynastic tradition since the mythical founding of the country, and no political equivalent of the loss of the "mandate of heaven" ever emerged by which a Japanese emperor could lose his throne. The Japanese were careful not to allow the political dictates of Confucianism to impinge on the prerogatives of the emperor and the ruling political class. Hence in Japan obligations to the emperor were superior to obligations to one's father, and a son facing the dilemma of reporting on his father would be required to favor the state over the family. In Chinese Confucianism, the family (or lineage) is a bulwark against the power of the state; in Japan, the family is a much weaker rival to political authority. Hence Huntington's characterization of Confucianism as inevitably supporting state power over subordinate social groups applies much more readily to Japanese than to Chinese Confucianism. Yet it is Japan, rather than China, that has been democratic for the past 45 years.

Granite and Sand

This contrast between Chinese and Japanese Confucianism has given rise to several important differences between the two countries' political cultures—differences that should have implications for the prospects of Western-style democracy. Given the strength of intrafamilial bonds within a traditional Chinese society, ties between people unrelated to each other are relatively weak. In other words, in a Chinese society there is a relatively high degree of distrust between people who are not related. The Chinese may be characterized as family-oriented, but they are not group-oriented, as the Japanese are frequently said to be. The competition between families frequently makes Chinese society appear more individualistic to Western observers than Japanese society, and is the basis for the famous remark that while the Japanese are like a block of granite, the Chinese are like a tray of sand, with each grain representing a single family.

Because of the primacy of the family in China, political authority there has always been weaker than in Japan, and political instability much closer to the surface. Chinese families have traditionally been suspicious of government authority, and many Chinese family businesses—both in the People's Republic of China (PRC) and among the overseas (or *nanyang*) Chinese—go through elaborate machinations to hide their affairs from the tax collector and other officials. Nationalism and national identity have traditionally been much weaker in China than in Japan: There is little sense in China of the "us-against-them" mentality that has at times characterized Japanese nationalism. In business relationships and even political affiliations, loyalties to family, lineage, and region frequently take precedence over the mere fact of being Chinese. It has often been remarked that the level of citizenship is lower in China than it is in many other societies: Provided the state leaves them alone, most

Chinese do not feel any particular obligations to the larger society in which they live. And there is certainly no generalized moral obligation to do right by strangers simply because they are human beings, as there is in Christian culture. Because they lack the intense feeling of natural unity that the Japanese have, the Chinese find political instability, in a sense, more psychologically threatening.

Paradoxically, the weaker Chinese deference to authority creates a greater need for an authoritarian political system in Chinese societies. Precisely because state authority is less respected in China, the danger of social chaos emerging in the absence of an overt, repressive state structure is greater there than in Japan. The fear of China's fragmenting and becoming dangerously unstable was clearly one of the factors motivating the Chinese Communist leadership in its crackdown on the prodemocracy movement at Tiananmen Square in June 1989. Fear of disintegration is what continues to make China's rulers reluctant to liberalize the political system significantly. One is led to suspect that the emphasis on political authoritarianism in Singapore and other Southeast Asian states is less a reflection of those societies' self-discipline—as they would have outsiders believe—than of their rather low level of spontaneous citizenship and corresponding fear of coming apart in the absence of coercive political authority. In Japan, by contrast, it is not necessary for the state to legislate against failing to flush public toilets or writing on walls, because the society itself has absorbed and internalized such rules.

The relationship between Confucianism and democracy, then, is far more complex than many commentators have indicated. Chinese Confucianism, in particular, does not legitimate deference to the authority of an all-powerful state that leaves no scope for the development of an independent civil society. If civil society is weak in China, that weakness is due not to a statist ideology, but rather to the strong familism that is basic to Chinese culture, and the consequent reluctance of the Chinese to trust people outside of their kinship groups. The problem that will confront the institutionalization of democracy in China in the future will not be a culturally ingrained deference to state authority, but a sense of citizenship too feeble to generate spontaneous coherence or call forth sacrifices for the sake of national unity. As in other familistic societies in Southern Europe or Latin America, there will be a need to bring the "morality of the street" more in line with the morality of the family.

The experience of communism in the PRC has done nothing to alter these cultural attitudes, despite decades of anti-Confucian indoctrination. Indeed, the importance of family obligations in the PRC has, if anything, deepened over the past few generations. The traditional Chinese family, after all, was essentially a defensive mechanism that served to protect its members against an arbitrary and capricious state: Although one could not trust the local authorities, one could trust members of one's own family.

Nothing in the chaotic political experience of China in the twentieth century has led the average Chinese to change this evaluation of relative risks. Hence we see even members of the communist elite in China securing educations, foreign bank accounts, and safe havens for their children in the event that the communist political edifice comes crashing down.

The statist, group-oriented attitudes toward authority that Huntington believes to be characteristic of Confucianism per se are more properly characteristic of Japan and Japanese Confucianism, and were indeed manifest in Japan in an extreme form during the 1930s. As a result of the disastrous experience of the Second World War, nationalism and statism have been delegitimized, and replaced by a workable democracy. Traditionally deferential attitudes toward political authority continued to be evident, however, in the long-unchallenged rule of the bureaucracy-LDP-business triangle in the postwar period. As noted earlier, however, it is not clear that these attitudes will continue to pose an insurmountable barrier to a more participatory, Western form of democracy featuring multiparty contestation for power.

The ways in which Confucian culture—both Chinese and Japanese—differs significantly from the Christian and democratic culture of the West have to do with the status of the individual. Although Chinese familism may appear individualistic in some respects, it is not the same as the individualism that undergirds the Western ideal. That is, individuals in China do not have a source of legitimate authority on the basis of which they can revolt against their families and the web of social ties into which they are born. Christianity provides the concept of a transcendent God whose Word is the highest source of right. God's laws take precedence over all other obligations—remember that God required Abraham to be willing to sacrifice his son—and this transcendent source of morality is what enables an individual in the West to repudiate all forms of social obligation, from the family all the way up to the state. In modern liberalism, the Christian concept of a universal God is replaced with the concept of an underlying human nature that becomes the universal basis of right. Liberal rights apply to all human beings as such, just as God's law did in Christianity, transcending any particular set of real-world social obligations. While not all of today's American human rights advocates working for organizations like Asia Watch or Amnesty International would describe themselves as believing Christians, they all share their Christian culture's emphasis on universal rights and, consequently, individual conscience as the ultimate source of authority. This, it is safe to say, does not have a counterpart in any Confucian society. It is this difference that is at the root of contemporary disagreements between Americans and Asians over human rights policy.

In evaluating the claim of a fundamental incompatibility between Confucianism and liberal democracy, we should remember that many experts once thought that Confucianism presented insuperable obstacles to capitalist economic modernization as well. While Huntington argues—correctly—that modern liberal democracy grew out of Christian culture, it is clear that democracy emerged only after a long succession of incarnations of Christianity that were inimical to liberal tolerance and democratic contestation. All in all, the obstacles posed by Confucian culture do not seem any greater than those posed by other cultures; indeed, when compared to those of Hinduism or Islam, they appear to be much smaller.

An Attitudinal Shift

The upshot of all this is that Confucianism by no means mandates an authoritarian political system. In Singapore, the current political authorities are appealing to Confucian traditions somewhat dishonestly to justify an intrusive and unnecessarily paternalistic political system. Other Confucian societies like Japan and South Korea have been able to accommodate a greater degree of political participation and individual liberty than Singapore without compromising their own fundamental cultural values, and Taiwan is moving rapidly in the same direction. I see no reason why Singapore should not be able to follow this path. If economic modernization does lead to demands for greater recognition, it will be the next generation of Singaporeans who will be voicing the strongest demands for greater political participation and individual freedom—not because these are Western values, but because they meet the needs of a middle-class, well-educated populace.

On the other hand, virtually no one in Asia today believes it likely that Asian societies will ultimately converge with the particular model of liberal democracy represented by the contemporary United States, or, indeed, that such a state of affairs is remotely desirable. This represents quite a change from the early postwar period, when many people—and not just in Asia—believed that the United States was the exemplar of a modern democracy, to be revered and emulated. This attitudinal shift can be traced to two subsequent developments. The first was East Asia's spectacular economic growth, which many people attributed to the region's Confucian traditions. The second was a perceived decline in the American standard of living, measured not in terms of per-capita GDP, but rather in terms of growing crime, the breakdown of the family, a loss of civility, racial tensions, and illegal immigration—problems that showed no sign of abating. In the view of many Asians, individualism was far too rampant in American society and was leading to social chaos, with potentially devastating economic and political consequences. Thus some began to argue that a "soft" authoritarian system—rooted in Confucian principles and characterized by less individual liberty and more social discipline—not only would result in faster economic growth, but would create a much more satisfying society in terms of overall quality of life.

There is both an element of truth and a great deal of exaggeration in this Asian analysis of what currently ails the United States. It is true that the individualism deeply ingrained in the theoretical principles underlying the U.S. Constitution and legal system has no counterpart in Asian culture. It is thus no accident that American political discourse is framed largely in terms of conflicting individual rights. Yet as Mary Ann Glendon has pointed out, this "rights talk" is a dialect unique to the United States, with its Lockean and Jeffersonian traditions; in most modern European countries, individual rights are carefully balanced in constitutional law against responsibilities to the community.[13] Moreover, even in the American tradition, the inherent individualism of the constitutional-legal system has always been counterbalanced in practice by strongly communitarian social habits. This high degree of communal participation derived originally from religion (that is, the sectarian form of Protestantism dominant in the United States) and later from the communal habits of America's ethnic groups as well. Alexis de Tocqueville noted in the 1830s that Americans were very good at associating with one another and subordinating their individualism to voluntary groups of one type or another.

It is only in the past couple of generations that the balance between individualism and communalism in the United States has been tipped decisively in favor of the former. For a variety of historical reasons, communal institutions have grown weaker—or have been deliberately undermined by the state—while the number and scope of basic individual rights to which Americans feel they are entitled have steadily increased. The causes of the problem—and possible solutions to it—are well beyond the scope of the present essay, but the result has been a diminution of the appeal to Asians of the American model of democracy. Nor are Asians alone in this view; judging from the positive reaction that many Americans exhibited to the caning of Michael Fay in Singapore, this model has become much less appealing to Americans themselves.

Finding a Balance

To many Asians, the social problems currently plaguing the United States are problems of liberal democracy per se. To the extent that this perception continues, the future of democracy in Asia will depend less on the theoretical compatibility or incompatibility of Confucianism with democratic principles than on whether people in Asia feel that they want their society to resemble that of the United States.

Asia is therefore at a very interesting crossroads. It is quite possible that the modernization hypothesis will continue to be borne out in the future, and that rising per-capita incomes and educational levels in the region will be accompanied by an increasing democratization of political systems. As noted above, this is because there is a universal tendency of human beings to seek recognition of their dignity through a political system that allows them to participate as adult human beings. On the other hand, people's choices are strongly influenced by the alternatives that they see directly at hand, and if East Asia continues to prosper and the United States makes little or no progress in solving its economic and social problems, the Western democratic model will become less and less attractive. Japan's experience will be critical. If Japan emerges from the current recession with its people believing that the country's economic problems were the result of the accumulated inefficiencies of the period of LDP domination, then there will be a sustained impetus for reform of the political system and enhanced prospects for a more genuinely democratic Japan. Yet there is a real possibility that the reform effort itself will become the scapegoat for Japan's economic woes, in which case a sentiment favoring restoration of a more authoritarian kind of political system may take root.

I do not have any particular prediction to make, concerning either Japan or Asia as a whole. What I hope to have shown, however, is that there is no fundamental cultural obstacle to the democratization of contemporary Confucian societies, and there is some reason to believe that these societies will move in the direction of greater political liberalization as they grow wealthier. We should regard assertions that authoritarian political systems are necessarily more Confucian than democratic systems with a certain amount of skepticism. In fact, Confucian values might work quite well in a liberal society (as they clearly do for many Asian immigrants to the United States), where they can serve as a counterbalance to the larger society's atomizing tendencies. On the other hand, the particular form that Asian democracy will ultimately take is unlikely to be identical to the model represented by the United States. If Asia's Confucian traditions allow it to find an appropriate and stable balance between the need for liberty and the need for community, in the end it will be a politically happy place indeed.

NOTES

1. See, for example, Lee's interview with Fareed Zakaria in *Foreign Affairs* 73 (March–April 1994): 109–27.

2. The basic texts outlining early postwar modernization theory include Daniel Lerner, *The Passing of Traditional Society* (Glencoe, Ill.: The Free Press, 1958), and the various works of Talcott Parsons, especially *The Structure of Social Action* (New York: McGraw-Hill, 1937); (with Edward Shils), *Toward a General Theory of Action* (Cambridge: Harvard University Press, 1951); and *The Social System* (Glencoe, Ill.: The Free Press, 1951). In this tradition were the nine volumes sponsored by the American Social Science Research Council between 1963 and 1975, beginning with Lucian Pye's *Communications and Political Development* (Princeton: Princeton University

Press, 1963) and ending with Raymond Grew's *Crises of Political Development in Europe and the United States* (Princeton: Princeton University Press, 1978).

3. Seymour Martin Lipset, "Some Social Requisites of Democracy: Economic Development and Political Legitimacy," *American Political Science Review* 53 (1959): 69–105.

4. For empirical evidence, see Larry Diamond, "Economic Development and Democracy Reconsidered," *American Behavioral Scientist* 15 (March–June 1992): 450–99.

5. Talcott Parsons, "Evolutionary Universals in Society," *American Sociological Review* 29 (June 1964): 339–57.

6. See my *The End of History and the Last Man* (New York: The Free Press, 1992), esp. pt. 2; and "Capitalism and Democracy: The Missing Link," *Journal of Democracy* 3 (July 1992): 100–10.

7. See especially Karel van Wolferen, *The Enigma of Japanese Power* (London: Macmillan, 1989).

8. On this subject see Barbara Geddes, "Challenging the Conventional Wisdom," *Journal of Democracy* 5 (October 1994): 104–18; and Minxin Pei, "The Puzzle of East Asian Exceptionalism," *Journal of Democracy* 5 (October 1994): 90–103.

9. One exception is Lucian Pye; see his "Political Science and the Crisis of Authoritarianism," *American Political Science Review* 84 (March 1990): 3–17.

10. Samuel P. Huntington, "Democracy's Third Wave," *Journal of Democracy* 2 (Spring 1991): 24.

11. Tu Wei-ming, *Confucian Ethics Today: The Singapore Challenge* (Singapore: Curriculum Development Institute of Singapore, 1984), 90.

12. Quoted in Marion J. Levy, *The Rise of the Modern Chinese Business Class* (New York: Institute of Pacific Relations, 1949), 1.

13. Mary Ann Glendon, *Rights Talk: The Impoverishment of Political Discourse* (New York: The Free Press, 1992).

4

MUSLIMS AND DEMOCRACY

Abdou Filali-Ansary

Abdou Filali-Ansary *is director of the King Abdul-Aziz al-Saoud Foundation for Islamic Studies and Human Sciences in Casablanca, Morocco, and editorial director of* Prologues: revue maghrébine du livre, *a French-Arabic journal of philosophy, literature, and the social sciences. His most recent book,* L'Islam: Est-il hostile à la laïcité?, *was published in 1997. This essay is based on a talk that he presented on 13 January 1999 at the International Forum for Democratic Studies in Washington, D.C.*

The past is often held to weigh especially heavily on Muslim countries, particularly as regards their present-day receptivity to democracy. I do not dispute that past history has had an overwhelming and decisive influence in shaping the contemporary features and attitudes of Muslim societies. But the past that is most relevant today is not, as is commonly thought, the early centuries of Islamic history, but rather the nineteenth-century encounter of Muslims with the modernizing West.

It is widely believed that the key to understanding contemporary Muslim societies is to be found in a structure of beliefs and traditions that was devised and implemented at (or shortly after) the moment at which they adopted Islam. This view, often labeled as "Muslim exceptionalism," holds that these societies are, as Ernest Gellner has elegantly put it, permeated by an "implicit constitution" providing a "blueprint" of the social order.[1] This view has been subjected to intense criticism by a number of scholars, but it still influences dominant attitudes in academia and, with much more devastating effects, in the media.

This theory rests on two assumptions: first, that the past is ever-present and is much more determining than present-day conditions; and second, that the character of Muslim societies has been determined by a specific and remote period in their past during which the social and political order that continues to guide them was established. This past has allegedly acquired such a strong grip that it can—and does—channel, limit, or even block the effects of technological, economic, or social change. In other words, for Muslims alone a remote past has defined, forever and without any possibility of evolution, the ways in which fundamental issues are perceived and addressed. The ultimate conclusion lurking behind these considerations is that, due to the overwhelming presence and influence of that particular part of their past, the societies in question are incapable of democratization. In other societies history may take the form of continual change, but in Muslim ones history is bound to repeat itself.

Apart from the many other criticisms that have been directed against this set of views, it should be emphasized that it is not based on any solid historical knowledge about the way in which this "implicit constitution" was shaped and implemented or imposed. Some of its proponents refer to a normative system that was never really enacted: They invoke the model of the "rightly guided" caliphate, which lasted, at most, for about three decades after the death of the Prophet. Many others cite instead the social order that prevailed during the Middle Ages in societies where Muslims were a majority or where political regimes were established in the name of Islam. In both of these versions, however, the power of this past to determine the present remains, by and large, mysterious. It is simply taken for granted, with no explanation given about why the past has had such a far-reaching and pervasive effect in these societies. To understand how the belief in these misconceptions was born and came to influence contemporary attitudes so powerfully, we must turn to a particular moment in modern times—the beginning and middle of the nineteenth century.

A Tenacious Misunderstanding

The earliest intellectual encounters between Muslims and Europeans in modern times took the form of sharp confrontations. Jamal-Eddin Al-Afghani (1838–97), one of the first and most prominent Muslim thinkers and activists in the struggle against despotism, became famous for engaging in a controversy against European secularists. He acquired a high reputation, especially for his efforts to refute European critics of religion in general and of Islam in particular. An essay that he wrote in reply to Ernest Renan bore the title *"Ar-Rad 'ala ad-Dahriyin"* ("The Answer to Temporalists"). He used the term *Dahriyin,* which literally means "temporalists," to refer to secularists. The word itself, which is of Qur'anic origin, had originally been applied to atheists. Al-Afghani attacked the positivist ideologues of his century, who were deeply convinced that religion was responsible for social backwardness and stagnation and that scientific progress would soon lead to its disappearance. Through his choice of terminology, Al-Afghani implicitly equated these nineteenth-century positivists with the seventh-century opponents of the Prophet. For Muslim readers, this formulation defined the terms of a large and enduring misunderstanding. From then on, secularism was seen as being intimately related to, if not simply the same thing as, atheism. The confusion was taken a step further when, some decades later, other Muslim authors wishing to coin a term for secularism, and either ignoring Al-Afghani's choice of the term *Dahriyin* or feeling that it was inappropriate, chose *ladini,* which literally means nonreligious or areligious.

These initial choices of terminology gave birth to the opposition in the mind of Muslims between, on the one hand, the system of belief and the social order that they inherited and lived in, and on the other, the alternative adopted by the Europeans. Although the term *ladini* was replaced later by another, *'ilmani* (this-worldly), the bipolar opposition between the two views was already deeply entrenched. The feeling that has prevailed since then among Muslims is that there is a strict and irreducible opposition between two systems—Islam and non-Islam. To be a secularist has meant to abandon Islam, to reject altogether not only the religious faith but also its attendant morality and the traditions and rules that operate within Muslim societies. It therefore has been understood as a total alienation from the constituent elements of the Islamic personality and as a complete surrender to unbelief, immorality, and self-hatred, leading to a disavowal of the historic identity and civilization inherited from illustrious ancestors. It is worth noting that the vast majority of Muslims in the nineteenth century, even those who were part of the educated elite, lived in total ignorance both of the debates going on in Europe about religion and its role in the social order and of the historical changes reshaping European societies. They were not aware of the distinction between atheism and secularism. The consequences of this misunderstanding still profoundly shape the attitudes of Muslims today.

Thus secularism became known to Muslims for the first time through a controversy against those who were supposed to be their "hereditary enemies." The original distinction within Christianity between "regular" and "secular" members of the clergy,[2] which was the initial step in the long evolution toward the establishment of a separate secular sphere, had no equivalent in the Muslim context. Hence the choice of a term for the concept of secularism was decisive. In the latter part of the nineteenth century and early in the twentieth, the confrontation with the colonial powers, thought to be the carriers and defenders of a mixture of aggressive Christian proselytism and of the new secularism, played an important role in strengthening this dualism. In the diverse conflicts that local populations waged to defend their independence, identity and religion became intimately fused. The oppositions between local and intruder, between Muslim and European, between believer and secularist were, in one way or another, conflated. The resulting polarization came to dominate all attitudes and approaches to questions related to religion, politics, and the social order.

One of the most striking consequences of this evolution is that Islam now appears to be the religion that is most hostile to secularization and to modernity in general. Yet intrinsically Islam would seem to be the religion closest to modern views and ideals, and thus the one that would most easily accommodate secularization. "The high culture form of Islam," writes Ernest Gellner, "is endowed with a number of features—unitarianism, a rule-ethic, individualism, scriptualism, puritanism, an egalitarian aversion to mediation and hierarchy, a fairly small load of magic—that are congruent, presumably, with requirements of modernity or modernisation."[3] In a similar vein, Mohamed Charfi observes that, on the level of principles, Islam should favor individual freedoms and the capacity for religious choice. The historical developments noted above, however, caused Muslim societies to evolve in the opposite direction—toward the loss of individual autonomy and total submission to the community and the state.[4]

This evolution gave birth at later stages to such dichotomies as "Islam and the West," "Islam and modernity," "Islam and human rights," "Islam and democracy," and others of the sort, which set the framework within which critical issues are addressed, whether in popular, journalistic, or even academic circles. This framework has imposed a particular way of raising questions and building conceptions, imprisoning attitudes in predefined and static formulas.[5] Muslim exceptionalism seems, therefore, to reside in the ways we raise questions about these matters. Although many studies on religion and its influence in the social and political spheres are undertaken in what were formerly referred to as Christian societies, nobody today poses the issue of "Christianity and democracy" in the same way that this question is formulated with respect to Islam. The fact that we still ask questions such as "Is Islam compatible with democracy?" shows how strong this polarization has become. It also shows that a dynamic was established, enabling the polarization that emerged in the nineteenth century to replicate itself as it extends to new fields or expresses itself in new terms.

From Settlement to System

This polarization, which still determines the type of questions that can be asked, rests on two main prejudices: The first is that Islam is a "system," and should be treated as a structure of rules. The dubious character of this assumption has been clearly pointed out by the eminent scholar of comparative religion Wilfred Cantwell Smith: "[T]he term *nizam* [or] 'system,' is commonplace in the twentieth century in relation to Islam. This term, however, does not occur in the Qur'an, nor indeed does any word from this root; and there is some reason for wondering whether any Muslim ever used this concept religiously before modern times. The explicit notion that life should be or can be ordered according to a system, even an ideal one, and that it is the business of Islam to provide such a system, seems to be a modern idea (and perhaps a rather questionable one)."[6] Once Islam has been defined in this way, it can be used to assess whether other new or alien concepts can be accommodated within it and to decide the degree of their compatibility with its presumed and predefined content. This stance, however, reflects a particular attitude toward religion, not a particular feature of Islam. In fact, as Leonard Binder has observed, any of the monotheistic religions, if adopted in this manner, can lead to similar conclusions: "In the light of modern liberal democratic thought, Islam is no more, nor any less democratic than Christianity or Judaism. All three monotheistic religions, if proposed as constitutional foundations of the state, and if understood as providing an ineluctable authority for the guidance of all significant human choice, are undemocratic or nondemocratic."[7]

The second prejudice is more insidious. It is based on the confusion of Islam as a religion with Islam as a civilization. This confusion is deeply entrenched, again because of prevailing linguistic usages both in Arabic and in European languages. For Islam, no distinction has been drawn comparable to that between "Christianity" and "Christendom." The same word was, and still is, used to refer both to a set of beliefs and rituals and to the life of the community of believers through time and space. Only recently, thanks to the work of historian Marshall G.S. Hodgson, has the necessity of drawing a sharp line between Islam and "Islamdom" been recognized as essential for explaining key phenomena in the history of Muslims.[8] Islamdom, in its golden age, was a social and political order built on norms adopted from Islamic sources but specifically adapted to the conditions of the time (only at a later stage were these formulated as explicit rules). This enabled Muslims in the Middle Ages to create and maintain a world civilization attuned to the circumstances of the era.

Muslims at that time lived within polities bound by *shari'a,* yet did not consider the political regimes to which they were subjected to be in conformity with Islamic principles. The rulers were considered to be legal but not really legitimate. Even though they were not fully legitimate, they had to be obeyed, but only to avoid a greater evil, the *Fitna* (the great rebellion or anarchy). For premodern societies of Muslims, the political model remained the early caliphate, which was not bound by *shari'a,* since *shari'a* had not yet been devised. The ideal was a kind of "republican" regime, where caliphs are chosen by members of the community rather than imposed by force, and where the behavior of rulers is clearly dedicated to serving the community instead of satisfying their personal ambitions. Nonetheless, Muslims came to understand that it was no longer possible to implement the fully legitimate system of

Khilafa rachida, the virtuous or rightly guided caliphate, that the republican ideal was out of reach, and that they had to accept the rule of despots. They could, however, limit the extent of the power accorded to autocratic rulers by invoking *shari'a,* to which a sacred character had come to be attributed. In this way, at least some degree of autonomy from the political authorities, and minimal protection against arbitrariness, could be attained. This is what one may label the "medieval compromise" or "medieval settlement." The sacralization of *shari'a* achieved through this process led to another far-reaching consequence: Ever since, Islam has been seen as a set of eternal rules, standing over society and history, to be used as a standard for judging reality and behavior.

In fact, *shari'a* was never a system of law in the sense in which it is understood nowadays. As was noted by Fazlur Rahman: "Islamic law . . . is not strictly speaking law, since much of it embodies moral and quasi-moral precepts not enforceable in any court. Further, Islamic law, though a certain part of it came to be enforced almost uniformly throughout the Muslim world (and it is primarily this that bestowed homogeneity upon the entire Muslim world), is on closer examination a body of legal opinion or, as Santillana put it, 'an endless discussion on the duties of a Muslim' rather than a neatly formulated code or codes."[9]

What happened in the nineteenth century was the transformation of the medieval settlement into a system in the modern sense of the word. The duality of fact and norm was inverted, as *shari'a*-bound societies were confused with fully legitimate Muslim communities and deemed to be fully realizable through voluntary political action, whether of a peaceful or violent character. We see therefore how the confusion between a "model" and a historical system could arise and spread among Muslims at a time when they were confronted by the challenge of modern ideas. The typical attitudes of premodern Muslims had been based on a sharp distinction between the norm (of the virtuous or rightly guided caliphate) and the actual conditions (including the implementation of the *shari'a*) under which they lived. In the face of this duality, people adopted an attitude of resignation, accepting that the norm was, at least temporarily, out of reach. By contrast, some modern Muslims have elevated the actual conditions and rules under which their medieval forefathers lived to the status of a norm, and decided that they too have to live by these rules if they are to be true Muslims.

This has led to the contradictions of the present day: Secularization has been taking place for decades in Muslim societies, yet prevailing opinion opposes the concept of secularism and everything that comes with it (like modernity and democracy). As a historical process, secularization has so transformed life in Muslim societies that religion, or rather traditions built on religion, no longer supply the norms and rules that govern the social and political order. In almost all countries with substantial communities of Muslims, positive law has replaced *shari' a* (except with regard to matters of "personal status," and more specifically the status of women, where the traditional rules generally continue to be maintained). Modern institutions—nation-states, modern bureaucracies, political parties, labor unions, corporations, associations, educational systems—have been adopted everywhere, while traditional institutions are, at best, relegated to symbolic roles. Similarly, prevailing conceptions and attitudes of everyday life are founded on modern rationality and on doctrines influenced by science and philosophy rather than on traditional or premodern worldviews. Most Muslims now have come to accept the "disenchantment of the world," and this has profoundly transformed expectations and models of behavior within their societies. The evolution from the premodern attitude, combining resignation toward despotism with millennial hopes, to the typically modern combination of sharp political determination and desire for this-worldly progress, is clearly a visible consequence of these very changes, that is, of the secularization that has actually been going on in Muslim societies.

Secularism, however, continues to be rejected as an alien doctrine, allegedly imposed by the traditional enemies of Muslims and their indigenous accomplices. Islam is seen as an eternal and immutable system, encompassing every aspect of social organization and personal morality, and unalterably opposed to all conceptions and systems associated with modernity. This creates an artificial debate and an almost surrealist situation. The changes that are evident in the actual lives of individuals and groups are ignored, while ideological stances are maintained with great determination. Secularists and, more generally, social scientists are often pushed into adopting defensive positions or withdrawing altogether from public debates. Frequently they feel obliged to prove that they are not guilty of hostility toward religious belief, morality, and the achievements of Islamic civilization.

As Mohamed Charfi has pointed out, the policies adopted by some modern states under the influence of nationalist ideologies are partly responsible for this state of affairs. The education systems in many Muslim countries have taught Islam not as a religion, but as an identity and a legal and political system. The consequence is that Islam is presented both as irreducibly opposed to other kinds of self-identification or of social and political organization and as commanding certain specific attitudes regarding political and social matters.[10]

Attitudes Toward Democracy

We saw that, as a consequence of the inversion of norms that occurred in Muslim societies during the nineteenth century, the traditional rules and usages grouped under the emblem of *shari' a* were transformed into a system and elevated into norms that define the "essence" of being Muslim—that is, simultaneously the ideal status and the specific identity of Muslims. Thus *shari'a*-bound societies are now equated with "truly" Islamic societies. Implementing the *shari'a* has become the slogan for those who seek a "return" to Islam in its original and pure form, which is held to embody the eternal truth and ultimate pattern for Muslims.

What could the status of democracy be in societies that have evolved in this manner? One first must perceive the difference between a question posed in this way, which attempts to interpret the actual evolution of particular societies and their prevailing conceptions, and the kinds of questions frequently asked by fundamentalists and by some scholars, such as: "What is the status of democracy with regard to Islam?" This latter formulation posits Islam as a system that one can use to evaluate everything else.

One can discern two possible answers to the question of democracy as I have posed it. The first accepts the strict identification between Islam and *shari'a*-bound systems, and thus rules out any possible future for democracy in this particular environment. The second identifies democracy itself with a kind of religious faith or "mystical ideal." As Tim Niblock has noted: "The Middle East related literature purveys a romanticized conception of the nature and characteristics of liberal democracy. This occurs not through any explicit description of liberal democracy, but precisely through the absence of any analysis of the concept and its practical application. The concept hovers, like a mystical symbol, in the background of the discussion on democratization in the Middle East, with an implied assumption that liberal democracy con- stitutes an ideal polity where the common good is realized by means of the population deciding issues through the election of individuals who carry out the people's will."[11]

There even appears to be a certain trend toward adopting this second attitude. More and more fundamentalists accept the idea that Islam is not opposed to democracy; some argue that by embracing the principle of *shura* (or "consultation"), for example, Islam has always favored the kind of relationship between rulers and ruled that democracy entails. Democracy may even end up being described as a Western adaptation of an originally Islamic principle. Many fundamentalists are prepared to go as far as possible to support democracy—with the notable reservation that it should be maintained only within the limits set by *shari'a*. A "guided democracy" is the system envisioned by many fundamentalists and traditionalists of different sorts. Iran may be considered as a case where this kind of doctrine has been implemented. In addition to institutions common in all democracies, like elected parliaments and executives, it also has a high council of experts and a religious guide who are entrusted with ensuring that the laws and decisions made by democratically elected bodies are in conformity with religious principles and rules.

This shows how much popularity, or rather prestige, democracy enjoys within contemporary Muslim societies. The renowned contemporary philosopher Mohamed Abed Jabri has said that democracy is the only principle of political legitimacy which is acceptable nowadays in Muslim societies, whatever their religious beliefs and attitudes may be. "Revolutionary" alternatives that postpone the implementation of democracy until other conditions are realized no longer seem to be acceptable to the masses.[12] This support for democracy reflects in some cases a realistic recognition that it responds to the needs of contemporary societies, that it is indeed the only alternative that really works and makes possible the peaceful and rational management of public affairs. In many other cases, however, this newly favorable reception of democracy arises from its being viewed as another utopia.[13] While this may have certain immediate advantages, especially in contexts where democratic systems are in place or where democratization is under way, it may also encourage attitudes that are harmful to the longer-range prospects for democratization. For it may lead to democracy's being seen as an alien or unattainable ideal, and thus strengthen the idea that the Islamic alternative is more workable and better adapted to the conditions of Muslim societies. In other words, democracy may be treated in the same way as other modern ideologies, such as nationalism and socialism, that recently enjoyed a brief ascendancy in some Muslim countries. Both nationalism and socialism were indeed endowed with a quasi-religious aura; they were adopted as ultimate worldviews and total beliefs, and considered as magical remedies to all the ills and problems of society. This kind of approach would only deepen the initial misunderstanding on the part of Muslims of both secularization and democracy. The result would be to strengthen the view that Islam and democracy represent two irreducibly separate and opposing outlooks, even if some mixture of Islam and democracy were to be envisaged and tentatively implemented.

Replacing Democracy with Its "Building Blocks"

What might be an appropriate strategy for democrats in this situation? For those who are convinced that democracy is not a new religion for humanity, but that it provides the most efficient means to limit abuses of power and protect individual freedoms, enabling individuals to seek their own path to personal accomplishment, there can be a variety of approaches. The most effective ones avoid the reified and "utopianized" version of democracy, either by highlighting such concepts as "good governance" or by supporting some of the "building blocks of democracy," that is, conceptions and systems that are linked to or part of democracy.

Replacing highly prestigious and, at the same time, highly contentious notions with terms that refer to easily understood facts and ideas is neither a retreat from conceptual clarity nor a defeatist position. A few years ago Mohamed Abed Jabri was bitterly attacked by a large number of Arab intellectuals for proposing to replace the slogan of secularization with such notions as rationality and democratization. Secularization, he contended, had become a charged issue for Arab public opinion because it was understood as being more or less equivalent to Westernization; its actual contents, however, such as rational management of collective affairs and democracy, could hardly be rejected once they were understood and accepted in their true meaning. In a similar vein, Niblock has observed: "Focusing on the 'big' issue of democratisation has detracted from the attention which can be given to a range of more specific issues which affect populations critically. Among these are the level of corruption, the effectiveness of bureaucratic organisation, the independence of the judiciary, the existence of well-conceived and clearly-articulated laws, freedom of expression, the respect given to minorities, attitudes to human rights issues, and the extent of inequalities which may create social disorder."[14]

In order to avoid a new and devastating misunderstanding that would present democracy as an alternative to religion and make its adoption appear to be a deviation from religious rectitude, it is essential to renounce quixotic confrontations and to accept some "tactical" concessions—especially when the use of appropriate terminology can bring greater clarification without sacrificing substance. Niblock's suggestion, stressing the importance of specific issues relevant to democracy, is one possible strategy, and it is certainly of real usefulness for the cases at hand. Yet it represents an external point of view, one that seems to be directed primarily at politicians and decision makers who attempt to influence political change in Muslim countries from the outside. It does not take into account the attitudes of Muslims themselves, and especially the need to foster their real acceptance and support of democracy. For this purpose, a more "conceptual" approach is required, one that would help present democracy in terms understandable and acceptable to Muslim publics, and thus bridge the gap between a "mystical" representation and a more realistic comprehension. It would answer the need for analytical terms that can clarify the conceptions and adjust the expectations of Muslims regarding democracy, and that can encourage the kind of *political* support that is equally distant from mythical or ideological fervor on the one hand, and egotistical or individualist attitudes on the other.

This approach, which should be understood not as an alternative but rather as a complement to the one proposed by Niblock, aims at clarifying the issue for a specific public that is influenced by particular worldviews and has expectations of its own. Finding the right terms is not easy. Interpretations of democracy and democratization are so rich and diverse that it may be difficult to reach a consensual view on the subject. All such interpretations, however, seem to point to some basic features as being essential conditions for achieving real democracy. It is possible to underscore at least three such conditions that seem to be required for the particular case of contemporary Muslim societies: 1) the updating of religious conceptions; 2) the rule of law; and 3) economic growth.

1) The *updating of religious conceptions* should be understood not in terms of the Reformation that occurred in sixteenth-century Christian Europe, but rather as the general evolution of religious attitudes that has affected Christians and Jews (except within limited circles of fundamentalists) since the seventeenth or eighteenth centuries and achieved its full effects only in the early decades of this century. The Reformation is a singular event in history, linked to a particular environment and to specific conditions. It cannot, as some observers are suggesting nowadays, be "replicated" in the context of another religion and under twentieth-century conditions.

There is, however, another process of change in religious attitudes that, although it first occurred in one particular environment, is of more universal scope and significance and seems to be related to modernization in general. This process leads the majority of the population to give religious dogmas a symbolic truth-value, and to consider religious narratives as contingent, historical manifestations or expressions of the sacred that are amenable to rational understanding and scientific scrutiny. Religious dogmas and narratives no longer define, in a monolithic way, people's ideas about the world and society, nor do they determine the views that believers are supposed to be guided by in their social and political interactions. This kind of "disenchantment" may discard the literal meaning of sacred words and rituals, but it maintains (and probably reinforces) the overall ethical and moral teachings. Religious attitudes are no longer defined in terms of a combination of strict observance of rituals and the adoption of premodern views, but rather as an informal but deeply felt adherence to principles of morality and a commitment to universal values. Faith becomes a matter of individual choice and commitment, not an obligation imposed upon all members of the community.

An evolution in this direction has proceeded quite far among Christians and Jews, but has made only limited headway among Muslims. The reification of Islam that began in the nineteenth century is the most important obstacle to such progress. Thus it is significant that a number of contemporary Muslim thinkers agree that new attitudes toward religion are now required both by a scrupulous interpretation of sacred sources and by modern conditions. Their teachings imply a strict separation between the sacred message of Islam and Muslim attempts to implement it in the course of history, including the political systems and legislation created in the "golden age." The Egyptian theologian Ali Abderraziq, for example, proposed to consider the early caliphate created by companions of the Prophet not as a religious institution but as a political one, amenable to critical scrutiny in the same way as any normal human institution.[15] Fazlur Rahman and Mohamed Mahmoud Taha suggested a tempered and modernized attitude toward revelation.[16] Mohamed Talbi and Mohamed Charfi introduced and defended a clear distinction between religious principles and the legal prescriptions devised in order to implement them.[17] This trend (if one can so label a collection of otherwise unrelated thinkers who come to similar conclusions) has received little coverage in the media. Its influence has also been restricted by the educational policies of modern states and by intimidation on the part of the fundamentalists.

2) The *rule of law* is a notion that expresses something that Muslims have longed for since the early phases of their history, and have felt to be part of the message of Islam. Muslim travelers to Europe in the nineteenth century were struck by Europeans' adhesion to rules and rule-bound behavior. This made some of them think that these societies were "Muslim" without being aware of it, as Islam was clearly identified with law-abiding attitudes. Fundamentalists claim that the only way of satisfying this aspiration for lawfulness is by implementing *shari'a*, which they present as the sole remedy for the arbitrariness and abuse of power common in most "Muslim" states. This argument can be countered by showing that the modern concept of "rule of law" is clearer, more operational, and easier to monitor, and thus that the dichotomy of "Islam (or rather *shari'a*) vs. despotism" trumpeted by fundamentalist propaganda is not the whole story. Experience has revealed that law-abidingness is rather a feature of truly modernized societies, where individuals feel that they have a voice in the making of public decisions.

3) *Economic growth* here refers to the idea of continuous progress, which is a basic component of modernity, replacing the messianic hopes and political resignation dominant in premodern societies with the voluntarism and this-worldly resourcefulness of modern times. Democracy, as an expression of the free will of the citizens, cannot thrive if no collective will is allowed to surface or to have a say about the changes that society is compelled to undergo. It is the direct and visible expression of what Alain Touraine called modernization (in contrast with modernity)—that is, the process through which societies take control of their own affairs, mobilize their forces and their resources, and seek to determine the course of their destiny.[18] Economic growth offers the prospect of an improvement in the conditions of life, which seems to be required in every modern society, and all the more so in "developing" ones. No prospect of democratization can be envisaged if no economic growth is actually taking place.

Toward a Universal Rule of Law

It seems obvious that democracy cannot be exported, much less imposed on peoples who are not prepared to accept it and to mobilize themselves to implement it. If great numbers of Muslims today invoke religion rather than democracy as the alternative to despotism, and others consider democracy itself (at least implicitly) as a kind of new religious belief, this is not because of some special characteristics either of Islam or of Muslims. It is rather because of the particular historical circumstances that I have tried to explain. Muslim confrontations with European colonial powers in the nineteenth century gave birth to some great and lasting misunderstandings, as a result of which Muslims have rejected key aspects of modernity (secularization and, to some degree, democratization) as an alienation and a surrender of the historical self to the "Other."

For those who believe that "civilizations" are hard-core realities that last throughout history and that have distinctive and irreducible features, such polarization is understandable, being the "normal" course of history. It should therefore be treated as such, and the appropriate behavior would be to prepare to defend one's own civilization against alien ones in the unavoidable confrontations of the future.

For those, however, who believe that modern history has, for better or worse, put an end to the separate life of different cultures, there can be convergent paths to establishing social and political systems that promote individual freedoms, human rights, and social justice. These convergent paths point to the crucial importance of the international context and especially of the ongoing relationships between established and would-be democracies.

The fact that democracy has been adopted only in some countries (where it defines the ways their interests are promoted) and not in others creates an asymmetry. The collective interests of some communities, and not of others, find a channel for their expression, and therefore for the promotion of their particular national interests. The moral values that prevail within these communities will not prevail in their relationships with others. This asymmetry will fuel deeper antagonism between nations and greater resentment from those who are weaker. It is therefore time to call for a universal rule of law, where law is not considered only as a means for defending selfish national interests, but is respected for its own sake in a "Kantian" way.

We are living, much more than did our ancestors of the nineteenth and early twentieth centuries, in a deeply integrated world. Some form of a "universal rule of law," creating a new balance between the selfish interests of nations and universal principles, would ease the evolution we are seeking. It would help to define a framework—political, cultural, and economic—that is truly compatible with democratic ideals on the scale of humanity, and favorable to their wider acceptance.

NOTES

1. "Islam is the blueprint of a social order. It holds that a set of rules exists, eternal, divinely ordained, and independent of the will of men, which defines the proper ordering

of society. . . . In traditional Islam, no distinction is made between lawyer and common lawyer, and the roles of theologian and lawyer are conflated. Expertise on proper social arrangements, and on matters pertaining to God, are one and the same thing." Ernest Gellner, *Muslim Society* (Cambridge: Cambridge University Press, 1981), 1.

2. Those priests who belong to monastic order and live according to its rules are considered "regular" clergy, while those priests living in the world and not bound by monastic vows or rules are considered "secular" clergy.

3. Quoted by Samuel Huntington, "Democracy's Third Wave," in Marc F. Plattner and Larry Diamond, eds., *The Global Resurgence of Democracy* (Baltimore: Johns Hopkins University Press, 1993), 19.

4. Mohamed Charfi, *Islam et liberté: le malentendu historique* (Paris: Albin Michel, 1998), 191.

5. Richard K. Khuri gives a very comprehensive description of the way this build-up was achieved. See Richard K. Khuri, *Freedom, Modernity and Islam: Toward a Creative Synthesis* (Syracuse, N.Y.: Syracuse University Press), 1998.

6. Wilfred Cantwell Smith, *The Meaning and End of Religion: A New Approach to the Religious Traditions of Mankind* (New York, 1962), 117.

7. Leonard Binder, "Exceptionalism and Authenticity: The Question of Islam and Democracy," *Arab Studies Journal* 6 (Spring 1998): 33–59.

8. Marshall G.S. Hodgson's main work is *The Venture of Islam,* 3 vols. (Chicago: University of Chicago Press, 1974). A summary of his conclusions appeared in a collection of articles published posthumously under the title *Rethinking World History: Essays on Europe, Islam and World History,* edited, with an introduction and a conclusion, by Edmund Burke III (Cambridge: Cambridge University Press, 1993).

9. Fazlur Rahman, *Islam and Modernity: Transformation of an Intellectual Tradition* (Chicago: University of Chicago Press, 1982), 32.

10. Mohamed Charfi, *Islam et liberté* (Paris: Albin Michel, 1998), 228.

11. Tim Niblock, "Democratisation: A Theoretical and Practical Debate," *The British Journal of Middle Eastern Studies* 25 (November 1998): 221–34.

12. Mohamed Abed Jabri, *Ad-Dimuqratiya wa Huquq al-Insan [Democracy and Human Rights]* (Beirut: Center for Arab Unity Studies, 1994).

13. Tim Niblock, "Democratisation," 226.

14. Ibid., 229.

15. Ali Abderraziq (1888–1966) attempted, in a famous and much debated essay published in 1925, to dispel the misunderstanding and confusions surrounding religion and politics in Islam. His demonstration—for it was intended to be a rigorous demonstration—aimed at showing the strict separation between, on the one hand, religious principles and rules relating to social and political matters and, on the other, the laws and regulations made by theologians and political leaders to implement the faith in the temporal life of their community. He rejected the view, widely held among Sunni Muslims, that the end of the 'rightly guided' caliphate (approximately three decades after the death of the Prophet), which allegedly saw the replacement of the initially religious community by a regular polity and of a religious order by a secular or temporal order, constituted a really basic turn in the history of Muslims. The initiative of Ali Abderraziq was a founding moment in contemporary Muslim thought and politics.

It did not succeed in dispelling the "big misunderstanding"; it is, however, the most radical attempt to show that a "new beginning" is possible for Muslims regarding such basic issues as the overall relation between faith and the social and political order. Ali Abderraziq, *L'Islam et les fondements du pouvoir* (Paris: La Découverte, 1994).

16. Fazlur Rahman did so in scholarly and measured terms, while Taha wrote a kind of manifesto calling for a reversal of the order of prominence that Muslims give to Qur'anic verses: Mahmoud Mohamed Taha, *The Second Message of Islam,* translated by Abdullahi Ahmed An-Na'im (Syracuse, N.Y.: Syracuse University Press, 1987).

17. For Talbi, see *Plaidoyer pour un Islam moderne* (Casablanca: Le Fennec, 1996). For Charfi, see *Islam et liberté: le malentendu historique* (Paris: Albin Michel, 1998).

18. Alain Touraine, "Modernité et spécificités culturelles," in *Revue Internationale des Sciences Sociales* 118 (November 1988): 497–512.

5

HOW FAR CAN FREE GOVERNMENT TRAVEL?

Giovanni Sartori

Giovanni Sartori *is Albert Schweitzer Professor Emeritus in the Humanities at Columbia University. He is the author of numerous books, including, most recently,* Comparative Constitutional Engineering: An Inquiry into Structures, Incentives and Outcomes *(1996). A version of this essay was presented at an October 1994 conference in Seoul sponsored by the Korean Association of International Studies.*

There is no doubt that the theory and practice of liberal democracy are a Western product rooted in Western history and culture. Thus as democracy is exported from the West to other areas and cultures we hear references made to "cultural imperialism" and to a "biased, Western-centric model." But I do not think that ideas should be rejected on the basis of where they originated. That democracy is a Western invention does not entail that it is a bad invention, or a product suitable only for Western consumption. That my own writings on democracy are Western-centric does not give me any particular guilt complex.[1] I do recognize, however, that the prescription of democracy for non-Western areas confronts us with "traveling issues." First, can democracy be exported to any place, regardless of "import conditions," that is, of conditions in the importing countries? Second, can and should democracy be exported *in toto* and in its most advanced (Western) formulation, or should we first break the concept of liberal democracy down into its *necessary* (defining) and *contingent* (variable) elements?

The question whether democracy can be implanted in any soil is generally answered by pointing to India and Japan—both decidedly non-Western cultures and yet convincing instances of a successful implant. I bow to this grand evidence; nonetheless, I am not entirely satisfied by it. What about Africa, for instance? Close study would reveal that India and Japan did meet "minimal conditions" for the import of democratic forms, conditions that may not exist in other areas. Further exploration of the exportability of democracy, however, requires that we first take up the second question and look at the component elements of the concept.

At the outset I referred to "liberal democracy," and I must emphasize that "democracy" is only a shorthand—and a misleading one at that—for an entity composed of two distinct elements: 1) freeing the people (liberalism) and 2) empowering the people (democracy). One could equally say that liberal democracy consists of 1) "demo-protection," meaning the protection of a people from tyranny, and 2) "demo-power," meaning the implementation of popular rule. Historically, the creation of a free people was the accomplishment of liberalism (from Locke to, say, Benjamin Constant, the major French constitutionalist), and this element is generally singled out by the notions of constitutional democracy and/or liberal constitutionalism. A free *demos,* however, is also a *demos* that gradually enters the house of power, asserts itself, "demands" and "obtains." And this is democracy per se.

Which of the aforementioned elements is the more important one? If this question implies that what is more important must supersede what is less important, then it is a misguided question. If we take this road, we generally arrive at the answer that *freedom to* is more important than *freedom from,* that demo-power is more important than demo-protection, and thus that the democratic element takes priority over the liberal element.[2] But this conclusion would be wrong. Regardless of our own personal feelings about which element is more important, the issue is one of *procedural sequencing,* and thus of what is a prior condition of what else. And it cannot be doubted that—procedurally—*freedom from* (what Hobbes referred to as the absence of external impediments) and demo-protection (liberal constitutionalism) are the *necessary condition* of democracy per se.[3]

Of the two component elements of liberal democracy, then, demo-protection is the necessary and defining element. And I would also hold that this is the global or universal element, the one that *can* be exported anywhere and implanted in any kind of soil. As this element is concerned primarily with the structural and legal means of limiting and controlling the exercise of power, and thus of keeping arbitrary and absolute power at bay, we have here a political form that can be superimposed (since it is only a *form*) on any culture regardless of underlying socioeconomic configurations. This is not the case with the demo-power element, for here we enter the arena of policy content, of concrete inputs and outputs processed by, and within, the political form. The constitutional state intimates *how* decisions are made; demo-power bears on *what* is decided. And, clearly, in the "will of the people" arena contingency and cultural factors are likely to engender a great deal of variance in the particular decisions that are made.

The standard objection to my argument for the universality (and hence exportability) of democracy as a constitutional form is that it assumes that freedom—as defined and protected by constitutionalism—is both a primary and a universal value, when in fact this may not be the case. In essence, then, the objection is that freedom is not "valued" by everybody everywhere. For instance, in theocratic and "submissive" cultures there is no place for valuing freedom.[4] The point is buttressed by arguing that the freedom in question actually is *individual* freedom, and therefore a freedom tainted by mean, even sordid, individualistic values. But the empirical evidence in support of this argument is invalid, and the individualistic indictment unwarranted.

How can we ascertain whether the state of "being free" is in fact appreciated by most people in most places? The caveat here is that, "if I ask someone whether he prefers to travel on horseback or by car, his reply is meaningless unless the respondent has at least seen a car and a horse. It is pointless to enquire about preferences vis-à-vis people who have never been offered alternatives, that is, anything to compare. . . . Innumerable people cannot prefer something to something else because they have no "else" in sight; they simply live with, and encapsulated within, the human (or inhumane) condition they find."[5]

Clearly, then, it is preposterous to assess the matter by asking illiterate peasants in primitive societies and Third World countries whether they "value freedom" and whether they prefer this value to others. The notions of value and freedom are highly abstract, analytic concepts that are utterly unintelligible to a large majority of the world's inhabitants.

This does not mean, however, that the issue must be dropped on the grounds that the universal desirability of freedom can be neither verified nor falsified by empirical findings. Rather, what must be dropped is the abstract (and surely Western-centric) vocabulary in which the case is being framed. Instead of speaking of *values,* let us speak of *harms,* thereby recasting the argument in terms of the harm principle. The contention thus becomes that nobody likes to be imprisoned, tortured, or killed, and that everybody tries to escape when confronted with harm. And political freedom is an abstract rendering of what the harm principle is concretely about. Liberal constitutionalism aims to ensure that no one can be harmed by the coercive instruments of politics without due process and in violation of *habeas corpus.*

The desirability, universality, and exportability of democracy as a constitutional form rest, then, on the *harm-avoidance* rule. This formulation clearly invalidates, *inter alia,* the "individualistic" charge. Individuals seek to avoid bodily harm (and what they perceive as harmful) in a communitarian setting just as much as in an atomistic one. A member of a tribal village will try to escape before allowing himself to be roasted over a fire or carved by a knife just as surely as his "individualistic," egocentric counterpart. Thus the contention that *freedom from* is of no interest to people whose belief system does not "value" the individual is without merit.

The analytic distinction that we are drawing between demo-protection and demo-power should not be understood, however, as amounting to a practical disjunction. The two are connected, a connection clearly established by voting and electing. Even so, the importance of voting tends to be exaggerated by authors who lack historical perspective. Take the claim—and by now the slogan—that full democracy is achieved only when universal (male and female) suffrage is achieved. Yes—but also no. For we should remind ourselves that liberal (constitutional) democracy was launched and long sustained by very small electorates. Voting is indeed a *necessary condition* of any free polity.[6] Yet the extent and extension of voting in a given polity are not as crucial as some would have us believe. Feminist outcries notwithstanding, I still hold that Switzerland was a full democracy in spite of its electoral exclusions. And if I had to choose between a country with universal suffrage but insecure rule of law and, conversely, a country with less-than-universal suffrage but secure rule of law, I would unhesitatingly choose the latter as a better democracy than the former.[7] Voting, then, is not *the* indicator of democracy. It does not adequately measure full democracy, and I will suggest below that it is a mistake to blindly impose voting on countries that are unfit for voting.

Preconditions of Democracy

Why deal extensively with the liberal *past* of liberal democracy? Because *initial* democracy in Asia and elsewhere confronts the same problems that democracy faced initially in the West. To be sure, once a political form has been invented and tried out somewhere, it takes less time to copy it elsewhere. Granted also that, in principle, creating a democracy "by imitation" is a relatively easy thing to do. The problem, however, is the gap between *calendar time* and *historical time*. Copying a political model is a synchronic process based on calendar time: We import today what exists today. But in terms of historical time, countries can be a thousand years apart. Historically, Afghanistan and millions of villages scattered across the underdeveloped (let alone the undeveloped) areas today are about where most of Europe was in the dark Middle Ages. Thus the import business is not as easy as it is often made to appear. Since it involves tricky "timing differences," it runs into trouble whenever an advanced model is abruptly imposed upon a lagging reality. Even though in calendar time today is the same day in Washington as it is in Kabul, a transplant from the former to the latter is a huge leap.

Let me rephrase this caveat in terms of preconditions. The notion of preconditions of democracy generally refers to economic preconditions. I will come to these shortly, but here I mean historical antecedents. There are two: One is secularization, and the other is what I call the "taming" of politics. Secularization occurs when the realm of God and the realm of Caesar—the sphere of religion and the sphere of politics—are separated. As a result, politics is no longer reinforced by religion: It loses both its religion-derived rigidity (dogmatism) and its religious-like intensity. Out of this situation arise the conditions for the taming of politics. By this I mean that politics no longer kills, is no longer a warlike affair, and that peacelike politics affirms itself as the standard *modus operandi* of a polity.

One need not look far to grasp the connection between these historical conditions and democracy. Democracy assumes that power is both given and revoked by electoral verdicts and thus routinely requires rotation in office. But if powerholders have reason to fear that relinquishing power could endanger their life and property, it is clear that they will not relinquish it. Therefore, until politics is secularized and "tamed"—that is, until there is sufficient protection for the human being as such—the stakes will be too high for politicians to surrender their power and step down.

All these preconditions were conspicuously absent in Algeria at the time of the 1991–92 elections. It was a grievous mistake, I believe, to cancel the second round and to nullify the elections. But the worse mistake was to call elections at all. The international community is ill-advised in asking countries currently facing the tide of Islamic fundamentalism to "certify" their democracy by calling for a vote. In a nonsecular-ized, warlike setting in which the loser expects to be killed, democracy of any kind is impossible.

It is possible, then, that nations coming late to democracy are actually *disadvantaged* by the availability of a prototype that they can simply copy. If the latecomers are expected to "catch up" (ignoring historical time) at an excessively rapid pace, they are likely to suffer from "over-load," an unmanageable situation arising from too many simultaneous crises or burdens.[8] In this regard it is important to keep in mind that a century ago democracy was only a political form, and that the con-stitutional state did not provide, nor was it expected to provide, economic "goodies"; rather, it provided freedom and the "good things" that come in its wake. For well over a century, the case was never made that democ-racy had economic preconditions and that its sustainability depended on economic growth and prosperity. The point is, then, that the nineteenth-century demo-protection afforded by the liberal state did not have wealth requirements. To the extent that liberal democracy is conceived as a political form, a "poor democracy" is equally conceivable and possible.

As Western democracies developed and attained higher levels of democratization, however, demo-power became demo-appetite, and the policy content of the liberal-constitutional forms increasingly centered around distributive issues, around "who gets how much of what." This shift was probably inevitable. It has been mightily reinforced, however, by the withering away of ethics, by Marxist "materialism," and by the strongly utilitarian bent that has shaped the theory and practice of democracy in its Anglo-American unfolding. These are, to be sure, cultural factors that may be countered as democracy takes root in other cultures. Yet the fact remains that if democracy is imported as a system of demo-power eminently concerned with demo-distributions, then the fate of democracy becomes intertwined with economic performance.[9] Therefore, the crucial issue almost everywhere today is whether democracy also supplies economic growth.

Does Democracy Work Best?

Let us turn, then, to the question: Does democracy work best, economically speaking? Many would boldly answer with a resounding yes. As *The Economist* puts it, the evidence shows that "across scores of countries and centuries of history, democracy has promoted growth far more effectively and consistently than any other political system."[10] I wish that I could believe that. Alas, what this account completely misses is that growth came with technological advancement, and that technology is a by-product not of democracy but of the kind of logic and rationality forged by the ancient Greeks, which eventually gave rise to the "scientific spirit" and, in its wake, to the prodigious development of technology that uniquely occurred in the last two centuries in the Western world. It is true that Chinese civilization was marked by outstanding skills, and for a long time outpaced the West in technical inventions. Yet the science and technology that "modernize" today's world never blossomed in other cultures—neither in China nor, to cite another major example, in India. Hence the observed correlation between Western liberal democracy and affluence turns out to be spurious.

Correlations aside, what is the argument behind the thesis of democracy's "economic superiority"? According to *The Economist,* "one of the main reasons why democracy promotes growth is that it offers the security of property rights that is necessary for capitalistic progress."[11] In the wake of the disastrous collapse of Soviet-type planned economies, however, even dictators well realize by now that "the invisible hand works better than the visible boot."[12] Thus dictators too will find that promoting market systems and respecting property rights are in their own best interests.

As I look around, I see democracies "in growth" and democracies that are backsliding, just as I see dictatorships that are in economic ruins and dictatorships that are enjoying economic success. Taiwan, Singapore, South Korea, and now Malaysia as well have engineered their "economic miracles" under authoritarian monitoring. And what of Hong Kong, which is not a democracy but a colony ruled by a British governor? In Latin America, the economies of Chile and Peru collapsed under democratic rule and owe their comebacks to authoritarian governance (in Peru, President Alberto Fujimori did wonders for the economy, but at the cost of suspending and subsequently rewriting a dubiously democratic constitution). The overall pattern of the region is that military dictatorships and democratic governments have equally poor developmental records.[13] In the former Soviet Union and Eastern Europe, democratization has preceded economic reform and made the latter more difficult. China under Deng Xiaoping, on the other hand, has followed the opposite approach—with economic liberalization handed down from above under strict dictatorial control—and the success has been remarkable.

So the contention that democracy is not only a superior political system (I certainly concur in that) but also an "economic winner" is easily countered by the argument that, given equal market mechanisms, governments that are spared gridlock and popular pressures are in a better position to promote growth than governments encumbered by demo-demands and demo-distributions. To be sure, as people grow richer, democracy is one of the things they are likely to demand. But in this argument it is growth that entails democracy, not democracy that generates growth.

That democracy works best is not, then, a sort of natural law. Democracies *must be made to work* (through structural incentives and constraints, not merely good will). And here I would stress that the model itself, the Western political form, is in crying need of repair.[14] The danger of bankrupt democracy, of so-called democracy in deficit, is a very real one, and one that present-day constitutional structures are not equipped to deal with.

Let me once again place the problem in historical perspective. When the liberal-constitutional polities were conceived, the single major driving force behind their implementation was the principle "no taxation without representation." (As James Otis bluntly put it in 1761, "taxation without representation is tyranny.") Therefore, when parliaments became one of the pillars of the constitutional state, they held the "power of the purse"—that is, the power of raising monies and of granting them to the holder of the "power of the sword" (that is, the king). This division of competencies between parliamentary guardianship and executive spending achieved its purpose as long as parliaments represented (as they did throughout the nineteenth century) the actual taxpayers—that is, the "haves," not the "have-nots." Under these conditions, parliaments have in fact been effective expense controllers. Over the last century, however, the equilibrium between parliamentary brakes and executive accelerators has been lost. With universal suffrage and the subsequent general shift from law and order (what the "small state" was expected to deliver) to the need-attending welfare state, parliaments have become even greater spenders than governments. The natural dam that kept national budgets in equilibrium up to the middle of the twentieth century was the belief that a budget by definition is a *balance,* a balancing of revenues and expenditures. And it is this belief that accounts for the fact that the enormous debts created by two world wars were gradually absorbed.

The spell was broken when the message of John Maynard Keynes— deficit spending—got through to politicians. Free riding on borrowed money has since become an irresistible temptation. Across the structures of the constitutional state one no longer finds, at any point, a fiscally responsible gatekeeper. And if free-riding politicians can get away with incurring debts "for consumption" (not for investment), and therefore, in the end, with simply printing more money, then bad politics, bad economics, or both are virtual certainties. It is therefore crucial that control of the purse be reestablished, for what we now have is, on this score, a state without checks and balances.

I cannot discuss here the possible remedies.[15] I can only underscore that whether or not democracy performs (in economic terms) is crucially determined at the "control of the purse" juncture. It is here, as we move from form (the constitutional structure) to policy content (resulting from demo-demands), that democracy currently faces its greatest challenge.

The formal rights set forth in the original bills of rights were, by and large, costless. As formal rights have expanded to encompass material entitlements, they have become ever more costly. In recent decades, Western democracies have been able to meet escalating welfare expenditures by two means: deficit spending and protectionism. Both resources have since dried up. Many Western democracies today end up with "rigid budgets"—that is to say, they are so deeply in debt that different or additional allocations are almost impossible. And to the extent that a global economy inevitably exposes formerly protected pro- ducers (which were able to pass their fiscal burdens on to their consum- ers) to worldwide competition, the welfare state becomes unaffordable. The years to come will thus have to be years of retrenchment. Now more than ever, then, democracies must be capable of sustaining growth. But even if worst comes to worst and we are drawn into a negative-sum vortex—a game in which everybody loses—the thought that I offer in consolation is that liberal democracy is still worthwhile on its own and that to have demo-protection is still infinitely better than to have nothing.

A Final Question

A final question remains, namely, whether Asia and Africa may need their own "models" of democracy. At the core—that is, the constitutional techniques for protecting citizens and controlling (limiting) the exercise of political power—no alternative model is in sight, and I equally fail to see why anyone would want to discard a well-tested mechanism that works. But at the periphery—for instance, when it comes to party systems and the processes of articulation and aggregation of interests—I grant that the multiparty arrangements originally resulting from Western class cleavages make little sense where the loyalties are exclusively tribal. African leaders who make this argument have a point, but they are wrong when their solution is to ban multiparty politics and, in practice, establish a one-man, one-party rule.

When we come, on the other hand, to the "will of the people" element of liberal democracy, it is difficult to generalize. The world is made up of very different people embedded in very different cultures, worldviews, and value systems, not to mention circumstances.[16] Even in the West, *vox populi* is not necessarily understood as *vox Dei;* and I for one hold not that the people are always right but that the people have the right to be mistaken. Similarly, should we permit democracy to be "demo-killed"—that is, should we allow a power of the people that eliminates itself? This and a host of similar questions prompt a number of different responses, which in turn deeply affect the policy outputs of democratic experiments. Walter Bagehot praised, in his time, the "deferential stupidity" of the English. Is democracy better served by undeferential arrogance? These are, I suggest, matters best left to each *Volksgeist,* to each distinctive "spirit of the people."

The Western theory of democracy has evolved (often normatively and even perfectionistically) to reflect advanced levels of democratization. As this theory travels to new democracies in the making (and is disseminated by students trained in Western universities), the foundations of Western democracy itself are either taken for granted or overlooked entirely. This is, I submit, a bad beginning for beginners. Historically, as I have argued above, liberal democracy has grown to encompass two component elements: 1) demo-protection (which results in a free people), and 2) demo-power (which results in a self-asserting people). Demo-protection is secured by the "form" of liberal democracy—that is, its constitutional structures and procedures—whereas demo-power is the input-output "content" delivered by policy decisions. The first element is—in my argument—a necessary condition of democracy, whereas the second is an open-ended set of implementations.

It follows from the aforementioned distinctions that: 1) the form (the liberal-constitutional element) is the universally exportable element, whereas the content (what a people wills and demands) is the contingent, culturally dependent element; 2) "tamed" and peacelike politics is an essential precondition of electoral verdicts that are respected and bring about rotation in political office; 3) demo-protection is indifferent to economic conditions and thus allows, *ex hypothesi,* for a "poor" democracy, whereas a demo-power that demands demo-benefits crucially requires wealth and economic growth; and, therefore, 4) the outright identification of democracy with demo-distributions makes the present-day fiscal crisis of democracy—wherever it occurs—particularly worrisome.

NOTES

1. In the main, three: *Democratic Theory* (Detroit: Wayne State University Press, 1962; New York: Praeger, 1965); *The Theory of Democracy Revisited* (Chatham, N.J.: Chatham House, 1987), which extends and revises the earlier volume; and *Democrazia: Cosa •E* (Milan: Rizzoli, 1992), in which a new part discusses democracy after communism—that is, in victory.

2. It must be borne in mind that in this essay "liberal" is always used in its historical sense, not in the sense in which it is currently used in the United States—that is, as a synonym for "left."

3. For a more detailed analysis, see my *Theory of Democracy Revisited,* 301–10, 357–58, 386–93.

4. I use the term "submissive culture" rather than "subject culture," "deferential culture," or similar expressions because the word Islam means "submission," and because Islamic culture is currently the main antagonist of what Gabriel Almond and others have called "civic culture."

5. See my *Theory of Democracy Revisited,* 272, 273–79 passim.

6. Even Edmund Burke, who championed "virtual representation"—that is, representation without election—qualified his stance by noting in a 1792 letter to Sir Hercules Langrishe that "this sort of virtual representation cannot have a long or sure existence, if it has not a substratum in the actual. The member must have some relation to the constituent." *Burke, Works,* 9 vols. (Boston: Little, Brown, 1839), 3:521.

7. In much of Latin America, for instance, the right to vote is extended to all, but the independence of the judiciary is often dubious; and I do marvel at how "electoral democratization" can be given precedence over the rule-of-law requirement.

8. Reference is made here to the "sequencing of crises" theory that was developed in a series of volumes sponsored by the Social Science Research Council and published by Princeton University Press, which is summarized in the concluding volume of the series, by Leonard Binder et al., *Crises and Sequences in Political Development* (1971), especially the last chapter by Sidney Verba.

9. The debate about the relationship between democracy and economic development goes back to the seminal work of Seymour Martin Lipset, *Political Man: The Social Bases of Politics* (Garden City, N.Y.: Doubleday, 1959), especially ch. 2. For a more recent assessment, see Larry Diamond, "Economic Development and Democracy Reconsidered," in Gary Marks and Larry Diamond, eds., *Reexamining Democracy* (Newbury Park, Calif.: Sage, 1992), 93–139.

10. "Democracy Works Best," *The Economist,* 27 August 1994, 9.

11. Ibid. A more sophisticated argument along the same lines is made (in terms of taxation) by Mancur Olson in "Dictatorship, Democracy, and Development," *American Political Science Review* 87 (September 1993): 567–76. According to Olson, a dictator (a "stationary bandit") will do well only "if he is taking an indefinitely long view," whereas the odds are that "an autocrat is only concerned about getting through the next year" (571). But is the time horizon of the democratic politician longer than that of the dictator? I very much doubt it.

12. "Democracy and Growth: Why Voting Is Good for You," *The Economist*, 27 August 1994, 17.

13. In this essay I do not deal with the sui generis problems surrounding the importation of democracy into Latin America. A good overview can be found in Abraham F. Lowenthal, ed., *Exporting Democracy: The United States and Latin America* (Baltimore: Johns Hopkins University Press, 1991).

14. I deal at length with the repairs that democratic systems need in my *Comparative Constitutional Engineering: An Inquiry into Structures, Incentives and Outcomes* (New York: New York University Press; London: Macmillan, 1994). Here I must confine the argument to the economic feebleness, so to speak, of Western constitutional structures.

15. With regard to the constitutional solutions proposed in the United States, see Aaron Wildavsky, *How to Limit Government Spending* (Berkeley: University of California Press, 1980); and R.E. Wagner et al., *Balanced Budgets: Fiscal Responsibility and the Constitution* (Washington, D.C.: Cato Institute, 1982). The introduction of a balanced-budget amendment into the U.S. Constitution is currently on the agenda of Congress.

16. For a broad, cross-national treatment of the role of the cultural factor, see Larry Diamond, ed., *Political Culture and Democracy in Developing Countries* (Boulder, Colo.: Lynne Rienner, 1993).

6

DEMOCRACY AND LIBERTY: THE CULTURAL CONNECTION

Russell Bova

Russell Bova *is professor of political science and director of the Russian Area Studies Program at Dickinson College in Carlisle, Pennsylvania. He has written widely on Soviet and postcommunist politics and is currently working with several colleagues on a book on the relationship between Russian culture and Western civilization.*

A close association between democracy and liberty has long been taken for granted. At least a minimal package of human freedoms, including rights of association, opposition, and free speech and expression, is in fact required if democratic institutions such as elections are to be meaningful. Most definitions of the term "democracy" include reference to such freedoms. Moreover, democracy is presumed to foster basic human liberties and freedoms to a degree that is unmatched by authoritarian regimes. Democratic checks on rulers make it much more difficult for them to abuse their power or oppress their subjects, and they provide the opportunity for citizens to act to expand the range of rights to which they are entitled. It is, in fact, this connection between democracy, on the one hand, and human rights and liberties, on the other, that constitutes the most powerful argument in favor of democratic government.

It is against the backdrop of this conventional thinking that Adrian Karatnycky, in the 1993–94 edition of Freedom House's annual global survey of political freedom, identified a paradox of the early 1990s. Specifically, he observed that while the number of democracies continued to grow, the state of freedom in the world was deteriorating.[1] His explanation for this troubling trend was that some democracies were facing acute economic, political, or social problems that were serving to undermine human rights and liberties. Such difficulties can certainly limit the quantity and quality of freedom that even a democratically constituted government can provide. Yet there is another possible explanation for the paradox: The close relationship observed between democracy and liberty may be contingent on culture.

The definition of democracy adopted in this essay is a minimalist, procedural one rooted in the notion, originally put forth by Joseph Schumpeter, that democracy is a method or process of selecting rulers and, at least indirectly, policies. More specifically, to be considered democratic a political system must, at a minimum, meet two criteria: 1) the criterion of *participation,* which assumes that all adult members of the political community have the right to participate in the political process, most importantly in the process of electing public officials; and 2) the criterion of *contestation,* which assumes that significant political decision makers are elected via competition among multiple candidates and parties that allows for some meaningful degree of voter choice. To the extent that part of the adult population is excluded from participation or that individuals or parties are prevented from competing fairly for public support, the quality of democracy may be said to suffer.

While democracy has to do with the selection of rulers or policies, liberty refers to the freedom to engage in certain behaviors or to hold and express views without governmental interference. For example, the freedom to travel, to practice one's religious faith, to look at pornography, and to buy and own property are measures of liberty rather than democracy. The bulk of what are commonly referred to as human rights involve precisely such questions of liberty. To some extent, of course, all governments limit individual liberties. They differ, however, in the amount of residual space left open for individuals to occupy free from governmental constraint.

A Complex Relationship

Both in theory and in practice, the relationship between democracy and liberty is a complex one that has spawned a certain degree of confusion among scholars. On the one hand, liberty is sometimes treated as a *consequence* of democracy; democratic governments, though varying among themselves in level of respect for human rights, are assumed to do a better job of protecting those rights than do their authoritarian counterparts.[2] On the other hand, liberty is frequently treated as a *precondition* of democracy, to the point that most scholars include civil and political liberties as a third element (beyond participation and contestation) of the definition of democracy itself.

To some extent, expanding the definition of democracy in this fashion seems reasonable. Absent at least a minimal package of civil liberties involving various freedoms of association and expression, what Larry Diamond has labeled "electoral democracy" may, in fact, prove to be quite hollow.[3] Yet an overly demanding definition of democracy that conflates democracy and liberty may fail to acknowledge that "electoral democracies," though they fall short of what Diamond calls "liberal democracies" in their level of respect for human rights, still may produce regular and peaceful transfers of political power that differentiate them from authoritarian regimes.

With this distinction between electoral and liberal democracy in mind, two questions must be addressed. First, to what extent is there an empirical relationship between democracy (minimally defined in terms of participation and contestation) and human rights and liberties? Second, what accounts for the variation in human rights performance among regimes that qualify as democracies in the minimalist sense? Why, in other words, are some democracies more "liberal" than others? Help in answering the first question is provided by Freedom House's annual survey of freedom, which distinguishes between "political rights" and "civil liberties." Freedom House's checklist for political rights deals largely with issues of participation and contestation, while its checklist for civil liberties deals mainly with issues of individual liberty.[4] Although the two checklists overlap to some degree (for example, freedom of organization appears as the fifth item on the political-rights checklist and the fourth item on the civil-liberties checklist), there remains enough of a difference to suggest that the Freedom House data provide at least an imperfect picture of the relationship between democracy and liberty. That picture shows the relationship to be strongly positive.

For 1993–94, Freedom House rated 190 countries on two separate 7-point scales, one for political rights and the other for civil liberties.[5] In 94 cases (49 percent), the scores on the two dimensions were exactly the same. For example, Canada received a score of 1 (the best possible score) on each dimension, while Syria received a score of 7 (the worst possible score) on each. In another 81 cases (43 percent), the difference in the two scores was only 1 point (for example, Russia received a 3 on political rights and a 4 on civil liberties). In only 15 cases (8 percent) was there a 2-point difference in the two scores (for example, Albania received a 2 on political rights and a 4 on civil liberties), and in no case did the scores differ by more than 2 points.

Other data also show a correlation between political rights and civil liberties. The 1992 edition of Charles Humana's *World Human Rights Guide* compares and ranks 104 independent states around the world on the basis of 40 human rights criteria specified in UN-sponsored international agreements.[6] On a 100-point scale (with 100 being the best possible score), the average human rights rating in this survey is 62. One of Humana's 40 criteria was the holding of multiparty elections by secret and universal ballot—an approximation of our minimalist definition of democracy as a political system based on participation and contestation. Correlating countries' performance on this criterion with their overall human rights records again points to a relationship between democracy on the one hand and human rights and liberties on the other. Countries demonstrating unqualified respect for the principle of multiparty elections by universal ballot had an average human rights

TABLE 1—DEMOCRACY AND HUMAN RIGHTS

MULTIPARTY ELECTIONS BY SECRET AND UNIVERSAL BALLOT *	NUMBER OF CASES	AVERAGE HUMAN RIGHTS RATING
"Yes"	42	85
Qualified "Yes"	27	63
Qualified "No"	11	53
"No"	24	35

Source: Charles Humana, World Human Rights Guide, 3rd ed. (New York: Oxford University Press, 1992). Average human rights ratings for the four categories were calculated on the basis of Humana's individual country data.
* According to Humana, "Yes" indicates unqualified respect for the principle of multiparty elections by secret and universal ballot; "Qualified Yes" indicates occasional breaches of such respect; "Qualified No" indicates frequent violations of the principle; and "No" indicates a constant pattern of violations of the principle.

score of 85. At the other extreme, countries that in practice utterly rejected the concept of multiparty elections by universal ballot had an average human rights rating of only 35 (see Table 1 above).

These data would seem to provide a very strong case for an essential connection between democracy and liberty. Yet this analysis leaves out an important part of the picture. Until very recently, most democratic regimes were found either in the West or in countries heavily influenced by Western political culture owing to Western colonialism. Samuel P. Huntington notes that there were, by his count, 58 democratic countries in 1990.[7] Of those, he points out, 37 were West European, European-settled, or Latin American countries, 6 were East European countries, and 9 were former colonies of Britain, the United States, or Australia. Of the remaining six (Japan, South Korea, Turkey, Mongolia, Namibia, and Senegal), the first two were heavily influenced by the United States as a consequence of war.

This relationship between democracy and Western culture at least raises the possibility that the correlation between democracy and liberty is spurious. Perhaps democracy and liberty are both products of Western culture, or, more to the point, perhaps democracy leads to liberty only in the specific cultural context of the West. The notion of cultural contingency is not far-fetched given that the emergence of the "democratic idea" in its modern form in the Europe of the Enlightenment was closely intertwined with—and, in fact, preceded by—the development of the doctrine of natural rights.

The idea of natural rights, as reflected in the writings of John Locke, was conceived as a limitation on tyranny, as a justification for religious tolerance, and as a general defense of individual rights and liberties. While some made the leap from the idea of natural rights to support for political democracy, others were more hesitant. Indeed, well into the nineteenth century, many European liberals resisted the idea of democracy, if only because it seemed to them to threaten the very advances in liberty that had already been achieved. In Democracy in

America, Alexis de Tocqueville noted along these lines that in the aristocratic ages that preceded the birth of democracy, "the sovereigns of Europe had been deprived of, or had relinquished, many of the rights inherent in their power."[8] In contrast, he argues, political equality and democracy bring with them a natural tendency toward governmental centralization and governmental intrusion into spheres of activity previously viewed as within the private domain.[9] Writing in the 1830s, Tocqueville believed that of the two opposite evils to which democracy could lead, servitude was a greater threat than anarchy, if only because the former threat was less readily discerned than the latter. With the perspective of hindsight, however, one might argue that precisely this Tocquevillean fear of democratic tyranny—rooted in decades of Enlightenment thought and reflected, for example, in the statesmanship of the framers of the U.S. Constitution—has helped to develop and maintain the essentially liberal character of Western democracy.

The question, therefore, is what happens when democracy is transplanted to cultural settings where the Enlightenment emphasis on natural rights, the individual, and liberty is less deeply rooted and where the threat of democratic servitude is therefore even less discernible than it was in the Europe of Tocqueville's time. While there is much variation among non-Western political cultures, the emphasis on individualism that grew out of the European Enlightenment and out of the doctrine of natural rights is nowhere as highly developed as in the West. Indeed, even in closely related political cultures like that of Orthodox Russia and Eastern Europe, duty, community, and *sobornost* (roughly, "populist collectivism") take precedence over individual rights. In such settings, electoral institutions may be imported while deficiencies in human rights and liberties remain. Indeed, as Tocqueville feared, electoral democracy in such illiberal settings may even become a tool for the suppression of certain human liberties.

The Impact of Culture

The impact of culture on human rights and liberties can be examined by grouping the 104 countries examined in Humana's survey of human rights into three different categories: 1) Western democracies, 2) non-Western democracies, and 3) non-Western authoritarian regimes. Once again, the analysis presented here is based on a minimalist definition of democracy emphasizing participation and contestation. All those countries that, in Humana's assessment, demonstrated either complete or qualified respect for the principle of multiparty elections by secret and universal ballot in 1991 are classified as democracies.

A more difficult question is on what basis to classify countries as "Western." One approach would require that they meet two criteria: first, whether a country is European or, owing to European colonization, characterized by significant European settlement; and second, whether the country has a Western Christian (or Jewish) majority. In many cases, the classifications that result from strict application of both these criteria are uncontroversial. All the West European countries and European-settled countries like the United States, Canada, and Australia are generally viewed as unambiguously Western. This approach, however, prompts questions when applied to two other parts of the world.

In Eastern Europe, this scheme leaves only Poland, Hungary, and Czechoslovakia classified as Western, since they were the only three independent countries in that region with Western Christian majorities at the beginning of 1991. (Subsequently, the three Baltic states, Croatia, and Slovenia achieved recognition as independent states, but as of 1991 they were still subsumed within larger countries with a dominant culture that was not rooted in Western Christianity.) This use of religion to separate Poland, Hungary, and Czechoslovakia from their Orthodox and Islamic neighbors to the East is not without scholarly support. For example, Huntington, citing William Wallace, suggests that the critical cultural dividing line in Europe today is the boundary of Western Christendom in 1500.[10] While Huntington is not entirely convinced that this religious divide will translate into a political divide between democracies and nondemocracies, he does accept that the penetration of Western culture across that religious boundary into areas of Orthodoxy and Islam has been relatively weak. Moreover, Huntington's sense of the region is consistent with the general distinction made by regional specialists between the culture of Central Europe and that of its neighbors to the south and east. While the latter have certainly been influenced by the West (and vice versa), their relationship to the West is more ambiguous than that of the former. Russia, for example, has always been torn between East and West and between Slavophiles and Westernizers, giving rise to a culture that is less unambiguously Western than that of the Czechs, for example.

The classification of most of Latin America as Western is also debatable, given that it too is a region of considerable cultural complexity. Despite this complexity, Latin America is an overwhelmingly Catholic region whose history and culture have been dominated by European colonialism and settlement since the sixteenth century. As Howard Wiarda has stated, "With strong roots in Roman law, Catholicism, and the Iberian sociopolitical tradition, Latin America is Western."[11] At the same time, Wiarda notes that Latin American culture represents a Hispanic variant of the Western tradition, different from the culture that the British brought to North America. There are, in addition, significant Indian cultural influences whose strength varies from country to country. While some countries of the region see themselves as "European," in others the Indian influence (and population) is more significant. None-

TABLE 2—DEMOCRACY, CULTURE, AND HUMAN RIGHTS

COUNTRY TYPE[1]	NUMBER OF CASES	AVERAGE HUMAN RIGHTS RATING
Western Democracies[2]	45	84
Non-Western Democracies	24	64
Non-Western Authoritarian Regimes	33	40

Source: See Table 1.
[1] On the basis of the definitions used here, two countries included in Humana's rankings—Cuba and Yugoslavia—did not fit into any of these three categories in 1991 and therefore are not included here.
[2] Includes all of Eastern Europe and Latin America.

theless, even in the latter cases the Iberian legacy has predominated,[12] and it is in fact a variant of Western religious, legal, political, and economic traditions. Indeed, Huntington includes Latin America among the cases that might be used to support the thesis that successful democratization is tied to Western culture; thus there is ample precedent for viewing Latin America as part of the West.[13]

Nevertheless, because of the ambiguity of both the East European and Latin American cases, it is useful to analyze the relationship between democracy and human rights employing several different definitions of "the West." Thus data are provided here for a definition based on strict application of the two criteria of European settlement and religion mentioned above, as well as for both more and less inclusive definitions. The most inclusive definition classifies as "Western" both Latin America and all of Eastern Europe (including the Orthodox countries). This definition yields the data presented in Table 2 (above), which shows differences in human rights performance on the Humana scale across the three categories of countries. On average, the human rights performance of non-Western democracies is significantly better than that of non-Western authoritarian regimes but significantly worse than that of Western democracies. Strict application of the criteria of European settlement and religion—which excludes regimes in Orthodox Eastern Europe from the "Western" category—results in no change in the average human rights rating of Western democracies, and only a slight increase in that of non-Western democracies, from 64 to 65.[14]

Adoption of the most restrictive definition of the West, which excludes Latin America and all of postcommunist Eastern Europe except for Hungary, Poland, and Czechoslovakia, produces significantly different results. On that definition, the average human rights rating of the Western democracies is 93, compared with 68 for the non-Western democracies. The difference in scores generated by shifting from the least to the most restrictive definition of "the West" reveals that, on average, the human rights performance of democracies in Latin America and Orthodox Eastern Europe falls somewhere in between that of the unambiguously Western states of the North Atlantic region and that of the unambiguously non-Western states of Africa and Asia. That middle position on the

Humana scale is exactly what a strict culturalist perspective would predict for those culturally ambiguous regions.

Problems of Transplantation

Thus, no matter how broadly or narrowly one defines "the West," two important points emerge. First, the data seem to confirm the conventional assumption that democracy—even limited "electoral democracy"—is associated with at least a minimal package of human rights and liberties. The two non-Western multiparty systems with the lowest overall human rights scores (Pakistan and Turkey) still scored better than 18 of the 33 non-Western authoritarian regimes. Second, the findings clearly indicate that the transplantation of democratic institutions to non-Western societies does not guarantee the same high level of respect for human rights and individual liberties found in the West. If democracy is an antidote to human rights abuses, it seems to be a much less effective one outside the West than within it.

The paradigmatic case here is Turkey. As Freedom House's 1993–94 survey noted, "Turks can change their government democratically, but the country is beset by widespread human rights abuses."[15] While, as noted above, Turkey scored better in Humana's rankings than did 18 authoritarian regimes, it also scored worse than 15 other authoritarian regimes. Its overall human rights score was only about average for the authoritarian world and was far below that of the Western democracies. The U.S. State Department characterized 1994 as a particularly bad year for human rights in Turkey; 1995 saw limited improvement. Still, the overall human rights picture remains grim. A 1995 State Department report indicates that human rights in Turkey continue to be undermined by torture; mystery killings and disappearances; harassment of human rights monitors, journalists, and lawyers; limits on free expression; and a general climate of police impunity.[16]

The spread of democratic government to additional countries in Africa and Asia in the 1990s may well add to the number of cases—of which Turkey is an example—in which democracy and widespread human rights abuses coexist. Akwasi Aidoo, a program officer for the Ford Foundation in Dakar, Senegal, observed in 1993 that the democratization process in Africa was not automatically putting an end to the human rights abuses that had long plagued the continent. While acknowledging that some of the worst violations have occurred under authoritarian rule, he noted that in many nations human rights problems persist even after democratization. As Aidoo points out, in many parts of Africa "it is considered acceptable to form or belong to a political party that would contest elections, but it is considered almost a crime to belong to an organization that campaigns against state abuses of human rights."[17]

The small nations of the British Caribbean and South Pacific are an apparent exception to this pattern. Though Humana excludes most of those cases from his rankings, the Freedom House survey ranks them higher on both political rights and civil liberties than most other non-Western countries. A possible explanation is the British connection. In former British colonies characterized by significant British settlement (for example, the United States, Canada, Australia, and New Zealand), performance on tests for democracy and human rights is better than in regions of Spanish and Portuguese settlement (Latin America). Moreover, the performance of the Caribbean countries indicates that British colonization even with less extensive British settlement may still be conducive to democracy and respect for human rights. If that is indeed the explanation of the Caribbean situation, however, the effect does not extend much beyond these small, largely island nations. If one examines the human rights performance of the 17 members of the British Commonwealth ranked in Humana's study (not including the Caribbean and British-settled North America, Australia, and New Zealand), the impact of the British connection appears minimal. Overall, those 17 countries have an average human rights rating of only 54. Excluding those that have made no effort to democratize raises the average rating only to 59, slightly below the average for non-Western democracies as a whole.

One can only speculate about the reasons for the disparity between the Caribbean and other former British colonies, but it may be related to the size of the Caribbean nations and the fact that the indigenous peoples and their cultures were largely eliminated in the process of first Spanish and then British colonization. Compared with India, for example—with its large size, enormous native population, and deeply rooted culture—the Caribbean, populated largely by settlers and slaves from outside the region, was probably more susceptible to long-term British influence. To the extent that this is indeed the case, it reinforces the argument that political culture is key to understanding the diffusion (or lack thereof) of human rights.

Time and Quality

Before resting the case, however, we must consider other possible factors affecting human rights performance. After all, African democracies, for example, not only are of relatively recent origin but are some of the world's poorest countries. Consequently, we must consider the extent to which the variation in human rights performance might be explained either as a function of the duration and quality of democratic government itself or as a reflection of a country's relative level of economic prosperity.

One might object that it is unfair to compare the human rights records of new non-Western democracies with those of long-consolidated

Western democratic systems, since it takes time to establish new patterns of respect for human rights and to navigate the difficult waters of the transition itself. Yet new democracies in both Central Europe and Latin America have, on average, turned around poor human rights records relatively quickly. Just two years after the collapse of communism in Eastern Europe, the three most culturally Western postcommunist states—Czechoslovakia, Hungary, and Poland—earned human rights scores of 97, 97, and 83, respectively, in Humana's rankings. Those numbers are far above the average for new non-Western democracies and, especially in the cases of Czechoslovakia and Hungary, are very impressive even by the standards of the long-established Western democracies.

In Latin America, the number of new democracies is larger and their human rights records more varied. Still, on the whole, new Latin American democracies turn in significantly better human rights performances than new democracies in Africa and Asia, scoring an average of 10 points higher on the Humana scale. Once again, it might be argued that Latin America is a hybrid of Western and non-Western culture. Yet however one classifies Latin America, it is certainly more Western than Asia and Africa. Indeed, the tendency of new democracies in Latin America to upgrade their human rights records more quickly than those in Africa and Asia but more slowly than those in Central Europe seems to reflect Latin America's status as more Western than the former but less Western than the latter. Thus while the vintage of a democratic government may account for part of its human rights record, the experience of some newly created democracies suggests that time is not the whole story.

If the Central European regimes and some Latin American regimes demonstrate that it is possible to reduce the number of human rights violations very quickly, the case of India illustrates that even a long-functioning democratic system does not guarantee an end to those violations. The 1995 human rights report of the U.S. State Department described India as "a longstanding parliamentary democracy with a free press, a civilian-controlled military, an independent judiciary, and active political parties and civic associations."[18] With the exception of the two-year state of emergency declared by Indira Gandhi in 1975, India has functioned as a democracy ever since the drafting of its 1950 Constitution. On the basis of Samuel Huntington's "two-turnover test," which assumes that a democracy can be considered consolidated following two democratic and peaceful transitions of power subsequent to the creation of the initial democratic government, India would have been considered a fully consolidated democracy by 1980. In that year, Gandhi and her Congress party made a comeback, having been turned out of office in the 1977 elections. Indeed, India has had additional democratic turnovers of power since 1980.

In spite of India's democratic regime, however, the country's human rights record leaves much to be desired. The U.S. State Department reports significant human rights abuses, including extrajudicial executions and political killings; arbitrary arrest; long-term detention without trial; and the torture, rape, and death of suspects in police custody. In Humana's 1991 assessment, India received a mediocre score of 54. That is better than the scores of most (though not all) authoritarian regimes included in the ratings, but it is nearly 30 points lower than the average for the Western democracies (broadly defined) and approximately 20 points lower than the average for the Latin American countries, a large number of which are relatively new, "third wave" democracies.

If the duration of democratic institutions cannot explain the difference in human rights performance between Western and non-Western countries, we are left with the question whether that difference can be explained by variation in the quality of democracy. The Humana data do indicate that respect for the principle of multiparty elections by a secret and universal ballot is less complete and more likely to be qualified in non-Western than in Western countries. Included among those non-Western countries that Humana views as having at least qualified respect for that principle are a large number of countries that others would tend to label as only semidemocratic. One can better control for variation in the quality of democracy by using Freedom House's finer 7-point scale for evaluating political rights (that is, rights of participation and contestation).

Included in Humana's rankings are seven Western (all Latin American) regimes that scored 3 or 4 on political rights in the 1991–92 Freedom House survey; their average human rights score on the Humana scale is 65.5. The ten non-Western regimes receiving a 3 or 4 on political rights from Freedom House and included in the Humana survey have an average human rights score of 61. Though the difference is small, the gap between Western and non-Western countries expands as the quality of democracy increases. Thus for Western countries scoring a 1 or 2 on political rights in the Freedom House survey (34 cases), the average human rights score on the Humana scale is 88. For the non-Western countries that were included in the Humana survey and received a 1 or 2 from Freedom House (12 cases), the average human rights score is only 71.

A partial explanation for this gap might be that among the Western democracies there are more countries that received a score of 1 on political rights than a score of 2, while for the non-Western democracies the distribution is reversed. Even controlling for that small difference in the quality of political rights, however, the human rights advantage of the West remains. Among countries that received a 2 on political rights, Western democracies outperform their non-Western counterparts by 11 points in the Humana rankings. And for the many Western countries that received the best possible score of 1 on political rights, the advantage over the few non-Western countries that received a 1 from Freedom House and were included in the Humana study is also 11 points. Thus while a higher score on political rights is associated with a higher average human rights performance in Western and non-Western nations alike, the cultural gap remains and even expands as the quality of democracy increases.

The Economic Factor

The countries with the best human rights records are not only disproportionately Western but also disproportionately wealthy. Thus it is important to try to disentangle the effects of culture and wealth. To this end, a number of interesting comparisons can be made. First, at the high end of the scale of national wealth, one finds a handful of non-Western nations located in East Asia and the Middle East. The World Bank's 1993 *World Development Report* indicates that in the non-Western world there were six upper-middle-income and high-income economies (defined as having GNP per capita of $6,000 or more) in 1991.[19] Of those six countries, four (Singapore, South Korea, Saudi Arabia, and Oman) have human rights ratings below the average for all of the countries scored on the Humana scale and even more substantially below the average score of the Western democracies. The two exceptions, Japan and Hong Kong, with their relatively high human rights scores of 82 and 79, respectively, actually help demonstrate the impact of culture. Although Japan and Hong Kong are not part of the West, the politics of both have been directly influenced by Western governments. In the case of Japan, one finds a political order largely crafted during the early post–World War II era in the context of American occupation, while Hong Kong has been a dependent territory of the United Kingdom.

Comparing Hong Kong and Singapore is especially instructive. Here are two small Asian city-states with comparable levels of GNP per capita, high enough to rank both among the world's richest two dozen countries. Moreover, each received a rating of 4 in Freedom House's 1991–92 assessment of political rights (that is, democracy). Yet while Singapore's score on the Humana human rights scale is a mediocre 60 (slightly below the global average of 62), Hong Kong's score is an impressive 79. The most compelling explanation for the difference is a cultural one. Though both have historical ties to the United Kingdom, the influence of Britain and its political culture have more directly shaped political life in Hong Kong, its dependent territory, than in independent Singapore.

The impact of culture can also be demonstrated at lower levels of economic development. On average, democratic and semidemocratic countries in Latin America score better on Humana's scale of human rights than do comparable regimes in Africa and Asia. The ten Latin American democracies or semidemocracies with a 1991 GNP per capita below $1,500 have an average human rights score of 67.1 on the Humana scale, while the 11 most politically and economically comparable cases in Asia and Africa have an average score of 64.5. Though the difference here is modest, it grows with increased prosperity. The eight Latin American cases with a 1991 GNP per capita of $1,500 or more have an average human rights score of 79.1, while the corresponding African and Asian cases score an average of only 61.3. Moreover, included among the relatively prosperous non-Western nations is Japan, with its special relationship to the West via the American connection and its high score on human rights.[20] Excluding Japan would make the comparative performance of the more developed Asian and African cases look worse still. Consequently, to the extent that there is a connection between economic prosperity and human rights performance, that connection seems strongest within the context of Western political culture. Once again, then, culture seems to be the crucial intervening variable.

Policy Implications

The evidence presented above suggests that a high level of respect for human rights and liberties is most likely to be found in relatively prosperous Western countries with a longstanding practice of democratic government that includes the consistent and unambiguous implementation of the principle of multiparty elections by secret and universal ballot. While culture is not the only factor influencing the level of human liberty, it is clear that culture does matter. At the same time, it is apparent that democracy can coexist with human rights abuses. While democratic government, almost by definition, incorporates a minimal (and not inconsequential) degree of liberty, the level of respect for liberty beyond that minimum can vary widely.

These findings have direct implications for governments that seek to foster human rights and democracy outside their own borders. For example, the 1995 statement of national-security strategy issued by the Clinton administration assumed that the promotion of democracy and the expansion of human rights are mutually supportive goals of U.S. foreign policy, consistent with the general effort to pursue the U.S. national interest.[21] Yet as the analysis presented here suggests, the promotion of human rights and the promotion of democracy are not always identical. Democratization does not by itself guarantee full respect for human rights, and in extreme cases, democratic elections can produce outcomes that are illiberal. Consider, for example, the January 1992 Algerian situation, in which military leaders, faced with the prospect of victory by the fundamentalist Islamic Salvation Front, decided to cancel the second round of elections and short-circuit the process of Algerian democratization. On the one hand, democracy was clearly sacrificed. On the other hand, a victory for the Islamic Salvation Front, which had indicated an intention to impose an Iranian-like theocratic state and society governed by Islamic law, would hardly have been a positive development for human rights, at least as they are understood and defined in the West.

A similar dilemma occurred in Russia in the fall of 1993. President Boris Yeltsin's decisions to close down the Russian Supreme Soviet and to employ military force to that end were viewed at the time by many in both the West and in Russia as unconstitutional and undemocratic acts. On the other hand, the Supreme Soviet and many of its supporters included significant numbers of individuals who were themselves ideologically opposed both to democracy and to the human rights and liberties that had been expanded in Yeltsin's Russia. Once again, supporters of democracy both inside the country in question and in Western capitals were faced with a dilemma in terms of how to respond. Indeed, some observers feared that the very same dilemma could have been repeated had the prospect of a Communist victory led Yeltsin to cancel Russia's 1996 presidential election on the grounds of preserving the liberties that Russians had only recently attained. While such a claim by Yeltsin might have appeared disingenuous, it could also have contained an important element of truth. Clichéd advice to worry less about the results of such elections than about the integrity of the democratic process itself is not particularly useful, for it ignores the fact that support for the democratic process is at least partly related to the results that it produces.

Such cases notwithstanding, there remain many reasons, related to both moral and pragmatic considerations, to support the diffusion of democratic government. Included among those reasons is that democratic governments, even outside the Western world, are more consistently likely than their authoritarian counterparts to maintain at least a minimal level of respect for basic human liberties. Yet it should be recognized that the correlation between democracy and liberty is not a perfect one, and there will continue to be situations, such as that of Algeria in 1992, in which maximizing both will be difficult.

NOTES

1. Freedom House, *Freedom in the World: The Annual Survey of Political Rights and Civil Liberties, 1993–1994* (New York: Freedom House, 1994), 5–6.

2. See George Sorensen, *Democracy and Democratization* (Boulder, Colo.: Westview, 1993), 87–88.

3. Larry Diamond, "Is the Third Wave Over?" *Journal of Democracy* 7 (July 1996): 21–24.

4. Freedom House, *Freedom in the World,* 672.

5. Ibid., 677–78.

6. Charles Humana, *World Human Rights Guide,* 3rd ed. (New York: Oxford University Press, 1992).

7. Samuel P. Huntington, *The Third Wave: Democratization in the Late Twentieth Century* (Norman: University of Oklahoma Press, 1991), 299.

8. Alexis de Tocqueville, *Democracy in America,* Thomas Bender, ed. (New York: Random House, 1981), 569.

9. Ibid., 569–72.

10. Samuel P. Huntington, *The Third Wave,* 299–300.

11. Howard Wiarda, *Latin American Politics and Development,* 3rd ed. (Boulder, Colo.: Westview, 1990), 4.

12. Howard Wiarda, *Latin American Politics* (Belmont, Calif.: Wadsworth, 1995), 29–30.

13. See Samuel P. Huntington, *The Third Wave,* 299.

14. The change here is modest because the number of countries that could be considered even qualified democracies in Orthodox Eastern Europe in 1991 was very small.

15. Freedom House, *Freedom in the World,* 553.

16. U.S. Department of State, *Country Reports on Human Rights Practices for 1995* (Washington, D.C.: U.S. Government Printing Office, 1996), 1060–79.

17. Akwasi Aidoo, "Africa: Democracy Without Human Rights," *Human Rights Quarterly* 15 (November 1993): 708–9.

18. U.S. Department of State, *Country Reports on Human Rights Practices for 1995,* 1310.

19. World Bank, *World Development Report 1993* (New York: Oxford University Press, 1993), 239. Not included on the World Bank list were Kuwait (owing to the Iraqi invasion and its aftermath), Qatar, the United Arab Emirates, and a few small but prosperous microstates with tiny populations.

20. Note that Japan's score on the Humana scale is 82. That is high by global standards but significantly below the 93 average for the most economically developed Western democracies.

21. The White House, "A National Security Strategy of Engagement and Enlargement" (Washington, D.C., February 1995), i, 22–24.

7

FROM LIBERALISM
TO LIBERAL DEMOCRACY

Marc F. Plattner

Marc F. Plattner *is coeditor of the* Journal of Democracy *and co-director of the International Forum for Democratic Studies. This essay is a revised version of a paper presented at a course on "Liberalism, Old and New" in Arrabida, Portugal, in October 1998. It appears in a volume coedited by João Carlos Espada, Marc F. Plattner, and Adam Wolfson entitled* The Liberal Tradition in Focus: Problems and New Perspectives *(2000).*

Today the most liberal regimes in the world, those of the advanced Western countries, are typically referred to either as liberal democracies or, more often, simply as democracies. This reflects one of the most striking ways in which twentieth-century liberalism differs from the older liberalism that emerged in the late seventeenth and eighteenth centuries. Today, wherever one finds liberalism (understood as constitutional and limited government, the rule of law, and the protection of individual rights), it is almost invariably coupled with democracy (understood as the selection of government officials by universal suffrage). The converse proposition, however, has in recent decades been becoming less and less true. With the downfall since 1975 of scores of authoritarian regimes and their replacement by more or less freely elected governments, there are now many regimes that can plausibly be called democratic but not liberal. As a result, the relationship between liberalism and democracy has once again become a subject of intense intellectual and policy debate.

Perhaps the most prominent example of this is Fareed Zakaria's 1997 article in *Foreign Affairs* on "The Rise of Illiberal Democracy."[1] Zakaria emphasizes a point that had already been made by other observers more sympathetic than he to the struggles of new would-be liberal democracies in the postcommunist and developing worlds: Even among those regimes that have succeeded in holding genuinely free elections, many have compiled a poor record in terms of such criteria of liberalism as the rule of law and the protection of individual rights. The more sympathetic observers tend to stress the importance of "consolidating" these new democracies, preserving their electoral achievements while strengthening their liberal features. Zakaria, however, concludes that the liberal deficit of these regimes has emerged not in spite of, but in some measure because of, their adoption of the democratic mechanism of popular elections. He thus questions the wisdom of encouraging countries to elect their rulers before the foundations of liberalism are firmly in place.

Zakaria puts heavy emphasis on the distinction between liberalism and democracy. Making it clear that he views the former as more important than the latter, he argues for the superiority of liberal autocracy over illiberal democracy. This in turn has prompted discussion of the viability of liberal autocracy (or, more generically, nondemocratic liberalism) in the contemporary world, for the only explicit twentieth-century example of liberal autocracy that Zakaria provides is Hong Kong under British colonial rule. His primary example is the constitutional monarchies of nineteenth-century Europe, which certainly did have many of the elements of liberalism in place before they adopted universal manhood suffrage. But it is also noteworthy that all of these pre–tweiltieth-century liberal nondemocracies have now become democratic. This raises the question of why liberal regimes have all tended to evolve in a democratic direction. Is it due merely to adventitious circumstances or extraneous factors, or is it somehow related to the intrinsic principles of liberalism? That is the issue I wish to explore.

Liberalism and Equality

Liberalism is essentially a doctrine devoted to protecting the rights of the individual to life, liberty, property, and the pursuit of happiness. Government is needed to protect those rights, but it can threaten them as well, so it is also essential to guard against their infringement by government. Thus liberalism entails a government that is limited by a constitution and by the rule of law. At first sight, however, there does not seem to be any reason in principle why such a government must be chosen by the people. A constitutional government of one man or of a few could rule in such a way as to protect the rights of individuals. Indeed, there is reason to fear that a government responsive to popular majorities will be tempted to violate the rights of unpopular individuals or minorities. Accordingly, many liberals in past centuries opposed the extension of the suffrage, fearing precisely such an outcome. Yet everywhere efforts to forestall the extension of the suffrage failed, and liberalism turned into liberal democracy. And far from being destroyed by its democratization, liberalism on the whole has flourished. This suggests that the tension between liberalism and democracy is not so great as some have thought. In fact, I would go further, and propose that the philosophy of liberalism contains within itself the seeds of its own democratization.

In the first place, one may point to the massive fact that the classic statements of liberal principles set forth not only the doctrines of individual rights and limited government but also the doctrine of human equality. The American Declaration of Independence proclaims as the first of its self-evident truths "that all men are created equal." The French Declaration of the Rights of Man and Citizen states in the very first of its 17 principles: "Men are born, and always continue, free and equal in respect of their rights." This intimate connection between the rights or freedom of men and their mutual equality can easily be traced back to the opening pages of the classic work of liberal political theory, John Locke's *Second Treatise of Government.* In elaborating the origins of legitimate political power, Locke begins by considering "what state all men are naturally in"; he argues that this is not only "a state of perfect freedom" but "a state also of equality, wherein all the power and jurisdiction is reciprocal, no one having more than another."[2]

> *Once other principles of political legitimacy are undermined, only the consent of the governed remains.*

The connection between natural liberty and natural equality is clear. If men are not equal in their natural rights, that is, if some men have a right to rule over other men, then men cannot naturally be free. And correspondingly, if all men are naturally free, then none can have a natural right to rule over others. Locke's *Second Treatise* is, of course, the sequel to his *First Treatise,* a refutation of Sir Robert Filmer's doctrine of paternal power. According to Locke, the ground of Filmer's system is as follows: "Men are not born free, and therefore could never have the liberty to choose either governors or forms of government."[3] After showing the flaws in Filmer's argument for the natural subjection of men, Locke begins the *Second Treatise* by asserting that if fraud and violence are not to be the only basis for government, a new origin for political power must be found. He finds it in the consent of the people. Precisely because men are "by nature all free, equal, and independent, no one can be put out of this estate and subjected to the political power of another without his own consent."[4] Once other principles of political legitimacy are undermined, only the consent of the governed remains.

To say that legitimate government rests on the consent of the governed is to say that the people—a term that for Locke means not the many as opposed to the nobles, but all those who belong to the society—are ultimately sovereign. They are the founders of political society; they decide where to invest the power of making laws; and they have "a right to resume their original liberty" and to choose a new legislative power if the existing one betrays their trust.[5] Yet despite these egalitarian or democratizing aspects of Locke's doctrine, he does not draw from it the conclusion that the people themselves (or their elected representatives) should necessarily govern. Instead, he argues that when men first unite into political society, the majority may choose to invest the legislative power not in themselves (which Locke says would constitute a "perfect democracy") but in a few men, or in a single man, or in such "compounded and mixed forms of government, as they think good."[6] In England, for example, he suggests that it is the attachment of the people to their old constitutional arrangements that keeps bringing them back to the "old legislative of king, lords, and commons."[7] In short, nondemocratic forms of government can be legitimate if they enjoy the consent of the people.

This is not unreasonable as theory, and it is a view that prevailed for at least a century among supporters of the rights of man and limited government. But gradually and inexorably the notion that government must be based on popular consent led to the notion that government must be of the people, by the people, and for the people. Why did this happen? Perhaps one may begin to address this question by asking why the people might consent to government that is *not* in the hands of themselves or their elected representatives. One may, of course, simply say that in earlier centuries the people were never really given a choice, and if they had been, they would have chosen popular government. Alternatively, one may conclude with Locke that "people are not so easily got out of their old forms as some are apt to suggest. They are hardly to be prevailed with to amend the acknowledged faults in the frame they have been accustomed to."[8] In the seventeenth and eighteenth centuries the monarchic and aristocratic principles still reigned not only in the world but in the minds of the people. One might say that the people were willing to consent to be ruled by others precisely because principles other than that of consent still held great sway. But the public espousal and growing acceptance of the principles of natural equality and government by consent were fated to erode the willingness of the people to consent to nondemocratic government.

In the American colonies, where Locke's teachings were most widely adopted and where monarchy and aristocracy enjoyed much less support than in the more traditional societies of Europe, it was clear after the Revolution that the people would accept nothing other than popular government.[9] The French Revolution quickly moved toward an outright rejection of any admixture of monarchy or aristocracy. Even in Britain, where popular attachment to the "old forms" remained much stronger, calls for universal manhood suffrage date back at least to the 1770s,[10] and the nineteenth century was marked by widespread and eventually successful agitation for expansion of the franchise.

Extending the Vote

One useful way to explore the dynamic that led to the democratization of liberalism is to consider the views expressed by some leading liberal thinkers of the late eighteenth and the nineteenth century. An early example of the invocation of natural equality and consent of the people as a basis for rejecting anything other than popular government can be found in the work of Thomas Paine, who can always be counted upon to draw the most radical conclusions from the Lockean teaching on natural rights. In his *Dissertation on First Principles of Government* (1795),[11] Paine argues that there are only two "primary divisions" of government: "First, government by election and representation; secondly, government by hereditary succession." The former, Paine contends, is "founded on the rights of the people," while the latter is "founded on usurpation." Hereditary government, according to Paine, "has not a right to exist." The English parliament may have had a right to call William and Mary to the throne in 1688, for "every Nation, for the time being, has a right to govern itself as it pleases." But Parliament had no right to bind future generations of Englishmen to be governed by the heirs of William and Mary.

As for representative government, its only true basis is equality of rights: "Every man has a right to one vote and no more in the choice of representatives." Though Paine does not address the question of female suffrage, he decries as unjust the view that property should be made the criterion for voting. Exclusion from voting is offensive because it "implies a stigma on the moral character of the persons excluded," and poverty does not justify such a stigma. "The right of voting for representatives," Paine holds, "is the primary right by which other rights are protected. To take away this right is to reduce a man to slavery, for slavery consists in being subject to the will of another, and he that has not a vote in the election of representatives is in this case."

Finally, I quote at some length a passage that, when allowances are made for Paine's excessive rhetoric, offers some insight into the historical process by which exclusion from voting came to seem intolerable:

> While men could be persuaded they had no rights, or that rights appertained only to a certain class of men, or that government was a thing existing in right of itself, it was not difficult to govern them authoritatively. The ignorance in which they were held and the superstition in which they were instructed furnished the means of doing it. But when the ignorance is gone and the superstition with it, when they perceive the imposition that has been acted upon them, when they reflect that the cultivator and the manufacturer are the primary means of all the wealth that exists in the world beyond what nature spontaneously produces, when they begin to feel their consequences by their usefulness and their right as members of society, it is then no longer possible to govern them as before. The fraud once detected cannot be reacted.

Another strand of support for extension of the suffrage came from utilitarianism, which, although it rejected the doctrine of natural rights, nonetheless took as a guiding principle Jeremy Bentham's dictum

"Everyone to count for one, nobody for more than one." The classic expression of utilitarian political thought is considered to be James Mill's *Essay on Government* (1820).[12] Like Paine, James Mill regards the system of representation as the key to good government. Eschewing any lang-uage claiming the *right* of individuals to vote for their representatives, he argues that "the benefits of the representative system are lost in all cases in which the interests of the choosing body are not the same with those of the community." This coincidence of interests, however, may exist with less than universal suffrage, provided that the interests of those excluded from voting "are indisputably included in those of other individuals" who can vote. On this basis Mill justifies the exclusion of women, "the interest of almost all of whom is involved in that of their fathers or in that of their husbands," and is prepared to accept the exclusion of men under the age of forty, because "the men of forty have a deep interest in the welfare of the younger men."

James Mill also presents a long and convoluted argument on the question of property qualifications for voting. He rejects a high property qualification on the grounds that it would lead to a government of the few, who, given human nature, would pursue their own interests at the expense of the community's. Though he concedes that a very low qualification permitting the great majority of the people to vote would be "no evil," he also concludes that it would be "of no use," since admitting the small remainder to the suffrage would not change things much. Thomas Babington Macaulay, in his famous review (1829) of Mill's *Essay,* interprets Mill as being opposed to any property qualifi-cation, and takes issue with him on this point.[13] (Macaulay also objects to Mill's reasoning on the question of women's suffrage, charging that the latter "placidly dogmatises away the interests of one half of the human race.")

For Macaulay, who also fundamentally objects to Mill's deductive approach to politics and his rapacious view of human nature, the issue of a "pecuniary qualification" for the vote is "the most important practical question in the whole essay." He argues, contrary to Mill, that since "it happens that in all civilised communities there is a small minority of rich men, and a great majority of poor men," it would indeed be in the interests of the latter, if they enjoyed the franchise, to use their political power to plunder the rich. In a marvelous rhetorical flight, Macaulay paints the dangers of enfranchising the poor:

[I]s it possible that in the bosom of civilisation itself may be engendered
the malady which shall destroy it? Is it possible that institutions may be
established which, without the help of earthquake, of famine, of pestilence,
or of the foreign sword, may undo the work of so many ages of wisdom
and glory, and gradually sweep away taste, literature, science, commerce,
manufactures, everything but the rude arts necessary to the support of animal
life? Is it possible that, in two or three hundred years, a few lean and half-

naked fishermen may divide with owls and foxes the ruins of the greatest
European cities, may wash their nets amidst the relics of her gigantic docks,
and build their huts out of the capitals of her stately cathedrals? If the
principles of Mr. Mill be sound, we say, without hesitation, that the form of
government which he recommends will assuredly produce all this. But, if
these principles be unsound, if the reasonings by which we have opposed
them be just, the higher and middling orders are the natural representatives
of the human race. Their interest may be opposed in some things to that of
their poorer contemporaries; but it is identical with that of the innumerable
generations which are to follow.

Macaulay's paeans to the splendors of civilization and his incompar-
able prose should not obscure the fact that this remains a dispute about
"pecuniary qualification," which turns essentially on the likely fate of
property under a regime of universal suffrage. This is a controversy
that, one might say, is carried on within a wholly Lockean framework.
The real issue is whether the right to property is endangered by the extension of the right to vote. As support for hereditary institutions faded
with the triumph of the principles of natural equality and government
by consent, the argument over democracy increasingly became an intra-
liberal dispute.

The Inevitability of Universal Suffrage

In the debate over the potential consequences of eliminating property
qualifications, the example of America often figured prominently. In
his critique of James Mill's argument for universal manhood suffrage,
Macaulay states, "The case of the United States is not in point," because
there, unlike in more settled countries, the poor have a reasonable hope
of becoming rich. Then, invoking the Malthusian doctrine that increased
population will lead to greater inequality of conditions, he concludes,
"As for America, we appeal to the twentieth century."

Tocqueville, of course, provided powerful ammunition in his *Democracy in America* for those who believed that universal suffrage would
be compatible with the security of property. Among the many passages
in which Tocqueville remarks upon the respect of the Americans for
property, we may cite the following: "In no country in the world is the
love of property more active and more anxious than in the United States;
nowhere does the majority display less inclination for those principles
which threaten to alter, in whatever manner, the laws of property."[14]

In addition to the more general argument he makes that the world has
for seven hundred years been undergoing a providential and irresistible
democratic revolution, Tocqueville also offers a more specific argument
as to why continuing expansion of the suffrage is inevitable:

When a nation begins to modify the elective qualification, it may easily be
foreseen that, sooner or later, that qualification will be entirely abolished.

> There is no more invariable rule in the history of society: the further electoral rights are extended, the greater is the need for extending them; for after each concession the strength of the democracy increases, and its demands increase with its strength. The ambition of those who are below the appointed rate is irritated in exact proportion to the great number of those who are above it. The exception at last becomes the rule, concession follows concession, and no stop can be made short of universal suffrage.[15]

In describing the process by which the property qualifications existing prior to the American Revolution were gradually eliminated, Tocqueville notes that it was men of the higher orders who voted these changes, pursuing the goodwill of the people at any price. This in some ways seems to have characterized the process in Britain as well. Historian Gertrude Himmelfarb describes the struggle over the Reform Act of 1867 between Disraeli's Tories and Gladstone's Liberals in the following terms: "What is interesting is the fact that it was not the reformers inside or outside the House who forced up the price of reform, but rather the party leaders themselves. [Liberal parliamentarian Robert] Lowe described the parties as competing against each other in a miserable auction with the constitution being 'knocked down to the lowest bidder.' A Conservative complained that his colleagues were trying to 'outbid the Liberal party in the market of liberalism.'"[16]

In the wake of the passage of the Reform Act, even those most dubious about universal suffrage acknowledged its inevitability. In *Liberty, Equality, Fraternity* (1873), James Fitzjames Stephen writes:

> The accepted theory of government appears to be that everybody should have a vote, that the Legislature should be elected by these votes, and that it should conduct all the public business of the country through a committee which succeeds for the time in obtaining its confidence. This theory, beyond all question, has gone forth, and is going forth conquering and to conquer. The fact of its triumph is as clear as the sun at noonday, and the probability that its triumphs will continue for a longer time than we need care to think about is as strong as any such probability can well be. . . . If I am asked, What do you propose to substitute for universal suffrage? Practically, What have you to recommend? I answer at once, Nothing. The whole current of thought and feeling, the whole stream of human affairs, is setting with irresistible force in that direction. The old ways of living, many of which were just as bad in their time as any of our devices can be in ours, are breaking down all over Europe, and are floating this way and that like haycocks in a flood. Nor do I see why any wise man should expend much thought or trouble on trying to save their wrecks. The waters are out and no human force can turn them back, but I do not see why as we go with the stream we need sing Hallelujah to the river god.[17]

Stephen's somewhat half-hearted criticisms of democracy mostly focus on the importance of specialized knowledge and steadiness in the business of government and on the ignorance and fickleness of the voting masses. He also echoes some of the concerns put forth by John

Stuart Mill regarding the "mediocrity" of contemporary society and government.[18] And he attributes the enthusiasm for equality in part to "the enormous development of wealth in the United States." Like Macaulay, Stephen raises the question of how long the Americans "will continue to be equal when the population becomes dense," and concludes by wondering in any case whether "the rapid production of an immense multitude of commonplace, self-satisfied, and essentially slight people is an exploit which the whole world need fall down and worship."

Stephen's resigned and ineffectual grumblings largely reflect the subsequent course of opposition to universal suffrage, which turned from a political program into a cultural lament. With the first half of the twentieth century the exclusion of women from the suffrage also began to be swept away. Thus when in 1948 the United Nations adopted the Universal Declaration of Human Rights, Article 21 stated, "Everyone has the right to take part in the government of his country, directly or through freely chosen representatives. . . . The will of the people shall be the basis of the authority of the government; this will shall be expressed in periodic and genuine elections which shall be by universal and equal suffrage and shall be held by secret vote or by equivalent free voting procedures." Obviously, most of the provisions of Article 21 have been consistently violated by many UN member states with one-party or other dictatorial governments, but even most of these (excepting, of course, South Africa under apartheid) have conducted their bogus elections under rules calling for universal and equal suffrage.

Democracy and the Liberal Revival

What conclusions may be drawn from this brief survey of the evolution of liberalism into contemporary liberal democracy? First, the spread of liberal ideas of the natural freedom and equality of all human beings doomed any special and substantial privileges enjoyed on the basis of heredity. Though monarchy and even an aristocratic branch of the legislature may in some places have been preserved in form, everywhere in the developed world they have been emptied of any substantial political power. Second, these same liberal ideas eventually undermined any effort to exclude people from political participation on the basis of such factors as race, religion, or sex. Third, the attempt to limit the franchise on the basis of property qualifications was the greatest potential obstacle to the democratization of liberalism, because it could claim some basis in the sacredness of private property endorsed by liberalism itself.

The real or perceived tension between political majoritarianism and policies that promote economic growth and prosperity is a theme that remains very much alive today, with many commentators claiming that effective economic reform requires the insulation of policy makers from electoral majorities. At the same time, the history of the past two centuries has made it unmistakably clear that the introduction of universal suffrage need not lead to the outright plunder of the rich and the destruction of a productive economy and a civilized society. Tocqueville was right and Macaulay was wrong. The case of the nineteenth-century United States was indeed "in point." Its economic vitality and political stability were not simply the product of a sparse population able to expand over a vast and fertile continent. In the Old World as well, liberal societies have tended to generate large middle classes rather than to become divided into a handful of the rich and a vast majority of the poor.

At the same time, until the past two decades it could plausibly have been argued that, due to the social and economic policies enacted by popular majorities, liberalism was dying a slow death. With the spread of state-owned industry, the seemingly irreversible growth of the welfare state, and the increasing tax burden necessary to pay for it, it was not unreasonable to view the political empowerment of the masses as proceeding in tandem with the gradual socialization of the economy. The idea of property rights seemed to be falling into increasing disrepute. One striking symptom of this was the omission from the UN International Covenant on Economic, Social, and Cultural Rights (1966) of any mention of the right to property (which had still featured in the 1948 Universal Declaration). Those political forces identifying themselves as liberals (in the European sense) were a dwindling minority, and ruling parties in many democracies identified themselves as socialists or social democrats. The term social (or even socialist) democracy often superseded the term liberal democracy. And of course, the democratic world was threatened by a powerful communist adversary that proclaimed both its egalitarianism and its hostility to liberalism.

The last two decades, however, have seen a remarkable revival of liberalism. Market economics has come back into vogue. State-owned industries are being privatized, and welfare benefits trimmed. The critical importance of protecting property rights has been recognized not only in international agreements and new national constitutions but by an influential academic literature. Right-of-center and explicitly promarket parties governed the leading democracies during the 1980s. Left-of-center parties, many of which have returned to power in the 1990s, have largely abandoned statist economics and rediscovered the virtues of markets and entrepreneurship. And all this has been accompanied and accelerated by the downfall of communism.

How have these developments and the liberal revival they have promoted affected the political role of popular majorities? Here I believe a crucial distinction must be made, one that is rooted in the very principles of liberalism. For I would say that the principle of universal inclusion— that no one should be deprived of an equal voice in choosing those who govern—has only become more sacrosanct. At the same time, however, there has been a clear weakening of the view that popular majorities should play a more active role in deciding on governmental policies.

The latter is reflected in many ways, but perhaps not least in the unfavorable connotation that the word "populism" has come to acquire in the new democracies of the developing and postcommunist worlds. More generally, there has been no tendency, in either new or long-established democracies, to make governments more directly responsive to the electorate through such traditional devices as shortening terms of office. In fact, there has been an increasing trend toward giving greater power to judiciaries and autonomous agencies, the parts of government most insulated from the people. Judicial review was long viewed as an "antidemocratic" institution, giving power to unelected judges at the expense of popular majorities. In recent years, however, judicial review, once a peculiarity of the United States, has spread to old and new democracies alike. Not only has it encountered very little opposition, but in many postcommunist countries, public opinion polls show that constitutional courts enjoy high levels of popular support.[19]

> *It is precisely the triumph of the liberal principle that all men are created equal that makes it virtually impossible for nondemocratic liberalism to flourish in the contemporary world.*

Perhaps even more striking has been the rise, especially in new democracies, of independent agencies explicitly meant to be free of control by the politically responsive branches of government. These include such institutions as central banks, electoral commissions, human rights commissions, anticorruption bodies, ombudsmen, and the like.[20] The new prominence of agencies of this kind obviously reflects in part a suspicion of the people's elected representatives, a sense that they cannot be trusted to refrain from seeking personal or partisan advantage at the expense of the public good. But it also reflects a triumph of liberal ways of thinking, a sense that limiting the excesses of government and protecting individual rights are of greater concern than translating immediate popular sentiment into public policy. Another sign of this same tendency is the increased emphasis being given today by political practitioners and political scientists alike to such concerns as constitutionalism, the rule of law, institutional checks and balances, and accountability. One may say that they are rediscovering the wisdom of the *Federalist* papers, seeking protection against the dangerous tendencies of popular government through remedies that are themselves compatible with popular government. In fact, the popularity of the attack on illiberal democracy may itself be regarded as a sign of the triumph of liberalism.

For the most part, the response to Zakaria's critique has not taken the form of arguments depreciating the importance of such liberal desiderata as constitutionalism, rule of law, and individual rights compared to that of popular elections. Virtually everyone joining the debate has agreed on the value of these liberal goals. The argument has instead focused on whether, in societies lacking a strong liberal tradition, authoritarian or elected government is a more promising road for achieving them. The real issue is whether the nineteenth-century sequence of first liberalism, then democracy, can work today, when the progress of liberal ideas has undermined traditional nondemocratic claims to political legitimacy.[21]

It is worth noting that, in contrast to the current widespread experimentation with various kinds of checks and balances and independent agencies, there have been virtually no experiments with limited suffrage (at least in liberal, self-governing societies). If anything, the right to universal and equal suffrage is more unchallenged today than it has ever been, and it is hard to see on what acceptable grounds limitations on suffrage might be introduced. If there is little clamor for more populist government, there is none at all for exclusionary government. It is precisely the triumph of the liberal principle that all men are created equal that makes it virtually impossible for nondemocratic liberalism to flourish in the contemporary world. For better or worse, the future of liberalism is indissolubly tied to the future of liberal democracy.

NOTES

1. Fareed Zakaria, "The Rise of Illiberal Democracy," *Foreign Affairs* 76 (November–December 1997), 22–43.

2. John Locke, *Second Treatise of Government,* ed. Thomas P. Peardon (Indianapolis: Bobbs-Merrill, 1952), ch. 2, sec. 4, p. 4.

3. John Locke, *First Treatise,* in Peter Laslett, ed., *Two Treatises of Government* (New York: New American Library, 1960), ch. 1, sec. 5, p. 178.

4. Locke, *Second Treatise,* ch. 8, sec. 95, p. 54.

5. Ibid., ch. 19, sec. 222, p. 124.

6. Ibid., ch. 10, sec. 132, p. 74.

7. Ibid., ch. 19, sec. 223, p. 125.

8. Ibid., ch. 19, sec. 223, p. 125.

9. See Clinton Rossiter, ed., *The Federalist* (New York: New American Library, 1961), no. 39, p. 240.

10. S. MacCoby, ed., *The English Radical Tradition, 1763–1914* (London: Nicholas Kaye, 1952), 31–32, 36, 39–40.

11.Thomas Paine, *Dissertation on First Principles of Government,* in Nelson F. Adkins, ed., *Common Sense and Other Political Writings* (New York: Liberal Arts Press, 1953), 155–74. All quotes from Paine come from this work.

12. James Mill, *An Essay on Government* (Indianapolis: Bobbs-Merrill, 1955). All quotes come from ch. 8, pp. 72–82.

13. Thomas Babington Macaulay, "Mill on Government," in *The Works of Lord Macaulay* (New York: Hurd and Houghton, 1878), 2:5–51. All quotes from Macaulay are taken from this essay.

14. Alexis de Tocqueville, *Democracy in America,* ed. Phillips Bradley (New York: Vintage, 1960) 2:270.

15. Ibid., 1:59.

16. Gertrude Himmelfarb, *Victorian Minds* (New York: Harper & Row, 1970), 348.

17. James Fitzjames Stephen, *Liberty, Equality, Fraternity* (Cambridge: Cambridge University Press, 1967), 210–12. This and subsequent quotes from Stephen are drawn from ch. 5, pp. 179–229.

18. John Stuart Mill occupies a curious place in the evolution of thinking about extension of the suffrage. In his *Considerations on Representative Government* (1861), he argues that "it is a personal injustice to withhold from anyone, unless for the prevention of greater evils, the ordinary privilege of having his voice reckoned in the disposal of affairs in which he has the same interest as other people." He not only opposes property qualifications, but vehemently rejects his father James Mill's argument for denying the suffrage to women. Nonetheless, he defends denying the vote to illiterates, those who pay no taxes, and those on relief. Moreover, he not only accepts these exceptions in practice to universal suffrage, but explicitly rejects the very principle of *equal* suffrage. Today his argument in favor of awarding multiple votes to those possessing "individual mental superiority" (as indicated by their profession or educational attainments) seems even more archaic than arguments for restricting the suffrage. See John Stuart Mill, *Considerations on Representative Government* (New York: Liberal Arts Press, 1958), 127–47.

19. On the spread of judicial review, see Nathan Brown, "Judicial Review and the Arab World" and Herman Schwartz, "Eastern Europe's Constitutional Courts," *Journal of Democracy* 9 (October 1998): 85–114.

20. On the rise of these institutions, see Andreas Schedler, Larry Diamond, and Marc F. Plattner, eds., *The Self-Restraining State: Power and Accountability in New Democracies* (Boulder, Colo.: Lynne Rienner, 1999).

21. See Marc F. Plattner, "Liberalism and Democracy," *Foreign Affairs* 77 (March–April 1998): 171–80.

II

Consolidating Democracy

8

TOWARD CONSOLIDATED DEMOCRACIES

Juan J. Linz and Alfred Stepan

Juan J. Linz *is Sterling Professor Emeritus of Political and Social Science at Yale University.* **Alfred Stepan,** *who was Gladstone Professor of Government at Oxford University in 1996–99, is now Wallace Sayre Professor of Government at Columbia University. This article is drawn from their book* Problems of Democratic Transition and Consolidation: Southern Europe, South America, and Post-Communist Europe *(1996). An earlier version of this article was presented in August 1995 at an international conference in Taipei, Taiwan, on "Consolidating Third Wave Democracies: Trends and Challenges." The conference was cosponsored by the Institute for National Policy Research of Taipei and the International Forum for Democratic Studies of Washington, D.C.*

It is necessary to begin by saying a few words about three minimal conditions that must obtain before there can be any possibility of speaking of democratic consolidation. First, in a modern polity, free and authoritative elections cannot be held, winners cannot exercise the monopoly of legitimate force, and citizens cannot effectively have their rights protected by a rule of law unless a state exists. In some parts of the world, conflicts about the authority and domain of the *polis* and the identities and loyalties of the *demos* are so intense that no state exists. No state, no democracy.

Second, democracy cannot be thought of as consolidated until a democratic transition has been brought to completion. A necessary but by no means sufficient condition for the completion of a democratic transition is the holding of free and contested elections (on the basis of broadly inclusive voter eligibility) that meet the seven institutional requirements for elections in a polyarchy that Robert A. Dahl has set forth.[1] Such elections are not sufficient, however, to complete a democratic transition. In many cases (for example, Chile as of 1996) in which free and contested elections have been held, the government resulting from elections like these lacks the de jure as well as de facto power to determine policy in many significant areas because the executive, legislative, and judicial powers are still decisively constrained by an interlocking set of "reserve domains," military "prerogatives," or "authoritarian enclaves."[2]

Third, no regime should be called a democracy unless its rulers govern democratically. If freely elected executives (no matter what the magnitude of their majority) infringe the constitution, violate the rights of individuals and minorities, impinge upon the legitimate functions of the legislature, and thus fail to rule within the bounds of a state of law, their regimes are not democracies.

In sum, when we talk about the consolidation of democracy, we are not dealing with liberalized nondemocratic regimes, or with pseudo-democracies, or with hybrid democracies where some democratic institutions coexist with nondemocratic institutions outside the control of the democratic state. Only democracies can become consolidated democracies.

Let us now turn to examining how, and when, new political systems that meet the three minimal conditions of "stateness," a completed democratic transition, and a government that rules democratically can be considered consolidated democracies.[3]

In most cases after a democratic transition is completed, there are still many tasks that need to be accomplished, conditions that must be established, and attitudes and habits that must be cultivated before democracy can be regarded as consolidated. What, then, are the characteristics of a consolidated democracy? Many scholars, in advancing definitions of consolidated democracy, enumerate all the regime characteristics that would improve the overall quality of democracy. We favor, instead, a narrower definition of democratic consolidation, but one that nonetheless combines behavioral, attitudinal, and constitutional dimensions. Essentially, by a "consolidated democracy" we mean a political regime in which democracy as a complex system of institutions, rules, and patterned incentives and disincentives has become, in a phrase, "the only game in town."[4]

Behaviorally, democracy becomes the only game in town when no significant political group seriously attempts to overthrow the democratic regime or to promote domestic or international violence in order to secede from the state. When this situation obtains, the behavior of the newly elected government that has emerged from the democratic transition is no longer dominated by the problem of how to avoid democratic breakdown. (Exceptionally, the democratic process can be used to achieve secession, creating separate states that can be democracies.) Attitudinally, democracy becomes the only game in town when, even in the face of severe political and economic crises, the overwhelming majority of the people believe that any further political change must emerge from within the parameters of democratic procedures.

Constitutionally, democracy becomes the only game in town when all of the actors in the polity become habituated to the fact that political conflict within the state will be resolved according to established norms, and that violations of these norms are likely to be both ineffective and costly. In short, with consolidation, democracy becomes routinized and deeply internalized in social, institutional, and even psychological life, as well as in political calculations for achieving success.

Our working definition of a consolidated democracy is then as follows: *Behaviorally,* a democratic regime in a territory is consolidated when no significant national, social, economic, political, or institutional actors spend significant resources attempting to achieve their objectives by creating a nondemocratic regime or by seceding from the state. *Attitudinally,* a democratic regime is consolidated when a strong majority of public opinion, even in the midst of major economic problems and deep dissatisfaction with incumbents, holds the belief that democratic procedures and institutions are the most appropriate way to govern collective life, and when support for antisystem alternatives is quite small or more-or-less isolated from prodemocratic forces. *Constitutionally,* a democratic regime is consolidated when governmental and nongovernmental forces alike become subject to, and habituated to, the resolution of conflict within the bounds of the specific laws, procedures, and institutions sanctioned by the new democratic process.

We must add two important caveats. First, when we say a regime is a consolidated democracy, we do not preclude the possibility that at some future time it could break down. Such a breakdown, however, would be related not to weaknesses or problems specific to the historic process of democratic consolidation, but to a new dynamic in which the democratic regime cannot solve a set of problems, a nondemocratic alternative gains significant supporters, and former democratic regime loyalists begin to behave in a constitutionally disloyal or semiloyal manner.[5]

Our second caveat is that we do not want to imply that there is only one type of consolidated democracy. An exciting new area of research is concerned with precisely this issue—the varieties of consolidated democracies. We also do not want to imply that consolidated democracies could not continue to improve their quality by raising the minimal economic plateau upon which all citizens stand, and by deepening popular participation in the political and social life of the country. Within the category of consolidated democracies there is a continuum from low-quality to high-quality democracies. Improving the quality of consolidated democracies is an urgent political and intellectual task, but our goal in this essay, though related, is a different one. As we are living in a period in which an unprecedented number of countries have completed democratic transitions and are attempting to consolidate democracies, it is politically and conceptually important that we understand the specific tasks of "crafting" democratic consolidation. Unfortunately, too much of the discussion of the current "wave" of democratization focuses almost solely on elections or on the presumed democratizing potential of market mechanisms. Democratic consolidation, however, requires much more than elections and markets.

Crafting and Conditions

In addition to a functioning state, five other interconnected and mutually reinforcing conditions must be present, or be crafted, in order for a democracy to be consolidated. First, the conditions must exist for the development of a free and lively *civil society*. Second, there must be a relatively autonomous *political society*. Third, throughout the territory of the state all major political actors, especially the government and the state apparatus, must be effectively subjected to a *rule of law* that protects individual freedoms and associational life. Fourth, there must be a *state bureaucracy* that is usable by the new democratic government. Fifth, there must be an institutionalized *economic society*. Let us explain what is involved in crafting this interrelated set of conditions.

By "civil society," we refer to that arena of the polity where self-organizing and relatively autonomous groups, movements, and individuals attempt to articulate values, to create associations and solidarities, and to advance their interests. Civil society can include manifold social movements (for example, women's groups, neighborhood associations, religious groupings, and intellectual organizations), as well as associations from all social strata (such as trade unions, entrepreneurial groups, and professional associations).

By "political society," we mean that arena in which political actors compete for the legitimate right to exercise control over public power and the state apparatus. Civil society by itself can destroy a nondemocratic regime, but democratic consolidation (or even a full democratic transition) must involve political society. Democratic consolidation requires that citizens develop an appreciation for the core institutions of a democratic political society—political parties, legislatures, elections, electoral rules, political leadership, and interparty alliances.

It is important to stress not only the difference between civil society and political society, but also their complementarity, which is not always recognized. One of these two arenas is frequently neglected in favor of the other. Worse, within the democratic community, champions of either civil society or political society all too often adopt a discourse and a set of practices that are implicitly inimical to the normal development of the other.

In the recent struggles against the nondemocratic regimes of Eastern Europe and Latin America, a discourse was constructed that emphasized "civil society vs. the state"—a dichotomy that has a long philosophical genealogy. More importantly for our purposes, it was also politically useful to those democratic movements emerging in states where explicitly political organizations were forbidden or extremely weak. In many countries, civil society was rightly considered to be the hero of democratic resistance and transition.

The problem arises at the moment of democratic transition. Democratic leaders of political society quite often argue that civil society, having played its historic role, should be demobilized so as to allow for the development of normal democratic politics. Such an argument is not only bad democratic theory, it is also bad democratic politics. A robust civil society, with the capacity to generate political alternatives and to monitor government and state, can help start transitions, help resist reversals, help push transitions to their completion, and help consolidate and deepen democracy. At all stages of the democratization process, therefore, a lively and independent civil society is invaluable.

But we should also consider how to recognize (and thus help overcome) the false opposition sometimes drawn between civil society and political society. The danger posed for the development of political society by civil society is that normative preferences and styles of organization perfectly appropriate to civil society might be taken to be the desirable—or indeed the only legitimate—style of organization for political society. For example, many civil society leaders view "internal conflict" and "division" within the democratic forces with moral antipathy. "Institutional routinization," "intermediaries," and "compromise" within politics are often spoken of pejoratively. But each of the above terms refers to an indispensable practice of political society in a consolidated democracy. Democratic consolidation requires political parties, one of whose primary tasks is precisely to aggregate and represent differences between democrats. Consolidation requires that habituation to the norms and procedures of democratic conflict-regulation be developed. A high degree of institutional routinization is a key part of such a process. Intermediation between the state and civil society, and the structuring of compromise, are likewise legitimate and necessary tasks of political society. In short, political society—informed, pressured, and periodically renewed by civil society—must somehow achieve a workable agreement on the myriad ways in which democratic power will be crafted and exercised.

The Need for a *Rechtsstaat*

To achieve a consolidated democracy, the necessary degree of autonomy of civil and political society must be embedded in, and supported by, our third arena, the rule of law. All significant actors—especially the democratic government and the state apparatus—must be held accountable to, and become habituated to, the rule of law. For the types of civil society and political society we have just described, a rule of law animated by a spirit of constitutionalism is an indispensable condition. Constitutionalism, which should not be confused with majoritarianism, entails a relatively strong consensus regarding the constitution, and especially a commitment to "self-binding" procedures of governance that can be altered only by exceptional majorities. It also requires a clear hierarchy of laws, interpreted by an independent judicial system and supported by a strong legal culture in civil society.[6]

The emergence of a *Rechtsstaat*—a state of law, or perhaps more accurately a state subject to law—was one of the major accomplishments of nineteenth-century liberalism (long before full democratization) in continental Europe and to some extent in Japan. A *Rechtsstaat* meant that the government and the state apparatus would be subject to the law, that areas of discretionary power would be defined and increasingly limited, and that citizens could turn to courts to defend themselves against the state and its officials. The modern *Rechtsstaat* is fundamental in making democratization possible, since without it citizens would not be able to exercise their political rights with full freedom and independence.

A state of law is particularly crucial for the consolidation of democracy. It is the most important continuous and routine way in which the elected government and the state administration are subjected to a network of laws, courts, semiautonomous review and control agencies, and civil-society norms that not only check the state's illegal tendencies but also embed it in an interconnecting web of mechanisms requiring transparency and accountability. Freely elected governments can, but do not necessarily, create such a state of law. The consolidation of democracy, however, requires such a law-bound, constraint-embedded state. Indeed, the more that all the institutions of the state function according to the principle of the state of law, the higher the quality of democracy and the better the society.

Constitutionalism and the rule of law must determine the offices to be filled by election, the procedures to elect those officeholders, and the definition of and limits to their power in order for people to be willing to participate in, and to accept the outcomes of, the democratic game. This may pose a problem if the rules, even if enacted by a majority, are so unfair or poorly crafted and so difficult to change democratically that they are unacceptable to a large number of citizens. For example, an electoral law that gives 80 percent of the seats in parliament to a party that wins less than 50 percent of the vote, or an ideologically loaded constitution that is extremely difficult to amend, is not likely to be conducive to democratic consolidation.

Finally, a democracy in which a single leader enjoys, or thinks he or she enjoys, a "democratic" legitimacy that allows him or her to ignore, dismiss, or alter other institutions—the legislature, the courts, the constitutional limits of power—does not fit our conception of rule of law in a democratic regime. The formal or informal institutionalization of such a system is not likely to result in a consolidated democracy unless such discretion is checked.

Some presidential democracies—with their tendency toward populist, plebiscitarian, "delegative" characteristics, together with a fixed term of office and a "no-reelection" rule that excludes accountability before the electorate—encourage nonconstitutional or anticonstitutional behavior that threatens the rule of law, often democracy itself, and certainly democratic consolidation. A prime minister who develops similar tendencies toward abuse of power is more likely than a president to be checked by other institutions: votes of no confidence by the opposition, or the loss of support by members of his own party. Early elections are a legal vehicle available in parliamentarianism—but unavailable in presidentialism—to help solve crises generated by such abusive leadership.

A Usable Bureaucracy

These three conditions—a lively and independent civil society; a political society with sufficient autonomy and a working consensus about procedures of governance; and constitutionalism and a rule of law—are virtually definitional prerequisites of a consolidated democracy. However, these conditions are much more likely to be satisfied where there are also found a bureaucracy usable by democratic leaders and an institutionalized economic society.

Democracy is a form of governance in which the rights of citizens are guaranteed and protected. To protect the rights of its citizens and to deliver other basic services that citizens demand, a democratic government needs to be able to exercise effectively its claim to a monopoly of the legitimate use of force in its territory. Even if the state had no other functions than these, it would have to tax compulsorily in order to pay for police officers, judges, and basic services. A modern democracy, therefore, needs the effective capacity to command, to regulate, and to extract tax revenues. For this, it needs a functioning state with a bureaucracy considered usable by the new democratic government.

In many territories of the world today—especially in parts of the former Soviet Union—no adequately functioning state exists. Insufficient taxing capacity on the part of the state or a weak normative and bureaucratic "presence" in much of its territory, such that citizens cannot effectively demand that their rights be respected or receive any basic entitlements, is also a great problem in many countries in Latin America, including Brazil. The question of the usability of the state bureaucracy by the new democratic regime also emerges in countries such as Chile, where the outgoing nondemocratic regime was able to give tenure to many key members of the state bureaucracy in politically sensitive areas such as justice and education. Important questions about the usability of the state bureaucracy by new democrats inevitably emerge in cases where the distinction between the communist party and the state had been virtually obliterated (as in much of postcommunist Europe), and the party is now out of power.

Economic Society

The final supportive condition for a consolidated democracy concerns the economy, an arena that we believe should be called "economic society." We use this phrase to call attention to two claims that we believe are theoretically and empirically sound. First, there has never been, and there cannot be, a consolidated democracy that has a command economy (except perhaps in wartime). Second, there has never been, and almost certainly will never be, a modern consolidated democracy with a pure market economy. Modern consolidated democracies require a set of sociopolitically crafted and accepted norms, institutions, and regulations—what we call "economic society"—that mediate between the state and the market.

No empirical evidence has ever been adduced to indicate that a polity meeting our definition of a consolidated democracy has ever existed with a command economy. Is there a theoretical reason to explain such a universal empirical outcome? We think so. On theoretical grounds, our assumption is that at least a nontrivial degree of market autonomy and of ownership diversity in the economy is necessary to produce the independence and liveliness of civil society that allow it to make its contribution to a democracy. Similarly, if all property is in the hands of the state, along with all decisions about pricing, labor, supply, and distribution, the relative autonomy of political society required for a consolidated democracy could not exist.[7]

But why are completely free markets unable to coexist with modern consolidated democracies? Empirically, serious studies of modern polities repeatedly verify the existence of significant degrees of market intervention and state ownership in all consolidated democracies.[8] Theoretically, there are at least three reasons why this should be so. First, notwithstanding certain ideologically extreme but surprisingly prevalent neoliberal claims about the self-sufficiency of the market, pure market economies could neither come into being nor be maintained without a degree of state regulation. Markets require legally enforced contracts, the issuance of money, regulated standards for weights and measures, and the protection of property, both public and private. These requirements dictate a role for the state in the economy. Second, even the best of markets experience "market failures" that must be corrected if the market is to function well.[9] No less an advocate of the "invisible hand" of the market than Adam Smith acknowledged that the state is necessary to perform certain functions. In a crucial but neglected passage in the *Wealth of Nations,* Adam Smith identified three important tasks of the state:

> First, the duty of protecting the society from the violence and invasion of other independent societies; secondly, the duty of protecting, as far as possible, every member of the society from the injustice or oppression of every other member of it, or the duty of establishing an exact administration of justice; and, thirdly, the duty of erecting and maintaining certain public works and certain public institutions which it can never be for the interest of any individual, or small number of individuals, to erect and maintain; because the profit could never repay the expense to any individual or small number of individuals, though it may frequently do much more than repay it to a great society.[10]

Finally, and most importantly, democracy entails free public contestation concerning governmental priorities and policies. If a democracy never produced policies that generated government-mandated public goods in the areas of education, health, and transportation, and never provided some economic safety net for its citizens and some alleviation of gross economic inequality, democracy would not be sustainable. Theoretically, of course, it would be antidemocratic to take such public policies off the agenda of legitimate public contestation. Thus, even in the extreme hypothetical case of a democracy that began with a pure market economy, the very working of a modern democracy (and a modern advanced capitalist economy) would lead to the transformation of that pure market economy into a mixed economy, or that set of norms, regulations, policies, and institutions which we call "economic society."[11]

Any way we analyze the problem, democratic consolidation requires the institutionalization of a politically regulated market. This requires an economic society, which in turn requires an effective state. Even a goal such as narrowing the scope of public ownership (that is, privatization) in an orderly and legal way is almost certainly carried out more effectively by a stronger state than by a weaker one. Economic deterioration due to the state's inability to carry out needed regulatory functions greatly compounds the problems of economic reform and democratization.[12]

In summary, a modern consolidated democracy can be conceived of as comprising five major interrelated arenas, each of which, to function properly, must have its own primary organizing principle. Rightly understood, democracy is more than a regime; it is an interacting system. No single arena in such a system can function properly without some support from another arena, or often from all of the remaining arenas. For example, civil society in a democracy needs the support of a rule of law that guarantees to people their right of association, and needs the support of a state apparatus that will effectively impose legal sanctions on those who would illegally attempt to deny others that right. Furthermore, each arena in the democratic system has an impact on other arenas. For example, political society manages the governmental bureaucracy and produces the overall regulatory framework that guides and contains economic society. In a consolidated democracy, therefore, there are constant mediations among the five principal arenas, each of which is influenced by the others.

Two Surmountable Obstacles

Two of the most widely cited obstacles to democratic consolidation are the dangers posed by ethnic conflict in multinational states and by disappointed popular hopes for economic improvement in states undergoing simultaneous political and economic reform. These are real problems. Democratic theorists and crafters alike must recognize that there is often more than one "awakened nation" present in the state, and that there can be prolonged economic reversals after democratic transition begins. Nonetheless, we are convinced, on both theoretical and empirical grounds, that democracy can still make significant strides toward consolidation under such conditions. We are furthermore convinced that if democratic theorists conceptualize what such obstacles mean and do not mean, this may lessen the dangers of democratic disenchantment and help to identify obstacle-reducing paths. That is our task in the rest of this essay.

Under what empirical conditions do "nation-states" and "democratization" form complementary logics? Under what conditions do they form conflicting logics? If they form conflicting logics, what types of practices and institutions will make democratic consolidation most, or least, likely?

Many political thinkers and activists assume that Weberian states, nation-states, and democracy cohere as part of the very grammar of modern polities. In a world where France, Germany, Portugal, Greece, and Japan are all Weberian states, nation-states, and democracies, such an assumption may seem justified. Yet in many countries that are not yet consolidated democracies, a nation-state policy often has a different logic than a democratic policy. By a nation-state policy we mean one in which the leaders of the state pursue what Rogers Brubaker calls "nationalizing state policies" aimed at increasing cultural homogeneity. Consciously or unconsciously, the leaders send messages that the state should be "of and for" the nation.[13] In the constitutions they write and in the politics they practice, the dominant nation's language becomes the only official language and occasionally the only acceptable language for state business and for education; the religion of the nation is privileged (even if it is not necessarily made the official religion); and the culture of the dominant nation is privileged in state symbols (such as the flag, national anthem, and even eligibility for some types of military service) and in state-controlled means of socialization (such as radio, television, and textbooks). By contrast, democratic policies in the state-making process are those that emphasize a broad and inclusive citizenship that accords equal individual rights to all.

Under what empirical conditions are the logics of state policies aimed at nation-building congruent with those aimed at crafting democracy? Empirically, conflicts between these different policies are reduced when almost all of the residents of a state identify with one subjective idea of the nation, and when that nation is virtually coextensive with the state. These conditions are met only if there is no significant irredenta outside the state's boundaries, if there is only one nation existing (or awakened) in the state, and if there is little cultural diversity within the state. In these circumstances (and, we will argue, virtually *only* in these circumstances) leaders of the government can simultaneously pursue democratization policies and nation-state policies. This congruence between the *polis* and the *demos* facilitates the creation of a democratic nation-state; it also virtually eliminates all problems of "stateness" and should thus be considered a supportive condition for democratic consolidation. Under modern circumstances, however, very few states will begin a possible democratic transition with a high degree of national homogeneity. This lack of homogeneity tends to exacerbate problems of "stateness."

Democracy is characterized not by subjects but by citizens; thus a democratic transition often puts the question of the relation between *polis* and *demos* at the center of politics. From all that has been said thus far, three assertions can be made. First, the greater the extent to which the population of a state is composed of a plurality of national, linguistic, religious, or cultural societies, the more complex politics becomes, since an agreement on the fundamentals of a democracy will be more difficult. Second, while this does not mean that consolidating democracy in multinational or multicultural states is impossible, it does mean that especially careful political crafting of democratic norms, practices, and institutions is required. Third, some methods of dealing with the problems of "stateness" are inherently incompatible with democracy.

Clear thinking on this subject demands that we call into question some facile assumptions. One of the most dangerous ideas for democracy is that "every state should strive to become a nation-state and every nation should become a state." In fact, it is probably impossible for half of the territories in the world that are not now democratic ever to become both "nation-states" and "consolidated democracies," as we have defined these terms. One of the reasons for this is that many existing nondemocratic states are multinational, multilingual, and multicultural. To make them "nation-states" by democratic means would be extremely difficult. In structurally embedded multicultural settings, virtually the only democratic way to create a homogeneous nation-state is through voluntary cultural assimilation, voluntary exit, or peaceful creation and voluntary acceptance of new territorial boundaries. These are empirically and democratically difficult measures, and hence are exceedingly rare.

The other possibilities for creating a homogeneous nation-state in such settings involve subtle (or not-so-subtle) sanctions against those not speaking the language, wearing the attire, or practicing the religion of the titular nation. Under modern circumstances—where all significant groups have writers and intellectuals who disseminate national cultures, where communication systems have greatly increased the possibility for migrants to remain continuously connected to their home cultures, and where modern democratic norms accept a degree of multiculturalism— such sanctions, even if not formally antidemocratic, would probably not be conducive to democratic crafting.[14] If the titular nation actually wants a truly homogeneous nation-state, a variant of "ethnic cleansing" is too often a temptation.

Another difficulty in the way of building nation-states that are also democracies derives from the manner in which humanity is spatially distributed across the globe. One building block for nations is language. But as Ernest Gellner observed, there are possibly as many as eight thousand languages (not counting important dialects) currently spoken in the world.[15] Even if we assume that only one out of every ten languages is a base for a "reasonably effective" nationalism, there could be as many as eight hundred viable national communities.[16] But cultural, linguistic, and religious groups are not neatly segmented into eight thousand or eight hundred nationalities, each occupying reasonably well-defined territories. On the contrary, these groups are profoundly intermixed and overlapping.

We are not arguing against democratically crafted "velvet divorces." We should note, however, that relatively clear cultural boundaries facilitate such territorial separations. Latvia would like to be a nation-state, but in none of its seven most-populous cities is Latvian spoken by a majority of the residents. In Tallinn, the capital of Estonia, barely half the people of this aspiring nation-state speak Estonian. For these and many other countries, no simple territorial division or "velvet divorce" is available.[17]

Democracy and Multinational States

Some analysts were happy when the separate nationalities of the USSR became 15 republics, all based on "titular nationalities," on the assumption that democratic nation-states might emerge. In fact, many political leaders in these republics sounded extreme nationalist (rather than democratic) themes in the first elections. One possible formula for diminishing conflict between titular nationalities and "migrants" is what David Laitin calls the "competitive-assimilation game." That is, it becomes in the best interests of some working-class migrants to assimilate in order to enhance the life chances of their children in the new environment. This may happen to Spanish working-class migrants in culturally and economically vibrant Catalonia, but is it likely to occur among Russians in Central Asia? In 1989 in Almaty, the capital of Kazakhstan, Russians constituted 59 percent of the population, and the Kazakhs, the titular nationality, only 22.5 percent. Less than 1 percent of the Russians spoke the titular language. In Bishkek, the capital of Kyrgyzstan, the comparable percentages were virtually identical. In such contexts, shaped by settler colonialism, it is utterly implausible that a nation-state would emerge voluntarily through a process of competitive assimilation.[18]

So how can democracy possibly be achieved in multinational states? We have a strong hypothesis about how *not* to consolidate democracy in multinational settings. The greater the percentage of people in a given state who either were born there or arrived without perceiving themselves as foreign citizens, and who are subsequently denied citizenship in the state (when their life chances would be hurt by such denial), the more unlikely it is that this state will consolidate democracy. Phrased more positively, our hypothesis is that in a multinational, multicultural setting, the chances of consolidating democracy are increased by state policies that grant inclusive and equal citizenship and give all citizens a common "roof" of state-mandated and state-enforced individual rights.

Such multinational states also have an even greater need than other polities to explore a variety of nonmajoritarian, nonplebiscitarian formulas. For example, if there are strong geographic concentrations of different groups within the state, federalism might be an option worth exploring. The state and the society might also allow a variety of publicly supported communal institutions—such as media and schools in different languages, symbolic recognition of cultural diversity, a variety of legally accepted marriage codes, legal and political tolerance for parties representing different communities, and a whole array of political procedures and devices that Arend Lijphart has described as "consociational democracy."[19] Typically, proportional representation, rather than large single-member districts with first-past-the-post elections, can facilitate representation of geographically dispersed minorities. Some strict adherents to the tradition of political liberalism, with its focus on universalism and individual rights, oppose any form of collective rights. But we believe that in a multinational, multicultural society and state, combining collective rights for nationalities or minorities with individual rights fully protected by the state is the least-conflictual solution.[20]

Where transitions occur in the context of a nondemocratic,

multinational federal system, the crafting of democratic federalism should probably begin with elections at the federal level, so as to generate a legitimate framework for later deliberations on how to decentralize the polity democratically. If the first competitive elections are regional, the elections will tend to favor regional nationalists, and ethnocracies rather than democracies may well emerge.[21] However, the specific ways of structuring political life in multinational settings need to be contextualized in each country. Along these lines, we believe that it is time to reevaluate some past experiments with nonterritorial autonomy such as the kinds of partially self-governing ethnic or religious communities exemplified by the Jewish Kabal of the Polish-Lithuanian Commonwealth, the millets of the Ottoman Empire, or the "national curias" of the late Habsburg Empire. These mechanisms will not eliminate conflict in multinational states, but they may moderate conflict and help make both the state and democracy more viable.

We also believe that some conceptual, political, and normative attention should be given to the possibility of "state-nations." We call "state-nations" those multicultural or even multinational states that nonetheless still manage to engender strong identification and loyalty from their diverse citizens. The United States is such a multicultural and increasingly multilingual country; Switzerland is another. Neither is strictly speaking a "nation-state," but we believe both could now be called "state-nations." Under Jawaharlal Nehru, India made significant gains in managing multinational tensions by the skillful and consensual use of numerous consociational practices. Through this process India became, in the 1950s and early 1960s, a democratic "state-nation"; but if Hindu nationalists were to attempt to turn India (with its 115 million Muslims) into a Hindu nation-state, communal violence would almost certainly increase and Indian democracy would be gravely threatened.

Multiple Identities

Let us conclude with a word about "political identities." Many writings on nationalism have focused on "primordial" identities and the need for people to choose between mutually exclusive identities. Our research into political identities, however, has shown two things. First, political identities are not fixed or "primordial" in the *Oxford English Dictionary*'s sense of "existing at (or from) the very beginning." Rather, they are highly changeable and socially constructed. Second, if nationalist politicians (or social scientists and census-takers with crude dichotomous categories) do not force polarization, many people may prefer to define themselves as having multiple and complementary identities.[22] In fact, along with a common political "roof" of state-protected rights for inclusive and equal citizenship, the human capacity for multiple and complementary identities is one of the key factors that make democracy in multinational states possible. Because political identities are not fixed and permanent, the quality of democratic leadership is particularly important. Multiple and complementary political identities can be nurtured by political leadership, as can polarized and conflictual political identities. Before the conscious use of "ethnic cleansing" as a strategy to construct nation-states in the former Yugoslavia, Sarajevo was a multinational city whose citizens had multiple identities and one of the world's highest interfaith-marriage rates.

Our central proposition is that, if successful democratic consolidation is the goal, would-be crafters of democracy must take into careful consideration the particular mix of nations, cultures, and awakened political identities present in the territory. Some kinds of democracy are possible with one type of *polis*, but virtually impossible if political elites attempt to build another type of *polis*. Political elites in a multinational territory could initiate "nationalizing policies" that might not violate human rights or the Council of Europe's norms for democracy, but would have the effect, in each of the five arenas of the polity, of greatly diminishing the chances of democratic consolidation.

An example of such "nationalizing policies" in each of five arenas would be the following: In the arena of civil society, schooling and mass media could be restricted to the official language. In the arena of political society, nationalizing citizenship laws could lead to a significant overrepresentation of the dominant nationality in elected offices. In the arena of the rule of law, the legal system could subtly privilege a whole range of nationalizing customs, practices, and institutions. In the arena of the state bureaucracy, a rapid changeover to one official language could decrease other nationalities' participation in, and access to, state services. Finally, in the arena of economic society, the titular nationality, as the presumed "owners" of the nation-state, could be given special or even exclusive rights to land redistribution (or voucher distribution, if there was privatization). In contrast, if the real goal is democratic consolidation, a democratizing strategy would require less majoritarian and more consensual policies in each of the above arenas.

A final point to stress concerns timing. Potentially difficult democratic outcomes may be achievable only if some preemptive policies and decisions are argued for, negotiated, and implemented by political leaders. If the opportunity for such ameliorative policies is lost, the range of available space for maneuver will be narrowed, and a dynamic of societal conflict will likely intensify until democratic consolidation becomes increasingly difficult, and eventually impossible.

Problems of Simultaneous Reform

The widely held view that market reform and privatization can legitimate new democracies is based on the dubious assumption that economic improvement can be achieved simultaneously with the installation and legitimation of democratic institutions. We believe that, in countries with imploded command economies, democratic polities can and must be installed and legitimized by a variety of other appeals before the possible benefits of a market economy fully materialize. Many analysts and political advisors dismiss the case for giving priority to state restructuring because they assume that, due to people's demands for material improvements, economic and political gains must not only be pursued but occur simultaneously. Some even argue that simultaneous economic and political reforms are necessary, but that such simultaneity is impossible.[23]

We can call the two opposing perspectives about the relationship between economics and democratization the "tightly coupled" hypothesis and the "loosely coupled" hypothesis. By "loosely coupled," we do not mean that there is no relationship between economic and political perceptions, only that the relationship is not necessarily one-to-one. For at least a medium-range time horizon, people can make independent, and even opposite, assessments about political and economic trends. We further believe that when people's assessments about politics are positive, they can provide a valuable cushion for painful economic restructuring.[24] Let us look at the evidence concerning the relationship between economic growth and democratization in the first five years of postcommunist Europe. Certainly, if we look only at relatively hard economic data, none of the 27 countries in postcommunist Europe except Poland experienced positive growth in 1992. Indeed, in 1993 all postcommunist countries were still well below their 1989 industrial-output levels.[25]

If we look at subjective impressions of economic well-being in six East Central European countries, the mean positive rating (on a +100 to −100 scale) among those polled between November 1993 and March 1994 was 60.2 for the communist economic system, but was only 37.3 for the postcommunist economic system—a drop of almost 23 points. The tightly coupled hypothesis would predict that attitudes toward the political system would also drop steeply, even if not by the full 23 points. What does the evidence show? The mean positive ranking of the communist political system was 45.7. Thus a one-to-one correlation between the political and economic evaluations would have yielded a positive evaluation of the political system of 22.6. Yet the mean positive ranking for the postcommunist political system, far from falling, rose to 61.5—or 38.9 points higher than a "perfectly coupled" hypothesis would have predicted.[26]

How can we explain such incongruence? First of all, human beings are capable of making separate and correct judgements about a basket of economic goods (which may be deteriorating) and a basket of political goods (which may be improving). In fact, in the same survey the respondents judged that, in important areas directly affected by the democratic political system, their life experiences and chances had overwhelmingly improved, even though they also asserted that their own personal household economic situations had worsened.[27]

We do not believe such incongruence can last forever; it does indicate, however, that in a radical transformation like that occurring in East Central Europe, the deterioration of the economy does not necessarily translate into rapid erosion of support for the political system. The perceived legitimacy of the political system has given democratic institutions in East Central Europe an important degree of insulation from the perceived inefficacy of the new economic system. Indeed, most people in East Central Europe in 1994 had a fairly long time horizon and expressed optimism that by 1999 the performance of both the new democracy and the new economic system would improve significantly.[28]

Thus the evidence in East Central Europe is strongly in favor of the argument that deferred gratification and confidence in the future are possible even when there is an acknowledged lag in economic improvement. Simultaneity of rapid political and economic results is indeed extremely difficult, but fortunately the citizens of East Central Europe did not perceive it as necessary.

Democracy and the Quality of Life

While we believe that it is a good thing for democracies to be consolidated, we should make it clear that consolidation does not necessarily entail either a high-quality democracy or a high-quality society. Democratic institutions—however important—are only one set of public institutions affecting citizens' lives. The courts, the central bank, the police, the armed forces, certain independent regulatory agencies, public-service agencies, and public hospitals are not governed democratically, and their officials are not elected by the citizens. Even in established democracies, not all of these institutions are controlled by elected officials, although many are overseen by them. These institutions operate, however, in a legal framework created by elected bodies and thereby derive their authority from them.

In view of all this, the quality of public life is in great measure a reflection not simply of the democratic or nondemocratic character of the regime, but of the quality of those other institutions.

Policy decisions by democratic governments and legislators certainly affect the quality of life, particularly in the long run, but no democracy can assure the presence of reputable bankers, entrepreneurs with initiative, physicians devoted to their patients, competent professors, creative scholars and artists, or even honest judges. The overall quality of a society is only in small part a function of democracy (or, for that matter, a function of nondemocratic regimes). Yet all of those dimensions of society affect the satisfaction of its citizens, including their satisfaction with the government and even with democracy itself. The feeling that democracy is to blame for all sorts of other problems is likely to be particularly acute in societies in which the distinctive contributions of democracy to the quality of life are not well understood and perhaps not highly valued. The more that democrats suggest that the achievement of democratic politics will bring the attainment of all those other goods, the greater will be the eventual disenchantment.

There are problems specific to the functioning of the state, and particularly to democratic institutions and political processes, that allow us to speak of the quality of democracy separately from the quality of society. Our assumption is that the quality of democracy can contribute positively or negatively to the quality of society, but that the two should not be confused. We as scholars should, in our research, explore both dimensions of the overall quality of life.

NOTES

This essay is largely drawn from excerpts from our book, *Problems of Democratic Transition and Consolidation: Southern Europe, South America, and Post-communist Europe* (Baltimore: Johns Hopkins University Press, 1996). Interested readers can find more detailed documentation, analysis, and references there. We thank the Ford Foundation and the Carnegie Corporation of New York for help in our research.

1. See Robert A. Dahl, *Polyarchy: Participation and Opposition* (New Haven: Yale University Press, 1971), 3.

2. We document the incomplete status of the Chilean democratic transition in chapter 13 of our book. For military prerogatives, see Alfred Stepan, *Rethinking Military Politics: Brazil and the Southern Cone* (Princeton, N.J.: Princeton University Press, 1988), 68–127. For the electoralist fallacy in Central America, see Terry Lynn Karl, "The Hybrid Regimes of Central America," *Journal of Democracy* 6 (July 1995): 72–86. Dahl in his *Polyarchy* has an eighth institutional guarantee, which does not address elections as such, but rather the requirement that "[Institutions] for making government policies [should] depend on votes and other expressions of preference," (p. 3). This addresses our concern about reserve domains.

3. Some readers have accused our work—and other studies of democratic transition and consolidation—of being teleological. If this means advocating a single end-state democracy, we decidedly do not share such a view. If, however, teleological means (as the *Oxford English Dictionary* says) "a view that developments are due to the purpose or design that is served by them," our analysis is in part teleological, for we do not believe that structural factors per se lead to democracy and its consolidation. Social actors (and in some measure particular leaders) must also act purposefully to achieve a change of regime leading to some form of governing that can be considered democratic. The design of democracy that these actors pursue may be different from the one resulting from their actions, but without action whose intent is to create "a" democracy (rather than the particular institutionalized form that results), a transition to and consolidation of democracy are difficult to conceive. The processes that we are studying do, therefore, involve a "teleological" element that does not exclude important structural factors (or many unpredictable events). In addition, there is not a single motive but a variety of motives for pursuing democracy (as we define it) as a goal.

4. For other discussions about the concept of democratic consolidation, see

Scott Mainwaring, Guillermo O'Donnell, and J. Samuel Valenzuela, eds., *Issues in Democratic Consolidation: The New South American Democracies in Comparative Perspective* (Notre Dame: University of Notre Dame Press, 1992).

5. In essence, this means that the literature on democratic breakdown, such as that found in Juan J. Linz and Alfred Stepan, eds., *The Breakdown of Democratic Regimes* (Baltimore: Johns Hopkins University Press, 1978), would be much more directly relevant to analyzing such a phenomenon than this essay or related books on democratic transition and consolidation. This is not a criticism of the transition literature; rather, our point is that the democratic-transition and democratic-breakdown literatures need to be integrated into the overall literature on modern democratic theory. From the perspective of such an integrated theory, the "breakdown of a consolidated democracy" is not an oxymoron.

6. On the relationships between constitutionalism, democracy, legal culture, and "self-bindingness," see Jon Elster and Rune Slagstad, eds., *Constitutionalism and Democracy* (Cambridge: Cambridge University Press, 1988), 1–18.

7. Robert A. Dahl, in a similar argument, talks about two arrows of causation that produce this result; see his "Why All Democratic Countries Have Mixed Economies," in John Chapman and Ian Shapiro, eds., *Democratic Community, Nomos XXXV* (New York: New York University Press, 1993), 259–82.

8. See, for example, John R. Freeman, *Democracies and Market: The Politics of Mixed Economies* (Ithaca, N.Y.: Cornell University Press, 1989).

9. For an excellent analysis of inevitable market failures, see Peter Murrell, "Can Neoclassical Economics Underpin the Reform of Centrally Planned Economies?" *Journal of Economic Perspectives* 5 (1991): 59–76.

10. Adam Smith, *The Wealth of Nations*, 2 vols. (London: J.M. Dent and Sons, Everyman's Library, 1910), 2: 180–81.

11. Robert A. Dahl's line of reasoning follows a similar development. See his "Why All Democratic Countries Have Mixed Economies," cited in note 7 above, 259–82.

12. In postcommunist Europe, the Czech Republic and Hungary are well on the way to becoming institutionalized economic societies. In sharp contrast, in Ukraine and Russia the writ of the state does not extend far enough for us to speak of an economic society. The consequences of the lack of an economic society are manifest everywhere. For example, Russia, with a population 15 times larger than Hungary's and with vastly more raw materials, only received 3.6 billion dollars of direct foreign investment in 1992–93, whereas Hungary received 9 billion dollars of direct foreign investment in the same two years.

13. See Rogers Brubaker's "National Minorities, Nationalizing States, and External National Homelands in the New Europe," *Daedalus* 124 (Spring 1995): 107–32.

14. See, for example, the outstanding monograph by Eugen Weber, *Peasants into Frenchmen: The Modernization of Rural France, 1870–1914* (Stanford, Calif.: Stanford University Press, 1976), which analyzes in extensive detail the wide repertoire of nation-state mandated policies in the schools, the civil service, and the military that were systematically designed to repress and eliminate multilingualism and multiculturalism and to create a nation-state. From today's perspective, similar endeavors of modern states appear far from admirable and represent a cost that many of us would not like to pay. However, it is not just a question of how we evaluate such efforts of state-based nation-building, but of how feasible these efforts are in the contemporary context.

15. See Ernest Gellner, *Nations and Nationalism* (Ithaca, N.Y.: Cornell University Press, 1983), 44.

16. This conjecture is developed by Ernest Gellner in *Nations and Nationalism*, 44–45.

17. See the excellent, and sobering, book by Anatol Lieven, *The Baltic Revolution: Estonia, Latvia, Lithuania and the Path to Independence* (New Haven: Yale University Press, 1993), 434.

18. For David Laitin's analysis of what he calls a "migrant competitive-assimilation game" in Catalonia, and his analysis of a possible "colonial-settler game" in the Central Asian republics of the former Soviet Union, see his "The Four Nationality Games and Soviet Politics," *Journal of Soviet Nationalities* 2 (Spring 1991): 1–37.

19. See Arend Lijphart's seminal article "Consociational Democracy," *World Politics* 21 (January 1969): 207–25.

20. For interesting arguments that some notion of group rights is, in fact, necessary to the very definition of some types of individual rights and necessary to the advancement of universal norms in rights, see the work by the Oxford philosopher Joseph Raz, *The Morality of Freedom* (Oxford: Oxford University Press, 1986), 165–217. Also see Will Kymlicka, *Multicultural Citizenship: A Liberal Theory of Minority Rights* (Oxford: Oxford University Press, 1995), 107–30.

21. We develop this point in greater detail in our "Political Identities and Electoral Sequences: Spain, the Soviet Union and Yugoslavia," *Daedalus* 121 (Spring 1992): 123–39; and in our *Problems of Democratic Transition and Consolidation* in the chapters on Spain, on "stateness" in the USSR, and on Russian speakers' changing identities in Estonia and Latvia.

22. In our *Problems of Democratic Transition and Consolidation*, we show how in Catalonia in 1982, when respondents were given the opportunity to self-locate their identities on a questionnaire offering the following five possibilities—"Spanish," "more Spanish than Catalan," "equally Spanish and Catalan," "more Catalan than Spanish," or "Catalan"—the most-chosen category, among respondents with both parents born in Catalonia, as well as among respondents with neither parent born in Catalonia, was the multiple and complementary category "equally Spanish and Catalan." We also show how identities in Catalonia were becoming more polarized and conflict-ridden before democratic devolution.

23. The title of a widely disseminated article by Jon Elster captures this perspective; see "The Necessity and Impossibility of Simultaneous Economic and Political Reform," in Douglas Greenberg, Stanley N. Katz, Melanie Beth Oliviero, and Steven C. Wheatley, eds., *Constitutionalism and Democracy: Transitions in the Contemporary World* (Oxford: Oxford University Press, 1993), 267–74.

24. The voters might, due to negative economic performance, vote incumbents out of office, but the overall economic policies of their successors might well continue to be roughly the same. Poland in 1993–95, and Hungary in 1994–95 come to mind.

25. See our *Problems of Democratic Transition and Consolidation*.

26. See Richard Rose and Christian Haerpfer, "New Democracies Barometer III: Learning from What is Happening," *Studies in Public Policy* No. 230 (1994), questions 22–23, 32–33. Percentages rounded off.

27. Richard Rose and Christian Haerpfer, "New Democracies Barometer II," questions 26, 35, 36, 39, 40, and 42.

28. Richard Rose and Christian Haerpfer, "New Democracies Barometer II," questions 24, 26, 35, 36, 39, 40, 42, and 34.

9

ILLUSIONS ABOUT CONSOLIDATION

Guillermo O'Donnell

Guillermo O'Donnell is Helen Kellogg Professor of Government and International Studies at the University of Notre Dame. An earlier version of this essay was first presented at a conference on "Consolidating Third Wave Democracies: Trends and Challenges," held on 27–30 August 1995 in Taipei, Taiwan, under the auspices of the Institute for National Policy Research of Taipei and the International Forum for Democratic Studies of Washington, D.C.

Democracies used to be few in number, and most were located in the northwestern quarter of the world. Over the last two decades, however, many countries have rid themselves of authoritarian regimes. There are many variations among these countries. Some of them have reverted to new brands of authoritarianism (even if from time to time they hold elections), while others have clearly embraced democracy. Still others seem to inhabit a gray area; they bear a family resemblance to the old established democracies, but either lack or only precariously possess some of their key attributes. The bulk of the contemporary scholarly literature tells us that these "incomplete" democracies are failing to become consolidated, or institutionalized.

This poses two tasks. One is to establish a cutoff point that separates all democracies from all nondemocracies. This point's location depends on the questions we ask, and so is always arbitrary. Many definitions of democracy have been offered.[1] The one that I find particularly useful is Robert Dahl's concept of "polyarchy." Once a reasonably well-delimited set of democracies is obtained, the second task is to examine the criteria that a given stream of the literature uses for comparing cases within this set. If the criteria are found wanting, the next step is to propose alternative concepts for these comparisons. This is what I attempt here, albeit in preliminary and schematic fashion.

Contemporary Latin America is my empirical referent, although my discussion probably also applies to various newly democratized countries

in other parts of the world. The main argument is that, contrary to what most
of current scholarship holds, the problem with many new polyarchies is not
that they lack institutionalization. Rather, the way in which political
scientists usually conceptualize some institutions prevents us from
recognizing that these polyarchies actually have two extremely important
institutions. One is highly formalized, but intermittent: elections. The other
is informal, permanent, and pervasive: particularism (or clientelism, broadly
defined). An important fact is that, in contrast to previous periods of
authoritarian rule, particularism now exists in uneasy tension with the formal
rules and institutions of what I call the "full institutional package" of
polyarchy. These arguments open up a series of issues that in future
publications I will analyze with the detail and nuance they deserve. My
purpose at present is to furnish some elements of what I believe are needed
revisions in the conceptual and comparative agenda for the study of all
existing polyarchies, especially those that are *informally institutionalized*.[2]

Polyarchy, as defined by Dahl, has seven attributes: 1) elected officials;
2) free and fair elections; 3) inclusive suffrage; 4) the right to run for
office; 5) freedom of expression; 6) alternative information; and 7) associational autonomy.[3] Attributes 1 to 4 tell us that a basic aspect of polyarchy is that elections are inclusive, fair, and competitive. Attributes 5
to 7 refer to political and social freedoms that are minimally necessary
not only during but also between elections as a condition for elections
to be fair and competitive. According to these criteria, some countries of
Latin America currently are not polyarchies: The Dominican Republic,
Haiti, and Mexico have all held elections marred by serious irregularities
before, during, and after the voting.

Other attributes need to be added to Dahl's list. One is that elected (and
some appointed) officials should not be arbitrarily terminated before the
end of their constitutionally mandated terms (Peru's Alberto Fujimori and
Russia's Boris Yeltsin may have been elected in fair elections, but they
abolished polyarchy when they forcefully closed their countries' congresses
and fired their supreme courts). A second addition is that the elected
authorities should not be subject to severe constraints, vetoes, or exclusion
from certain policy domains by other, nonelected actors, especially the
armed forces.[4] In this sense, Guatemala and Paraguay, as well as probably
El Salvador and Honduras, do not qualify as polyarchies.[5] Chile is an odd
case, where restrictions of this sort are part of a constitution inherited from
the authoritarian regime. But Chile clearly meets Dahl's seven criteria of
polyarchy. Peru is another doubtful case, since the 1995 presidential
elections were not untarnished, and the armed forces retain tutelary powers
over various policy areas. Third, there should be an uncontested national
territory that clearly defines the voting population.[6] Finally, an appropriate
definition of polyarchy should also include an intertemporal dimension:
The generalized expectation that a fair electoral process and its surrounding
freedoms will continue into an indefinite future.

These criteria leave us with the three polyarchies—Colombia, Costa Rica, and Venezuela—whose origins date from before the wave of democratization that began in the mid-1970s, and with nine others that resulted from this wave: Argentina, Bolivia, Brazil, Ecuador, Nicaragua, Panama, Uruguay and, with the caveats noted, Chile and Peru. Only in the oldest Latin American polyarchy (Costa Rica) and in two cases of redemocratization (Chile and Uruguay) do the executive branch, congress, parties, and the judiciary function in a manner that is reasonably close to their formal institutional rules, making them effective institutional knots in the flow of political power and policy. Colombia and Venezuela used to function like this, but do so no longer. These two countries, jointly with Argentina, Bolivia, Brazil, Ecuador, Nicaragua, Panama, and Peru—a set that includes a large majority of the Latin American population and GNP—function in ways that current democratic theory has ill prepared us to understand.

We must go back to the definition of polyarchy. This definition, precise in regard to elections (attributes 1 to 4) and rather generic about contextual freedoms (attributes 5 to 7), is mute with respect to institutional features such as parliamentarism or presidentialism, centralism or federalism, majoritarianism or consensualism, and the presence or absence of a written constitution and judicial review. Also, the definition of polyarchy is silent about important but elusive themes such as if, how, and to what degree governments are responsive or accountable to citizens between elections, and the degree to which the rule of law extends over the country's geographic and social terrain.[7] These silences are appropriate: The definition of polyarchy, let us recall, establishes a crucial cutoff point—one that separates cases where there exist inclusive, fair, and competitive elections and basic accompanying freedoms from all others, including not only unabashed authoritarian regimes but also countries that hold elections but lack some of the characteristics that jointly define polyarchy.

Among polyarchies, however, there are many variations. These differences are empirical, but they can also be normatively evaluated, and their likely effect on the survival prospects of each polyarchy may eventually be assessed. These are important issues that merit some conceptual clarification.

By definition, all the Latin American cases that I have labeled polyarchies are such because of a simple but crucial fact: Elections are institutionalized. By an institution I mean a regularized pattern of interaction that is known, practiced, and accepted (if not necessarily approved) by actors who expect to continue interacting under the rules sanctioned and backed by that pattern.[8] Institutions are typically taken for granted, in their existence and continuity, by the actors who interact with and through them. Institutions are "there," usually unquestioned regulators of expectations and behavior. Sometimes, institutions become complex organizations: They are supposed to operate under highly formalized and explicit rules, and materialize in buildings, rituals, and officials. These are the institutions on which both "prebehavioral" and most of contemporary neo-institutionalist political science focus. An unusual characteristic of elections *qua* institutions is that they are highly formalized by detailed and explicit rules, but function intermittently and do not always have a permanent organizational embodiment.

In all polyarchies, old and new, elections are institutionalized, both in themselves and in the reasonable[9] effectiveness of the surrounding conditions of freedom of expression, access to alternative information, and associational autonomy. Leaders and voters take for granted that in the future inclusive, fair, and competitive elections will take place as legally scheduled, voters will be properly registered and free from physical coercion, and their votes will be counted fairly. It is also taken for granted that the winners will take office, and will not have their terms arbitrarily terminated. Furthermore, for this electoral process to exist, freedom of opinion and of association (including the freedom to form political parties) and an uncensored media must also exist. Countries where elections do not have these characteristics do not qualify as polyarchies.[10]

Most students of democratization agree that many of the new polyarchies are at best poorly institutionalized. Few seem to have institutionalized anything but elections, at least in terms of what one would expect from looking at older polyarchies. But appearances can be misleading, since other institutions may exist, even though they may not be the ones that most of us would prefer or easily recognize.

Theories of "Consolidation"

When elections and their surrounding freedoms are institutionalized, it might be said that polyarchy (or political democracy) is "consolidated," that is, likely to endure. This, jointly with the proviso of absence of veto powers over elected authorities, is the influential definition of "democratic consolidation" offered by Juan J. Linz, who calls it a state of affairs "in which none of the major political actors, parties, or organized interests, forces, or institutions consider that there is any alternative to democratic processes to gain power, and . . . no political institution or group has a claim to veto the action of democratically elected decision makers. . . . To put it simply, democracy must be seen as the 'only game in town.'"[11] This minimalist definition has important advantages. Still, I see little analytical gain in attaching the term "consolidated" to something that will probably though not certainly endure—"democracy" and "consolidation" are terms too polysemic to make a good pair.

Other authors offer more expanded definitions of democratic consolidation, many of them centered on the achievement of a high degree of "institutionalization."[12] Usually these definitions do not see elections as an institution.[13] They focus on complex organizations, basically the executive, parties, congress, and sometimes the judiciary. Many valuable studies have been conducted from this point of view. By the very logic of their assessment of many new polyarchies as noninstitutionalized, however, these studies presuppose, as their comparative yardstick, a generic and somewhat idealized view of the old polyarchies. The meaning of such a yardstick perplexes me: Often it is unclear whether it is something like an average of characteristics observed within the set of old polyarchies, or an ideal type generated from some of these characteristics, or a generalization to the whole set of the characteristics of some of its members, or a normative statement of preferred traits. Furthermore, this mode of reasoning carries a strong teleological flavor. Cases that have not "arrived" at full institutionalization, or that do not seem to be moving in this direction, are seen as stunted, frozen, protractedly unconsolidated, and the like. Such a view presupposes that there are, or should be, factors working in favor of increased consolidation or institutionalization, but that countervailing "obstacles" stymie a process of change that otherwise would operate unfettered.[14] That some of these polyarchies have been in a state of "protracted unconsolidation"[15] for some 20 years suggests that there is something extremely odd about this kind of thinking.

One book on the subject, entitled *The Politics of Democratic Consolidation: Southern Europe in Comparative Perspective,* is a case in point.[16] This is the first in a series of five volumes, resulting from an eight-year project that involved, as coauthors and discussants, many of the most active and distinguished students of democratization. The introduction (pp. 1–32) and the conclusions (pp. 389–413) by the coeditors and codirectors of the project offer an impressively learned distillation of these extensive scholarly exchanges. These texts are also paradigmatic of the views that I am criticizing. The editors use the concept of "*trajectories* of democratic transitions and consolidations," with which, even though they warn that it "should in no way be understood as implying a deterministic conceptual bias," they intend to "capture and highlight the particular combination and interplay of freedom and constraint *at each successive stage of the democratization process*" (p. xvi, emphasis added). Further on, they state, "We regard *continued movement towards the ideal type of democratic consolidation* as very significant" (p. 9, emphasis added). Consistent with this view, most of Latin America—in contrast to Southern European countries that the authors say became consolidated democracies in part because they "leap-frogged" democratization and developmental *stages*— is seen as "*still* struggling with transitional problems of varying, and often major, magnitude and intensity" (p. xiv–xvi, emphasis added). An exception is Chile, where the transition is "*moving towards consolidation*" (p. 19, emphasis added), and "seems to be *well on its way to successful completion*" (p. 389, emphasis added). The Southern European countries, after achieving consolidation, are said to be entering yet another stage of "democratic persistence," which is the "end product of a long democratization process" (p. xiii, passim).

One way or the other, polyarchies that are seen as unconsolidated, noninstitutionalized, or poorly institutionalized are defined negatively, for what they lack: the type and degree of institutionalization presumably achieved by old polyarchies. Yet negative definitions shift attention away from building typologies of polyarchies on the basis of the specific, positively described traits of each type.[17] Such typologies are needed, among other purposes, for assessing each type's likelihood of endurance, for exploring its patterns of change, and for clarifying the various dimensions on which issues of quality and performance of polyarchy may be discussed and researched.

There is no theory that would tell us why and how the new polyarchies that have institutionalized elections will "complete" their institutional set, or otherwise become "consolidated." All we can say at present is that, as long as elections are institutionalized, polyarchies are likely to endure. We can add the hypothesis that this likelihood is greater for polyarchies that are formally institutionalized. But this proposition is not terribly interesting unless we take into account other factors that most likely have strong independent effects on the survival chances of polyarchies.[18] Consequently, calling some polyarchies "consolidated" or "highly institutionalized" may be no more than saying that they are institutionalized in ways that one expects and of which one approves. Without a theory of how and why this may happen, it is at best premature to expect that newer polyarchies will or should become "consolidated" or "highly institutionalized." In any event, such a theory can only be elaborated on the basis of a positive description of the main traits of the pertinent cases.

The Importance of Informal Rules

Polyarchy is the happy result of centuries-long processes, mostly in countries in the global Northwest. In spite of many variations among these countries, polyarchy is embodied in an institutional package: a set of rules and institutions (many of them complex organizations) that is explicitly formalized in constitutions and auxiliary legislation. Rules are supposed to guide how individuals in institutions, and individuals interacting with institutions, behave. The extent to which behavior and expectations hew to or deviate from formal rules is difficult to gauge empirically. But when the fit is reasonably close, formal rules simplify our task; they are good predictors of behavior and expectations. In this case, one may conclude that all or most of the formal rules and institutions of polyarchy are fully, or close to fully, institutionalized.[19] When the fit is loose or practically nonexistent, we are confronted with the double task of describing actual behavior and discovering the (usually informal) rules that behavior and expectations do follow. Actors are as rational in these settings as in highly formalized ones, but the contours of their rationality cannot be traced without knowing the actual rules, and the common knowledge of these rules, that they follow. One may define this situation negatively, emphasizing the lack of fit between formal rules and observed behavior. As anthropologists have long known, however, this is no substitute for studying the actual rules that are being followed; nor does it authorize the assumption that somehow there is a tendency toward increasing compliance with formal rules. This is especially true when informal rules are widely shared and deeply rooted; in this case, it may be said that these rules (rather than the formal ones) are highly institutionalized.[20]

To some extent this also happens in the old polyarchies. The various laments, from all parts of the ideological spectrum, about the decay of democracy in these countries are largely a consequence of the visible and apparently increasing gap between formal rules and the behavior of all sorts of political actors. But the gap is even larger in many new polyarchies, where the formal rules about how political institutions are supposed to work are often poor guides to what actually happens.

Many new polyarchies do not lack institutionalization, but a fixation on highly formalized and complex organizations prevents us from seeing an extremely influential, informal, and sometimes concealed institution: clientelism and, more generally, particularism. For brevity's sake, I will put details and nuances aside[21] and use these terms to refer broadly to various sorts of nonuniversalistic relationships, ranging from hierarchical particularistic exchanges, patronage, nepotism, and favors to actions that, under the formal rules of the institutional package of polyarchy, would be considered corrupt.[22]

Particularism—like its counterparts, neopatrimonial[23] and delegative conceptions and practices of rule—is antagonistic to one of the main aspects of the full institutional package of polyarchy: the behavioral, legal, and normative distinction between a public and a private sphere. This distinction is an important aspect of the formal institutionalization of polyarchy. Individuals performing roles in political and state institutions are supposed to be guided not by particularistic motives but by universalistic orientations to some version of the public good. The boundaries between the public and the private are often blurred in the old polyarchies, but the very notion of the boundary is broadly accepted and, often, vigorously asserted when it seems breached by public officials acting from particularistic motives. Where particularism is pervasive, this notion is weaker, less widely held, and seldom enforced.

But polyarchy matters, even in the institutional spheres that, against their formal rules, are dominated by particularism. In congress, the judiciary, and some actions of the executive, rituals and discourses are performed as if the formal rules were the main guides of behavior. The consequences are twofold. On one side, by paying tribute to the formal rules, these rituals and discourses encourage demands that these rules be truly followed and that public-oriented governmental behavior prevail. On the other side, the blatant hypocrisy of many of these rituals and discourses breeds cynicism about the institutions of polyarchy, their incumbents, and "politicians" in general. As long as this second consequence is highly visible, particularism is taken for granted, and practiced as the main way of gaining and wielding political power. In such polyarchies, particularism is an important part of the regime.[24] Polyarchies are regimes, but not all polyarchies are the same kind of regime.

Here we see the ambiguity of the assertion made by Juan J. Linz, Adam Przeworski,[25] and others who argue that consolidation occurs when democracy becomes "the only game in town." It is clear that these authors are referring to the formal rules of polyarchy. More generally, even though they may not refer to "institutionalization," authors who limit themselves to the term "consolidation" also assert, more or less implicitly, the same close fit between formal rules and actual behavior.[26] For example, Przeworski argues that democratic consolidation occurs "when no one can imagine acting outside the democratic institutions." But this does not preclude the possibility that the games played "inside" the democratic institutions are different from the ones dictated by their formal rules. Przeworski also states: "To put it somewhat more technically, democracy is consolidated when compliance—acting within the institutional framework—constitutes the equilibrium of the decentralized strategies of all the relevant forces."[27] Clearly, Przeworski is assuming that there is only one equilibrium, the one generated by a close fit between formal rules and behavior. Yet however inferior they may be in terms of performances and outcomes that we value, the situations that I am describing may constitute an equilibrium, too.[28]

A Theoretical Limbo

If the main criterion for democratic consolidation or institutionalization is more or less explicitly a reasonably close fit between formal rules and actual behavior, then what of countries such as Italy, Japan, and India? These are long-enduring polyarchies where, by all indications, various forms of particularism are rampant. Yet these cases do not appear problematic in the literature I am discussing. That they are listed as "consolidated" (or, at least, not listed as "unconsolidated") suggests the strength—and the inconsistency—of this view. It attaches the label "consolidated" to cases that clearly do not fit its arguments but that have endured for a significantly longer period than the new polyarchies have so far. This is a typical paradigmatic anomaly. It deals with these cases by relegating them to a theoretical limbo,[29] as if, because they are somehow considered to be "consolidated," the big gaps between their formal rules and behavior were irrelevant. This is a pity, because variations that are theoretically and empirically important for the study of the whole set of existing polyarchies are thereby obscured.

Another confusing issue is raised by the requirement of "legitimacy" that some definitions of consolidation add. Who must accept formal democratic rules, and how deep must this acceptance run? Here, the literature oscillates between holding that only certain leaders need adhere to democratic principles and arguing that most of the country's people should be democrats, and between requiring normative acceptance of these principles and resting content with a mere perception that there is no feasible alternative to democracy. The scope of this adherence is also problematic: Is it enough that it refers to the formal institutions of the regime, or should it extend to other areas, such as a broadly shared democratic political culture?

Given these conceptual quandaries, it is not surprising that it is impossible clearly to specify when a democracy has become "consolidated." To illustrate this point, consider the "tests" of democratic consolidation that Gunther, Diamandouros, and Puhle propose. These tests supposedly help them to differentiate the consolidated Southern European cases from the unconsolidated Latin American, as well as East European and Asian, ones. The indicators that "may constitute evidence that a regime is consolidated" are: 1) "alternation in power between former rivals";[30] 2) "continued widespread support and stability during times of extreme economic hardship"; 3) "successful defeat and punishment of a handful of strategically placed rebels"; 4) "regime stability in the face of a radical restructuring of the party system"; and 5) "the absence of a politically significant antisystem party or social movement" (pp. 12–13).

With respect to Latin America, it bears commenting in relation to each of these points that: 1) alternations in government through peaceful electoral processes have occurred in Latin America as frequently as in Southern Europe; 2) in the former, support for regime stability has persisted—in Argentina, Brazil, and Bolivia, among other countries—even in the face of far more acute recessions than Southern Europe has seen, and in the midst of quadruple-digit inflation; 3) the record of punishment is poor, albeit with important exceptions in both regions; 4) even when thinking about Italy today, it is hard to imagine party-system restructurings more radical than the ones that occurred in Bolivia, Brazil, and Ecuador; and 5) "antisystem" political parties are as absent from the Latin American as from the Southern European polyarchies. The indicators of democratic consolidation invoked by these authors (and shared by many others) suffer from extreme ambiguity.[31] Finally, one might note that their argument points toward a *reductio ad absurdum,* for one could in following its logic argue that Latin America's polyarchies are actually "more consolidated" because they have endured more "severe tests" (p. 12) than their Southern European counterparts.

Polyarchies, Particularism, and Accountability

It almost goes without saying that all actual cases exhibit various combinations of universalism and particularism across various relevant dimensions. This observation, however, should not lead to the Procrustean solution of lumping all cases together; differences in the degree to which each case approximates either pole may justify their separate classification and analysis. Of course, one may for various reasons prefer a political process that adheres quite closely to the formal rules of the full institutional package of polyarchy. Yet there exist polyarchies—some of them as old as Italy, India, and Japan, or in Latin America, Colombia, and Venezuela—that endure even though they do not function as their formal rules dictate. To understand these cases we need to know what games are really being played, and under what rules.

In many countries of the global East and South, there is an old and deep split between the *pays réel* and the *pays légal*. Today, with many of these countries claiming to be democracies and adopting a constitutional framework, the persistence and high visibility of this split may not threaten the survival of their polyarchies—but neither does it facilitate overcoming the split. Institutions are resilient, especially when they have deep historical roots; particularism is no exception. Particularism is a permanent feature of human society; only recently, and only in some places and institutional sites, has it been tempered by universalistic norms and rules. In many new polyarchies, particularism vigorously inhabits most formal political institutions, yet the incumbency of top government posts is decided by the universalistic process of fairly counting each vote as one. This may sound paradoxical but it is not; it means that these are polyarchies, but they are neither the ones that the theory of democracy had in mind as it grew out of reflection on the political regimes of the global Northwest, nor what many studies of democratization assume that a democracy should be or become.

That some polyarchies are informally institutionalized has important consequences. Here I want to stress one that is closely related to the blurring of the boundary between the private and the public spheres: Accountability, a crucial aspect of formally institutionalized polyarchy, is seriously hindered. To be sure, the institutionalization of elections means that retrospective electoral accountability exists, and a reasonably free press and various active segments of society see to it that some egregiously unlawful acts of government are exposed (if seldom punished). Polyarchy, even if not formally institutionalized, marks a huge improvement over authoritarian regimes of all kinds. What is largely lacking, however, is another dimension of accountability, which I call "horizontal." By this I mean the controls that state agencies are supposed to exercise over other state agencies. All formally institutionalized polyarchies include various agencies endowed with legally defined authority to sanction unlawful or otherwise inappropriate actions by other state agents. This is an often-overlooked expression of the rule of law in one of the areas where it is hardest to implant, that is, over state agents, especially high-ranking officials. The basic idea is that formal institutions have well-defined, legally established boundaries that delimit the proper exercise of their authority, and that there are state agencies empowered to control and redress trespasses of these boundaries by any official or agency. These boundaries are closely related to the private-public boundary, in that those who perform public roles are supposed to follow universalistic and public-oriented rules, rather than their own particular interests. Even though its actual functioning is far from perfect, this network of boundaries and accountabilities is an important part of the formal institutionalization of the full package of polyarchy.[32]

By contrast, little horizontal accountability exists in most new polyarchies. Furthermore, in many of them the executive makes strenuous, and often successful, efforts to erode whatever horizontal accountability does exist. The combination of institutionalized elections, particularism as a dominant political institution, and a big gap between the formal rules and the way most political institutions actually work makes for a strong affinity with delegative, not representative, notions of political authority. By this I mean a caesaristic, plebiscitarian executive that once elected sees itself as empowered to govern the country as it deems fit. Reinforced by the urgencies of severe socioeconomic crises and consonant with old *volkisch,* nonindividualistic conceptions of politics, delegative practices strive headlong against formal political institutionalization; congress, the judiciary, and various state agencies of control are seen as hindrances placed in the way of the proper discharge of the tasks that the voters have delegated to the executive. The executive's efforts to weaken these institutions, invade their legal authority, and lower their prestige are a logical corollary of this view.[33] On the other hand, as Max Weber warned, institutions deprived of real power and responsibility tend to act in ways that seem to confirm the reasons adduced for this deprivation. In the cases that concern us here, particularism becomes even more rampant in congress and parties, courts ostensibly fail to administer justice, and agencies of control are eliminated or reduced to passivity. This context encourages the further erosion of legally established authority, renders the boundary between public and private even more tenuous, and creates enormous temptations for corruption.

In this sea of particularism and blurred boundaries, why does the universalistic process of fair and competitive elections survive? Governments willing to tamper with laws are hardly solid guarantors of the integrity of electoral processes. Part of the answer, at least with respect to elections to top national positions, is close international attention and wide reporting abroad of electoral irregularities. Fair elections are the main, if not the only, characteristic that certifies countries as democratic before other governments and international opinion. Nowadays this certification has important advantages for countries and for those who govern them. Within the country, elections are a moment when something similar to horizontal accountability operates: parties other than the one in government are present at the polling places, sharing an interest in preventing fraud. Elections create a sharp focus on political matters and on the symbols and rituals that surround the act of voting. At this moment, the citizens' sense of basic fairness manifests itself with special intensity. Violations are likely to be immediately reported. Faced with the protests that might ensue and their repercussions in the international media, and considering the further damage that would come from trying to impose obviously tainted results, most governments are willing to run the risks inherent in fair and competitive elections.

Pervasive particularism, delegative rule, and weak horizontal accountability have at least two serious drawbacks. The first is that the generalized lack of control enables old authoritarian practices to reassert themselves.[34] The second is that, in countries that inaugurated polyarchy under conditions of sharp and increasing inequality, the making and implementation of policy becomes further biased in favor of highly organized and economically powerful interests.

In the countries that occupy us here, the more properly political, *democratic* freedoms are effective: uncoerced voting; freedom of opinion, movement, and association; and others already listed. But for large sections of the population, basic *liberal* freedoms are denied or recurrently trampled. The rights of battered women to sue their husbands and of peasants to obtain a fair trial against their landlords, the inviolability of domiciles in poor neighborhoods, and in general the right of the poor and various minorities to decent treatment and fair access to public agencies and courts are often denied. The effectiveness of the whole ensemble of rights, democratic and liberal, makes for full civil and political citizenship. In many of the new polyarchies, individuals are citizens only in relation to the one institution that functions in a manner close to what its formal rules prescribe—elections. As for full citizenship, only the members of a privileged minority enjoy it.[35] Formally institutionalized polyarchies exhibit various mixes of democracy, liberalism, and republicanism (understood as a view that concurs with liberalism in tracing a clear public-private distinction, but that adds an ennobling and personally demanding conception of participation in the public sphere). Informally institutionalized polyarchies are democratic, in the sense just defined; when they add, as they often do, the plebiscitarian component of delegative rule, they are also strongly majoritarian. But their liberal and republican components are extremely weak.

Freeing Ourselves from Some Illusions

I have rapidly covered complicated terrain.[36] Lest there be any misunderstanding, let me insist that I, too, prefer situations that get close to real observance of the formal rules of polyarchy, a citizenry that firmly approves democratic procedures and values, fair application of the law in all social and geographical locations, and low inequality. Precisely because of this preference, I have argued for the need to improve our conceptual tools in the complex task of studying and comparing the whole set of existing polyarchies. It is through a nonteleological and, indeed, nonethnocentric, positive analysis of the main traits of these polyarchies that we scholars can contribute to their much-needed improvement. This is especially true of the polyarchies that are institutionalized in ways we dislike and often overlook, even if they do not—and some of them may never—closely resemble the "consolidated democracies" of the Northwest.

For this purpose, we must begin by freeing ourselves from some illusions. As an author who has committed most of the mistakes I criticize here, I suspect that we students of democratization are still swayed by the mood of the times that many countries have more or less recently passed through. We believe that democracy, even in the rather modest guise of polyarchy, is vastly preferable to the assortment of authoritarian regimes that it has replaced. We shared in the joy when those regimes gave way, and some of us participated in these historic events. These were moments of huge enthusiasm and hope. Multitudes demanded democracy, and international opinion supported them. The demand for democracy had many meanings, but in all cases it had a powerful common denominator: "Never Again!"[37] Whatever confused, utopian, or limited ideas anyone held concerning democracy, it was clear that it meant getting rid of the despots once and for all. Democracy, even if— or perhaps precisely because—it had so many different meanings attached to it, was the central mobilizing demand that had to be achieved and preserved forever. Somehow, it was felt, this democracy would soon come to resemble the sort of democracy found in admired countries of the Northwest—admired for their long-enduring regimes and for their wealth, and because both things seemed to go together. As in these countries, after the transition democracy was to be stabilized, or consolidated; the Northwest was seen as the endpoint of a trajectory that would be largely traversed by getting rid of the authoritarian rulers. This illusion was extremely useful during the hard and uncertain times of the transition. Its residue is still strong enough to make democracy and consolidation powerful, and consequently pragmatically valid, terms of political discourse.[38] Their analytical cogency is another matter.

On the other hand, because the values that inspired the demands for democracy are as important as ever, the present text is an effort toward opening more disciplined avenues for the study of a topic—and a concern—I share with most of the authors that I have discussed: the quality, in some cases rather dismal, of the social life that is interwoven with the workings of various types of polyarchy. How this quality might be improved depends in part on how realistically we understand the past and present situation of each case.

NOTES

For their comments on an earlier version of this text, I am grateful to Michael Coppedge, Gabriela Ippolito-O'Donnell, Scott Mainwaring, Sebastián Mazzuca, Peter Moody, Gerardo Munck, and Adam Przeworski.

1. Reflecting the lack of clearly established criteria in the literature, David Collier and Steven Levitsky have inventoried and interestingly discussed the more than 100 qualifiers that have been attached to the term "democracy." Many such qualifiers are intended to indicate that the respective cases are in some sense lacking the full attributes of democracy as defined by each author. See Collier and Levitsky, "Democracy 'With Adjectives': Finding Conceptual Order in Recent Comparative Research" (unpubl. ms., University of California–Berkeley, Political Science Department, 1995).

2. I have tried unsuccessfully to find terms appropriate to what the literature refers to as highly vs. noninstitutionalized (or poorly institutionalized), or as consolidated vs. unconsolidated democracies, with most of the old polyarchies belonging to the first terms of these pairs, and most of the new ones to the second. For reasons that will be clear below, I have opted for labeling the first group "formally institutionalized" and the second "informally institutionalized," but not without misgivings: in the first set of countries, many things happen outside formally prescribed institutional rules, while the second set includes one highly formalized institution, elections.

3. This list is from Robert Dahl, *Democracy and Its Critics* (New Haven: Yale University Press, 1989), 221; the reader may want to examine further details of these attributes, discussed by Dahl in this book.

4. See, especially, J. Samuel Valenzuela, "Democratic Consolidation in Post-Transitional Settings: Notion, Process, and Facilitating Conditions," in Scott Mainwaring, Guillermo O'Donnell, and J. Samuel Valenzuela, eds., *Issues in Democratic Consolidation: The New South American Democracies in Comparative Perspective* (Notre Dame: University of Notre Dame Press, 1992), 57–104; and Philippe C. Schmitter and Terry Lynn Karl, "What Democracy Is . . . and Is Not," *Journal of Democracy* 2 (Summer 1991): 75–88.

5. See Terry Lynn Karl, "The Hybrid Regimes of Central America," *Journal of Democracy* 6 (July 1995): 73–86; and "Imposing Consent? Electoralism vs. Democratization in El Salvador," in Paul Drake and Eduardo Silva, eds., *Elections and Democratization in Latin America, 1980–85* (San Diego: Center for Iberian and Latin American Studies, 1986), 9–36.

6. See, especially, Juan J. Linz and Alfred Stepan, *Problems of Democratic Transition and Consolidation: Southern Europe, South America, and Postcommunist Europe* (Baltimore: Johns Hopkins University Press, 1996); and Philippe Schmitter, "Dangers and Dilemmas of Democracy," *Journal of Democracy* 5 (April 1994): 57–74.

7. For a useful listing of these institutional variations, see Schmitter and Karl, "What Democracy Is . . . and Is Not."

8. For a more-detailed discussion of institutions, see my "Delegative Democracy," *Journal of Democracy* 5 (January 1994): 56–69.

9. The term "reasonable" is admittedly ambiguous. Nowhere are these freedoms completely uncurtailed, if by nothing else than the political consequences of social inequality. By "reasonable" I mean that there are neither de jure prohibitions on these freedoms nor systematic and usually successful efforts by the government or private actors to annul them.

10. On the other hand, elections can be made more authentically competitive by, say, measures that diminish the advantages of incumbents or of economically powerful parties. These are, of course, important issues. But the point I want to make at the moment is that these differences obtain among countries that already qualify as polyarchies.

11. Juan J. Linz, "Transitions to Democracy," *Washington Quarterly* 13 (1990): 156. The assertion about "the only game in town" entails some ambiguities that I discuss below.

12. Even though most definitions of democratic consolidation are centered around "institutionalization" (whether explicitly or implicitly, by asserting acceptance or approval of democratic institutions and their formal rules), they offer a wide variety of additional criteria. See Doh Chull Shin, "On the Third Wave of Democratization: A Synthesis and Evaluation of Recent Theory and Research," *World Politics* 47 (October 1994): 135–70.

13. Even though he does not use this language, an exception is the definition of democratic consolidation offered by J. Samuel Valenzuela, which is centered in what I call here the institutionalization of elections and the absence of veto powers; see his "Democratic Consolidation in Post-Transitional Settings," 69.

14. It is high time for self-criticism. The term "stunted" I used jointly with Scott Mainwaring and J. Samuel Valenzuela in the introduction to our *Issues in Democratic Consolidation,* 11. Furthermore, in my chapter in the same volume (pp. 17–56), I offer a nonminimalist definition of democratic consolidation, and propose the concept of a "second transition," from a democratically elected government to a consolidated democratic regime. These concepts partake of the teleology I criticize here. This teleological view is homologous to the one used by many modernization studies in the 1950s and 1960s; it was abundantly, but evidently not decisively, criticized at the time. For a critique of the concept of "democratic consolidation" that is convergent with mine, see Ben Ross Schneider, "Democratic Consolidations: Some Broad Comparisons and Sweeping Arguments," *Latin American Research Review* 30 (1995): 215–34; Schneider concludes by warning against "the fallacy of excessive universalism" (p. 231).

15. Philippe C. Schmitter with Terry Lynn Karl, "The Conceptual Travels of Transitologists and Consolidologists: How Far to the East Should They Attempt to Go?" *Slavic Review* 63 (Spring 1994): 173–85.

16. Richard Gunther, P. Nikiforos Diamandouros, and Hans-Jürgen Puhle, eds., *The Politics of Democratic Consolidation: Southern Europe in Comparative Perspective* (Baltimore: Johns Hopkins University Press, 1995).

17. We should remember that several typologies have been proposed for formally institutionalized polyarchies; see, especially, Arend Lijphart, *Democracies: Patterns of Majoritarian and Consensus Government in Twenty-one Countries* (New Haven: Yale University Press, 1984). This work has been extremely useful in advancing knowledge about these polyarchies, which underscores the need for similar efforts on the now greatly expanded whole set of polyarchies. For an attempt in this direction see Carlos Acuña and William Smith, "Future Politico-Economic Scenarios for Latin America," in William Smith, Carlos Acuña, and Eduardo Gamarra, eds., *Democracy, Markets, and Structural Reform in Latin America* (New Brunswick, N.J.: Transaction, 1993), 1–28.

18. Adam Przeworski and his collaborators found that higher economic development and a parliamentary regime increase the average survival rate of polyarchies. These are important findings, but the authors have not tested the impacts of socioeconomic inequality and of the kind of informal institutionalization that I discuss below. Pending further research, it is impossible to assess the causal direction and weight of all these variables. I suspect that high socioeconomic inequality has a close

relationship with informal institutionalization. But we do not know if either or both, directly or indirectly, affect the chances of survival of polyarchy, or if they might cancel the effect of economic development that Przeworski et al. found. See Adam Przeworski and Fernando Limongi, "Modernization: Theories and Facts" (Working Paper No. 4, Chicago Center for Democracy, University of Chicago, November 1994); and Adam Przeworski, Michael Alvarez, José Antonio Cheibub, and Fernando Limongi, "What Makes Democracies Endure?" *Journal of Democracy* 7 (January 1996): 39–55.

19. A topic that does not concern me here is the extent to which formal rules are institutionalized across various old polyarchies and, within them, across various issue areas, though the variations seem quite important on both counts.

20. The lore of many countries is filled with jokes about the naive foreigner or the native sucker who gets in trouble by following the formal rules of a given situation. I have explored some of these issues with reference to Brazil and Argentina in "Democracia en la Argentina: Micro y Macro" (Working Paper No. 2, Kellogg Institute for International Studies, University of Notre Dame, 1983); "Y a mí qué me importa? Notas Sobre Sociabilidad y Política en Argentina y Brasil" (Working Paper No. 9, Kellogg Institute for International Studies, University of Notre Dame, 1984); and "Micro-Escenas de la Privatización de lo Público en Brasil" (Working Paper No. 21, with commentaries by Roberto DaMatta and J. Samuel Valenzuela, Kellogg Institute for International Studies, University of Notre Dame, 1989).

21. For the purposes of the generic argument presented in this essay, and not without hesitation because of its vagueness, from now on I will use the term "particularism" to refer to these phenomena. On the contemporary relevance of clientelism, see Luis Roniger and Ayse Gunes-Ayata, eds., *Democracy, Clientelism, and Civil Society* (Boulder, Colo.: Lynne Rienner, 1994). For studies focused on Latin America that are germane to my argument, see especially Roberto DaMatta, *A Case e a Rua*: *Espaço, Cidadania, Mulher e Morte no Brasil* (São Paulo: Editora Brasiliense, 1985); Jonathan Fox, "The Difficult Transition from Clientelism to Citizenship," *World Politics* 46 (January 1994): 151–84; Francis Hagopian, "The Compromised Transition: The Political Class in the Brazilian Transition," in Scott Mainwaring et al., *Issues in Democratic Consolidation*, 243–93; and Scott Mainwaring, "Brazilian Party Underdevelopment in Comparative Perspective," *Political Science Quarterly* 107 (Winter 1992–93): 677–707. These and other studies show that particularism and its concomitants are not ignored by good field researchers. But, attesting to the paradigmatic force of the prevalent views on democratization, in this literature the rich data and findings emerging from such case studies are not conceptually processed as an intrinsic part of the *problématique* of democratization, or are seen as just "obstacles" interposed in the way of its presumed direction of change.

22. Particularistic relationships can be found in formally institutionalized polyarchies, of course. I am pointing here to differences of degree that seem large enough to require conceptual recognition. One important indication of these differences is the extraordinary leniency with which, in informally institutionalized polyarchies, political leaders, most of public opinion, and even courts treat situations that in the other polyarchies would be considered as entailing very severe conflicts of interest.

23. For a discussion of neopatrimonialism, see my "Transitions, Continuities, and Paradoxes," in Scott Mainwaring et al., *Issues in Democratic Consolidation*, 17–56. An interesting discussion of neopatrimonialism is Jonathan Hartlyn's "Crisis-Ridden Elections (Again) in the Dominican Republic: Neopatrimonialism, Presidentialism, and Weak Electoral Oversight," *Journal of Interamerican and World Affairs* 34 (Winter 1994): 91–144.

24. By "regime" I mean "the set of effectively prevailing patterns (not necessarily legally formalized) that establish the modalities of recruitment and access to governmental roles, and the permissible resources that form the basis for expectations of access to such roles," as defined in my *Bureaucratic Authoritarianism: Argentina,*

1966–1973, in Comparative Perspective (Berkeley: University of California Press, 1988), 6.

25. Adam Przeworski, *Democracy and the Market: Political and Economic Reforms in Eastern Europe and Latin America* (Cambridge: Cambridge University Press, 1991).

26. See, among many others that could be cited (some transcribed in Shin, "On the Third Wave of Democratization"), the definition of democratic consolidation proposed by Richard Gunther, P. Nikiforos Diamandouros, and Hans-Jürgen Puhle in *Politics of Democratic Consolidation,* 3: "the achievement of substantial attitudinal support for and behavioral compliance with the new democratic institutions and the rules which they establish." A broader but equivalent definition is offered four pages later.

27. Adam Przeworski, *Democracy and the Market,* 26.

28. In another influential discussion, Philippe C. Schmitter, although he does not use this language, expresses a similar view of democratic consolidation; see his "Dangers and Dilemmas of Democracy," *Journal of Democracy* 5 (April 1994): 56–74. Schmitter begins by asserting, "In South America, Eastern Europe, and Asia the specter haunting the transition is . . . nonconsolidation. . . . These countries are 'doomed' to remain democratic almost by default." He acknowledges that the attributes of polyarchy may hold in these countries—but these "patterns never quite crystallize" (pp. 60–61). To say that democracy exists "almost by default" (that is, is negatively defined) and is not "crystallized" (that is, not formally institutionalized) is another way of stating the generalized view that I am discussing.

29. An exception is Richard Gunther et al., *Politics of Democratic Consolidation,* where Italy is one of the four cases studied. But the way they deal with the events in Italy is exemplary of the conceptual problems I am discussing. They assert that in Italy "several important partial regimes . . . were challenged, became deconsolidated, and entered into a significant process of restructuring beginning in 1991" (p. 19). On the same page, the reader learns that these partial regimes include nothing less than "the electoral system, the party system, and the structure of the state itself." (Added to this list later on is "the basic nature of executive-legislative relations" [p. 394].) Yet the "Italian democracy remains strong and resilient"—after practically every important aspect of its regime, and even of the state, became "deconsolidated" (p. 412). If the authors mean that, in spite of a severe crisis, the Italian polyarchy is likely to endure, I agree.

30. Actually, the authors are ambiguous about this first "test." Just before articulating their list of tests with this one at its head, they assert that they "reject [peaceful alternation in government between parties that were once bitterly opposed] as a *prerequisite* for regarding a regime as consolidated." See Richard Gunther et al., *Politics of Democratic Consolidation,* 12 (emphasis added).

31. In the text on which I am commenting, the problem is further compounded by the use of categories such as "partial consolidation" and "sufficient consolidation" (which the authors say preceded "full consolidation" in some Southern European cases). They even speak of a stage of "democratic persistence" that is supposed to follow the achievement of "full [democratic] consolidation."

32. I may have sounded naive in my earlier comments about how individuals performing public roles are supposed to be guided by universalistic orientations to some version of the public good. Now I can add that, as the authors of the *Federalist Papers* knew, this is not only, or even mostly, a matter of the subjective intentions of these individuals. It is to a large extent contingent on institutional arrangements of control and accountability, and on expectations built around these arrangements, that furnish incentives (including the threats of severe sanctions and public discredit) for that kind of behavior. That these incentives are often insufficient should not be allowed to blur the difference with cases where the institutional arrangements are

nonexistent or ineffective; these situations freely invite the enormous temptations that always come with holding political power. I wish to thank Adam Przeworski and Michael Coppedge for raising this point in private communications.

33. The reader has surely noticed that I am referring to countries that have presidentialist regimes and that, consequently, I am glossing over the arguments, initiated by Juan J. Linz and followed up by a number of other scholars, about the advantages of parliamentarism over the presidentialist regimes that characterize Latin America. Although these arguments convince me in the abstract, because of the very characteristics I am depicting I am skeptical about the practical consequences of attempting to implant parliamentarism in these countries.

34. For analyses of some of these situations, see Paulo Sérgio Pinheiro, "The Legacy of Authoritarianism in Democratic Brazil," in Stuart S. Nagel, ed., *Latin American Development and Public Policy* (New York: St. Martin's, 1995), 237–53; and Martha K. Huggins, ed., *Vigilantism and the State in Modern Latin America: Essays on Extralegal Violence* (New York: Praeger, 1991). See also the worrisome analysis, based on Freedom House data, that Larry Diamond presents in his "Democracy in Latin America: Degrees, Illusions, and Directions for Consolidation," in Tom Farer, ed., *Beyond Sovereignty: Collectively Defending Democracy in the Americas* (Baltimore: Johns Hopkins University Press, 1995). In recent years, the Freedom House indices reveal, more Latin American countries have regressed than advanced. For a discussion of various aspects of the resulting obliteration of the rule of law and weakening of citizenship, see Guillermo O'Donnell, "On the State, Democratization, and Some Conceptual Problems: A Latin American View with Glances at Some Post-Communist Countries," *World Development* 21 (1993): 1355–69.

35. There is a huge adjacent theme that I will not discuss here: the linkage of these problems with widespread poverty and, even more, with deep inequalities of various sorts.

36. Obviously, we need analyses that are more nuanced, comprehensive, and dynamic than the one that I have undertaken here. My own list of topics meriting much further study includes: the opportunities that may be entailed by demands for more universalistic and public-oriented governmental behavior; the odd coexistence of pervasive particularism with highly technocratic modes of decision making in economic policy; the effects of international demands (especially regarding corruption and uncertainty in legislation and adjudication) that the behavior of public officials should conform more closely to the formal rules; and the disaggregation of various kinds and institutional sites of clientelism and particularism. Another major issue that I overlook here, raised by Larry Diamond in a personal communication, is locating the point at which violations of liberal rights should be construed as cancelling, or making ineffective, the political freedoms surrounding elections. Finally, Philippe C. Schmitter makes an argument worth exploring when he urges that polyarchies be disaggregated into various "partial regimes"; most of these would surely look quite different when comparing formally versus informally institutionalized cases. See Schmitter, "The Consolidation of Democracy and Representation of Social Groups," *American Behavioral Scientist* 35 (March–June 1992): 422–49.

37. This is the title of the reports of the commissions that investigated human rights violations in Argentina and Brazil. For further discussion of what I call a dominant antiauthoritarian mood in the transitions, see my "Transitions, Continuities, and Paradoxes," in Scott Mainwaring et al., *Issues in Democratic Consolidation,* 17–56; and Nancy Bermeo, "Democracy and the Lessons of Dictatorship," *Comparative Politics* 24 (April 1992): 273–91.

38. Symptomatically illustrating the residues of the language and the hopes of the transition as well as the mutual influences between political and academic discourses, on several occasions the governments of the countries that I know more closely (Argentina, Brazil, Chile, and Uruguay) triumphantly proclaimed that their democracies had become "consolidated."

10

O'DONNELL'S "ILLUSIONS": A REJOINDER

Richard Gunther, P. Nikiforos Diamandouros, and Hans-Jürgen Puhle

Richard Gunther *is professor of political science at Ohio State University.* **P. Nikiforos Diamandouros** *is professor of political science at the University of Athens, and is the National Ombudsman of Greece.* **Hans-Jürgen Puhle** *is professor of political science at the University of Frankfurt.*

Now that the "third wave" of democratization has apparently ended, the research agenda for many social scientists logically shifts from the processes through which new democratic regimes come into being to a greater concern with the viability and prospects for long-term survival of those new regimes, as well as to various aspects of the performance of democratic institutions and the quality of political and social life following the transition from nondemocratic rule. The three Southern European countries of Greece, Portugal, and Spain were the first to initiate and complete transitions to democracy in this so-called third wave. Recognizing that they therefore represent an important laboratory for the systematic study of these research questions, a group of social scientists established a Committee on the Nature and Consequences of Democracy in the New Southern Europe under the auspices of the American Council of Learned Societies and the Social Science Research Council. Its principal function was to commission explicitly comparative research on the various dimensions of political, economic, social, and cultural change that have unfolded with such great speed within the region. The first product of this collaborative endeavor was a book that we edited entitled *The Politics of Democratic Consolidation: Southern Europe in Comparative Perspective.*[1]

In chapter 9 of this volume, Guillermo O'Donnell takes issue with some of the concepts set forth in that book, and, indeed, with the very notion of democratic consolidation. The concept, he contends, is inherently teleological and based on a narrow Northern European view of democracy that may not be easily adaptable to non-European settings. We fundamentally disagree with these assertions.

Before dealing with O'Donnell's main points, we must correct a significant error in his interpretation of our concept of democratic consolidation. Our definition begins with the recognition that the concept is necessarily double-barreled—it joins two distinct dimensions that must be assessed separately in analyzing the status of political regimes. In order to conclude that democratic consolidation has taken place in a particular country, it is necessary first to ascertain whether the country's new political regime is fully democratic, and then to determine whether that democracy is consolidated. In our conceptualization, both democracy and consolidation are ideal types, and both must be closely approximated before one can conclude that democratic consolidation has occurred. The definition of democracy that we use is the procedural conceptualization set forth by Juan Linz in his classic essay on regime typologies. Accordingly, a regime can be regarded as democratic "when it allows for the free formulation of political preferences, through the use of basic freedoms of association, information and communication, for the purpose of free competition between leaders to validate at regular intervals by nonviolent means their claim to rule . . . without excluding any effective political office from that competition or prohibiting any members of the political community from expressing their preference."[2] It should be noted that this is a very demanding definition that goes well beyond the mere convening of elections as the criterion for determining that a system is democratic. It is also entirely compatible with Robert Dahl's operationalization of the concept of "polyarchy," on which O'Donnell bases his critique.

Consolidation involves a second dimension, relating to the stabilization, routinization, institutionalization, and legitimation of patterns of politically relevant behavior. Specifically, we consider a democratic regime to be consolidated when all politically significant groups regard its key political institutions as the only legitimate framework for political contestation, and adhere to democratic rules of the game. This definition thus includes an attitudinal dimension, wherein existing political institutions are regarded as acceptable and without legitimate alternatives, as well as a behavioral criterion, according to which a specific set of norms is respected and adhered to by all politically significant groups. It also involves an institutional criterion that is broader than the electoral process per se; it encompasses all of those governmental or representative institutions over which disagreement among politically significant groups—for example, debates about monarchy vs. republic, or parliamentarism vs. presidentialism—could undermine the legitimacy of the regime.

The term "politically significant," we should note, builds into the definition a degree of flexibility—a necessary feature of all ideal-type conceptualizations. As with all ideal types, there is no real-world case in which *all* citizens or political groups strictly obey democratic rules of the game and fully acknowledge the legitimacy of the political institutions and principles under which they live: Every fully democratic society will include some political dissidents or social deviants who reject or violate these criteria (examples would be the "Montana Freemen" in the United States, or the Red Brigades in Italy in the 1970s). While these inevitable departures from strict conformity with the ideal type do not undermine the utility of such concepts in comparative analysis, they do sometimes make it difficult to locate with precision the dividing line (or what O'Donnell calls the "cutting point") between (in this instance) consolidated and unconsolidated democratic regimes. Since regime sustainability over the long term is the principal concern of those who utilize the concept of consolidation, we focus our attention primarily but not exclusively on politically mobilized sectors of society, and on organized groups and their leaders: These are the individuals and groups who have the capacity (owing to their strategic locations or organizational resources) to destabilize a democratic system.

Consensus, Stability, and Survival

When all the politically significant groups in a new democracy acknowledge its political institutions as the only legitimate arena for political contestation and adhere to their behavioral norms, we regard the system as sufficiently consolidated: Even though it falls short of "full consolidation" (the unachievable end point of our ideal-type continuum, where all individuals in a society join in the democratic consensus), the regime has sufficient support and resilience to be able to survive and remain stable in the face of serious challenges. In this respect, our definition is not as demanding as some others (such as Geoffrey Pridham's "positive consolidation")[3] that insist upon adherence to democratic norms and values by virtually all individuals in a society, whether they are politically mobilized and organized or not. Those other conceptualizations usually require the complete transformation of a society's political culture—a process that may require generations. We contend, in contrast, that regimes can become sufficiently consolidated in a relatively short period of time (five years after the first democratic elections in the case of Spain, between three and seven years in the case of Greece), and that the nature of politics within such regimes is fundamentally different than in those that are unconsolidated. This is not to say that the broadening and deepening of the democratic consensus to include unorganized, unmobilized sectors of society is unimportant: Continued progress toward "full consolidation" at the extreme end of the continuum can further reinforce the resilience of the regime, and reduce the prospects that it might become destabilized in the future. As long as marginalized and alienated sectors of a society exist, there remains the possibility that at some point in the future they may be mobilized and organized, thereby posing a threat to regime stability. But over the short and medium term, it is the stance of organized, active groups that has the most direct relevance for the prospects for regime stability and survival.

How does one determine whether a regime is consolidated? It is over this question of indicators that O'Donnell most seriously misstates our argument. He attributes to us the following view (p. 121):

> The indicators that "may constitute evidence that a regime is consolidated" are: 1) "alternation in power between former rivals"; 2) "continued widespread support and stability during times of extreme economic hardship"; 3) "successful defeat and punishment of a handful of strategically placed rebels"; 4) "regime stability in the face of a radical restructuring of the party system"; and 5) "the absence of a politically significant antisystem party or social movement."

Actually, only the fifth of these points correctly restates our argument. In fact, we explicitly *reject* the other four as indicators of consolidation, arguing that the use of these kinds of criteria commonly runs the risk of leading the analyst into tautological argumentation. Our book states:

> It is commonly argued that peaceful alternation in government between parties that were once bitter rivals constitutes such a test. We reject the use of this as a prerequisite for regarding a regime as consolidated, not only because we believe it reflects conceptual confusion, but also because it leads to some rather absurd applications to the real world: according to this criterion, the democratic regimes of Japan and Italy . . . would not have been regarded as consolidated until the 1990s. While the passing of a severe test (alternation in power between former rivals, continued widespread support and stability during times of extreme economic hardship, successful defeat and punishment of a handful of strategically placed rebels, or regime stability in the face of a radical restructuring of the party system) may constitute evidence that a regime is consolidated, that test should not be confused with the concept of consolidation itself (p. 12).

We add: "The absence of sufficient regime consolidation may be *confirmed* by subsequent acts such as a military coup or mass-level protest and rebellion, but in order to avoid tautological argumentation these kinds of obvious behavioral manifestations should never be relied upon as the sole measure of a lack of consolidation" (p. 13). Instead, given our concern that such *post hoc* indicators are conducive to tautological argument, we insist that the extent of consolidation achieved by a given democracy should be determined through the use of "unequivocal empirical measures" that have predictive value. These include "public statements by leaders of political parties, social movements, and large secondary organizations, by official documents and ideological declarations made by such groups, and by symbolic gestures and behavioral habits that reflect a denial of the legitimacy of a regime's representative institutions and its behavioral norms." We add that, while the existence of a sizeable antisystem party is a very useful indicator of the absence of consolidation, the extent to which a party is or is not antisystem must not be ascertained on the basis of accusations by rival parties, but must be independently confirmed by the analyst "on the basis of [the antisystem party's] official ideological and programmatic declarations, speeches by their elites, or probing interviews with party leaders" (p. 13). We think that only on the basis of a misreading of these theoretical ground rules would one conclude (as O'Donnell did) that they are "ambiguous" or inconsistent.

Our main argument with O'Donnell involves his claim that our notion of consolidation is inherently teleological. If by "teleological" he means that we (and others who treat consolidation as a central issue) assume some kind of automatic or "natural" progression toward some ultimate, *a priori* specified objective, then we must vigorously disagree. Indeed, in our concluding chapter, we point to important features of the Italian and Portuguese democratization experiences (not to mention the Basque regional exception to Spain's otherwise rapid and successful consolidation) as "powerful reminders that consolidation is not and should not be conceived of as a linear process, moving inexorably towards successful completion. Empirical reality has amply demonstrated in recent years that protractedness, stagnation, temporary reversal, and, quite often, deconsolidation are equally, if not more likely outcomes" (p. 392). We explicitly argue that consolidation should be conceived of not as a "phase" that follows transition in a neat temporal sequence, but rather as a "process" that may temporally overlap with that of transition, and the outcome of which is entirely indeterminate.

Beyond Institutions

Not only do we reject the notion that consolidation is inherently teleological, but we also remain convinced that the concept captures an extremely important dimension of the democratization process. As the ultimate fates of large numbers of new democracies established in Europe after the First World War or in Africa following decolonization clearly reveal, merely creating democratic institutions and holding elections captures only part of the process through which stable, viable democratic systems come into being. All but two of those new interwar democracies, and all but one of the postcolonial African democracies, collapsed in less than two decades. Clearly there is something beyond the creation of these institutions that must be taken into consideration in assessing the success of the democratization process. We believe that consolidation represents an extraordinarily important part of that process, and that reliable empirical indicators can be used to measure the success or failure of new democratic regimes in becoming institutionalized and legitimate in the eyes of politically powerful groups or of the general public.

We are struck, for example, by the tremendous differences in levels of public support for democratic regimes in Southern Europe and in certain Latin American and East European countries that have redemocratized in the course of the third wave. In three successive public opinion surveys conducted between 1988 and 1992, for example, the percentages of Brazilians agreeing with the statement "Democracy is preferable to any other form of government" never exceeded 48 percent. In sharp contrast, a 1992 Eurobarometer survey found that fully 78 percent of Spaniards (a figure equivalent to the average of all European Union countries) and 90 percent of Greeks endorsed that statement. Conversely, in the aforementioned surveys, between 17 percent and 24 percent of Brazilians opted for the alternative statement "Under some circumstances, an authoritarian regime, a dictatorship, is preferable to a democratic system," while only 9 percent of Spaniards (again, equal to the EU average) and 4 percent of Greeks did so.[4] Indeed, in accord with our hypothesis that consolidation *can* occur rather quickly, mass-level attitudinal support for democracy in Spain just five years after Franco's death had achieved levels that were indistinguishable from those in the established democracies in Western Europe. In a nationwide survey conducted in 1982, only 7 percent of Spaniards agreed with the statement "It is better to have only one person to make decisions for us" (down from 18 percent eight years earlier), while fully 81 percent of Spaniards endorsed the notion "It is better to have decisions made by a group of persons elected by the citizens" (up from 60 percent in 1974 and 35 percent in 1966).[5]

These mass-level survey data are matched by statements by key political elites. All politically significant nationwide Spanish parties unequivocally endorsed the new democratic system and its key institutions in 1978. In contrast, even some mainstream Brazilian political leaders have made flagrantly semiloyal statements that might help to undermine support for the current regime.[6] The magnitude of these differences in both mass and elite orientations is so substantial as to suggest that there are some extremely important qualitative differences between consolidated and unconsolidated regimes.

As a more detailed examination of the Spanish case indicates, these attitudinal indicators of consolidation have proved to be of considerable utility in predicting behavior directly relevant to the stability and long-term survival of democratic regimes. Having, in 1978, unequivocally endorsed the new regime, all nationwide parties, including Alianza Popular (founded by leading figures of the Franco regime), remained steadfast in their support of democracy in the face of a coup attempt in 1981 by segments of the military that were not at that time part of the democratic consensus.[7] More importantly, the partial, regional exception to the success of the Spanish transition—in the Basque region—lends even greater support to the validity of our concept of consolidation: Basque nationalist parties publicly adopted stands that were semiloyal (Basque Nationalist Party) or outright antisystem (Herri Batasuna) vis-à-vis the new regime. This lack of elite-level consolidation within the region is entirely compatible with the extremely high level of polarization and political violence that unfolded over the decade following enactment of the constitution (between 1979 and 1988, 465 persons were killed by the Basque-nationalist terrorist organization ETA). Thus the political evolution of the Basque region is the mirror image of the moderation and unwavering support for democracy that has characterized the rest of Spain (even in the face of unemployment levels that sometimes exceeded 23 percent of the labor force).

Why Elections Are Not Enough

Our disagreements with O'Donnell go beyond our differing assessments of the validity and utility of the concept of democratic consolidation, and extend to what he proposes as an alternative to that concept. While he objects primarily to the term "consolidation," most of his article seems to be questioning our definition of democracy. In this he is quite inconsistent, discussing at one point the holding of elections as the only institution relevant to the study of democratization, and elsewhere broadening his focus from "formal" institutions and rules to "informal polyarchies," including clientelistic structures and procedures. If he is placing greatest stress on the former, we would regard his concept as excessively minimalist, and incapable of capturing meaningful dimensions of the institutionalization and stabilization of democracy. Merely institutionalizing free elections is insufficient, in our view, to classify a system as fully democratic. There are other, more demanding criteria that must be met under Linz's and our definition: Even after two rounds of democratic elections had been held in Chile, for example, we regarded that country's democratization as incomplete, insofar as General Augusto Pinochet still retained significant reserve powers that violated basic tenets of democracy and the key principle of civilian, democratic control of the military.

Similarly, the range of institutions that we regard as relevant to regime consolidation and long-term stability goes beyond the electoral process (which O'Donnell argues should suffice as an alternative to our concept of democratic consolidation). Many debilitating and potentially destructive fights have erupted among contending forces that accept the electoral process but reject other key democratic institutions. The polarization and violence that characterized the Spanish Basque region throughout the first decade of the new regime's existence did not derive from

differences of opinion over the electoral process: The structure of the
state was the primary bone of contention. This leads us to conclude that
the core representative and governmental institutions of the new regime
must also be institutionalized and legitimate in order for the regime to
qualify as consolidated.

We are also puzzled by O'Donnell's references to informal polyarchies as complements or even alternatives to the formal institutions
that customarily serve as foci for studies of democratization. To be sure,
all democracies (formally defined) include to varying degrees informal
structures of the kind O'Donnell discusses. Given the emphasis he places
on these networks (even to the extent that they might serve as alternatives
to formal institutions—see pp. 121–23 of this volume), his argument
seems to shade over into the conventional debate between "substantive"
and "procedural" definitions of democracy. On the one hand, his
insistence on elections as the major requirement for calling a polity
democratic leads him in the direction of a minimalist definition of the
procedural kind. On the other, in making the degree of fit between formal
rules and actual behavior a central attribute of his definition of democracy, he implicitly moves in the direction of a maximalist definition
that not even the most advanced industrial democracies (around which
he accuses us of building our ideal type) can meet. But this is clearly
self-contradictory, because it pulls his argument in conceptually
opposite directions that, in the final analysis, are difficult to reconcile.

Finally, we are most perplexed by the argument that "a fixation on
highly formalized and complex organizations prevents us from seeing
an extremely influential, informal, and sometimes concealed institution:
clientelism and, more generally, particularism . . . [that is,] various sorts
of nonuniversalistic relationships, ranging from hierarchical particularistic exchanges, patronage, nepotism, and favors to actions that, under
the formal rules of the institutional package of polyarchy, would be
considered corrupt" (p. 119). O'Donnell suggests that a substantial analytical advance can be secured by expanding our definition of democracy
beyond the "ethnocentric" formal definition that we use to include such
informal hierarchies. While under no circumstances would we deny the
prevalence and political importance of clientelism and particularism,
we do question O'Donnell's unstated assumption that these phenomena
are not incompatible with the stability of democracy. To be sure, political
systems within which elections are regularly held and are institutionalized have often coexisted with and been penetrated by clientelism in
many countries and at many periods in history—from American big-
city machines to the *cacique*-ridden "limited democracies" and "pseudo-
democracies" of Southern Europe and Latin America in the late
nineteenth and twentieth centuries. In fact, it is certainly the case that
particularistic arrangements exist in all democratic systems, albeit to
greatly varying degrees. We contend, however, that over the long run

such practices are antithetical to the quality of democracy, and that if these practices become too pervasive, they could result in the delegitimation of democracy. By definition, particularism and clientelism seem to us incompatible with the unhindered exercise of suffrage: particularism, because it involves and perpetuates unequal treatment of individuals or groups; clientelism, because it entails systematic and persistent power imbalances within society, polity, and economy. Over the long term, moreover, resentment over these exploitative relationships breeds discontent that can help to undermine the stability of the regime—as the demise of the Southern European limited democracies in the early twentieth century clearly attests. Indeed, we regard the inherent incompatibilities between the internal logics of "formal" democracy and pervasive particularism as so significant that they render O'Donnell's proposed reconceptualization theoretically problematic.

NOTES

1. Richard Gunther, P. Nikiforos Diamandouros, and Hans-Jürgen Puhle, eds., *The Politics of Democratic Consolidation: Southern Europe in Comparative Perspective* (Baltimore: Johns Hopkins University Press, 1995).

2. Juan J. Linz, "Totalitarian and Authoritarian Regimes," in Fred I. Greenstein and Nelson W. Polsby, eds., *Handbook of Political Science,* 8 vols. (Reading, Mass.: Addison-Wesley, 1975), 3:182–83.

3. Geoffrey Pridham, "The International Context of Democratic Consolidation: Southern Europe in Comparative Perspective," in Richard Gunther, P. Nikiforos Diamandouros, and Hans-Jürgen Puhle, eds., *Politics of Democratic Consolidation,* 169.

4. Brazilian data from José María Maravall, *Los resultados de la democracia: Un estudio del sur y el este de Europa* (Madrid: Alianza Editorial, 1995), 272; Spanish and Greek data from Eurobarometer 37 (Brussels: European Union, 1992).

5. Rafael López Pintor, *La opinión pública española: Del franquismo a la democracia* (Madrid: Centro de Investigaciones Sociológicas, 1982), 84.

6. Leonel Brizola, for example, was quoted by the *Jornal do Brasil* (Rio de Janeiro) as having said that "if there is no civil reaction [against privatizations], there will be a military one" (18 May 1995, 1), and by the *Fôlha de São Paulo* as explaining that he would consider a military intervention against privatizations as a positive act (18 May 1995, 1). The following day, the Rio de Janeiro newspaper *O Globo* published an article under the headline "Cardoso Criticizes Brizola for Defending a Military Coup" (19 May 1995, 3). These kinds of exchanges between top-ranking national political elites have been completely absent from Spain's political discourse since the early 1980s, reflecting an important qualitative difference between the two regimes.

7. Felipe Agüero's study entitled *Soldiers, Civilians and Democracy: Post-Franco Spain in Comparative Perspective* (Baltimore: Johns Hopkins University Press, 1995) found that the potential threat to democracy posed by the Spanish military disappeared after 1982, reinforcing our conclusion that democratic consolidation at the national level was completed at that time.

11

ILLUSIONS AND CONCEPTUAL FLAWS: A RESPONSE

Guillermo O'Donnell

Guillermo O'Donnell is Helen Kellogg Professor of Government and International Studies at the University of Notre Dame. This essay is a response to the critique offered by Richard Gunther, P. Nikiforos Diamandouros, and Hans-Jürgen Puhle in chapter 10 of this volume.

In their rejoinder, Richard Gunther, P. Nikiforos Diamandouros, and Hans-Jürgen Puhle (henceforth "the authors") discuss several issues: those pertaining to my critique of their use of "democratic consolidation"; those related to my doubts about the idea of democratic consolidation more generally; and their own critique of the alternative criteria sketched in my essay. The first set of issues is most relevant to this exchange, although I will briefly discuss the others as well.

The authors define democratic consolidation as "the achievement of substantial attitudinal support and behavioral compliance with the new democratic institutions and rules of the game they establish."[1] Since "full consolidation" is an ultimately unattainable "ideal type" (p. 5 and rejoinder), it suffices that "all politically significant groups" (p. 7) provide such support and compliance. When this is the case, a democracy is "sufficiently consolidated." The authors locate the "dividing line" between "consolidated and unconsolidated democratic regimes" where "democratic regimes are *sufficiently consolidated* so as to survive and remain stable in the face of such serious challenges as major economic or international crises, or even serious outbreaks of terrorist violence" (p. 8, italics in original).

This approach has several flaws. It fails to distinguish between survival and stability as a *definitional* component of sufficient consolidation and as a *consequence* of the consolidation resulting from the attitudinal and behavioral acceptance of the regime (p. 3). It also fails to distinguish between democratic consolidation as a *process* and as a *regime attribute* achieved after "successful completion" of the former (p. 389). Lastly, if "all politically significant actors" accept a regime's "rules of the game," it is not astounding news to assert that, other things being equal, this regime is consolidated—or likely to endure, or stable, or any equivalent idea.[2]

The authors view consolidation as a several-stage process. It begins, and may overlap, with the transition from an authoritarian regime (pp. xii–xiii; we are not told how to distinguish processes pertaining to the one or the other). The democracy resulting from the transition may be simply unconsolidated, but it may also be "partially consolidated," or "substantially consolidated"; or it may be consolidated at the national but not the regional level—all this before eventually reaching "sufficient consolidation."[3] In turn, partial consolidation may mean that only some of the "partial regimes"[4] have consolidated (p. 410), or it may refer to a *stage* between nonconsolidation and sufficient consolidation. Nor need the latter stage be the end, for then may come "the stage of democratic persistence" (p. 413), which "represents the end product of a long democ-ratization process" (p. xiii). Surprisingly, we read that at this stage "entirely new theoretical and practical concerns move to center stage, as the imperatives of transition and consolidation fade into the back-ground of social inquiry" (p. 412). Presumably this applies in the cases of "Greece, Portugal, and Spain [which] are examples of consolidation and continuing [sic] democratic persistence" (p. 413).

Still other possibilities exist: A consolidated or even a persistent democracy may deconsolidate and break down, or it may deconsolidate and reequilibrate, as in contemporary Italy (p. 15), or, in a different interpretation of this same case, see some of its partial regimes decon-solidate (p. 394)—in these cases we are not told if regimes are just reconsolidated or if they can return directly to the stage of persistence. Additionally, in categories even more casually drawn, a consolidated democracy may be "mired in its own contradictions and, hence [sic], become frozen" as a result of pacts (p. 406), or there may be "consol-idated limited democracies" (p. 413), or even democracies that, puzzlingly, are "by and large consolidated" (p. 25).

I find all this confusing. How can we know when a democracy is substantially consolidated (that is, no longer simply unconsolidated but not yet sufficiently consolidated), or substantially but "not yet" suffic-iently consolidated, or partly consolidated, or when some of its partial regimes have consolidated or deconsolidated, or when it has moved from consolidation to persistence? Now I examine how the authors treat cases.

Cases and Indicators

Beyond their own assertions, the authors give no indication that would allow us to recognize when most of their "stages" have been reached. We do get some concrete references when they discuss Spain, but these lead to the further expansion of confusing and empirically untraceable categories. We are told that in Spain before 1982–83, "substantial progress towards consolidation had been achieved" (p. 10), but that it "cannot be argued that full consolidation had been achieved by that time" (p. 11).[5] Then we read that Spanish democracy "has been substantially consolidated since about 1982 or 1983" (p. 21). At first sight, "substantial" would seem to be a synonym for "sufficient," yet it is not: The authors tell us that in Spain by 1982–83, consolidation had reached "completion at the national level" (p. 390), but this had not yet happened at the regional one, considering the antisystem opposition based in the Basque region (p. 11).[6] Further inklings that "substantial" and "sufficient" are not intended as synonyms come when we read that Greece (p. 31) and Italy were also cases of "substantial but incomplete levels of consolidation" (p. 22) before reaching a sufficient one. Furthermore, assuming that "incomplete" is equivalent to "partial" (otherwise the former would be still another "stage"), it seems that there is something more to substantial than to partial consolidation even if it still falls short of sufficient consolidation. Partial consolidation is not to be taken lightly, however, as it "constituted an essential resource that enabled the [Spanish] regime to survive [the] extreme test" of the 1981 coup attempt (p. 11). But surviving an "extreme test" is exactly the criterion that the authors propose for recognizing sufficient consolidation! How can we know, then, what is indicated by these "unequivocal empirical measures that have predictive value" (rejoinder)?

The authors' other criterion for sufficient consolidation, the absence of an important antisystem party or social movement, underlies the surprising argument that Italian democracy remained at "substantial but incomplete levels of consolidation" (p. 22) for about 30 years, in contrast to the speedy achievement of sufficient consolidation, and even democratic persistence, by the other three countries studied.[7]

We are left without indications for recognizing most of the consolidation stages the authors envisage. Yet the authors' rejoinder denies that the first four criteria I transcribed from their book (p. 12) should be considered as indicators of (sufficient) consolidation. In their book they correctly assert that these criteria "should not be confused with the concept of consolidation itself"; they say on the same page that "the passing of a severe test . . . may constitute evidence that a regime is consolidated" (p. 12), adding that this and other kinds of information "should never be relied upon as the *sole* measure of a lack of [sufficient] consolidation" (p. 13, italics added). If one is looking for indicators of "sufficient consolidation," these seem reasonably good ones (although not the only ones), particularly considering the convenience of using a multi-indicator approach to map so complex and multidimensional a concept as "consolidation," whether sufficient or not. Although the authors' book proposes crisis stability as a criterion for (sufficient) consolidation, in their rejoinder they weaken their case by asserting that they accept only "the absence of a politically significant antisystem party or social movement" as an adequate indicator of such a "stage." These two criteria may sometimes overlap, but they are different and may operate independently; using both gives the authors a stronger case. Let us see how these criteria operate.

In relation to Southern Europe, the authors are consistent when they consider the lack of antisystem actors, or regime survival or stability in the face of major crises, as prime indicators of sufficient consolidation. Yet their book explicitly intends to be broadly comparative, so we should look at how these criteria function in other areas of the world. Their picture is dismal. Only Uruguay and Costa Rica are considered (sufficiently, I gather) consolidated democracies. "Chile's transition seems to be well on its way to successful completion"; the rest of Latin America is "still struggling with transition problems of varying, and often major, magnitude and intensity"—but the situation in the postcommunist countries is "even worse" (p. 389). Elsewhere only South Korea "seems to have made considerable progress towards consolidation," while the other East Asian countries "still find themselves in various stages of their uncertain democratic transitions" (p. 390).

What are the grounds for these sweeping statements? Let us remember the criteria proposed by the authors: regime survival without destabilization, and no important antisystem actors. If these are the criteria, the authors' universe of sufficiently consolidated democracies would have to be broadened to include, among the new Latin American democracies, at least Argentina, Bolivia, and Brazil. These countries survived, without becoming politically destabilized or generating important antisystem actors, far more severe social and economic crises than Southern Europe has. The authors' error regarding some postcommunist countries is even more blatant. The Czech Republic, Hungary, Poland, and Slovenia have seen no significant antisystem party or social movement, have survived *"simultaneous* transition to democracy and to a market economy" (p. 390, italics in original; see also p. 396), including severe social and economic crises, and have even moved toward increasingly stable party and electoral systems. It is surprising that the authors do not apply their own criteria and conclude that these countries have worked the miracle of near-instantaneous "consolidation."

I must conclude that the authors do not use their own criteria consistently, or that these "reliable empirical indicators" (rejoinder) lack the analytical and empirical edge they claim.

Teleology

By a teleological concept I mean one which posits, explicitly or implicitly, that a given entity inherently tends to move from lower (or immature or incomplete) to higher (or more mature, or complete) stages, up to an end point that marks the full development of its potentialities. Characteristically, the stages are understood from their end point: A seed is "basically" a potential tree, or a given democracy is, as the authors put it, "not yet" sufficiently consolidated. Entities are defined negatively, characterized not by their specific attributes but by what they lack in relation to the paradigmatic end point of their presumed trajectory. Negative definitions generate residual categories: Cases are classified together on the basis of their sharing the lack of attributes that the more developed specimens of the same genus supposedly have. Furthermore, such a view usually entails conceiving of progress as movement through various "stages" along the posited "trajectory" toward "successful completion," that is, "'full consolidation' at the extreme end of the continuum"[8] (rejoinder). Consequently, other kinds of changes are deemed deviations from the proper trajectory, and factors that apparently hinder upward changes are seen merely as "obstacles" to such changes.

Thus democracies are classified not as positively defined types X or Y, but as (sufficiently) consolidated, or unconsolidated, or partially consolidated, or substantially but not sufficiently consolidated, and other references to what they lack in relation to the ideal type. The location of each case in the presumed "trajectory"—its "stage"—determines how it is conceptualized. Of course, if such a trajectory does not exist, or cannot be mapped with even minimal precision, analyses based on this view will be theoretically flawed and most probably misleading.[9]

We have seen that teleological thinking abounds in the authors' book. Furthermore, they properly, if perhaps unwittingly, emphasize their use of "the concept of trajectory [which] is meant to capture and highlight the particular combination and interplay of freedom and constraint at each successive stage of the democratization process" (p. xvi), adding that they "regard continued movement towards the ideal type of democratic consolidation . . . as very significant" (p. 9), a movement that leads to the "successful completion" of (sufficient) consolidation (pp. 389, 405). The rejoinder strongly reiterates these views.

I argued that teleological views entail negative definitions of lower-end cases that wind up in analytically useless residual categories; this book is an extreme instance of this flaw. The authors describe "unconsolidated" democracies as cases where "important and powerful elites and their supporters deny the legitimacy of the existing regime and may seek to overthrow it," where "few political actors are prepared to stake their futures on the workings of democratic institutions . . . [in part] because they also perceive rival political parties as conditional in their support for democracy," and where "mass mobilizations in the streets take the place of bargaining among representative elites," as a consequence of which a cycle "may be set in motion that progressively polarizes relations among groups and raises the overall level of violence within the polity" (p 10). But here the authors describe situations that simply do not fit a definition of democracy—neither the authors' nor the one I proposed in my essay. The cases that meet the authors' somber description are not consolidated democracies because, to begin with, they are not democracies. They correspond to Samuel P. Huntington's "mass praetorian" regimes, or they may be liberalized authoritarianisms or electoralist regimes—but they are not democracies.[10] Even if they have reasonably competitive elections and a fair count of the votes, they do not qualify as democracies, or polyarchies, because they lack other definitional attributes of this type of regime.

For a work that claims to have comparative import, the authors' book features a remarkable number of unwarranted generalizations about many of the new (and, in fact, also the old) democracies outside the Northwestern quarter of the globe. Many of these countries have serious problems derived from particularism and inequality (both of which are far from alien to Southern Europe). Yet even though several of these new democracies—including at least the Czech Republic, Hungary, Poland, Slovenia, Argentina, Bolivia, Brazil, Ecuador, Panama, Benin, and Malawi—show no signs of mass praetorianism or sheer electoralism, the authors lump them with nondemocratic countries in the residual, negatively defined category of "unconsolidated democracies." This is not a good way to forge the theoretical and comparative tools that the authors proclaim as one their goals.

Southern Europe and Latin America

In their rejoinder, the authors argue a truism. Obviously, before deciding if a democracy is consolidated, or if it belongs to type X, Y, or Z, one must define what one means by democracy. Against the opinion of the authors, we happen to agree on this matter. They use Juan Linz's definition, which, as they note, is similar to Robert Dahl's definition of polyarchy, which I adopted in my essay for reasons and with some additions explained there.[11]

Having cleared up this point, I now turn to the rejoinder's arguments about "Latin America," which actually refer only to Chile and Brazil. The authors see Chile as a case of "incomplete democratization"; they seem to use this argument to refute me, but, as should be clear from my essay, I agree with them. They further mention "the tremendous differences in levels of public support for democratic regimes" in Southern Europe vs. Latin America.[12] But public opinion data from several Latin American countries do not show this. The rejoinder cites only Brazilian surveys in which a proportion of respondents that "never exceeded 48 percent" agreed that "democracy is preferable to any other form of government." This they contrast with 78 and 90 percent agreement figures from Spain and Greece, respectively. Yet they fail to mention that 80 percent in Uruguay, 76.6 in Argentina, and 52.2 in Chile agreed with this same statement.[13] Again, the authors do not give even one clear and consistent indicator of (sufficient) consolidation, to say nothing of its various "stages."

The rejoinder also contains a misinformed allusion to "mainstream Brazilian political leaders [who] have made flagrantly semi-loyal statements." The only such leader turns out to be Leonel Brizola, who at the time had already fared dismally in elections, lost control of his party, and become a completely marginal figure. Furthermore, Brazil underwent a series of very "severe tests"[14] without politically destabilizing or generating any important antisystem party or social movement. According to the authors' own criteria, Brazil should be considered at least "substantially" consolidated.

On the subject of clientelism and, more generally, particularism, as important informal institutions in many new polyarchies, the rejoinder makes two points that I not only readily admit but elaborated in my essay. These are that all democracies "include to varying degrees informal structures of the kind O'Donnell discusses," and that widespread particularistic practices "are antithetical to the quality of democracy." But the authors go too far in claiming that these practices are "incompatible with the unhindered exercise of suffrage." This is simply empirically untrue. Furthermore, if the authors are right in drawing this conclusion because particularism "involves and perpetuates unequal treatment of individuals or groups" and clientelism "entails systematic and persistent power imbalances within society, polity, and economy," then they are implicitly making a radical critique of any democracy: Can they ignore the pervasive consequences of class, status, bureaucratic power, and so on that everywhere also perpetuate unequal treatment and generate systematic and persistent imbalances?

The authors also argue that "over the long term, resentment over these exploitative relationships . . . can help to undermine the stability of the regime." Yet in their own account, the "undermining of stability" may lead not to breakdown but to "reequilibration" at a higher point in the "consolidation trajectory." As for the relative likelihood of breakdown in informally institutionalized vs. formally institutionalized polyarchies, in my essay I declared myself agnostic pending better research. At least, I noted there that particularistic relationships are very important and pervasive in such long-lasting polyarchies as India and Japan and, indeed, Italy. With the exception of their already-quoted reference to Spain, the authors downplay in their book and ignore in their rejoinder a large literature showing the major role various kinds of particularistic phenomena play in the actual workings of the Southern European polyarchies.[15] I do not know how far these phenomena approximate those cases to the Latin American ones on which my essay focused. We will never know the answer, however, if we join the authors in dismissing these phenomena as pathologies that afflict cases that have not reached the fortunate status of "sufficient consolidation," and which they do not deem worth noting as "consolidated" cases.

NOTES

1. Richard Gunther, P. Nikiforos Diamandouros, and Hans-Jürgen Puhle, eds., *The Politics of Democratic Consolidation: Southern Europe in Comparative Perspective* (Baltimore: Johns Hopkins University Press, 1995), 3. Except when otherwise noted, all page references in parentheses are to this volume.

2. Assuming that a settlement can be reached regarding the eventually thorny issue of who are, or should be, the "politically significant actors."

3. The authors are inconsistent in the use of their terminology. Since they regard "full consolidation" as "the unachievable end point of our ideal-type continuum" (rejoinder), they deal with "sufficient consolidation" as the higher point in the consolidation "trajectory." On many occasions, however, they merely refer to "consolidation" or to a case as "consolidated," when in the context it seems that they should have added the qualifier "sufficient." In these cases, I add this term in parentheses or brackets.

4. See Philippe Schmitter, "Organized Interests and Democratic Consolidation in Southern Europe," in Richard Gunther, P. Nikiforos Diamandouros, and Hans-Jürgen Puhle, eds., *Politics of Democratic Consolidation*, 284–315.

5. Since "full" consolidation is an unattainable "ideal type," I gather that the text actually refers to "sufficient" consolidation.

6. The possibility of such a national-regional consolidation split, and its practical and theoretical consequences, are not elaborated.

7. The authors assert that "democracy in Italy was by and large consolidated" when "by the end of the 1970s, the PCI [Italian Communist Party] had demonstrated its reliability as a loyal democratic competitor" (p. 25). Until then, "concern over the PCI's commitment to democracy and its perceived antisystem stance constituted the major obstacles to consolidation" (p. 391). One could argue no less plausibly that since the Svolta de Salerno in 1944, the PCI had stubbornly demonstrated democratic loyalty (see Gianfranco Pasquino, "The Demise of the Fascist Regime and Italy's Transition to Democracy: 1943–1948," in Guillermo O'Donnell, Philippe Schmitter, and Laurence Whitehead, eds., *Transitions from Authoritarian Rule: Southern Europe* [Baltimore: John Hopkins University Press, 1986], 45–70), and that it was in the cynical interest of other political actors to raise the "specter of communism" to hinder the electoral chances of the former. The position of the authors in this matter seems influenced by another criterion of sufficient consolidation that they introduce entirely ad hoc. In their discussion of Portugal they refer to provisions of the 1976 Constitution, including those "guaranteeing the irreversibility of the nationalizations carried out during the revolutionary period," as the "last obstacle" to (sufficient) consolidation "removed through the May 1989 constitutional reform" (p. 28; see also p. 390). The rationale for this argument is that such clauses removed "important substantive policy issues from the everyday give and take of democratic politics" (p. 28). Here the authors give us a narrow and ahistorical implicit definition of democracy, according to which only issues of private property can be removed from political "give and take," and which has no place for a constitution that gives the state an important role in the economy. Their arguments about Greece are also indicative. In arguing "for using 1977 as the date signaling the end *[sic]* of consolidation," the authors point out as decisive the Greek Socialists' abandonment of their "erstwhile Third World orientations towards Greek foreign policy" (p. 30). Apparently democracies cannot exist, much less consolidate, if all politically significant actors do not share "the requisite conditions of moderation and restraint" (p. 391; see also p. 402) that the authors prefer—in this view India's and Israel's democracies cannot possibly have existed. These criteria are too ad hoc and subject to too many comparative variations across time and space to merit further discussion.

8. Notice, however, that according to the authors "the extreme end" is the "stage

of democratic persistence"; the criteria and even the end points of this "trajectory" seem to be in permanent oscillation.

9. Against the authors' disclaimers in both their book and rejoinder, a teleological view does not imply that all cases reach maturity, or that they cannot "freeze" at an intermediate stage, or that they cannot degenerate after reaching maturity. The point is that these events are seen as deviations from the proper, somehow preexistent path (p. 398). Moreover, a teleological view does not preclude asserting that a given entity has somehow "leap-frogged" some developmental stages (pp. xiv–xx), or that different objects may travel "quite different routes" (p. 19) toward the end point, or that progress toward the end point should be "unilinear" (p. 20).

10. On "mass praetorian" regimes, see Samuel P. Huntington, *Political Order in Changing Societies* (New Haven: Yale University Press, 1968). On "electoralist" regimes, see Terry L. Karl, "Imposing Consent? Electoralism vs. Democratization in El Salvador," in Paul Drake and Eduardo Silva, eds., *Elections and Democratization in Latin America, 1980–85* (San Diego: Center for Iberian and Latin American Studies, 1986), 9–36.

11. Because of space limitations, I refer the reader to this definition in my essay. Whatever its merits, this definition should suffice to show that only an extremely casual reading of my essay could have led the authors to assert that I regard "the holding of elections as the only institution relevant to the study of democratization," or to attribute to me a term ("informal polyarchies") that I never wrote and that bears no relation to the "informally institutionalized polyarchies" discussed in my essay.

12. Actually, in their book the authors are rather dismissive of the significance of this factor, and probably would have vigorously denied it if I had seen them using it as an indicator of consolidation. Furthermore, in their book they note that "pervasive cynicism at the mass level and extraordinarily low levels of mass-level involvement with politics reflect the incomplete status of efforts to resocialize the Spanish public" (p. 22). The reference is to Spain, but similar phenomena have been found in the other Southern European cases; see especially José María Maravall, *Los resultados de la democracia: Un estudio del sur y el este de Europa* (Madrid: Alianza Editorial, 1995), 257–302.

13. Data from Latino Barometer, 1995, transcribed by Juan Linz and Alfred Stepan, *Problems of Democratic Transition and Consolidation: Southern Europe, South America, and Postcommunist Europe* (Baltimore: Johns Hopkins University Press, 1996); I thank these authors for facilitating my access to these data. Should we conclude from these data that Uruguay and Argentina are "as consolidated" as Spain, while Greece is even more "consolidated" than these three countries, or that Chile, the only newly democratized Latin American country that the authors see as "well on its way" to consolidation, may not be so? Obviously, this does not seem a promising kind of discussion.

14. In addition to several years of four-digit inflation, one should count at least: the premature death of a very popular elected president (Tancredo Neves), five years of an extremely inept presidency (José Sarney), the impeachment for corruption of another president (Fernando Collor de Mello), and the indictment on similar charges of several prominent legislators—all without rumor or fear of military intervention. It should be noted, too, that Argentina not only weathered even higher inflation rates than Brazil but, when faced with a military-coup threat similar to Spain's, saw all political and social leaders (also as in Spain) rally unequivocally to democracy, with mass demonstrations supporting their stand. It seems that to the authors, surviving "severe tests" indicates "substantial" or "sufficient" consolidation in Southern Europe, but only "unconsolidation" in the rest of the world.

15. For an assessment and bibliographical references on these and related matters, see Maurizio Ferrera, "Il modello sud-europeo di welfare state," *Rivista italiana di scienza politica* 26 (April 1996): 21–66.

12

WHAT IS DEMOCRATIC CONSOLIDATION?

Andreas Schedler

Andreas Schedler, *professor of political science at the Facultad Latino-americana de Ciencias Sociales (FLACSO) in Mexico City, chairs the Research Committee on Concepts and Methods (C&M) of the International Political Science Association. His latest book (coedited with Larry Diamond and Marc F. Plattner) is* The Self-Restraining State: Power and Accountability in New Democracies *(1999). His current research focuses on democratization and electoral governance in Mexico in comparative perspective.*

During the past quarter-century, the "third wave" of global democratization has brought more than 60 countries around the world from authoritarian rule toward some kind of democratic regime.[1] This is no small achievement, of course, but it has also become apparent that sustaining democracy is often a task as difficult as establishing it. In the immediate aftermath of all these democratic transitions, pressing concerns have quickly arisen about how to strengthen and stabilize these new regimes. With the extension of democracy to additional countries now having slowed, political scientists—and political actors in new democracies—have been increasingly focusing on what has come to be called "democratic consolidation."

Originally, the term "democratic consolidation" was meant to describe the challenge of making new democracies secure, of extending their life expectancy beyond the short term, of making them immune against the threat of authoritarian regression, of building dams against eventual "reverse waves." To this original mission of rendering democracy "the only game in town," countless other tasks have been added. As a result, the list of "problems of democratic consolidation" (as well as the corresponding list of "conditions of democratic consolidation") has expanded beyond all recognition. It has come to include such divergent items as popular legitimation, the diffusion of democratic values, the neutralization of antisystem actors, civilian supremacy over the military, the elimination of authoritarian enclaves, party building, the organi-

zation of functional interests, the stabilization of electoral rules, the
routinization of politics, the decentralization of state power, the
introduction of mechanisms of direct democracy, judicial reform, the
alleviation of poverty, and economic stabilization.

At this point, with people using the concept any way they like, nobody can be sure exactly what it means to others, but all maintain the
illusion of speaking to one another in some comprehensible way.
While "democratic consolidation" may have been a nebulous concept
since its very inception, the conceptual fog that veils the term has only
become thicker and thicker the more it has spread through the academic
as well as the political world. If it is true that "[n]o scientific field can
advance far if the participants do not share a common understanding of
key terms in the field,"[2] then the study of democratic consolidation—at
its current state of conceptual confusion—is condemned to stagnation.
The aspiring subdiscipline of "consolidology" is anchored in an unclear, inconsistent, and unbounded concept, and thus is not anchored at
all, but drifting in murky waters. The use of one and the same term for
vastly different things only simulates a shared common language; in
fact, the reigning conceptual disorder is acting as a powerful barrier to
scholarly communication, theory building, and the accumulation of
knowledge.

I believe that we can order and comprehend the multiple usages and
meanings of "democratic consolidation" by looking at the concrete
realities as well as the practical tasks the term is meant to address. The
meaning that we ascribe to the notion of democratic consolidation
depends on where we stand (our empirical viewpoints) and where we
aim to reach (our normative horizons). It varies according to the contexts
and the goals we have in mind.

Viewpoints and Horizons

When students of democratization seek to classify regimes, the key
distinction, of course, runs between those that are democratic and those
that are not (the latter often generically labeled as "authoritarian"). The
most widely accepted criteria for identifying a country as democratic
have been put forward by Robert Dahl—civil and political rights plus
fair, competitive, and inclusive elections.[3] Dahl calls countries that meet
these criteria "polyarchies," but they are more commonly referred to as
"liberal democracies."

Two other subtypes of democracy have gained wide recognition in the
scholarly literature on new democracies. On the one hand, there are all
those borderline cases that possess some but not all of liberal democracy's
essential features, and therefore fall somewhere in between democracy
and authoritarianism. I call such semidemocratic regimes "electoral
democracies." This term is now generally used to describe a specific type

of semidemocracy—one that manages to hold (more or less) inclusive, clean, and competitive elections but fails to uphold the political and civil freedoms essential for liberal democracy. Here, however, I will use the term "electoral democracy" more broadly as a convenient shorthand for any kind of "diminished subtype" of democracy.[4]

On the other hand, there are those "advanced democracies" that presumptively possess some positive traits over and above the minimal defining criteria of liberal democracy, and therefore rank higher in terms of democratic quality than many new democracies. This term risks idealizing and reifying the wealthy Western democracies, but even if we recognize that admiring references to "established Western democracies" often rely on stereotypes, we have to acknowledge that discursive constructs (such as "democratic normality") are social realities too.

This four-fold classification—authoritarianism, electoral democracy, liberal democracy, advanced democracy—basically corresponds to the way David Collier and Steven Levitsky have ordered the semantic universe of democracy and its subtypes. In their admirable effort to bring order to the chaos of innumerable subtypes of democracy that circulate in contemporary democratization studies (they stopped counting at 550), they have distinguished precisely these four broad regime categories (even if they label them differently).[5] I want to show that these broad categories also provide a basis for reordering the conceptual map of consolidation studies, and for comprehending the manifold ways students of democracy use the term "democratic consolidation."

The Figure on the following page presents this classification of regime families graphically along a one-dimensional continuum of "democratic-ness," with authoritarian regimes placed at one end and advanced democracies at the other.[6] It depicts in a graphical way how these four regime types define the empirical contexts as well as the normative horizons and practical tasks that characterize distinct conceptualizations of democratic consolidation. The two middle categories, electoral and liberal democracy, represent the empirical referents of all debate on democratic consolidation. In normative terms, authoritarianism forms the outer negative horizon that democrats in both these kinds of regimes try to avoid, and advanced democracy forms the outer positive horizon that they try to approach. In addition, electoral democracy and liberal democracy constitute normative horizons for each other. While electoral democracy appears as liberal democracy's proximate horizon of avoidance, liberal democracy appears as electoral democracy's proximate horizon of attainment.

Now, those scholars who look (fearfully) from electoral or liberal democracy to authoritarianism equate democratic consolidation with avoiding an authoritarian regression, a "quick death" of democracy.

FIGURE—CONCEPTS OF DEMOCRATIC CONSOLIDATION

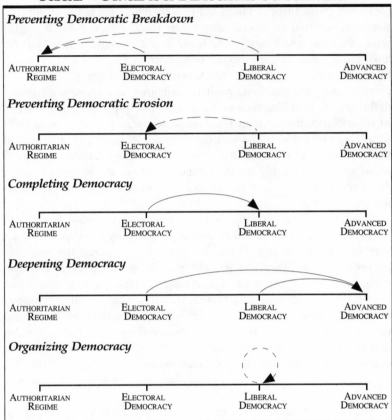

Those who look (hopefully) from electoral or liberal democracy to advanced democracy equate democratic consolidation with democratic deepening, with advances in the quality of democracy. Those who look (with concern) from liberal democracy to electoral democracy equate democratic consolidation with avoiding a "slow death" of democracy, the erosion of certain fundamental democratic features. And those who look (with impatience) from electoral democracy to liberal democracy equate democratic consolidation with completing democracy, with supplying its missing features.

We might say, tentatively, that those who are concerned with democratic stability and try to avoid regressions to either nondemocratic or semidemocratic regimes support "negative" notions of democratic consolidation, while those who are concerned with democratic advances and try to attain progress toward either liberal or high-quality democracy sponsor "positive" notions of democratic consolidation.[7]

In a way, this contextual and perspective-dependent approach tries to reconstruct the concept's teleological core. Of course, I am not the first to note the teleological quality of democratic consolidation. Both Ben Schneider and Guillermo O'Donnell have repeatedly criticized the notion's "strong teleological flavor."[8] These critics are right. Democratic consolidation is indeed an intrinsically teleological concept. Yet I think there is nothing inherently wrong with teleology, provided that three conditions are met: First, we have to avoid veiling or obscuring it; hidden teleology is indeed bad teleology. Second, we have to dissociate teleology from any belief in inevitable progress: Supporting some telos, some normative goal or practical task, is one matter; assuming "some kind of automatic or 'natural' progression" toward that goal is quite another.[9] Third, we have to acknowledge that the notion of democratic consolidation knows not merely one characteristic telos but many, and that this plurality of teloi accordingly defines a plurality of concepts of democratic consolidation.

Avoiding Democratic Breakdown

Once a transition from authoritarian rule in a given country has reached a point where (more or less) free, fair, and competitive elections are held, democratic actors usually cannot afford to relax and enjoy the "bounded uncertainty" of democratic rule. More often than not, regime-threatening "unbounded uncertainties" persist, and the democrats' fundamental concern shifts from establishing democracy's core institutions to securing what they have achieved. For these actors, consolidating democracy means reducing the probability of its breakdown to the point where they can feel reasonably confident that democracy will persist in the near (and not-so-near) future. This preoccupation with regime survival describes the "classical" meaning of democratic consolidation. It gives coherence to a broad and crowded semantic field where a wide range of semantic labels defines this telos in either positive or negative ways. In its positive formulations, this branch of consolidation studies speaks about reaching the goal of democratic continuity, maintenance, entrenchment, survival, permanence, endurance, persistence, resilience, viability, sustainability, or irreversibility. By contrast, negative formulations invoke the necessity of moving beyond democratic fragility, instability, uncertainty, vulnerability, reversibility, or the threat of breakdown. Whatever the differences in nuance, the unifying purpose beneath this multifaceted vocabulary is straightforward: It is basically preoccupied with keeping democracy alive, with preventing its sudden death.

In accordance with its focus on the danger of coups, this first notion of democratic consolidation is concerned above all with deviant or antisystem actors who harbor antidemocratic motives. In principle, the range of actors who actually or potentially fall into this category of dangerous elements is unlimited. In Latin America, with its recent history of bureaucratic-authoritarian regimes, fears of democratic breakdown have tended to focus on the professionals of state violence, as well as the business class, which had also acquired a solid antidemocratic reputation (until the latest cycle of democratization). But in fact, the list of (either suspected or convicted) assassins or gravediggers of democratic rule is much longer. It includes private men-at-arms (guerrillas, drug cartels, violent street protesters), elected presidents who stage military-backed *autogolpes,* and even disenchanted populations who may become tired of a democracy that has not delivered, in material terms, much more than economic hardship and social inequality.[10]

Eliminating, neutralizing, or converting disloyal players represents the primary task of democratic-breakdown prevention. Yet taming the enemy is by no means the only practical concern associated with the stabilization of democracy. Since democratic stability is a noble and un-controversial goal, some scholars tend to invoke anything positively valued in the name of democratic sustainability. They discuss, for example, economic performance, nation building and state building, the creation of mass legitimacy, the diffusion of democratic values, the elimination of authoritarian legacies, the institutionalization of party systems, and so forth. The list is endless. Sometimes these items are accompanied by plausible causal theories about how they affect chances for democratic survival, though often only through indirect and long chains of causation.[11]

Avoiding Democratic Erosion

As students of democratic consolidation have been quick to recognize, focusing on the military and on classical coup politics as privileged objects of research may be morally, politically, and empirically questionable insofar as it diverts attention from other pressing issues. Moreover, it may even turn out to be a misleading perspective that looks for danger in the wrong places, and therefore overlooks real threats that hide at less traditional and less obvious sites.

Many new democracies do face the threat of illegal or pseudolegal overthrow by antidemocratic forces. But in addition to the risk of breakdown—of dramatic, sudden, and visible relapses to authoritarian rule—many new democracies have to contend with the danger of decay, of less spectacular, more incremental, and less transparent forms of regression. While the former provokes a radical discontinuity with democratic politics (leading to open authoritarianism), the latter implies a gradual corrosion leading to fuzzy semidemocracy, to a hybrid regime somewhere between liberal democracy and dictatorship. If democratic breakdown is the dominant concern and defining horizon of avoidance of our first concept of democratic consolidation, democratic erosion occupies the same role with respect to this second concept of consolidation.

It was Guillermo O'Donnell who at the end of the 1980s put forward the first explicit formulation of this extended understanding of democratic consolidation. In his seminal essay "Transitions, Continuities, and Paradoxes," he drew attention to the threat of silent regressions from democracy to semidemocratic rule and incorporated the overcoming of this threat into his (broad) definition of democratic consolidation. Emphasizing the temporal dimension of his observation, he proposed to distinguish between "rapid deaths" and "slow deaths" of democracy. While the former referred to classical coup politics, O'Donnell described the latter as "a progressive diminuition of existing spaces for the exercise of civilian power and the effectiveness of the classic guarantees of liberal constitutionalism," as a "slow and at times opaque" "process of successive authoritarian advances," which in the end would lead to a *democradura,* a repressive, facade democracy.[12]

What has happened since the publication of O'Donnell's article? A cynic could make the point that a few new democracies no longer face the danger of retrogressing to semidemocratic rule because they have already arrived there. For such polities, democratic erosion is no longer a risk because it has become a reality. Irony aside, the continuing political relevance of the issue is quite evident. In a recent article, Samuel P. Huntington even went so far as to assert that with third-wave democracies, "the problem is not overthrow but erosion: the intermittent or gradual weakening of democracy by those elected to lead it."[13]

In recent years, students of democratic consolidation have improved their knowledge about different routes the "slow deaths" of democracies may take. The reassertion of military supremacy emphasized by O'Donnell is only one possibility, even if a very real one. Other forms of erosion attack other institutional pillars of democracy. For example, state violence as well as state weakness may subvert the rule of law; the rise of hegemonic parties may suffocate electoral competition; the decay of electoral institutions may affect the honesty of vote counting; incumbents may use their privileged access to state resources and to the mass media in ways that violate minimum standards of electoral fairness and equal opportunity; or the introduction of exclusionary citizenship laws may violate democratic norms of inclusiveness.

Completing Democracy

While liberal democracies face the "negative" challenge of preventing democratic erosion and regression to semidemocratic rule, "electoral democracies" face the symmetrical "positive" challenge of democratic completion, the attainment of full democratic rule. Students of electoral democracies often associate the notion of democratic consolidation with this task, with the telos of moving away from some "diminished subtype" of democracy toward a "nondiminished" democracy—or, as Guillermo O'Donnell once put it, with the accomplishment of a "second transition" from a democratic government to a democratic regime.[14] When they speak of democratic consolidation they tend to refer to the goal of completing a pending (that is, incomplete) transition to democracy. In graphical terms, they tend to look not just backward to the dangers of authoritarian regression, but also forward to the promises of democratic progress. When such expectations of democratic progress do not materialize, students of consolidation tend to express this frustrating institutionalization of semidemocratic rule with notions such as democratic "freezing" or "sclerosis."

Which are the basic actors, conflicts, and sites of democratic completion? It depends on the type of "electoral democracy" in place. In Latin America, three configurations have been of special relevance. To begin with, there are those countries where the outgoing authoritarian regime was able to write certain nondemocratic rules into the constitution. In such cases of constitutional defects, full democratization requires these formal authoritarian legacies to be removed. The prototypical Latin American case of constitutional semidemocracy has been Chile after 1990, and the classical study that modeled a general notion of democratic consolidation along the Chilean fault lines was J. Samuel Valenzuela's "Democratic Consolidation in Post-Transitional Settings."[15] In his perspective, abolishing "tutelary powers," "reserved domains," and "major discriminations" in the electoral law appeared as necessary ingredients of democratic consolidation. Since then, this notion of democratic consolidation has received widespread scholarly attention. For instance, Juan Linz and Alfred Stepan extensively analyze this constitution-centered type of democratic completion under the heading of "constitutional consolidation."[16]

Another kind of semidemocracy that has raised peculiar challenges of democratic consolidation-as-completion is the hegemonic-party system in crisis. The Latin American cases are (or were) Mexico and Paraguay. In essence, the problem is how to tell at what point (authoritarian) hegemonic parties have become (democratic) dominant parties. Hegemonic parties, given their reliance on state patronage, media control, repression, and ("in the last instance") electoral fraud, do not and cannot lose elections. Dominant parties, by contrast, do not but can, in principle, lose at the polls. Yet as long as alternation in power, the ultimate proof of any democratic electoral system, remains a mere possibility and does not occur in fact, entrenched suspicions will persist as to whether the incumbent party would really accept losing a national election.

While the constitutional legacies of military regimes as well as the structural legacies of hegemonic-party systems pose formidable "threshold problems" to democratizers, they involve only a handful of cases. In comparison, a third variety of democratic completion appears of more general relevance for Latin American countries: the transformation of "illiberal democracies," where the rule of law is biased and selective (or even aleatory), into liberal democracies that effectively guarantee basic political, civil, and human rights. With the notable (and debatable) exception of the three Southern Cone countries, Latin America's contemporary democracies have not followed Western Europe's historical sequence of political development: first, state building; second, legal domestication of the state; and third, democratic domestication of the state. Instead, as with many third-wave democracies in other regions, the sequence has been the reverse. Democracies have been created in the context of states whose presence looks partial and precarious (in both territorial and social terms) and with judicial systems in place that often cannot do much more than administer the rule of lawlessness. Correspondingly, the two keys to transcending "the illiberal nature of 'democracy' in Latin America today"[17] are "state reform" and "judicial reform"—both fashionable terms that have already entered the vocabulary even of international financial agencies.

Deepening Democracy

The notion of democratic consolidation just discussed—completing the democratic transition by traveling from electoral to liberal democracy—represents one progress-oriented, "positive" version of democratic consolidation. Moving further on the "continuum of democracy"—by deepening liberal democracy and pushing it closer to advanced democracy—represents a second positive version. When we compare Latin America's contemporary democracies with more or less rosy pictures of established Western democracies, the former seem to fall short on many counts. They appear to possess (or to be possessed by) "comparative disadvantages" in virtually every field of democratic politics. The list of presumptive structural deficits covers fields as diverse as governmental performance, public administration, judicial systems, party systems, interest groups, civil society, political culture, and styles of decision making. In all these and many other areas, most Latin American democracies look "underdeveloped" by comparison with the "advanced democracies."

Most authors who write about democratic consolidation either think about our very first notion of democratic consolidation, the stabilization of democracy, or about this last notion of democratic consolidation, the deepening of democracy. These two concepts of democratic consolidation are by far the most popular ones. In fact, the academic popularity of the former comes as no surprise. Most of Latin America's aging new democracies still have to worry about their long-term survival. As rule, however, this is no longer an immediate concern, but just one issue among many others that command political attention. Today, issues of democratic quality tend to be much more salient in everyday politics than issues of democratic survival.

Organizing Democracy

The variants of "negative" consolidation that I have discussed try to prevent democratic regression toward feared horizons of avoidance. Symmetrically, the two variants of "positive" consolidation try to achieve democratic progress toward valued horizons of attainment. *Tertium non datur?* I do not think so. In between the two pairs of concepts one can distinguish, in an uneasy intermediate position, a "neutral" usage of democratic consolidation, which comprehends democratic consolidation as the "organization" of democracy.

From this perspective, consolidating democracy calls for more than institutionalizing democracy's basic ground rules. It demands establishing democracy's specific rules and organizations. In other words, this concept of consolidation turns its attention from the procedural minima that define democratic regimes to the concrete rules and organizations that define various forms of democracy. It switches the level of analysis from regimes to subsystems, or in Philippe Schmitter's terms, to "partial regimes."[18] Thus democratic consolidation comes to be synonymous with "institution building." It implies constructing all those big organizations that make up the characteristic infrastructure of modern liberal democracies: parties and party systems, legislative bodies, state bureaucracies, judicial systems, and systems of interest intermediation.

While Schmitter, to my knowledge, deserves the credit for introducing and developing this concept of democratic consolidation, others have followed his track, especially subdisciplinary specialists to whom this notion of democratic consolidation provides an opportunity to link up their particular scholarly concerns with the general discussion on democratic consolidation.[19]

This fifth notion of democratic consolidation is "self-referential" insofar as liberal democracy serves as its point of both departure and arrival. It looks, so to speak, from liberal democracy to nowhere else. Some authors are emphatic in stressing its neutrality in normative terms. Yet rather than being normatively neutral, the concept appears to be normatively ambivalent. "Organizing" democracy may bring us closer to the normative goals of preventing democratic regressions and effecting democratic advances. But it may also pull us farther away. It all depends on the concrete forms in which democracy becomes organized.

Post-Transitional Blues

What picture emerges from this "teleological" reconstruction of coexisting and competing concepts of democratic consolidation? One basic finding is that the consolidation of democracy, as scholars use the term, represents a cluster concept with an intelligible structure but without a core, without a meaningful common denominator. All the notions in use part from some type or other of democratic regime, and they all aim at improving the democratic status quo. Yet their empirical context may be either liberal ("real") democracy or electoral ("semi-") democracy, and their normative horizon may be either democratic survival or democratic progress. In fact, these varying ideas of democratic consolidation do not have very much in common.

Thus the consolidation of democracy emerges as an omnibus concept, a garbage-can concept, a catch-all concept, lacking a core meaning that would unite all modes of usage. If it is indeed the case that it provides the foundation for what Schmitter has called "an embryonic subdiscipline" of political science, this discipline shares neither a substantive concern nor a methodological core. It is held together by no more than a shared domain of application. It covers all new democracies (including semidemocracies), which by definition enter the "phase of democratic consolidation" (or at least face the "problems of consolidation") as soon as they complete some sort of democratic transition. In this sense, "consolidology" is no more than a label for the study of new democracies.

Worst of all, students of democratic consolidation tend to ignore the concept's irritating multiplicity of meanings. They tend to ignore the vagueness and inconsistency of usage. All use the term in whatever way best fits their own research purposes, funding needs, and advertising strategies, while the usage of the same key term maintains the illusion of a common theoretical enterprise, a common purpose, a common language, a common "dependent variable."

One can understand the practical reasons for the current situation, but in terms of scholarly research, this uncontrolled coexistence of inconsistent meanings, this case of homonymity (one word meaning many things) running wild, is an unhappy state of affairs. It is not only inimical to theory building and the accumulation of knowledge, it even frustrates such elementary operations as case classification. In terms of democratic consolidation as the term is used today, countries such as Argentina and Poland may be ranked almost anywhere. Whether to describe them as "highly consolidated" or "persistently unconsolidated" depends entirely on the notion of democratic consolidation one chooses. As matters now stand, the concept's classificatory utility is close to zero. Its boundaries are fuzzy and fluid. It does not allow us to order reality in any reliable way.

How can we change this lamentable state of affairs? A minimal solution would be to practice "transparent toleration," to recognize the multiple meanings of democratic consolidation and to be clear and expli-cit about them. As Christoph Kotowski said about the concept of revo-lution, "If scholars do not attach the same meaning to the concept . . . they can at least specify which 'meaning' they 'mean.'"[20]

Such open recognition of differences may represent the only realistic way out of the conceptual mess. Perhaps democratic consolidation's "strange multiplicity" of meanings is here to stay. So long as the notion of democratic consolidation works as a generic label for the study of new democracies (and near-democracies), it would be surprising to see the scholarly community privileging one theme to the exclusion of others, and converging toward a more narrow and precise definition of the term. Most scholars would rapidly denounce such a one-sided agenda as empirically inappropriate, normatively annoying, politically unwise, and academically boring. As a consequence, any ambition to "legislate" the semantic field of democratic consolidation into unity may be doomed to failure.

In this spirit, the preceding "teleological" reconstruction of democratic consolidation would at least allow us to trace clear and distinct melodies in the current Babylonian chorus of voices singing songs of democratic consolidation. Its farewell to "the consolidation of democracy" in the singular, and its corresponding embrace of "types of democratic con-solidation" in the plural, would help us to compose our discordant songs of democratic consolidation in more conscious, more precise, and, in many cases, more modest ways.

Back to the Roots

The peaceful coexistence and mutual recognition of various concepts of democratic consolidation would be preferable to the status quo of con-ceptual confusion. The same would be true for another option: to abandon the concept and stop talking about it. Yet both alternatives are only second-best solutions. My first-order preference would be to exercise self-restraint and to stop using the term for whatever we would like to see happen in new democracies ("the conditions of democratic consolida-tion") or for whatever we think is problematic in these polities ("the prob-lems of democratic consolidation"). Rather than using the term in ambigu-ous and inconsistent ways, we should attach one clear meaning to it. As Giovanni Sartori declared, "different things should have different names."[21]

I think we should return to the concept's original concern with demo-cratic survival. We should restore its classical meaning, which is securing achieved levels of democratic rule against authoritarian regression. That means we should restrict its use to the two "negative" notions described above: avoiding democratic breakdown and avoiding democratic erosion. The term "democratic consolidation" should refer to expectations of regime continuity—and to nothing else. Accordingly, the concept of a "consolidated democracy" should describe a democratic regime that relevant observers expect to last well into the future—and nothing else. Why should one restrict the use of "democratic consolidation" in this particular way and not another? The main reason is that all other usages of democratic consolidation (completing, organizing, and deepening democracy) are problematic and can be replaced by superior alternative concepts.

First, the process (and the challenge) of putting a partial, blocked, derailed, or truncated transition back on track falls within the purview of transition studies. There is no need to confuse matters and introduce another term for it. In addition, in semidemocracies which face the task of democratic completion, any talk about "the consolidation of democracy" is misleading. It suggests that a democratic regime is already in place (and only needs to be "consolidated") when in fact the issue at hand is constructing a fully democratic regime.

Second, the development of democracy's subsystems, collective actors, and working rules is clearly a timely and relevant topic. But confounding the consolidation of "partial regimes" with the consolidation of democracy as a whole deprives us of an important analytic distinction. It binds together by definition two things that in fact are only loosely coupled. For example, a democracy may be secure against reversals even if its party system is still inchoate and fluid; and conversely, a democracy may break down even if its party system is highly institutionalized. Moreover, if we fuse the two levels of analysis we cannot issue reasonable judgments anymore about the consolidation of democracy's core institutions or a democratic regime as such. For, from this perspective, as long as any subsystem of democracy (be it the party system, interest organizations, the parliament, the system of government) does not show the requisite degree of consolidation (which is difficult to define other than by reference to "best" or "normal" practices in advanced democracies), we have to classify the democracy in question as "unconsolidated." And as soon as any subsystem experiences radical structural change (as Italy's party system did in the early 1990s), we are compelled to describe the polity in question as "deconsolidating." This does not seem to make much sense.

Finally, the association of democratic consolidation with improvements in the quality of democracy or with democratic deepening represents the most popular "positive" notion of democratic consolidation. But it also seems to be the most problematic one. Both the concepts of "democratic quality" and "democratic deepening" are still unclear and controversial. While we have tons of literature as well as a great deal of consensus about liberal democracy's minimum standards, discussion about the standards of democratic quality is still very preliminary. Therefore, in the current state of debate, conceptualizing democratic consolidation as democratic deepening amounts to inviting a free-for-all. It permits importing into the definition of democratic consolidation, in a subjective and arbitrary way, any kinds of goals and criteria that one deems to be indispensable for a high-quality and thus "consolidated" democracy (which becomes just another vague label for "real" democracy). This cannot but lead, of course, to uncontrolled and incongruous conclusions about empirical states of democratic consolidation.

On a more fundamental level, "democracy precludes closure regarding its own identity."[22] It is a moving target, an open-ended, developmental kind of thing—and so is democratic deepening. Any fixed meanings we may attach to the concepts of democratic quality and democratic deepening, and any consensus we may reach about them, can only be "temporary equilibria" open to future revision. As a result, if we associate democratic consolidation with democratic deepening, we get a concept of democratic consolidation that is open and boundless as well. In this sense, no democracy will ever be "fully consolidated," and it is quite understandable that authors who support such a notion of democratic consolidation are highly reluctant to extend the "certificate" of democratic consolidation at all.

NOTES

I am grateful to the Austrian Academy of Science for supporting work on this article through the Austrian Program for Advanced Research and Technology (APART). A previous version of this article was presented under the title "Concepts of Democratic Consolidation" at the 1997 meeting of the Latin American Studies Association in Guadalajara, Mexico, 17–19 April 1997. For more extensive bibliographic references, the reader may consult this longer original version. To obtain a copy, send an e-mail to the author *(andreas@dis1.cide.mx)*.

1. See Larry Diamond, *Developing Democracy: Toward Consolidation* (Baltimore: Johns Hopkins University Press, 1999), ch. 2.

2. Elinor Ostrom, "An Agenda for the Study of Institutions," *Public Choice* 48 (1986): 4.

3. Robert Dahl, *Polyarchy: Participation and Opposition* (New Haven: Yale University Press, 1971).

4. On "diminished subtypes" of democracy, see David Collier and Steven Levitsky, "Democracy with Adjectives: Conceptual Innovation in Comparative Research," *World Politics* 49 (April 1997): 430–51.

5. See David Collier and Steven Levitsky, "Democracy 'with Adjectives': Finding Conceptual Order in Recent Comparative Research" (paper presented at the annual meeting of the American Political Science Association, Chicago, 31 August–3 September 1995). This discussion does not appear in the published version of their paper, cited in note 4 above.

6. Positioning authoritarian and democratic regimes along a single continuum suggests that only quantitative differences separate these regime types. This is not a compelling assumption, however. For even if one thinks, as I do, that the distinction between democracy and authoritarianism is a qualitative one, a distinction of kind, a question of certain institutions being absent or present, one may concede that intricate problems of thresholds arise as soon as certain elements of democracy's institutional core package are either weak or absent. I should also note that the continuum looks closed on both sides while in fact it is closed only on its authoritarian side (by totalitarianism) but open on its democratic side (to future developments of democracy). In this sense, the metaphor of a horizon that I use below is "realistic" only for this open-ended side of the figure—a horizon, after all, can never be reached but recedes before the walker.

7. Note that this distinction between "positive" and "negative" consolidation is different from Geoffrey Pridham's. He associates "negative consolidation" with securing democratic survival and "positive consolidation" with legitimizing democracy at elite and mass levels. Yet the theoretical grounds of this distinction as well as the relation between the two types of democratic consolidation seem unclear. See Geoffrey Pridham, "The International Context of Democratic Consolidation: Southern Europe in Comparative Perspective," in Richard Gunther, P. Nikiforos Diamandouros, and Hans-Jürgen Puhle, eds., *The Politics of Democratic Consolidation: Southern Europe in Comparative Perspective* (Baltimore: Johns Hopkins University Press, 1996), 169.

8. Guillermo O'Donnell, "Illusions About Consolidation," p. 117 in this volume. See also idem, "Illusions and Conceptual Flaws," pp. 140–48 in this volume; and Ben Ross Schneider, "Democratic Consolidations: Some Broad Comparisons and Sweeping Arguments," *Latin American Research Review* 30 (1995): 215–34.

9. Richard Gunther, P. Nikiforos Diamandouros, and Hans-Jürgen Puhle, "O'Donnell's 'Illusions': A Rejoinder," *Journal of Democracy* 7 (October 1996): 155. When asked, anyone will agree with this cautious note against facile assumptions of linear progress. The literature is full of warnings that nothing is certain, that reversals can happen any time, and that even "consolidated" democracies are not immune to crises, "deconsolidation," and breakdown. However, "democratic consolidation" is one of those terms that refer both to a dynamic process (a consolidating democracy) and to its result (a consolidated democracy). And when authors use it to describe not the desired outcome—the telos—of democratic consolidation but the process that leads to its attainment, it is hard to avoid connotations of progressive certainties creeping into the language. For instance, common expressions such as "the process of democratic consolidation," "the dynamics of democratic consolidation," or "the logic of democratic consolidation" tend to suggest an underlying reality that propels itself toward the promised land of consolidation.

10. See, for example, Samuel P. Huntington, *The Third Wave: Democratization in the Late Twentieth Century* (Norman: University of Oklahoma Press, 1991); and Laurence Whitehead, "The Consolidation of Fragile Democracies: A Discussion with Illustrations," in Robert A. Pastor, ed., *Democracy in the Americas: Stopping the Pendulum* (New York: Holmes and Meier, 1989), 76–95.

11. For a critique of causal concepts that mix up the definition of democratic consolidation with its explanation, see Andreas Schedler, "Expected Regime Stability: Rethinking Democratic Consolidation" (Centro de Investigación y Docencia Económicas, Department of Political Studies, 1998, Working Paper 81).

12. See Guillermo O'Donnell, "Transitions, Continuities, and Paradoxes," in Scott Mainwaring, Guillermo O'Donnell, and J. Samuel Valenzuela, eds., *Issues in Democratic Consolidation: The New South American Democracies in Comparative Perspective* (Notre Dame: University of Notre Dame Press, 1992), 17–56. The quotes are from pages 19 and 33.

13. Samuel P. Huntington, "Democracy for the Long Haul," *Journal of Democracy*

7 (April 1996): 9. Note, however, that Huntington's notion of democratic erosion is substantially wider than the one developed here and includes, for instance, executive-led coups.

14. See Guillermo O'Donnell, "Transitions, Continuities, and Paradoxes," 18–19.

15. See J. Samuel Valenzuela, "Democratic Consolidation in Post-Transitional Settings: Notion, Process, and Facilitating Conditions," in Scott Mainwaring et al., *Issues in Democratic Consolidation,* 57–104.

16. See Juan J. Linz and Alfred Stepan, *Problems of Democratic Transition and Consolidation: Southern Europe, South America, and Post-Communist Europe* (Baltimore: Johns Hopkins University Press, 1996). However, Linz and Stepan's actual analysis is often inconsistent with their own term. For example, they classify Chile (correctly, I think) as an "incomplete democracy" and not as a "constitutionally unconsolidated" one (as their notion of "constitutional consolidation" would suggest). In essence, their idea of "constitutional consolidation" is at odds with their own prior assumption on pp. 3–6 that liberal democracy forms the indispensable starting point of democratic consolidation.

17. Larry Diamond, "Democracy in Latin America: Degrees, Illusions, and Directions for Consolidation," in Tom Farer, ed., *Beyond Sovereignty: Collectively Defending Democracy in the Americas* (Baltimore: Johns Hopkins University Press, 1996), 73. It is instructive to take a look at the "Map of Freedom" published regularly in Freedom House's *Annual Survey of Political Rights and Civil Liberties.* In the 1995–96 report, of all Latin America, only Chile, Argentina, Uruguay, Ecuador, Costa Rica, and Panama are colored white, indicating their status as "free" countries. All the remaining countries appear in gray shades, expressing their lower ranking as no more than "partly free" polities. See Freedom House, *Freedom in the World: The Annual Survey of Political Rights and Civil Liberties 1995–1996* (New York: Freedom House, 1996), 99.

18. See, for example, Philippe C. Schmitter, "Organized Interests and Democratic Consolidation in Southern Europe," in Gunther et al., *The Politics of Democratic Consolidation,* 284–314. I think it is misleading to describe this change in the level of analysis as "disaggregation" (Schneider, *Democratic Consolidations,* 220–21). After all, the relation between fundamental rules and secondary rules is not a relation between sum and parts (as the term disaggregation suggests) but more a relation between, say, basis and superstructure.

19. See Philippe C. Schmitter, "Organized Interests." See also, for example, Geoffrey Pridham, "Political Parties, Parliaments and Democratic Consolidation in Southern Europe: Empirical and Theoretical Perspectives," in Ulrike Liebert and Maurizio Cotta, eds., *Parliament and Democratic Consolidation in Southern Europe* (London: Pinter Publishers, 1990), 225–48. This "organizational" notion of democratic consolidation often comes together with the idea that actors have to accept and become habituated to these meso- and micro-arrangements. Linz and Stepan, for example, see the "constitutional consolidation" of democracy accomplished when all political actors "become subjected to, and habituated to, the resolution of conflict within the specific laws, procedures, and institutions sanctioned by the new democratic process." See Juan J. Linz and Alfred Stepan, *Problems of Democratic Transition and Consolidation,* 6.

20. Christoph M. Kotowski, "Revolution," in Giovanni Sartori, ed., *Social Science Concepts: A Systematic Analysis* (Beverly Hills: Sage Publications, 1984), 440.

21. Giovanni Sartori, "Guidelines for Concept Analysis," in Sartori, *Social Science Concepts,* 50 (see also 37–40).

22. Laurence Whitehead, "The Vexed Issue of the Meaning of 'Democracy'" (unpubl. ms., Oxford University, 1997), 17.

III

Foundations of Successful Democracy

13

WHAT MAKES DEMOCRACIES ENDURE?

Adam Przeworski, Michael E. Alvarez, José Antonio Cheibub, and Fernando Limongi

Adam Przeworski is professor of political science at New York University. *Michael E. Alvarez* is assistant professor of political science at DePaul University. *José Antonio Cheibub* is assistant professor of political science at Yale University. *Fernando Limongi* is assistant professor in the political science department at the University of São Paulo. This essay is a revised version of a paper presented at a conference on "Consolidating Third Wave Democracies: Trends and Challenges," held in Taipei, Taiwan, on 27–30 August 1995. The work was supported in part by National Science Foundation grant SES–9022605.

If a country, any randomly selected country, is to have a democratic regime *next* year, what conditions should be present in that country and around the world *this* year? The answer is: democracy, affluence, growth with moderate inflation, declining inequality, a favorable international climate, and parliamentary institutions.

This answer is based on counting instances of survival and death of political regimes in 135 countries observed annually between 1950 or the year of independence or the first year when economic data are available ("entry" year) and 1990 or the last year for which data are available ("exit" year), for a total of 4,318 country-years.[1] We found 224 regimes, of which 101 were democracies and 123 dictatorships, observing 40 transitions to dictatorship and 50 to democracy. Among democratic regimes, there were 50 parliamentary systems, 46 presidential systems, and 8 mixed systems.[2]

Our definition of democracy is a minimalist one. We follow Robert A. Dahl's 1971 classic *Polyarchy* in treating as democratic all regimes that hold elections in which the opposition has some chance of winning and taking office. When in doubt, we err in the direction of calling a regime dictatorial. Our classification is not idiosyncratic, but is closely related to several alternative scales of democracy. The rationale and the rules for classifying regimes are discussed in the Appendix below.

Democracy. It may seem tautological to say that a country should have a democratic regime this year in order to have a democracy next year. We do so in order to dispel the myth, prevalent in certain intellectual and political circles (particularly in the United States) since the late 1950s, that the route to democracy is a circuitous one. The claim is that 1) dictatorships are better at generating economic development in poor countries, and that 2) once countries have developed, their dictatorial regimes will give way to democracy. To get to democracy, then, one had to support, or at least tolerate, dictatorships.

Both of the above propositions, however, are false:

1) While analyses of the impact of regimes on economic growth have generated divergent results, recent econometric evidence fails to uncover any clear regime effect. The average rate of investment is in fact slightly higher in poor democracies than in poor dictatorships; population growth is higher under dictatorships but labor productivity is lower; and investment is more efficiently allocated under democracies. Dictatorships are no more likely to generate economic growth than democracies.[3] Indeed, the 56 dictatorships with annual per-capita income of less than $1,000 when we first observed them simply failed to develop.[4] By the exit year, only 18 of them had made it (whether under democracy or continued dictatorship) to $1,000, only 6 to $2,000, and only 3 to more than $3,000. South Korea and Taiwan are exceptional: They are the only two dictatorships that started under $1,000 in 1950 and had annual per-capita income exceeding $5,000 by 1990. If we consider as "initially poor" those countries with less than $2,000, we find that among 98 dictatorships first observed below this level, by the exit year only 26 had made it to $2,000, 15 to $3,000, 7 to $4,000, and 4 to $5,000. These figures should be enough to dispel any notion that dictatorship somehow promotes economic growth in poor countries.

2) Democracies are not produced by the development of dictatorships.[5] If they were, the rate at which dictatorships make the transition to democracy would increase with the level of development: Analyses of the survival prospects of dictatorships, however, indicate that this is not the case. Indeed, transitions to democracy are random with regard to the level of development: Not a single transition to democracy can be predicted by the level of development alone.[6]

Since poor dictatorships are no more likely to develop than poor democracies and since developed dictatorships are no more likely to become democracies than poor ones, dictatorships offer no advantage in attaining the dual goal of development and democracy. In order to strengthen democracy, we should strengthen democracy, not support dictatorships.

Affluence. Once a country has a democratic regime, its level of economic development has a very strong effect on the probability that democracy will survive. Poor democracies, particularly those with annual per-capita income of less than $1,000, are extremely fragile: Based on our study, the probability that one will die during a particular year is 0.12. This rate falls to 0.06 in the $1,000 to $2,000 range, to 0.03 between $2,000 and $4,000, and to 0.01 between $4,000 and $6,000. These numbers mean that a democracy can be expected to last an average of about 8.5 years in a country with per-capita income under $1,000 per annum, 16 years in one with income between $1,000 and $2,000, 33 years between $2,000 and $4,000, and 100 years between $4,000 and $6,000.

Whatever their theoretical and political differences, both Samuel P. Huntington and Guillermo O'Donnell claim that there is a level beyond which further development actually *decreases* the probability that democracy will survive.[7] Huntington argues that both democracies and dictatorships become unstable when a country undergoes modernization, which occurs at some intermediate level of development. O'Donnell, in turn, claims that democracies tend to die when a country exhausts "the easy stage of import substitution," again at some intermediate level. Our finding, however, is that there is *no* income level at which democracies become more fragile than they were when they were poorer. Only in the Southern Cone countries of Latin America have authoritarian regimes arisen at the intermediate levels of development. Four out of the nine transitions to authoritarianism above $3,000 transpired in Argentina. Adding Chile and Uruguay, we see that the instances in which democracy fell at medium levels of development are to a large extent peculiar to the Southern Cone.[8]

Above $6,000, democracies are impregnable and can be expected to live forever: No democratic system has ever fallen in a country where per-capita income exceeds $6,055 (Argentina's level in 1976). Hence Seymour Martin Lipset was correct to assert that "the more well-to-do a nation, the greater the chances that it will sustain democracy."[9] Once established in a developed country, democracy endures regardless of how it performs and regardless of all the exogenous conditions to which it is exposed.

Why democracies are more durable in more-developed countries has been the subject of extensive speculation. One reason, put forward by Lipset in *Political Man,* is that the intensity of distributional conflicts is lower at higher income levels. Another plausible hypothesis, suggested to us by Larry Diamond, focuses on institutions: Political actors in more-developed countries may be more likely to adopt a superior institutional framework at the moment when democracy is established. Later, we will examine this hypothesis with regard to parliamentarism and presidentialism. First, however, we will take up consideration of our third condition for the maintenance of democracy—economic performance.

Economic performance. For some countries, therefore, the story ends here: Once democracy is in place, affluence is a sufficient condition for it to survive regardless of anything else. But democracies can survive in poorer countries, if they generate economic growth with a moderate rate of inflation.

While Lipset, economist Mancur Olson, and Huntington all thought that democracy becomes destabilized when a country grows rapidly, they could not have been more wrong.[10] Rapid growth is not destabilizing for democracies (or for dictatorships): Indeed, democracies are always more likely to survive when they grow faster than 5 percent annually than when they grow slower. In turn, the fragility of democracy at lower levels of development flows largely from its vulnerability in the face of economic crisis.[11] Poor democracies, those under $1,000, have a 0.22 probability of dying in a year after their income falls (giving them a life expectancy of less than five years) and a 0.08 probability (or an expected life of 12.5 years) if their income rises. Between $1,000 and $6,000— the middle range—democracies are less sensitive to growth but more likely to die if they stagnate: They die at the rate of 0.059 when they decline, so that their expected life is about 17 years, and at the rate of 0.027, with an expected life of about 37 years, when they grow. Thus Larry Diamond and Juan J. Linz are correct to argue that "Economic crisis represents one of the most common threats to democratic stability."[12] Conversely, economic growth is conducive to the survival of democracy. Indeed, the faster the economy grows, the more likely democracy is to survive.

Inflation also threatens democratic stability. A democratic regime has a 0.023 chance of dying and an expected life of 44 years when the annual inflation rate is under 6 percent; a 0.014 chance and an expected life of 71 years when inflation is between 6 and 30 percent; and a 0.064 chance and an expected life of about 16 years when inflation is above 30 percent. Note that these results appear to confirm Albert Hirschman's 1981 hypo- thesis that a moderate rate of inflation promotes democratic stability.[13]

Economic performance, then, is crucially important for the survival of democracy in less-affluent countries. When the economy grows rapidly with a moderate rate of inflation, democracy is much more likely to last even in the poorest lands.

Income inequality. The study of the political effects of income inequality is hampered by the paucity and poor quality of the available data. The best collection of internationally comparable data, generated by the World Bank, includes 266 observations, scattered over time for 84 countries.

We tried to assess the impact of income inequality (measured by the income ratio between the richest and the poorest quintiles) on the probability that a democracy will survive for three and for five years following the time for which data are available. Unlike Edward N. Muller, we could find no pattern.[14] Since income inequality tends to be lower in poor countries, where most of the labor force is employed in self-sufficient agriculture, and in wealthy countries, where most workers are wage earners, and since democracy is brittle in poor countries and impregnable in rich ones, no overall pattern emerged from this analysis. The scantiness of our data, moreover, prevented us from controlling for the level of development.

On the other hand, we did find that democracy is much more likely to survive in countries where income inequality is declining over time. For those democratic regimes for which we had more than one observation of income distribution, we calculated the probability that democracy would die should inequality either increase or decrease. We found that the expected life of democracy in countries with shrinking inequality is about 84 years, while the expected life of democracies with rising income inequality is about 22 years (these numbers are based on 599 democratic years, with inequality increasing during 262 and declining during 337). Note that these findings contradict any notion that distributional pressures threaten the survival of democracy: People expect democracy to reduce income inequality, and democracies are more likely to survive when they do.

International climate. Economic factors are not the only ones that matter for the durability of democracy. Indeed, international conditions predict regime survival better than does the level of development. While we cannot statistically distinguish different mechanisms by which the international climate becomes transmitted to particular countries, the proportions of other democracies in the region and in the world matter separately for the survival of democracy in any particular country: The larger the proportion of democracies on the globe and in the region during a particular year, the more likely is democracy to survive in any particular country. The global effect is about twice as large as the regional effect, but these findings indicate that contagion operates independently of the direct influence of Western governments and various international institutions.

Political learning. It is frequently argued—Russia is a favorite example—that the absence of democratic traditions impedes the consolidation of new democratic institutions and, conversely, that democracy is more stable in countries (like Chile) that have enjoyed it in the past. What this argument misses is that if a country *had* a democratic regime (note the past tense), it is a veteran not only of democracy but of the *successful subversion* of democracy. Political learning, in other words, cuts both ways. Democrats may find the work of consolidation easier when they can rely on past traditions, but antidemocratic forces also have an experience from which they can draw lessons: People know that overthrowing democracy is possible, and may even know how to do it. If the failed Russian hardliners' coup of 1991 was more of a *coup de théâtre* than a *coup d'état*, it was perhaps because the coup plotters simply did not know what they were doing—an ignorance for which they were justly ridiculed by their more-experienced Latin American soul mates.

An overthrow of democracy at any time during the past history of a country shortens the life expectancy of any democratic regime in that country. To the extent that political learning does occur, then, it seems that the lessons learned by antidemocratic forces from the past subversion of democracy are more effective than the traditions that can be relied on by democrats.[15]

The effect of institutions. Democracies are not all the same. Systems of representation, arrangements for the division and supervision of powers, and methods of organizing interests, as well as legal doctrines and the rights and duties associated with citizenship, can and do vary widely among regimes that are generally recognized as democratic. These differences, expressed in the details of institutions, generate effects that two millennia of reflection and investigation have still not enabled us to grasp fully. We are far from knowing any clear answer to the question that Rousseau posed in his *Constitution of Poland:* Which institutions have which effects under which historical conditions?

Should we expect democracy to last longer under one institutional system than under another? Our analysis is limited to only one set of institutional features, summarized as parliamentarism vs. presidentialism (we leave "mixed" systems aside as presenting too small a sample to yield any robust estimate). We thus test the hypotheses of Juan Linz, who offers several reasons why parliamentary democracies should prove more durable than presidential ones.[16]

One of Linz's arguments is that the stakes are higher under presidentialism, since a race for the presidency can have but a single winner. Linz observes that a defeated presidential candidate has no official role in politics, and most likely will not even be a member of the legislature, while in a parliamentary system the defeated candidate for the premiership will be leader of the opposition.[17] Moreover, it is likely that the fixed term of office under a presidential system is longer than the expected term of office under a parliamentary system. Finally, under presidentialism the chief executive is at the same time the head of state, thus being able to portray the president's partisan interest as the national interest and thereby undermine the legitimacy afforded to the opposition.

The second reason why presidential democracies may be less durable is that they are more likely to generate legislative paralysis. Such paralysis can occur under either system: under parliamentarism when no majority coalition can be formed, and under presidentialism when the legislature is controlled by a majority that is hostile to the president but not large enough to override presidential vetoes routinely. Under presidential systems the executive, by virtue of the fixed term of office, can survive alongside hostile legislatures, leading to stalemates between the executive and the legislative branch. As the great nineteenth-century English political writer Walter Bagehot observed, "when a difference of opinion arises, the legislature is forced to fight the executive, and the executive is forced to fight the legislature; and so very likely they contend to the conclusion of their respective terms."[18] In several contemporary presidential systems the main line of political conflict is between the president and the congress, rather than among political parties. Under such conditions, no one can govern.

Legislative majorities are more frequent under presidentialism than under parliamentarism: 57.9 percent of the time under the former and 49.0 percent under the latter.[19] But in 24.2 percent of the presidential years, the share of the largest party in the legislature was smaller than one-half and larger than one-third. Since the proportion needed to override a presidential veto is typically two-thirds, these figures indicate that the conditions for executive-legislative deadlock are common under presidentialism. The average number of effective parties is about the same under the two systems: 3.10 under parliamentarism and 3.05 under presidentialism. Yet extreme fractionalization—in which no party controls more than a third of the seats—is more frequent under presidentialism (occurring 18 percent of the time) than under parliamentarism (where it occurs only 8.9 percent of the time).

Linz is right about the durability of alternative institutional arrangements. During the period under consideration, 14 democracies (or 28 percent of the 50 cases) died under a parliamentary system. Only one (12.5 percent of 8 cases) died under a mixed system, and 24 (52 percent of 46 cases) died under presidentialism.[20] Among those democracies that died during the period under our scrutiny, the parliamentary systems lasted an average of eight years, while their presidential counterparts lasted nine. But the parliamentary systems that were still around as of 1990 were much older: on the average about 43 years, as compared with 22 for presidential regimes. The probability that a democracy would die under presidentialism during any particular year of our study was 0.049; the comparable probability under parliamentarism was 0.014. If this difference appears small, think in terms of expected lives: Democracy's life expectancy under presidentialism is less than 20 years, while under parliamentarism it is 71 years.

This difference in durability is not an effect of the levels of economic development at which parliamentary and presidential regimes operated. While parliamentary systems are on the average found in wealthier countries, presidential democracies are less durable at almost every level. Excluding countries with a 1990 population of fewer than one million (many of which have parliamentary systems) changes nothing: The hazard rates—conditional probabilities that a regime would die given that it survived thus far—are exactly the same. Nor is this difference due to some hidden features of Latin America: In fact, presidential regimes in Latin America live much longer than those in other regions, the United States excepted. Hence presidential democracies are not shorter-lived because they are in Latin America.

Scott Mainwaring, like Alfred Stepan and Cindy Skach, is also correct: Democracies are less likely to survive when they combine presidentialism with a fragmented party system.[21] Combining presidentialism with a legislature where no single party has majority status is a kiss of death: Such systems can expect to live only 15 years. Presidential democracies in which a single party does have a legislative majority can expect to live 26 years. "Deadlock," a situation in which the share of seats of the largest party is between one-third and one-half, is even more deadly to presidential regimes. They die at the rate of 0.038 (with an expected life of 26 years) when there is no deadlock and at the rate of 0.091 (with an expected life of 11 years) when there is. Furthermore, descriptive information on parliamentarism supports Scott Mainwaring and Matthew Shugart's argument that "Parliamentary systems with disciplined parties and a majority party offer the fewest checks on executive power, and hence promote a winner-takes-all approach more than presidential systems."[22] Single-party majorities are not conducive to the survival of parliamentary democracies—those in which one party had a majority of seats in the lower house of the legislature have an expected life of 55 years, while parliamentary systems without a one-party majority have an expected life of 111 years. Yet this difference is not statistically significant.

How good are the alternative institutional arrangements at coping with economic crises? When the economy declines during a particular year, parliamentary democracies die at the rate of 0.039: They can expect to live 26 years under such conditions. When the economy grows, their death rate is 0.007 and the expected life is 143 years. Hence parliamentary systems are vulnerable to economic crises. Presidential systems are less sensitive, but they die at much higher rates under any conditions. When the economy declines, they die at the rate of 0.064, with an expected life of 16 years. When the economy grows, they die at the rate of 0.042, with an expected life of 24 years. Democracy is vulnerable to economic crisis under either institutional system, but presidential systems are less likely to survive under good economic conditions than parliamentary systems are under bad conditions.

Statistical analyses provide even stronger evidence in favor of parliamentarism. The expected life of presidential systems depends on the level of development, on economic growth, and on the presence of legislative majorities. Perhaps most startlingly, statistical analysis confirms that presidential systems are highly vulnerable to legislative-executive deadlocks. By contrast, in spite of the descriptive numbers cited above, for parliamentary systems neither the distribution of seats nor economic growth is a statistically significant predictor of the survival of democracy.

Statistics confirm as well that presidential regimes are less likely to survive in those countries that were not independent by 1950 (which is another way of saying "outside Latin America"), while parliamentary systems are equally likely to survive in either the "old" or the "new" countries. In turn, only parliamentary systems are sensitive to the ethnic fragmentation of the population. But this effect, while statistically significant, makes little difference for their expected lives. Thus presidential democracies are simply more brittle.

To summarize, the survival of democracies does depend on their institutional systems. Parliamentary regimes last longer, much longer, than presidential ones. Majority-producing electoral institutions are conducive to the survival of presidential systems: Presidential systems facing legislative deadlock are particularly brittle. Both systems are vulnerable to bad economic performance, but presidential democracies are less likely to survive even when the economy grows than are parliamentary systems when the economy declines. The evidence that parliamentary democracy survives longer and under a broader spectrum of conditions than presidential democracy thus seems incontrovertible.

The choice of institutions. Since parliamentary democracies last longer, it is puzzling why so many democracies adopt presidentialism. What determines the initial choice of democratic institutions? Much of the answer can be gleaned from a casual glance at history. Countries that had monarchies but experienced no revolution transferred governmental responsibility from crown to parliament, ending up with parliamentary systems. Countries in which monarchy was abolished (France in 1848 and again in 1875, Germany in 1919) and colonies that rebelled against monarchical powers (the United States and Latin America in the late eighteenth and early nineteenth centuries) replaced monarchs with presidents. As Simon Bolívar once put it, "We elect monarchs whom we call presidents." Countries that emerged from colonial domination after the Second World War typically inherited parliamentarism from the colonizers. Characteristically, however, these same countries instituted presidential systems if and when the initial democracy fell. Just as characteristically, democratizing dictatorships tended to retain presidentialism.

According to our count, among the 35 countries that democratized between 1974 and 1990, 19 adopted presidential systems, 13 chose parliamentarism, and 3 opted for mixed systems. If the political stakes are indeed higher under presidentialism, it is hard to see why this system would emerge under conditions in which the political parties are perfectly well informed and not risk-prone. One explanation might be that the parties are unduly optimistic: Each projects itself as a winner at the polls and assumes that it will gain the presidency. Still, we suspect that the choice of presidentialism is not just a decision of political parties.

Note that among the countries which were democratic at some time before the current transition to democracy, almost all chose the same system as the last time around.[23] This continuity, particularly in Latin America, may please those who like to find explanations in culture or traditions.[24] Yet it is more likely that it reflects the continuing political role of the military, which appears to have a preference for presidential regimes, perhaps because such regimes offer a clearer hierarchy. This reason is sufficient for the military to bargain for presidentialism when the issue of democratic institutions appears on the transitional agenda. The empirical patterns appear to support this expectation: While 10 of the 17 democratic regimes that emerged from civilian dictatorships went for presidentialism, an overwhelming 22 of the 28 democracies that surfaced from military dictatorships made the same choice. Thus presidentialism appears to be at least partly a legacy of military rule.

Once we learn that presidential systems are more likely to be adopted whenever the previous regime was military, the obvious question is whether all the findings concerning the longevity of presidential democracies are not spurious. Democracy may be more brittle under presidentialism precisely because this set of institutions is chosen where the military plays an active role in politics. To some extent this is the case: While the expected life of presidential democracies that emerge from civilian dictatorships is about 24 years, presidential systems that follow military dictatorships can expect to last only 17 years. Yet parliamentary democracies that follow military rule simply last much longer—71 years.[25] Hence it would seem to be presidentialism per se that makes democracy more brittle.

Once we exclude the institutions inherited from the colonial rulers, the level of development at which the transition to democracy occurs does appear to have some impact on the institutions that are chosen: Between 1950 and 1990, the average levels at which parliamentary institutions were chosen was $2,945, while presidential institutions were chosen at the average level of $2,584. The mode of transition, at least as indicated by strikes and other forms of social unrest (as coded by Arthur S. Banks), appears not to affect the choice of institutions.[26]

We focus on the moment of transition since particular institutional frameworks tend to persist once established, as if "renegotiation-proof." As the recent Brazilian referendum rejecting a proposed change to parliamentarism shows, the difficulty of changing complex institutional arrangements is that the status quo, whatever it happens to be, is favored. If the proponents of change offer only a slogan, "parliamentarism," then the defenders of the status quo can call for details of the new institutional arrangement; if the proponents of change offer such details, then the defenders can always find innumerable faults with the new system. During the entire period from 1950 to 1990, there were only three instances in which democratic regimes passed from one institutional system to another: France changed in 1958 from a parliamentary to a mixed system, while Brazil changed in 1960 from a presidential to a mixed system, only to return to presidentialism in 1963. Both cases occurred under exceptional circumstances. Countries that adopt presidential institutions when they transit to democracy are stuck with them.[27]

Conclusions. Our central finding is the importance of economic factors in sustaining democracies. While the modernization theory was wrong in thinking that development under dictatorship breeds democracies, Lipset was correct to argue that once established in a wealthy country, democracy is more likely to endure. Indeed, we have found that once a country is sufficiently wealthy, with per-capita income of more than $6,000 a year, democracy is certain to survive, come hell or high water. And while international factors as well as political institutions are important for the durability of democracy in less affluent countries, economic performance does matter: Indeed, democracy is more likely to survive in a growing economy with less than $1,000 per-capita income than in a country where per-capita income is between $1,000 and $4,000, but which is declining economically. Democracies can survive even in the poorest nations if they manage to generate development, if they reduce inequality, if the international climate is propitious, and if they have parliamentary institutions.

For a variety of reasons, however, this is not an optimistic conclusion. Poverty is a trap. Few countries with annual per-capita income below $1,000 develop under any regime: Their average rate of growth is less than 1 percent a year; many experience prolonged economic decline. When poor countries stagnate, whatever democracies happen to spring up tend to die quickly. Poverty breeds poverty and dictatorship.

Institutional choice offers a partial escape from this trap: Parliamentary systems in the poorest countries, while still very fragile, are almost twice as likely to survive as presidential democracies, and four times as likely when they grow economically. Yet since it appears that poor countries are more likely to choose presidentialism, little solace is offered by the possibility of institutional engineering. Equally little solace is offered by political learning. Most countries returning to democracy usually go back to whatever constitution they had in the past, even if it never worked, as in Argentina, where the first democratic alternation in office under the revived 1853 Constitution already violated its letter.[28]

Finally, we find no evidence of "consolidation." A democracy becomes "consolidated" if its aforementioned "hazard rate" declines with its age, so that, as Robert Dahl has argued, democracies are more likely to survive if they have lasted a while.[29] We find some evidence that this is true, but also that democracies are heterogeneous. Once we control for the level of development, the heterogeneity disappears and the hazard rates become independent of age, meaning that for a given level of development, democracies are about equally likely to die at any age. Since democracies are much more likely to survive when they occur in developed countries, these findings would indicate that hazard rates (uncorrected for the level of development) drop because countries develop economically, and not because a democracy that has been around is more likely to continue being around.

Clearly, we do not think that "consolidation" is just a matter of time, of some kind of "habituation" or mechanical "institutionalization."[30] We discovered that democracies are more likely to survive at higher levels of development. But we also found that democracies survive if they generate economic growth and if they control distributional pressures by allowing some inflation and reducing income inequality. This is not to deny that institutions matter: In fact they do, and not just parliamentarism and electoral systems but others that we have left out of consideration because we lack data. Democracy's ability to survive is a matter of politics and policy, as well as luck. Yet, conversely, if democracies become "consolidated" for whatever reasons, then we should observe that at any level of development the mere passage of time makes their demise less likely. This, however, we do not observe, and so conclude that "consolidation" is an empty term.

In sum, the secret of democratic durability seems to lie in economic development—not, as the theory dominant in the 1960s had it, under dictatorship, but under democracy based on parliamentary institutions.

Appendix: Classifying Regimes

We define democracy as a regime in which governmental offices are filled as a consequence of contested elections. Only if the opposition is allowed to compete, win, and assume office is a regime democratic. To the extent to which it focuses on elections, this is obviously a minimalist definition.

This definition has two parts—"offices" and "contestation." In no regime are all governmental offices filled as a consequence of elections. What is essential to consider a regime as democratic is that two kinds of offices are filled by elections— the chief executive office and the seats in the effective legislative body.

Contestation occurs when there exists an opposition that has some chance of winning office as a consequence of elections. We take quite literally Przeworski's dictum that "Democracy is a system in which parties lose elections": Whenever in doubt, we classify as democracies only those systems in which incumbent parties actually did lose elections. Alternation in office constitutes prima facie evidence of contestation.

Contestation, in turn, entails three features: 1) *ex ante* uncertainty, 2) *ex post* irreversibility, and 3) repeatability.

By "*ex ante* uncertainty," we mean that there is some positive probability that at least one member of the incumbent coalition can lose office in a particular round of elections. Uncertainty is not synonymous with unpredictability: The probability distribution of electoral chances is typically known. All that is necessary for outcomes to be uncertain is that some incumbent party could lose.

By "*ex post* irreversibility" we mean the assurance that whoever wins elections will be allowed to assume office. The outcome of elections must be irreversible under democracy even if the opposition wins. The practical consequence of this feature is to exclude sham elections as well as periods of liberalization. Liberalization is typically intended by dictatorial regimes to be a controlled opening of the political space. When it fails—that is, when the opposition does win—a clampdown sometimes follows. Hence there is no certainty that the opposition would be able to celebrate its victory.

The final feature of contestation is that elections must be expected to be repeated. Whoever wins the current round of elections cannot use office to make it impossible for the competing political forces to win next time. Democracy, as Juan Linz once said, is government *pro tempore*. All political outcomes must be temporary: Losers do not forfeit the right to compete in the future, to negotiate again, to influence legislation, to pressure the bureaucracy, or to seek recourse to courts. Even constitutional provisions are not immutable; rules, too, can be changed according to rules.

Operationally, a regime was classified as a democracy if it did not fail under any of the four rules listed below. (Our timing rules are as follows: We code the regime that prevailed at the end of the year, even if it came to power on December 31, as, for example, dictatorship arrived in Nigeria in 1983. Transitions to authoritarianism are signaled by a coup d'état. Transitions to democracy are dated by the time of the inauguration of the newly elected government, not of the election. In the few cases, like those of the Dominican Republic in 1963, where a democratic regime lasted six months, or Bolivia in 1979, where the situation changed several times, the information about regimes that began and ended within the same year is lost.) A regime is classified as a dictatorship if at least one of these conditions holds:

- *Rule 1: "Executive Selection." The chief executive is not elected.*
- *Rule 2: "Legislative Selection." The legislature is not elected.*
- *Rule 3: "Party." There is no more than one party. Specifically, this rule applies if 1) there were no parties or 2) there was only one party, or 3) the current tenure in office ended up in the establishment of nonparty or single-party rule, or 4) the incumbents unconstitutionally closed the legislature and rewrote the rules in their favor.* Alternation in office overrides the party rule: Jamaica, where a single party at one time held 100 percent of the seats in the legislature yet subsequently yielded office after losing an election, was classified as democratic during the entire period.

These three rules are not sufficient, however, to classify those regimes which repeatedly hold elections, allow varying degrees of freedom for the opposition, and always win. There are some regimes which cannot be unambiguously classified on the basis of all the evidence produced by history: We have no way of telling whether the incumbents would have held elections if they were not certain to win. In such cases we must decide which error we prefer to avoid: classifying as democracies regimes that may not be ones or rejecting as democracies regimes that may in fact be ones. Err we must; the only question is which way. We decided to err on the conservative side, disqualifying as democracies regimes that pass the previous three rules but not the following:

- *Rule 4: "Type II Error." The incumbents held office in the immediate past by virtue of elections for more than two terms or without being elected, and until today or the time when they were overthrown they have not lost an election.*

Throughout this discussion, we have focused on democracy. We treat dictatorship simply as a residual category, perhaps better denominated as "not democracy."

Since we are often told that democracy "is" a continuous variable, here are the reasons we insist on dichotomizing political regimes: 1) While some democracies are more democratic than others, unless offices are contested, no regime should be considered democratic. Kenneth A. Bollen and Robert W. Jackman, in their 1989 *American Sociological Review* essay "Democracy, Stability, and Dichotomies," confuse the argument that some democracies are more democratic than others with the claim that one can distinguish the degree of "democracy" for any pair of regimes. 2) The idea that we should, as Bollen and Jackman suggest in their discussion of "borderline cases," place the cases that cannot be unambiguously classified given our rules into an "intermediate" category, halfway between democracy and dictatorship, strikes us as ludicrous. 3) "Borderline cases" constitute either systematic or random errors. Systematic errors can be treated by explicit rules, such as our Type II Error rule, and their consequences can be examined statistically. Once this decision is made, the classification is unambiguous. 4) In turn, some errors random with regard to the rules will remain and we have to live with them. But there are no a priori reasons to think that a more refined classification will have a smaller measurement error. A finer scale generates smaller errors but more of them, a rougher scale generates larger errors but fewer of them. If the distribution of true observations is unimodal and close to symmetric, a more refined classification will have a smaller error, but in fact observations on all the polychotomous scales tend to be U-shaped, which advantages a dichotomous classification.

Whatever the peculiarities of our rules, the resulting classification differs little from alternative approaches: the Coppedge-Reinecke scale for 1978 predicts 92 percent of our regimes, the Bollen 1965 scale predicts 85 percent, and the Gurr scales of autocracy and democracy for 1950–86 jointly predict 91 percent. The Gastil scale of political liberties, covering the period from 1972 to 1990, predicts 93.2 percent of our classification; his scale of civil liberties predicts 91.5 percent; and the two scales jointly predict 94.2 percent of our regimes. Hence there is no reason to think that our results are idiosyncratic in the particular classification of regimes.

Since the distinction between parliamentary and presidential systems is uncontroversial, we state it only briefly. In parliamentary systems, the legislative assembly can dismiss the government, while under presidential systems it cannot. This criterion coincides perfectly with the mode of selection of the government: by the legislature in parliamentary systems, by the voters (directly or indirectly) in presidential systems. Within each type of institutional design there are important differences. Most important among these differences is the electoral system, some varieties of which may or may not be prone to generate legislative majorities.

Some institutional arrangements, however, do not fit either pure type: They are "premier-presidential," "semipresidential," or "mixed," according to different terminologies. In such systems, the president is elected for a fixed term and has some executive powers, but governments serve at the discretion of the parliament. These "mixed" systems are not homogeneous: Most lean closer to parliamentarism insofar as the government is responsible to the legislature; others, notably Portugal between 1976 and 1981, grant the president the power to appoint and dismiss governments and therein lean closer to presidentialism.

Among the 135 countries which are included in our sample, there were 50 parliamentary democracies, 46 presidential, and 8 mixed. Outside the Americas, there were nine presidential democracies: Congo (1960–62), Ghana (1979–80), Nigeria (1979–82), Uganda (1980–84), Bangladesh (1986–90), South Korea (1988–present), Pakistan (1972–76), and the Philippines (before 1964 and then from 1986 to the present).

In Latin America, the only parliamentary regimes were the short-lived attempt in Brazil, preceding the 1964 coup, and Suriname. Most West European countries have parliamentary systems, but parliamentary democracies can also be found in most other parts of the world.

NOTES

1. Most of the political data were collected by the authors, but some are taken from Arthur S. Banks, *Cross-National Time-Series Data Archive* (Binghamton, N.Y.: Center for Social Analysis, State University of New York at Binghamton, magnetic tape, 1993). They are described in Michael Alvarez, José Antonio Cheibub, Fernando Limongi, and Adam Przeworski, "Classifying Political Regimes for the ACLP Data Set" (Working Paper No. 3, Chicago Center on Democracy, University of Chicago, 1994). Most of the economic data are derived from Penn World Tables, version 5.6; other data are from the World Bank and the International Monetary Fund. We refer to this collection of data as the ACLP data base. Saudi Arabia and the five Persian Gulf states were excluded because oil revenues accounted for more than 50 percent of their GDP most of the time.

2. These numbers add up to 104 democratic institutional systems since there were three democratic regimes that changed their institutional framework without passing through a dictatorial spell.

3. Adam Przeworski and Fernando Limongi, "Democracy and Development" (paper presented at the Nobel Symposium on Democracy, Uppsala, Sweden, 27–30 August 1994). For divergent assessments of how regimes affect growth, see the overview presented in Przeworski and Limongi, "Political Regimes and Economic Growth," *Journal of Economic Perspectives* 7 (1993): 51–69. For recent econometric evidence, see John F. Helliwell, "Empirical Linkages Between Democracy and Economic Growth," *British Journal of Political Science* 24 (1993): 225–48; Robert J. Barro, "Democracy and Growth" (Working Paper No. 4909, National Bureau of Economic Research, Cambridge, Mass., 1994).

4. All figures for annual per-capita income are expressed in purchasing power parity (PPP) U.S. dollars in 1985 international prices, as given by version 5.5 of the Penn World Tables. In some cases, these numbers differ significantly from the 5.6 release, used in the remainder of this paper to measure the "level of development."

5. The results reported in this paragraph are treated at length in Adam Przeworski and Fernando Limongi, "Modernization: Theories and Facts" (Working Paper No. 8, Chicago Center on Democracy, University of Chicago, 1995).

6. After the fact, it may appear that development led to democracy. Suppose that we observe a dictatorship with a per-capita income of $2,000 a year in a country that grows at 2.5 percent per year. Assume further that at $2,000 any dictatorship faces each year the same risk of dying, equal to 0.025. If this dictatorship died exactly 28 years after its birth, at $4,000, we would be tempted to attribute its demise to development. But this dictatorial regime would have had a 50 percent cumulative chance of making it all the way to $4,000 *even if the marginal chance of surviving (the hazard rate) was exactly the same at $4,000 as at $2,000.* Conversely, take Spain, which we observe for the first time in 1950 at $1,953 per-capita income and which grew under the dictatorship at the average rate of 5.25 percent per annum, to reach $7,531 by 1976. Suppose that the Spanish dictatorship faced during the entire period a 0.03 chance of dying during each year, so that, assuming an exponential hazard function, it had about a 50 percent chance of not being around by 1974 *even if it had not developed at all.*

7. Samuel P. Huntington, *Political Order in Changing Societies* (New Haven: Yale University Press, 1968); Samuel P. Huntington and Joan Nelson, *No Easy Choice: Political Participation in Developing Countries* (Cambridge: Harvard University Press,

1976); and Guillermo O'Donnell, *Modernization and Bureaucratic-Authoritarianism: Studies in South American Politics* (Berkeley: Institute of International Studies, University of California, 1973).

8. In addition to the transitions in Argentina in 1955, 1962, 1966, and 1976, they occurred in Chile in 1973, Uruguay in 1973, Suriname in 1980, Turkey in 1967, and Fiji in 1987.

9. Seymour Martin Lipset, "Some Social Requisites of Democracy: Economic Development and Political Legitimacy," *American Political Science Review* 53 (1959): 56. Our best guess is that the European countries which succumbed to fascism between the wars had per-capita incomes not higher than $2,000 in the 1985 international prices. See Przeworski and Limongi, "Modernizations," 1995.

10. Lipset, *Political Man: The Social Bases of Politics* (Baltimore: Johns Hopkins University Press, 1981 [orig. publ. 1960]), esp. 27–63, 459–76, and 488–503; Mancur Olson, "Rapid Growth as a Destabilizing Force," *Journal of Economic History* 23 (1963): 453–72; and Huntington, *Political Order in Changing Societies.*

11. This finding parallels again the results of John B. Londregan and Keith T. Poole with regard to coups, which they found to be less likely when the economy grows. See John B. Londregan and Keith T. Poole, "Poverty, the Coup Trap, and the Seizure of Executive Power," *World Politics* 42 (1990): 151–83.

12. Larry Diamond and Juan J. Linz, "Introduction: Politics, Democracy, and Society in Latin America," in Larry Diamond, Juan J. Linz, and Seymour Martin Lipset, eds., *Democracy in Developing Countries: Latin America* (Boulder, Colo.: Lynne Rienner, 1989).

13. Hirschman's argument was that a moderate rate of inflation allows governments to pacify the most militant groups. See "The Social and Political Matrix of Inflation: Elaborations on the Latin American Experience," in *Essays in Trespassing: Economics to Politics and Beyond* (New York: Cambridge University Press, 1981), 177–207.

14. Edward N. Muller, "Democracy, Economic Development, and Income Inequality," *American Sociological Review* 53 (1988): 50–68.

15. Note again the parallel finding of John B. Londregan and Keith T. Poole in "Poverty, the Coup Trap, and the Seizure of Executive Power" that coups breed coups.

16. Juan J. Linz, "The Perils of Presidentialism," *Journal of Democracy* 1 (Winter 1990): 51–69 and "The Virtues of Parliamentarism," *Journal of Democracy* 1 (Fall 1990): 84–91.

17. Juan J. Linz, "Democracy: Presidential or Parliamentary—Does It Make a Difference?" (paper prepared for the Workshop on Political Parties in the Southern Cone, Woodrow Wilson International Center for Scholars, Washington, D.C., 1984). Linz's claim is disputed by Scott Mainwaring and Matthew Shugart, "Juan Linz, Presidentialism, and Democracy: A Critical Appraisal" (Working Paper No. 200, Helen Kellogg Institute for International Studies, University of Notre Dame, 1993).

18. Walter Bagehot, "The English Constitution: The Cabinet," in Arend Lijphart, ed., *Parliamentary Versus Presidential Government* (Oxford: Oxford University Press, 1992), 18. Woodrow Wilson's 1884 essay "Committee or Cabinet Government?"—reprinted in the same volume—makes an argument similar to Bagehot's. Also to be found in Lijphart's collection is an analysis of the U.S. political structure done to mark the 1976 Bicentennial by the U.S. Committee on the Constitutional System. The Commit-tee notes that "the separation of powers, as a principle of constitutional structure, has served us well in preventing tyranny and

the abuse of high office, but it has done so by encouraging confrontation, and deadlock, and by diffusing accountability for the results."

19. Note that throughout we refer only to the share of the largest party in the legis-lature, whether or not it has been the same as the party of the president. In the United States, since 1968, the control of at least one house of the Congress has rested in the hands of the party other than that of the president 80 percent of the time.

20. Mainwaring counted democratic breakdowns since 1945, finding 27 under presidentialism, 19 under parliamentarism, and 4 under other types. "Presidentialism, Multipartism, and Democracy: The Difficult Combination," *Comparative Political Studies* 26 (1993): 198–228.

21. Mainwaring, "Presidentialism in Latin America," *Latin American Research Review* 25 (1990): 157–79. Alfred Stepan and Cindy Skach, "Meta-Institutional Frameworks and Democratic Consolidation," *World Politics* 46 (1993): 1–22.

22. Mainwaring and Shugart, in "Juan Linz, Presidentialism, and Democracy," take issue with Linz: in their view it is majoritarian parliamentarism, rather than presidentialism, that increases the political stakes. Yet even if majoritarian parliamentary systems last shorter than minoritarian ones, parliamentary democracies of any kind last longer than presidential regimes. Whether this difference is due to the intensity of political conflicts, however, we do not know.

23. Only Pakistan went from parliamentarism in 1950–55 to presidentialism in 1972–76 and back to parliamentarism in 1988. Only Ghana, Nigeria, South Korea (which was a parliamentary democracy for one year in 1960), and Turkey chose a presidential system after having experienced parliamentary democracies. Lastly, only Suriname opted for a mixed system after having experienced democratic presidentialism.

24. This is the argument of the Nigerian Constitution Drafting Committee of 1976: "The tendency indeed of all people throughout the world is to elevate a single person to the position of ruler. In the context of Africa the division [of powers] is not only meaningless, it is difficult to maintain in practice. No African head of state has been known to be content with the position of a mere figurehead." See the Committee's report in Lijphart, *Parliamentary Versus Presidential Government*.

25. Only two parliamentary democracies emerged from a civilian dictatorship and died before 1991. Their expected life is 22 years, but the tiny number of countries involved greatly diminishes confidence in this number.

26. See Banks, *Cross-National Time-Series Data Archive*. Among the 35 transitions that occurred after 1973, parliamentary institutions were chosen in 13 cases at the average level of $3,414, presidential institutions in 19 cases at the average level of $2,591, making the effect even more pronounced.

27. This is not to argue that countries that have adopted presidential institutions during recent transitions to democracy should immediately attempt to move to parliamentarism. Whenever institutional choice is present on the political agenda, substantive conflicts, even minor ones, tend to spill over to institutional issues. Such situations are dangerous for democracy, since they signify that there are no clear rules by which substantive conflicts can be terminated. Hence having a clear and stable institutional system is more important than having a perfect one. We owe this observation to Hyug Baeg Im.

28. The 1853 Constitution sets the period between the election and the inauguration at nine months because that is how long it took electors to travel from the interior to Buenos Aires. The transfer of office from President Raúl Alfonsín to the President-elect Carlos Menem was shortened as a result of a mutual agreement under the pressure of an inflationary crisis.

29.Robert A. Dahl, "Transitions to Democracy" (address delivered to the symposium on "Voices of Democracy," University of Dayton, Center for International Studies, 16–17 March 1990).

30. Guillermo O'Donnell, "Partial Institutionalization: Latin American and Elsewhere" (paper presented at the conference on "Consolidating Third Wave Democracies: Trends and Challenges," Taipei, Taiwan, 27–30 August 1995), implies that "institutionalization" can be understood in two ways: either as a process of gradual stabilization of expectations that a particular institutional system will orient political actions or as an increasing fit between formal institutions and real practices. If "institutionalization" is taken in the first sense, it is tautologically related to "consolidation." But whether democracy can survive when the formal institutions do not describe real practices is an empirical question.

14

PARTY SYSTEMS IN THE THIRD WAVE

Scott Mainwaring

Scott Mainwaring *is professor of government and director of the Helen Kellogg Institute for International Studies at the University of Notre Dame. His two most recent books are* Presidentialism and Democracy in Latin America *(1997) and* Rethinking Party Systems in the Third Wave of Democratization *(1999).*

One of the most difficult obstacles facing the new post-1974 democracies in their efforts at democratic consolidation is weakly institutionalized party systems. The importance of this distinctive characteristic of party systems in the third-wave democracies has not been sufficiently recognized. Although analyses of Latin American and East European party systems have proliferated in the past decade, they have generally not attempted to challenge the manner in which political scientists typically think about and compare party systems. Such a challenge is in order.

The conventional criteria by which party systems are usually compared are the number of parties and the degree of ideological polarization. Along these two dimensions, the party systems of the third-wave democracies often resemble those of Western Europe. But if we bring in a third dimension—that of institutionalization—the contrast between West European systems and those of new democracies is substantial. Party systems in the third-wave democracies are markedly less institutionalized than those in most long-established democracies. This difference should not be obscured by the fact that parties in the advanced industrial democracies are facing new challenges and experiencing some erosion.

Of course, what is true in general is not true in every case: Not all third-wave democratizers have weakly institutionalized party systems. Portugal, Greece, and Spain, the Southern European countries where the third wave began, took relatively little time to develop systems with a greater degree of institutionalization than is found in most other third-

TABLE—IDEAL TYPE CHARACTERISTICS OF WELL AND WEAKLY INSTITUTIONALIZED PARTY SYSTEMS

	WELL INSTITUTIONALIZED SYSTEMS	*WEAKLY INSTITUTIONALIZED (INCHOATE) SYSTEMS*
STABILITY IN PATTERNS OF INTERPARTY COMPETITION	Highly stable. Major parties remain on the scene for decades. Electoral volatility is low.	Quite volatile. Some parties suffer precipitous declines, while other parties enjoy sudden electoral upsurges.
PARTY ROOTS IN SOCIETY	Parties are strongly rooted in society. Most citizens vote for the same party over time and vote because of party. Organized interests tend to be associated with a party.	Parties are weakly rooted in society. Only a minority of citizens regularly vote for the same party. Instead, citizens vote according to candidates or, if they vote because of the party label, they switch party preferences.
LEGITIMACY OF PARTIES AND ELECTIONS	Parties and elections enjoy unassailable legitimacy. Parties are seen as a necessary and desirable democratic institution.	Many individuals and groups question the legitimacy of parties and elections. A significant minority of citizens believes that parties are neither necessary nor desirable.
PARTY ORGANIZATION	Parties have significant material and human resources. Party processes are well institutionalized. Individual leaders, while important, do not overshadow the party.	Parties have few resources. Parties are the creation of, and remain at the disposal of, individual political leaders. Intraparty processes are not well institutionalized.

wave democracies. Not coincidentally, democratic consolidation also moved along briskly in these three countries. In Uruguay, old party patterns reasserted themselves after the reestablishment of democracy in 1984. Much the same thing happened in Chile after 1990; in both countries the "new" party systems are reasonably well institutionalized. Among long-established democracies, cases of weak party institutionalization occur rarely and briefly; among third-wave democratizers, they occur more often and have more staying power.

Institutionalization means the process by which a practice or organization becomes well established and widely known, if not universally accepted. Samuel P. Huntington calls it "the process by which organizations and procedures acquire value and stability."[1] The belief that a given ensemble of procedures and organizations will endure shapes expectations, attitudes, and behavior. In particular, party-system institutionalization means that actors entertain clear and stable expectations about the behavior of other actors, and hence about the fundamental contours and rules of party competition and behavior.

In an institutionalized party system, there is stability in who the main parties are and in how they behave. Change, while not completely precluded, is limited. The notion of institutionalization implies nothing teleological, no necessary progression from weaker to greater institutionalization. Party systems can deinstitutionalize, as they have done in Canada, Italy, Peru, and Venezuela during this decade. Nor is it inevitable that most third-wave democracies will move toward more institutionalized party systems. On the contrary, it seems likely that many will retain weakly institutionalized party systems.

Although weak institutionalization is typically associated with a variety of problems, this does not imply that greater institutionalization is always better. To the contrary, very high levels of institutionalization may result from a stultified party system. The relationship between party-system institutionalization and the quality of democracy, then, is far from linear, and an institutionalized party system is far from a panacea.

We can conceptualize four dimensions of party-system institutionalization, which are shown in summary form in the Table on the facing page.

First, more institutionalized party systems enjoy considerable stability; patterns of party competition manifest regularity. A system in which major parties regularly appear and then disappear or become minor parties is weakly institutionalized, as is one in which parties' vote totals often fluctuate widely.

Second, more institutionalized systems are ones in which parties have strong roots in society. The ties that bind parties and citizens are firmer; otherwise, parties do not structure political preferences over time and there is limited regularity in how people vote. Strong party roots in society help provide the regularity that institutionalization implies.

Similarly, links between organized interests and parties are generally more developed, although even in institutionalized systems there are considerable variations along this dimension.

Partly as a consequence of these links, parties in more institutionalized systems tend to be consistent in their relative ideological positions. A party that is markedly to the left of another party does not suddenly move to its rival's right simply to gain short-term electoral advantage, for parties are constrained by their need to maintain the support of activists. If major parties change their relative ideological position, it usually signals weak ties between parties and society and a lack of regularity in the process of how parties compete and how they relate to social actors.

Third, in more institutionalized systems, the major political actors accord legitimacy to parties. Elites and the citizenry in general believe in parties as fundamental, necessary, and desirable institutions of democratic politics. Legitimacy is a dimension of institutionalization because the latter concept implies that actors base their behavior on the expectation that a practice will continue. Legitimacy reinforces the tendency of actors to expect and to perpetuate a pattern of behavior.

Finally, in more institutionalized systems, party organizations matter. Parties are not subordinated to the interests of a few ambitious leaders, but possess an independent status and value of their own. Institutionalization is limited as long as a party is the personal instrument of a leader or a small coterie. As institutionalization grows, parties become autonomous vis-à-vis individuals who initially may have created them as mere instruments. It is a sign of greater system institutionalization if parties have firmly established structures; if they are territorially comprehensive; if they are well organized; if they have clearly defined internal structures and procedures; and if they have resources of their own. In more institutionalized systems, there is a routinization of intraparty procedures, including procedures for selecting and changing the party leadership.

Peaceful transfer of the leadership from one person or a small coterie to a different group indicates a process of institutionalization. The situation in Mexico under the long-ruling Institutional Revolutionary Party (PRI) reflected a form of institutionalization: Mexico's president dominated the PRI, but every sixth year brought turnover in the presidency (and frequently in the party leadership, too). There was a clear limit to the period during which a particular individual can dominate the party. Conversely, weak institutionalization was manifested in examples such as Juan Perón's Justicialist Party in Argentina, Fernando Collor de Mello's Party of National Reconstruction in Brazil, and Alberto Fujimori's Cambio 90 in Peru. In each of these cases, a single leader created and continued to dominate a party.

Party-system institutionalization implies a commitment to an organization and to some minimal collective goals (especially winning elections); it requires loyalty beyond allegiance to a single leader. In more institutionalized systems, politicians as a rule are loyal to their party on two basic issues: They do not change parties, and they do not publicly support candidates of other parties. A few politicians may change parties, but in institutionalized systems this practice is unusual.

Party systems characterized by lesser degrees of institutionalization can be termed inchoate. This implies less regularity in patterns and rules of party competition; weaker party roots in society; less legitimacy accorded to parties and elections; and weaker party organizations, often dominated by personalistic leaders.

Electoral Volatility

My claim that party systems differ profoundly along the dimension of institutionalization is buttressed by the application of the four criteria listed above to an array of cases drawn from Western Europe, Southern Europe, East Central Europe, and Latin America. The data reveal sharp differences in the degree of party-system institutionalization. These differences have important implications for democratic politics.

The first criterion of institutionalization, regularity in patterns of party competition, lends itself readily to measurement and comparison. The yardstick is electoral volatility, which is computed by adding the net change in percentage of votes gained or lost by each party from one election to the next, then dividing by two. For example, in a three-party system, if Party A wins 38 percent in one election and 43 percent in the next, while Party B sees its share drop from 47 to 27 percent, and C increases from 15 percent to 30 percent, then $V=(5+20+15)\div2$, or 20. Thus electoral volatility figures provide us with an index of the aggregate turnover of votes among parties from one election to the next in a given country.

I calculated lower-chamber electoral volatility for eight established advanced industrial democracies, three Southern European cases, the three old democracies in Latin America, eight third-wave Latin American cases, and four post-Soviet cases.[2] Mean country (as opposed to election) volatility was 9.7 for the advanced industrial democracies, 20.5 for the older Latin American democracies, 15.7 for the three Southern European cases, 30.0 for the eight newer Latin American cases, and 35.3 for the four post-Soviet cases. Volatility ranged from an average of 4.0 in the United States to 58.5 in Peru.

These dramatic differences in the stability of patterns of party competition have far-reaching consequences for democratic politics. With low volatility, electoral outcomes are stable from one election to the next, lending a high degree of predictability to a crucial aspect of democratic politics. Parties are long-lasting, and citizens know what they stand for. Opportunities for new parties are restricted, not legally, but rather as a result of the low turnover.

With high volatility, outcomes are less stable. The electoral market is more open and unpredictable. Major parties can suffer big losses, while new or minor ones can come out of nowhere to score large gains. The rapid rise and fall of parties make the system more opaque to citizens, who have less time to get a fix on where the different contenders stand. The probability of major policy changes is greater under high volatility, as is legislative turnover; lawmaking bodies in high-volatility systems are usually not hotbeds of political experience.

Parties' Roots in Society

In more institutionalized systems, parties put down deep roots in society. Where parties have such roots, most voters feel connected to a party and regularly vote for its candidates. Links between organized interest groups and parties tend to be tighter.

Party roots in society and electoral volatility, while analytically distinct, are closely related because the former limit the latter. If most citizens support the same party from one election to the next, there are relatively few of the floating voters whose shifts in allegiance are reflected in high electoral volatility. Where parties are deeply rooted in society, most voters support the same party over time and across different kinds of elections. Survey and voting data provide indications of the extent to which voters cast their ballots on a partisan basis (and hence the extent to which parties are rooted in the electorate). Parties are more deeply rooted if most voters state that they voted or intend to vote for candidates of the same party in consecutive elections.

Similarly, data from the local to the national level may indicate congruence or divergence between voting patterns for one position and another. For example, in presidential systems, the difference between presidential and legislative voting provides relevant information in assessing how deeply parties penetrate society. Where parties shape the political preferences of most voters, the difference between presidential and legislative voting should be less pronounced. Citizens more frequently vote on the basis of party labels, and therefore they tend to vote for the same label in legislative and presidential elections. In the United States between 1944 and 1992, the mean difference between the presidential and the lower-chamber vote was 10.3 percent. In Brazil in 1994, by contrast, it was 44.1 percent, indicating that large numbers of votes are not party-oriented. In Russia, surveys indicate that 70 percent of all voters planned to split their tickets in their country's 1993 national elections.[3]

The percentage of respondents who report having a party preference also helps us to assess the rootedness of parties in society. Although the precise level of party identification varies according to how the question is asked, the data again show a chasm between most of the advanced industrial democracies and most of the third-wave countries other than Greece and Uruguay, where party identification approaches West European levels. In most West European countries, 60 to 70 percent of voters identify at least somewhat with a party, though this figure has declined in recent decades. According to Stephen White, Richard Rose, and Ian McAllister, only 22 percent of Russian respondents report identifying with a party. Rose gives a figure of 80 percent reporting a party preference in England, compared to 40 percent for the Czech Republic, 30 percent for Slovakia, 20 percent for Hungary, and only 15 percent for Poland. He writes of "demobilized" voters in East Central Europe, referring to individuals who have no preferred party and do not trust parties; such voters form the clear majority in the entire region.[4]

In Southern Europe in 1989, rates of party identification ranged from a low of 30 percent in Spain to 63 percent in Italy. In Latin America, according to a Latinobarómetro survey, the percentage of party identifiers in the eight countries for which data are available (Argentina, Brazil, Chile, Mexico, Paraguay, Peru, Uruguay, and Venezuela) ranged from 67 percent of respondents in Uruguay to under 40 percent in Argentina (38 percent), Chile (36 percent), Venezuela, and Brazil (both 33 percent). In a 1995 poll taken in Lima, Peru, only 20 percent of respondents said that they identified with a party.[5] Thus while most voters in virtually all of the advanced industrial democracies have a party preference, large majorities in many third-wave democracies do not.

The ability of parties to survive a long time indicates that they have probably captured the long-term loyalties of some social groups. Consequently, in more institutionalized systems, parties are likely to have longer organizational histories. Comparing the same groups of countries once again shows sharp differences. On average, 71 percent of national legislative seats in all eight advanced industrial democracies were occupied during 1993–96 by parties that had been in existence at least since 1950. This figure was lowered by Italy, where the collapse of the party system left older parties in control of only a little more than a fifth of all seats. For Greece, Portugal, and Spain, the average was 18 percent. For Latin America's three oldest democracies it was 58 percent, while for that continent's nine third-wave democracies it was 40 percent. This comparison excludes the post-Soviet cases because the duration and massive impact of communist rule made it more difficult for older parties to survive. Still, the rapidity with which parties have appeared and disappeared in Russia and Poland is notable. Robert G. Moser observes that "of the 13 electoral blocs participating in the 1993 [Russian] parliamentary elections only four existed under the same label a year earlier."[6]

The contrasts among individual cases are stunning. In the 1994 U.S.

midterm elections, parties whose founding predated 1950 captured 97 percent of the vote; Norway, Sweden, and Finland were close behind at 90, 89, and 82 percent, respectively. At the other end of the scale, Bolivia, Brazil, Ecuador, and Peru have few pre-1950 parties that matter much electorally. In Peru, only one party created by 1950, APRA, ran in the 1995 elections, capturing a feeble 4 percent share of the lower-chamber vote. Most of the other Latin American cases fall somewhere in the middle.

Another way to examine party longevity is to consider the ages of parties that won at least 10 percent of the seats in recent legislative elections.[7] In the United States, the mean age of these parties (that is, Democrats and Republicans) was 154 years in 1996. In Peru, meanwhile, such parties had a mean age of only four years. The country mean was 88 years for the eight advanced industrial democracies, 29 for the three Southern European democracies, 74 for the three old Latin American democracies, and 44 for the nine third-wave Latin American cases.

Party Rootedness vs. Personalism

The ability of nonpartisan and antiparty candidates to win office serves as another indicator of party rootedness in society. Where citizens are attached to a party, such candidates rarely win high office. While nonpartisan or antiparty candidates rarely do well in consolidated democracies, such independent office-seekers can succeed in new democracies with inchoate party systems. Space for populists is especially available in presidential systems, where candidates can appeal directly to voters without needing to become head of a party in order to become a governor or president. For example, Brazil's Fernando Collor de Mello ran for president in 1989 at the head of a party that he had created for the purpose, and he ran as an *antiparty* figure. In the October 1990 congressional elections, held just seven months after his inauguration, his party won only 40 of 503 lower-chamber seats, and it evaporated within months of his December 1992 resignation (submitted to avoid impending impeachment proceedings). In 1990, Peru's Alberto Fujimori created an ad hoc party as part of his successful presidential run. He too campaigned against parties and has subsequently eschewed efforts to build a party. In Peru, political independents dominated the 1995 municipal elections. Hoping to imitate Fujimori's success at winning popular support, a new cohort of antiparty politicians has emerged.

Personalism and antiparty politicians are also common in some post-Soviet cases. Russian president Boris Yeltsin is not a member of a party and has undermined parties. Aleksandr Lebed, the former Soviet air force general who finished third in the 1996 Russian presidential election, ran as a quasi-independent. So did Stanisław Tymiński, who finished second in the 1990 Polish presidential election. Nonpartisan candidates have fared well in the plurality races for both chambers of the Russian parliament. In the 1993 elections, well over half of the single-member–district candidates for the lower chamber had no partisan affiliation, and only 83 of the 218 deputies elected in these races belonged to a party. In 1995, more than 1,000 of the 2,700 candidates for the single-member–district seats were independents. Independents won 78 of the 225 single-member seats; the largest single party could muster only 58 seats.[8]

In more institutionalized party systems, such personalism is the exception. Prime ministers in Western Europe and presidents in the Latin American countries with more institutionalized systems are almost always longtime members of major parties.

These indicators show that there are profound differences in the rootedness of parties in society. In most of the advanced industrial democracies, despite some erosion in party voting over recent decades, more than half the voters identify with and vote for the same party over time.[9] In Brazil, Peru, and Russia, only a small minority of voters stick with the same party through election after election. The weakness of parties' social roots means that democratic political competition, rather than being channeled through parties and other democratic institutions, assumes a personalized character.

These differences in party rootedness have significant implications for democratic politics. In more institutionalized systems, voters are more likely to identify with a party, and parties are more likely to dominate patterns of political recruitment. In inchoate systems, a larger share of the electorate votes more according to personal image or personal connections than party, and antiparty politicians find it easier to win office. Thus populism and "antipolitics" are more common in countries with weakly institutionalized systems. Personalities rather than party organizations dominate the political scene. Given the propensity toward personalism and the comparative weakness of parties, mechanisms of democratic accountability are usually weaker. Weak party roots in society and a high degree of personalism enhance the role of television in campaigns, especially for executive positions. Democracies with weak party systems tend to take on what Guillermo O'Donnell calls "delegative" characteristics, as mechanisms of accountability grow weaker, personalism increases, and the executive branch claims sweeping powers.[10]

Because they rely on direct links to the masses, populist leaders are more likely than others to act with an eye toward publicity rather than long-range policy impact. Tied to parties loosely if at all, they are more likely to be erratic and to violate unspoken "rules of the game." A vicious cycle can set in as the inchoate nature of the party system creates opportunities for populists, who then govern without attempting to create more solid institutions. In an inchoate system, predictability is low while the potential for erratic leadership is high. Politics tends to be more personalized and patrimonial.

In more institutionalized systems, party labels are powerful symbols, and party commitments are important. Parties give citizens a way of understanding who is who in politics without needing to read all the fine print. By doing so, they help to facilitate accountability, a central element of democratic politics. Even if voters cannot evaluate individual legislative candidates, they can evaluate party labels and can differentiate among the parties.

With inchoate party systems, there is less institutional control over leadership recruitment. Even in this era of instant mass communications (which makes it easier for candidates to reach the public directly) and of skepticism about parties (which makes it easier for antiparty politicians to gain currency), countries with more institutionalized party systems are less likely to have antiparty leaders.

Because of the greater probability that a populist with a weak party base might be elected, institutional impasses are more likely in democracies with inchoate party systems. In institutionalized systems, candidates from minor parties have little prospect of being elected president. Most voters are loyal to a party, and they generally cast their ballots for candidates from that party. This reduces the likelihood that a candidate from a minor party could win the election, and also lengthens the odds facing populist, antiparty candidates.

An election is personalistic if citizens cast their ballots more on the basis of a candidate's personal appeal than on the basis of party profile. Of course, some citizens in all democracies vote this way, but where personalistic disputes are decisive and party labels are less entrenched, those who win elections are likely to feel less restrained in how they govern. They are more prone to demagoguery and populism, both of which can have deleterious effects on democracy.

The Legitimacy of Parties and Elections

Legitimacy usually refers to attitudes about the political regime as a whole, but the concept can also be attached to particular democratic institutions. Parties are legitimate to the extent that political actors view them favorably, or at least consider them necessary parts of a good political regime. Comparatively positive attitudes toward parties increase the likelihood that the system will be stable.

Although there is growing citizen disaffection with parties even in institutionalized systems, parties have still lower legitimacy in most third-wave democratizers. White, Rose, and McAllister report that in Russia parties are the least trusted among the 16 institutions evaluated in a series of public-opinion surveys. On a scale of 1 (no trust) to 7 (great trust), only 2 percent of respondents gave parties a 6 or 7, compared to

60 percent who gave them a 1 or 2. Moreover, 43 percent agreed with the statement, "We do not need parliament or elections, but instead a strong leader who can make decisions and put them into effect fast."[11]

Parties also ranked as the institution (among eight) that commanded least sympathy in Portugal, Spain, Greece, and Italy, but nevertheless "the legitimacy of parties is high in all four countries." On a sympathy-index scale ranging from 1 (least sympathy) to 10 (greatest), parties scored a mean 4.4 in Portugal, 4.2 in Spain, 4.1 in Italy, and 4.9 in Greece in 1985. Greek parties scored only 11 percent below the midway point (5.5) of the scale.[12] On White, Rose, and McAllister's trust index, which ranged from 1 (least trust) to 7, Russian parties scored only 2.3, a figure that put them almost 43 percent below the midpoint of the scale.[13]

In a survey in Central Europe, pollsters asked several questions that tapped the comparative legitimacy of parties. One question asked citizens whether they approved of the dissolution of parties and parliament: 40 percent said yes in Poland, compared to only 8 percent in Austria. Thirty-one percent of Polish respondents said that they would prefer a one-party system, as compared with 8 percent in the Czech Republic. Thirty-nine percent in Poland said that they approved of rule by a strongman, as compared to 22 percent in Austria and only 19 percent in Slovakia.[14]

Although a 1995 Latinobarómetro survey question found that parties were generally the least trusted institution, the variance across cases was significant. In Uruguay, which has one of the more institutionalized party systems in Latin America, 41 percent of respondents expressed a lot of trust or some trust in parties, compared to only 21 percent in Peru and 17 percent in Brazil. In Venezuela, where the party system underwent a major crisis and deinstitutionalized in the 1990s, only 16 percent expressed some trust or a lot of trust. The level of trust in parties at the low end of the Latin American range is much lower than in the Southern European democracies.

The Latinobarómetro also asked respondents whether they believed that democracy could exist without political parties. A high percentage of respondents expressing the belief that parties are necessary for democracy suggests greater legitimacy of parties. In Uruguay and Argentina, both of which have moderately institutionalized party systems, more than 70 percent of respondents agreed that parties are necessary for democracy. Coming in at the low end (about 47 percent in both cases) were Brazil, which has a weakly institutionalized party system, and Paraguay, where democracy arrived only in 1993.

How do these differences in the legitimacy of parties affect democratic politics? The discrediting of parties explains the significant numbers of antiparty voters in many third-wave countries. Where parties are particularly discredited, it is easier for antiparty politicians to win office. The problems associated with antiparty politicians, including further attacks on democratic institutions and a somewhat greater likelihood of erratic leadership, are consequently more common in these countries.

The limited legitimacy of parties in inchoate party systems also hinders democratic consolidation, which involves not only outward obedience to the "rules of the game," but also a positive acceptance of certain beliefs and norms regarding the regime. The authors of a recent work on the subject consider a democracy consolidated "when all politically significant groups regard its key institutions as the only legitimate framework for political contestation, and adhere to democratic rules of the game."[15] Democracy is generally more consolidated when actors accord legitimacy to parties, since they constitute the main means of competing for state power in virtually all democratic systems.

Party Organization

With the partial exception of the United States, party organizations have long been relatively robust in countries with more institutionalized party systems. Parties in West European democracies have historically been well financed, had active (though now declining) mass memberships, maintained fairly sizable and professionalized staffs, and commanded strong loyalty on the part of elected representatives. Parties developed relatively clear and stable procedures for selecting leaders. In more institutionalized systems, the party is not subordinate to the leader. Although there have been important organizational differences between centrist and conservative parties, on the one hand, and leftist parties on the other, these differences pale in comparison to those between parties in more and less institutionalized systems.

In countries such as Bolivia, Brazil, Ecuador, Peru, and Russia, parties suffer from thin resources and weak professionalization. Party labels, though not devoid of ideological content, are often diffuse; many parties are little more than personalistic vehicles for their leading figures. In Peru and Russia, parties exercise little control over nominations. In Peru, for example, President Fujimori used focus groups and surveys to decide whom to put on his party's ticket.[16] Such personal control over congressional nominations is the antithesis of an institutionalized system. Moreover, as is also true in Russia, candidates in Peru can gain ballot access without a party and can win election as independents.

Politicians in some inchoate systems have little party loyalty, and switching allegiance is common. For example, in the Brazilian Congress of 1991–94, the 503 deputies changed parties 260 times. Between the December 1993 Russian parliamentary elections and October 1995, 128 of 450 Duma members switched parties. Similarly, in the weeks following the December 1995 Duma election, 142 Duma members switched parties.[17] The political elites' lack of party loyalty is mirrored by the citizenry at large. Organizational loyalty is much greater among politicians in countries with more institutionalized party systems. Party discipline is more frequently relaxed in countries with weakly institutionalized systems than in countries with stronger institutionalization. For example, in Latin America party discipline is strong in Argentina and Venezuela, which have comparatively institutionalized systems, and looser in Brazil, which has a less institutionalized system.

In sum, the solidity of party organization varies markedly across cases, with significant consequences for democratic politics. In some countries, party organizations have significant resources and command deep loyalty among the political elite; these organizations still dominate political campaigns. In others, party organizations are flimsy; party loyalties are frequently shallow, and politicians focus on cultivating personal followings among voters.

The Distinctiveness of Third-Wave Cases

Throughout most of the twentieth century, democratic politics has been rooted in the soil of relatively well-institutionalized party systems. Even the U.S. system, long considered weak compared to most of its West European counterparts, fits this description. Notwithstanding important differences among the party systems of the advanced industrial democracies, they are all relatively institutionalized.

Among the third-wave democracies, competitive political regimes exist in many countries with weakly institutionalized party systems. Democratic polities with inchoate party systems display traits that set them apart from democracies with more institutionalized systems: more personalism, weaker mechanisms of accountability, greater electoral volatility, more floating voters, more uncertainty. Although Guillermo O'Donnell does not discuss "delegative" democracy in terms of party-system characteristics, the phenomenon that he has identified is improbable if not impossible in more institutionalized party systems. It has become apparent that democracy can survive with weakly institutionalized party systems, but weak institutionalization harms the quality of democracy and the prospects for democratic consolidation.

It is possible that in some new democracies, an early period of low institutionalization will be followed by the construction of a more stable and deeply rooted party system. Yet cases such as those of Bolivia since 1980, Brazil since 1985, Ecuador since 1978, and especially Peru since 1980 show that institutionalization is not an inevitable product of time. In none of these cases has there been a clear move toward greater institutionalization, and electoral volatility remains at very high levels with no trend (that is, showing declining volatility in at least the last two elections) toward diminishing. In Peru, the old party system collapsed between the late 1980s and 1995.

Electoral volatility in the post-Soviet region also remains high and in most cases shows no clear sign of diminishing. The intuitively sensible idea that institutionalization will increase over time may still prove correct, but it is not yet supported by the empirical evidence, which rather suggests the continuing distinctiveness of Latin American and post-Soviet party systems.

To compare patterns of institutionalization, we can examine what occurred in earlier waves of democratization. A particularly useful comparison is with Austria, Germany, and Italy after World War II because it is clear which elections to use as the starting point for democracy. In Austria, electoral volatility in the first five democratic electoral periods after 1945 was 12.0, 3.6, 5.8, 3.0, and 1.7 percent; in Germany, 21.2, 9.2, 11.5, 7.6, and 6.0 percent; and in Italy, 23.0, 14.1, 5.2, 8.5, and 7.8 percent. Thus in a short time, patterns of party competition became highly stable. We can safely conclude, then, that even in the seemingly unlikely (based on developments so far) case that electoral volatility were to drop significantly in most Latin American and post-Soviet cases, the process of building a stable party system would have taken much longer than it did in Austria, Germany, and Italy—as well as in the rest of Western Europe.[18]

NOTES

1. Samuel P. Huntington, *Political Order in Changing Societies* (New Haven: Yale University Press, 1968), 12.

2. The eight advanced industrial democracies are Belgium, Finland, France, Italy, Norway, Sweden, Switzerland, and the United States. The three Southern European cases are Greece, Portugal, and Spain. The old Latin American democracies are Colombia, Costa Rica, and Venezuela, and the new ones are Argentina, Bolivia, Brazil, Chile, Ecuador, Mexico, Paraguay, Peru, and Uruguay. The Czech Republic, Poland, Russia, and Slovakia are the post-Soviet cases.

3. Stephen White, Richard Rose, and Ian McAllister, *How Russia Votes* (Chatham, N.J.: Chatham House, 1997), 139.

4. Stephen White, Richard Rose, and Ian McAllister, *How Russia Votes,* 135; Richard Rose, "Mobilizing Demobilized Voters in Post-Communist Societies" (Instituto Juan March de Estudios e Investigaciones, Working Paper 1995/96, September 1995), 22.

5. The Southern European data are reported in Hermann Schmitt, "On Party Attachment in Western Europe, and the Utility of Eurobarometer Data," *West European Politics* 12 (April 1998): 122–39. The Latinobarómetro data reported in this paper are printed with the permission of Marta Lagos. These data are provisional and subject to change. The Lima data are reported in Catherine M. Conaghan, "The Irrelevant Right: Alberto Fujimori and the New Politics of Pragmatic Peru," in Kevin Middlebrook, ed., *Conservative Parties and Democracy in Latin America* (Baltimore: Johns Hopkins University Press, 2000).

6. Robert G. Moser, "The Emergence of Political Parties in Post-Soviet Russia" (Ph.D. diss., University of Wisconsin–Madison, 1995), 10.

7. This idea was suggested by Robert H. Dix, "Democratization and the Institu-

tionalization of Latin American Political Parties," *Comparative Political Studies* 24 (January 1992): 488–511.

8. Robert G. Moser, "The Emergence of Political Parties in Post-Soviet Russia," 98; Stephen White, Richard Rose, and Ian McAllister, *How Russia Votes*, 203, 224.

9. Russell J. Dalton, Scott C. Flanagan, and Paul Allen Beck, eds., *Electoral Change in the Advanced Industrial Democracies: Realignment or Dealignment?* (Princeton: Princeton University Press, 1984).

10. Guillermo O'Donnell, "Delegative Democracy," *Journal of Democracy* 5 (January 1994): 55–69.

11. Stephen White, Richard Rose, and Ian McAllister, *How Russia Votes*, 51–52, 46.

12. Leonardo Morlino and José R. Montero, "Legitimacy and Democracy in Southern Europe," in Richard Gunther, P. Nikiforos Diamandouros, and Hans-Jürgen Puhle, eds., *The Politics of Democratic Consolidation: Southern Europe in Comparative Perspective* (Baltimore: Johns Hopkins University Press, 1995), 256–58.

13. Stephen White, Richard Rose, and Ian McAllister, *How Russia Votes*, 52–53.

14. Juan J. Linz, and Alfred Stepan, *Problems of Democratic Transition and Con-solidation: Southern Europe, South America, and Post-Communist Europe* (Baltimore: Johns Hopkins University Press, 1996), 285, citing Fritz Plasser and Peter A. Ulram, "Zum Stand der Demokatisierung in Ost-Mitteleuropa," in Fritz Plasser and Peter A. Ulram, eds., *Transformation oder Stagnation? Aktuelle Politische Trends in Osteuropa* (Vienna: Schriftenreihe des Zentrums für angewandte Politikforschung, 1993), 46–47.

15. Richard Gunther, P. Nikiforos Diamandouros, and Hans-Jürgen Puhle, "Introduction," in idem, eds., *Politics of Democratic Consolidation*, 7. See also Linz and Stepan, *Problems of Democratic Transition and Consolidation*, 5–6.

16. See Catherine M. Conaghan, "The Irrelevant Right."

17. Data on Brazil come from David J. Samuels, "Incentives to Cultivate a Party Vote in Candidate-Centric Electoral Systems: Evidence from Brazil," *Comparative Political Studies* 32 (June 1999): 487–518. Data on Russia come from Stephen White, Richard Rose, and Ian McAllister, *How Russia Votes*, 184, 238.

18. Data on Austria, Germany, Italy, and ten other West European countries come from Stefano Bartolini and Peter Mair, *Identity, Competition and Electoral Availability: The Stabilisation of European Electorates, 1885–1985* (Cambridge: Cambridge University Press, 1990), appendix 2.

15

WHAT MAKES ELECTIONS FREE AND FAIR?

Jørgen Elklit and Palle Svensson

Jørgen Elklit *is professor of political science at the University of Aarhus, Denmark. He has worked with elections and democratization in Africa, Asia, and Europe. In 1994 he was a member of the South African Independent Electoral Commission, and he is now advisor to the Lesotho Independent Electoral Commission.* ***Palle Svensson*** *is professor of political science at the University of Aarhus and has advised on and monitored elections in African countries. An earlier version of this essay was presented at the Nordic Political Science Association's Triennial Conference in Helsinki in August 1996.*

It was late in the afternoon in Kampala on 31 March 1994. Journalists were waiting impatiently for an announcement from international election observers. United Nations officials stated for the third time their argument that the observers should declare the March 28 elections for Uganda's Constituent Assembly "free and fair." But the election observers avoided that phrase. They had monitored only part of the electoral process; moreover, they knew that calling the election "free and fair" would hinder or preclude discussion of the problems they had discovered. In the end, the elections in Uganda—which were no worse than many other elections that have taken place in emerging democracies—were not declared "free and fair."

As this incident shows, election observers encounter great pressure—and not just from overeager journalists—to judge whether the elections in question were "free and fair." Indeed, sometimes it seems that this is all people want to know. "Free and fair" has become the catchphrase of UN officials, journalists, politicians, and political scientists alike. It exemplifies what Giovanni Sartori once called "conceptual stretching": "The wider the world under investigation, the more we need conceptual tools that are able to travel."[1] But what actually constitutes a "free and fair" election? Does the phrase mean only that the election was "acceptable," or does it imply something more?

International organizations have long been involved in monitoring and assessing elections and referendums. Especially notable has been the UN's role in referendums on independence, which began to take place in the late 1950s. Before the UN could recognize former colonies and trust territories as independent states, it had to know whether these votes had been "free and fair."[2] This concept supposedly made its first appearance in a report on Togoland's 1956 independence referendum.[3]

The UN's involvement in the November 1989 referendum in Namibia was fundamentally different: In that case the vote was not just an element of the colony's long liberation process but also an integral part of the UN's peacekeeping efforts in the area. In February 1990, the UN supervised presidential and legislative elections in Nicaragua. Interestingly, this was done at the request of the country itself, and as part of an assessment of the entire electoral process, not just of election-day events. Thus the UN acquired a major role in the electoral process of an independent member country—something that not all UN members saw as a positive development.

Subsequent elections and referendums in which the UN has been directly involved, either as part of peacekeeping efforts or because the countries in question sought its approval, include those in Haiti (December 1990), Angola (September 1992), Cambodia (May 1993), and Mozambique (October 1994). One might add to that list Eritrea (April 1993), South Africa (April 1994), and Malawi (June 1993 and May 1994), though the UN's involvement in these cases was less extensive and due in part to other factors.[4]

Besides the civil war–torn countries noted above, many other nations have taken dramatic steps toward democracy during the past decade. In many cases, individual Western countries have provided support for these developments; in other cases, the primary actors have been international organizations other than the UN (especially the Organization of American States, the European Union, the Organization for Security and Cooperation in Europe, the Inter-Parliamentary Union, and the Commonwealth Secretariat). Both national and international nongovernmental organizations (NGOs) have also become involved. Many of these NGOs have received substantial funding from governments and other public sources.[5]

Over the past decade, countless election observers have been dispatched to every region of the globe. This increased activity has been accompanied by an intensified demand for standardized assessment criteria, but the development of "checklists" has been hindered by disagreement over what should be included.[6] In addition, cooperation among different countries, organizations, and election authorities has been uneven. Thus a discussion of the basis on which an election or referendum can be labeled "free and fair," or at least "acceptable," is long overdue.

Although criteria for declaring an election "free and fair" have been developed in various contexts, translating such theoretical concepts into a comprehensive list of factors to consider has proved difficult. Equally daunting are the methodological problems of determining whether a particular electoral process meets the established criteria and combining the different "measurements" on various dimensions into a single score.[7] One approach is to study various aspects of the process (for example, the electoral system, the voter-registration system, media access, campaign rules, ballot counting) and then assess whether conditions within each area promote or hamper the freedom and fairness of the election.[8] Here we take a different approach. Drawing on the work of Robert Dahl, we start by examining the relationship between elections and democratic development. This provides a basis for defining the concepts "free" and "fair." We then present a list of assessment criteria and examine the value of such a list in actual practice.

Voting and Democratic Transitions

It is not surprising that politicians and voters in formerly colonized or nondemocratic countries—as well as individuals, countries, and international organizations that subscribe to democratic principles—take a great interest in elections and referendums. Yet this has contributed to the development of a distorted picture of the process of democratic transition: The poll itself has become the focus of attention, acquiring an importance that has no basis in either democratic theory or practical politics.[9]

A common misperception is that any country in which elections have been held without too many obvious irregularities can be called a "democracy." This attitude has been most easily discerned in U.S. policy toward some South and Central American countries, but it can also be identified in the foreign policy of other nations.[10] Yet if the ultimate objective is to encourage continuous development toward a well-functioning democracy, the *prerequisites* of democratic elections must not be ignored.

Robert Dahl has identified a number of "institutional prerequisites" of democracy. One of these is free and fair elections. Yet Dahl does not indicate what he means by "free and fair," other than that "elected officials are chosen in frequent and fairly conducted elections in which coercion is comparatively uncommon."[11] This leaves several questions unanswered: Can elections be free and fair if part of the adult population has no right to vote? What if not all adult citizens have the opportunity to run for office? And what if there is no freedom of speech, assembly, or movement? In other words, do "free and fair" elections not require the fulfillment of all of Dahl's other prerequisites of democracy? Dahl himself has argued that elections should be held later in the democratic-transition process than has often been the case. This implies that a number of other preconditions of democracy must be met, at least in part, before free and fair elections can be held.[12]

The concepts "free" and "fair," then, must be clearly defined and distinguished from other preconditions of democracy. They must also be translated into specific criteria that can be used to evaluate elections. The electoral process itself must be broken down into its component phases, each of which corresponds with certain evaluation criteria.

Freedom, as Dahl notes, contrasts with coercion. Freedom entails the right and the opportunity to choose one thing over another. Coercion implies the absence of choice, either formally or in reality: Either all options but one are disallowed, or certain choices would have negative consequences for one's own or one's family's safety, welfare, or dignity.

Fairness means impartiality. The opposite of fairness is unequal treatment of equals, whereby some people (or groups) are given unreasonable advantages. Thus fairness involves both *regularity* (the unbiased application of rules) and *reasonableness* (the not-too-unequal distribution of relevant resources among competitors).

In practice, it is not always easy to distinguish between freedom and fairness, and any categorization of various elements of the electoral process should be approached with caution. In general, however, the "freedom" dimension should include elements relating to voters' opportunity to participate in the election without coercion or restrictions of any kind (with the possible exception of economic limitations). Thus "freedom" primarily deals with the "rules of the game."

Which of the two dimensions is more important? We hold that freedom must be given priority, because it is a precondition for democracy and for elections as a means to that end. Without rules granting formal political freedoms, the question of the fair application of rules is meaningless, and the question of equality of resources, irrelevant.

It may be just as difficult to distinguish between the two aspects of fairness as between freedom and fairness, because both regularity and reasonableness involve the notion of impartiality. Yet they should be separated to the extent possible. Regularity—which involves impartial application of the election law, constitutional provisions, and other regulations—is the more specific of the two and must be present in a high degree before an election can be accepted. Reasonableness—which concerns securing roughly equal opportunities for the exercise of political freedoms—is more general, and is impossible to achieve in full or even to a high degree. In fact, we know of no democracy that has distributed relevant political resources equally among political competitors.

Thus in assessing the fairness of an election or a referendum, it is more important to discern how the rules are applied than to determine whether individuals and groups have ideal opportunities. This does not

TABLE—CHECKLIST FOR ELECTION ASSESSMENT

TIME PERIOD	DIMENSION	
	"FREE"	"FAIR"
BEFORE POLLING DAY	Freedom of movement Freedom of speech (for candidates, the media, voters, and others) Freedom of assembly Freedom of association Freedom from fear in connection with the election and the electoral campaign Absence of impediments to standing for election (for both political parties and independent candidates) Equal and universal suffrage	A transparent electoral process An election act and an electoral system that grant no special privileges to any political party or social group Absence of impediments to inclusion in the electoral register Establishment of an independent and impartial election commission Impartial treatment of candidates by the police, the army, and the courts of law Equal opportunities for political parties and independent candidates to stand for election Impartial voter-education programs An orderly election campaign (observance of a code of conduct) Equal access to publicly controlled media Impartial allotment of public funds to political parties (if relevant) No misuse of government facilities for campaign purposes
ON POLLING DAY	Opportunity to participate in the election	Access to all polling stations for representatives of the political parties, accredited local and international election observers, and the media Secrecy of the ballot Absence of intimidation of voters Effective design of ballot papers Proper ballot boxes Impartial assistance to voters (if necessary) Proper counting procedures Proper treatment of void ballot papers Proper precautionary measures when transporting election materials Impartial protection of polling stations
AFTER POLLING DAY	Legal possibilities of complaint	Official and expeditious announcement of election results Impartial treatment of any election complaints Impartial reports on the election results by the media Acceptance of the election results by everyone involved

mean that reasonableness is unimportant. Indeed, a broadening of access to relevant political resources and opportunities is a clear indication of a regime's progress toward democracy. In competitive elections, the opportunities available to various groups are especially important. There should be no question of any particular group or political party having a greater chance of winning the election than any other group. The standard formulation used in the preparatory phase of the April 1994 elections in

South Africa—the notion of "leveling the playing field"—epitomizes this aspect of "fairness."[13]

In addition to clarifying core concepts, it is important to distinguish among events before, during, and after the actual polling. The election day itself is only part of the electoral process; thus observation missions consisting of short stays around election day are fundamentally flawed. The preelection period is especially important: It is at this stage that observers must assess whether the election law and the constitution guarantee the freedom of the voters, and verify that relevant resources are not too unequally distributed among competing parties and candidates. The importance of evaluating pre–election day events has been increasingly acknowledged by the UN and other organizations, particularly since the Nicaraguan operation of 1990.

The period after the actual polling must also be considered. At this stage, the crucial issue is the fair and regular application of rules. The counting of ballots should be carefully controlled to prevent fraud, the results should be reported immediately, and complaints about the electoral process should be handled impartially.

The Assessment Process

Combining the two principal dimensions of election assessment with the three observational phases yields the checklist presented in the Table on the preceding page. The checklist is a useful device, but it is not without problems. Although it is based both on relevant literature[14] and on practical experience, it is certainly not exhaustive. Moreover, it represents a schematic outline of the assessment process, not a detailed and unambiguous set of instructions. This gives rise to a twofold problem of reliability. First, election observers may disagree on the extent to which the individual criteria have been fulfilled. Second, the list does not indicate the relative importance of the various criteria. If some criteria have been fulfilled, while others have not, or if a certain criterion has been fulfilled only partially, the observers must rely heavily on their own judgment. Nevertheless, some general guidelines can be provided.

Although the election law (and related regulations) of the country in question may not be ideal in the eyes of international election observers, the observers' main duty is to determine whether or not the electoral process conforms to that law. The checklist in the Table should prove useful in this regard: It can help observers keep track of the various components of the electoral process and compare them against the election law (with which the observers should be thoroughly familiar).

Of course, electoral processes differ, as do political and social conditions and democratic-transition processes themselves. Thus it is not possible to attach absolute weights to the various criteria listed in the Table, for their importance varies with the electoral context. In general, however, items in the "free" column are more important than those in the "fair" column, and within the "fair" column, correct and impartial application of the election law and other relevant regulations is more important than ideal opportunities for political competition. Whereas freedom is a necessary—though not sufficient—condition for an election's acceptability, the combination of freedom *and* the fair application of electoral rules is both necessary and sufficient for such acceptability. For an election to be free and fair, however, the main competitors should have had at least some access to campaign resources and the media, even if that access was not fully equal.

What happens before and after polling day is at least as important as what happens on polling day itself. In particular, the observance of political freedoms in the preelection period is a prerequisite for the acceptability of an election, and even for the mounting of an electoral observation. If these rules are broken, the election cannot be declared acceptable, much less free and fair. After the election, all that is required is voluntary acceptance of the outcome by all serious political contenders. If the results are disputed, it is essential to analyze the reasons for the disagreement and to observe how complaints are treated.

Of course, what happens on polling day is also important. Yet election-day activities are often overemphasized; moreover, they are not always reported adequately. It is not enough merely to observe and report irregularities; rather, they must be evaluated in relation to reasonable expectations. What matters is how widespread they are, how serious they are, whether they represent a clear tendency (especially in favor of current officeholders), and how significant they are in affecting the final results.

To be sure, irregularities should be noted, and suggestions for remedying them should be given. But irregularities that are a result of deficits in technical capacity or experience are less serious than deliberate attempts to manipulate the results. In fact, irregularities on polling day seriously threaten freedom and fairness only to the extent that they are extensive, systematic, or decisive in a close race.

In addition to determining which criteria have been fulfilled and deciding on the relative importance of the various items, observers should also judge whether the election or referendum under the given circumstances reflects the expressed will of the people. This is, after all, the main reason for conducting elections, and irregularities and technical problems should be assessed from this perspective.

Observers should also evaluate the election in the context of the specific democratic-transition process. Will the election—despite possible "technical" shortcomings—stimulate further democratization by increasing respect for political freedoms, strengthening adherence to the election law, enhancing political contestation through broader access to relevant resources, involving more people in the political process, or improving the quality of the political debate? Although some would categorize this as a "political" judgment, it can be argued that it legitimately falls within the domain of election observation. If observers are to view an election not as an isolated event but as part of the democratization process, they cannot avoid considering whether and how it contributes to that process.

It should be emphasized, however, that while observers may go beyond a narrow technical assessment of elections to evaluate the degree to which the preferences of the electorate have been expressed and the role that the election played in the democratization process, they still do not have license to pass judgments of a broader nature. An election should not be deemed acceptable *because* it contributes to political stability or law and order in the country or the region. Such judgments may be both relevant and expedient, but it is not the role of election observers to make them. All they can do is deliver relevant information about the electoral component of the overall situation; it is up to national governments and international bodies to draw the appropriate political conclusions.

It is not easy to establish the precise line between legitimate and illegitimate assessments; moreover, not all election observers acknowledge the distinction. This is readily apparent when a delegation of election observers includes a number of parliamentarians, who are used to making political judgments and willing to take responsibility for them. Such observers often refuse to accept the inherent limitations of their role. A similar problem of demarcation arises when international organizations or national governments have difficulty separating the electoral assessment from an analysis of the political consequences of that assessment. Again, these are two different kinds of activities, which should be carried out by different organizations.

Some Examples

A few examples will illustrate some of the problems of election observation and assessment mentioned above.

The June 1992 parliamentary elections in Mongolia were praiseworthy in at least one respect: The only slightly reformed, former communist Mongolian People's Revolutionary Party (MPRP) had introduced a by-and-large exemplary election law, which was observed in all essentials. Yet the MPRP had also installed an electoral system that was perhaps the most undemocratic in the world (majority elections in multimember constituencies, with each voter required to cast exactly the same number of votes as the number of parliamentary seats to be filled by the constituency).[15] Predictably, the MPRP won 93 percent of the available seats with only 57 percent of the vote. Of course, 57 percent is a clear majority. Yet this left more than 40 percent of the electorate virtually without parliamentary representation at a time when their country's social and political systems were being totally reformed. What does this mean for the election's status as "free and fair"? Can an election conducted under such a system even be termed "acceptable"? Fortunately, the electoral system was replaced with an ordinary first-past-the-post system for the June 1996 parliamentary elections.

In the case of Kenya's December 1992 presidential, parliamentary, and local elections, many elements of the electoral process were questionable.[16] There was considerable evidence of manipulation on the part of President Daniel arap Moi and his party, the Kenya African National Unity (KANU). Yet the situation appeared to improve as polling day approached, resulting in a relatively orderly vote, all things considered. The poor showing of the opposition parties was due largely to their own failure to work together and only in part to the various tricks of KANU, the chairman of the electoral commission, and others. Can such elections be termed "free and fair"?[17] To what extent can a degree of progress toward democracy compensate for irregularities and disregard of the rules?

In elections for Uganda's Constituent Assembly in March 1994, political parties—which had been associated with the country's bloody ethnic clashes—were forbidden to field candidates, while individual candidates were given *carte blanche,* a decision that provoked considerable dissatisfaction. Moreover, a serious voter-registration problem arose. The plan was to complete the voting in one day and count the ballots before dark. The voters were therefore distributed among polling stations of no more than 600 electors. Technical difficulties, however, prevented the voter lists from being published; consequently, people did not know which polling station to go to. This resulted in a good deal of confusion on election day. Does the exclusion of political parties from the electoral process preclude an election from being "free and fair?" And do technical problems with voter registration render an election unacceptable?

In South Africa's April 1994 elections for parliament and regional assemblies, considerable efforts were made to involve all citizens and parties in the process of democratization and reconciliation. Yet it was difficult to ensure equality of opportunity for the country's many different political formations and social groups. There were plenty of administrative and procedural problems as well. What are we to make of the dual character of this particular electoral process? Was it appropriate that the South African Independent Electoral Commission (IEC) itself issued the verdict of "substantially free and fair"?

In Tanzania's October 1994 local elections, only about half the electorate registered to vote—a disappointing figure compared with those of previous local elections. On the other hand, candidates from parties other than the autocratic Revolutionary Party of Tanzania (CCM) were nominated, and some were actually elected. Yet because the full election results were not reported, it was impossible to know the extent to which the opposition had succeeded in wresting local-council seats from the CCM, and how strong the opposition parties were nationally. It is difficult to regard such an election as "free and fair," but might it not pass as "acceptable?"

Making Analytical Distinctions

These and other cases make it clear that it is difficult—perhaps impossible—to establish precise guidelines for assessing elections wherever they occur. Nevertheless, it is possible to establish some analytical distinctions.

If we consider the two main dimensions of freedom and fairness, it seems evident that some elections can be characterized as free and fair, even if they are not perfect. All or almost all elections in well-established democracies presumably fit this description. In these cases, however, there is no perceived need to invite international observers, making this first category mainly of academic interest.

It is also evident that some elections are not "free and fair" owing to the violation of a large number of key criteria. In many cases the countries conducting such elections do not even bother to invite international observers, who would in any case be unlikely to come, for fear of being seen as endorsing the elections. In other cases, observers may declare the election not free and fair. Albania's parliamentary balloting of May 1996 is a recent case in point. Most village-committee elections in the People's Republic of China also fall into this category.[18]

Between the extremes, however, lie many cases in which elections cannot be labeled "free and fair" because of any number of shortcomings, but in which it would be unreasonable explicitly to declare them *not* "free and fair." Perhaps they are free in a formal sense, but fairness is limited in practice—or perhaps they are free only to some extent, but rather fairly conducted within those particular limits.

When observers take circumstances into account and adopt a broad view—especially in terms of the possibility of progress toward greater political competition and participation—they may deem such elections "acceptable," even if they fall short of being "free and fair." These are not only the most difficult cases to assess, but also the ones that international observers are most likely to witness: The governments in these countries are eager to obtain the international community's stamp of approval as a means of boosting their internal legitimacy and gaining external recognition.[19]

In practice, then, elections and referendums are most likely to fall within the shaded area (between curves a and c) of the Figure on the following page, representing balloting that is neither clearly free and fair nor clearly *not* free and fair, but acceptable when technical limitations and prospects for progress toward democracy are taken into account. In these cases, analysis of the application of a country's election law should take into account not only the criteria listed in the Table, but other factors that may help observers determine how strictly those criteria should be applied. For example, if the election is the first in a country undergoing a transition from authoritarianism to democracy, a relatively loose application of the criteria may be indicated (curve a).

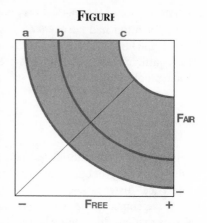

FIGURE

On the other hand, if there is reason to believe that the authorities have rigged the election, a stricter application is justified (curve b). Even under more favorable conditions, it is neither reasonable nor methodologically feasible to insist on complete fulfillment of all the criteria before declaring an election or a referendum "free and fair." Something less (curve c) may suffice, as long as basic freedoms exist, the election law is for the most part applied impartially, and the main competitors have reasonable access to campaign resources and the media.

Given the prevalence of elections and referendums that fall within the shaded area (between curves a and c), these special considerations deserve close attention. Because of the difficulty of distinguishing clearly between the dimensions of "free" and "fair," assessments of such ballots can be represented by a straight line connecting the two most extreme points (the diagonal line in the Figure). Thus the crucial point is where the diagonal leaves the shaded area (in a southwestern direction): It is here that we find the threshold between "acceptable" and "not acceptable."

In determining the acceptability of a given election, observers should focus on the degree of conformance to the country's election law and related regulations, considering not just election-day events but also the periods before and after the balloting. Also important are whether the preferences of the voters have been adequately expressed and what contribution the electoral process has made to the overall process of democratization.

Yet another issue to consider is the closeness of the electoral race. Should observers be more permissive in cases in which the winner triumphs by a wide margin, possibly indicating that irregularities would not have affected the outcome? This argument, while plausible, is nevertheless problematic. Even huge wins can be manufactured; moreover, the distinction between wide and narrow margins is subjective. Finally, given the importance of elections as learning opportunities for voters as well as for candidates, political parties, and election authorities, a strong case can be made for not setting electoral standards too low in newly emerging democracies.

A Complex Process

The phrase "free and fair" cannot denote compliance with a fixed, universal standard of electoral competition: No such standard exists, and the complexity of the electoral process makes the notion of any simple formula unrealistic. Election observation requires the simultaneous use of multiple scales to achieve valid and reliable measurements of complex phenomena. These problems especially affect the large segment of elections that are neither clearly free and fair nor clearly *not* free and fair.

Election observers, therefore, face a dilemma. They might simply avoid using the phrase "free and fair," but at the cost of opening the door to its use by others who have less knowledge or understanding of the situation. Alternatively, observers can elect to use the phrase as a convenient shorthand, but at the cost of exposing themselves to all manner of criticism grounded in intellectual or moral considerations.

This does not mean, however, that election observation and assessment are hopeless tasks. It is indeed possible to draw general conclusions about how best to conduct such activities. In the borderline cases described above—the crucial "in-between" category—observers should identify their evaluation criteria as clearly as possible while at the same time acknowledging that their conclusions rest to some degree on estimates and subjective judgments. In arriving at a conclusion, it is vital that they consider whether electoral competition shows qualitative improvements over previous elections (especially in terms of the freedom dimension and the regulatory aspect of the fairness dimension). Of course, it goes without saying that the course of events should reflect the preferences of the electorate.

The fulfillment of this last criterion is one reason for the widespread acceptance of the IEC's designation of the April 1994 elections in South Africa as "substantially free and fair."[20] This factor is also emphasized by Guy Goodwin-Gill, who tries to strike a balance between explicit standards (which he claims do indeed exist) and what he calls "the special conditions of the general situation"—that is, whether the elections reflect the will of the people and are conducted in a positive atmosphere.[21]

The decision to declare an election "acceptable" also involves the election observer's willingness to enter into a dialogue, not with the political authorities of the country in question, but with himself as to the possibilities of the situation. If the election, despite irregularities, seems to reflect progress toward a more democratic government, observers may choose to give it the benefit of the doubt. This may displease more moralistic observers who take a black-and-white view of the world, but so be it.

This essay has sought to develop a checklist with greater practical application than the ones that have emerged so far. Yet we do not consider it possible to develop a set of guidelines that is equally applicable to all elections and referendums in emerging democracies. The September 1996 elections in Bosnia-Herzegovina provide a good illustration of the complexity of the electoral process and the difficulty of rendering a final judgment. Before polling day, many freedoms were grossly violated, both in the Bosnian Federation and in Republika Srpska. Among them was the freedom of movement, which is usually taken for granted and therefore not included on checklists of assessment criteria.[22] The election authorities were, of course, aware of this state of affairs, but decided to proceed cautiously in order to avoid jeopardizing the entire electoral process, which was seen as crucial to achieving peace and stability in the long term. Other major preelection problems concerned voter registration, freedom of speech, media access, and intimidation of voters. On polling day itself, local reports of orderly elections abounded; at the counting stage, however, rumors of fraud in some areas began to circulate.

Questions can also be raised about the situation after polling day, especially with regard to the electoral authorities' willingness to address complaints and the acceptance of the election results. Of course, the problems that arose in the latter area may have been due to some people's refusal to acknowledge the legitimacy of the new political institutions.

On the whole, then, the evidence would seem to indicate that the elections in Bosnia-Herzegovina were not free and fair, or even acceptable. Yet they were accepted by the international community owing to their presumed importance for stability and peace in the region. The lesson is clear: Elections vary so much from one case to another, with new and complicated political situations constantly arising, that previous observation experiences can provide only limited help. Despite the rapid growth of election observation over the past decade, the task of establishing criteria for evaluating elections still has a long way to go.

NOTES

1. Giovanni Sartori, "Concept Misformation in Comparative Politics," *American Political Science Review* 64 (December 1970): 1034.

2. A good overview of such efforts is provided in Yves Beigbeder, *International Monitoring of Plebiscites, Referenda and National Elections: Self-Determination and Transition to Democracy* (Dordrecht, the Netherlands: Martinus Nijhoff, 1994), 94–143.

3. Jon M. Ebersole, "The United Nations Response to Requests for Assistance in Electoral Matters," *Virginia Journal of International Law* 13 (Fall 1992): 94. See

also Beigbeder, *International Monitoring of Plebiscites, Referenda and National Elections.*

4. Larry Garber and Clark Gibson, *Review of United Nations Electoral Assistance 1992–93* (Project INT/91/033, United Nations Development Programme, 18 August 1993).

5. Jon M. Ebersole, "United Nations Response"; Jennifer McCoy, Larry Garber, and Robert Pastor, "Pollwatching and Peacemaking," *Journal of Democracy* 2 (Fall 1991): 102–14.

6. See also *Lessons Learnt—International Election Observation: Seventeen Organizations Share Experiences on Electoral Observation* (Stockholm: International Institute for Democracy and Electoral Assistance, 1995), 13.

7. Jørgen Elklit, "Is the Degree of Electoral Democratization Measurable? Experiences from Bulgaria, Kenya, Latvia, Mongolia and Nepal," in David Beetham, ed., *Defining and Measuring Democracy* (London: Sage, 1994), 89–111.

8. Guy S. Goodwin-Gill, *Free and Fair Elections: International Law and Practice* (Geneva: Inter-Parliamentary Union, 1994), 27–80; William C. Kimberling, "A Rational Approach to Evaluating Voter Registration," in John C. Courtney, ed., *Registering Voters: Comparative Perspectives* (Cambridge, Mass.: Center for International Affairs, Harvard University, 1991), 3–11.

9. A good discussion of this point is found in Georg Sørensen, *Democracy and Democratization: Processes and Prospects in a Changing World* (Boulder, Colo.: Westview, 1993).

10. Philippe C. Schmitter and Terry Lynn Karl, "What Democracy Is . . . and Is Not," *Journal of Democracy* 2 (Summer 1991): 75–88.

11. Robert A. Dahl, *Democracy and Its Critics* (New Haven: Yale University Press, 1989), 221. Dahl actually refers not to "democracies" but to "polyarchies." We use the term "democracy" here—both for the ideology and for existing political regimes—in order to conform to ordinary usage.

12. Robert A. Dahl, "Democracy and Human Rights Under Different Conditions of Development," in Asbjørn Eide and Bernt Hagtvet, eds., *Human Rights in Perspective: A Global Assessment* (Oxford: Basil Blackwell, 1992), 235–51.

13. See, for example, Ron Gould and Christine Jackson, *A Guide for Election Observers* (Dartmouth, Aldershot, England: Commonwealth Parliamentary Association, 1995).

14. For example, Gould and Jackson, *A Guide for Election Observers;* Guy S. Goodwin-Gill, *Free and Fair Elections;* material on election monitoring from the South African IEC and a number of monitoring organizations; and *Democracy Forum: Report on the "Democracy Forum" in Stockholm, June 12–14, 1996* (Stockholm: International Institute for Democracy and Electoral Assistance, 1996), esp. 14–21.

15. This electoral system (the "mandatory bloc vote") is considered undemocratic because it produces particularly great discrepancies between the parties' vote shares and seat shares.

16. See, for example, Joel D. Barkan, "Kenya: Lessons from a Flawed Election," *Journal of Democracy* 4 (July 1993): 85–99; Gisela Geisler, "Fair? What Has Fairness Got to Do with It? Vagaries of Election Observation and Democratic Standards," *Journal of Modern African Studies* 31 (December 1993): 613–37; Patrick F.J. Macrory, Jørgen

Elklit, and Rafael Sabat Mendez, *Facing the Pluralist Challenge: Human Rights and Democratization in Kenya's December 1992 Multi-Party Election* (Washington, D.C.: International Human Rights Law Group, 1992); and Jørgen Elklit, "Et valg i Afrika: Kenya 1992 som eksempel" (An election in Africa: Kenya 1992 as an example), in Gorm Rye Olsen, ed., *Afrika—det ukuelige kontinent* (Africa—the indomitable continent) (Copenhagen: Danmarks Radio Forlaget, 1994), 115–36.

17. None of the observer groups reporting on the elections used the words "free and fair." Subsequent discussion of the elections has focused on whether or not the criticism should have been more explicit.

18. See Melanie Manion, "The Electoral Connection in the Chinese Countryside," *American Political Science Review* 90 (December 1996): 736–48; and Jørgen Elklit, "The Chinese Village Committee Electoral System," *China Information* 11 (Spring 1997): 1–13.

19. Christopher Clapham, *Africa and the International System: The Politics of State Survival* (Cambridge: Cambridge University Press, 1996), 200.

20. Elling N. Tjønneland, "The Birth of Democracy in South Africa," in Tjønneland, ed., *South Africa's 1994 Elections: The Birth of Democracy, Its Future Prospects and Norwegian Development Aid* (Oslo: Norwegian Institute of Human Rights, 1994), 7–47; Jørgen Elklit, "Historisk valg med mange problemer" (Historical elections with many problems), *udenrigs* (Foreign) 49 (Summer 1994): 1–11; Ron Gould, "Towards Free and Fair Elections—The Role of International Observers," *In Focus* 2 (1994): 4–7. For a more equivocal view, see R.W. Johnson, "How Free? How Fair?" in R.W. Johnson and Lawrence Schlemmer, eds., *Launching Democracy in South Africa: The First Open Election, April 1994* (New Haven: Yale University Press, 1996), 323–52.

21. Guy S. Goodwin-Gill, *Free and Fair Elections*, 81.

22. It does figure, however, in the discussion of liberalization in Guillermo O'Donnell and Philippe C. Schmitter, *Transitions from Authoritarian Rule: Tentative Conclusions About Uncertain Democracies* (Baltimore: Johns Hopkins University Press, 1986), 7.

16

FEDERALISM AND DEMOCRACY: BEYOND THE U.S. MODEL

Alfred Stepan

Alfred Stepan, who was Gladstone Professor of Government at Oxford University in 1996–99, is now Wallace Sayre Professor of Government at Columbia University. This essay is based on a lecture he delivered at George Washington University in November 1998 in a series cosponsored by the Mário Soares Foundation, the Luso-American Foundation, and the International Forum for Democratic Studies. A more extensive version of this essay appears in his book Arguing Comparative Politics *(2001). He is working with Juan J. Linz on a larger project on federalism that will culminate in a jointly authored book,* Federalism, Democracy and Nation.

For those of us interested in the spread and consolidation of democracy, whether as policy makers, human rights activists, political analysts, or democratic theorists, there is a greater need than ever to reconsider the potential risks and benefits of federalism. The greatest risk is that federal arrangements can offer opportunities for ethnic nationalists to mobilize their resources. This risk is especially grave when elections are introduced in the subunits of a formerly nondemocratic federal polity prior to democratic countrywide elections and in the absence of democratic countrywide parties. Of the nine states that once made up communist Europe, six were unitary and three were federal. The six unitary states are now five states (East Germany has reunited with the Federal Republic), while the three federal states—Yugoslavia, the USSR, and Czechoslovakia—are now 22 independent states. Most of postcommunist Europe's ethnocracies and ethnic bloodshed have occurred within these postfederal states.

Yet in spite of these potential problems, federal rather than unitary states are the form most often associated with multinational democracies. Federal states are also associated with large populations, extensive territories, and democracies with territorially based linguistic fragmentation. In fact, every single longstanding democracy in a territorially based multilingual and multinational polity is a federal state.

Although there are many multinational polities in the world, few of them are democracies. Those multinational democracies that do exist, however (Switzerland, Canada, Belgium, Spain, and India), are *all* federal. Although all these democracies, except for Switzerland, have had problems managing their multinational polities (and even Switzerland had the Sonderbund War, the secession of the Catholic cantons in 1848), they remain reasonably stable. By contrast, Sri Lanka, a territorially based multilingual and multinational unitary state that feared the "slippery slope" of federalism, could not cope with its ethnic divisions and plunged headlong into a bloody civil war that has lasted more than 15 years.

American-style federalism embodies some values that would be very inappropriate for many democratizing countries, especially multinational polities.

In addition to the strong association between multinational democracies and federalism, the six longstanding democracies that score highest on an index of linguistic and ethnic diversity—India, Canada, Belgium, Switzerland, Spain, and the United States—are all federal states. The fact that these nations chose to adopt a federal system does not *prove* anything; it does, however, suggest that federalism may help these countries manage the problems that come with ethnic and linguistic diversity. In fact, in my judgment, if countries such as Indonesia, Russia, Nigeria, China, and Burma are ever to become stable democracies, they will have to craft workable federal systems that allow cultural diversity, a robust capacity for socioeconomic development, and a general standard of equality among their citizens.

Consider the case of Indonesia, for example. It seems to meet all the indicators for a federal state. It has a population of over 200 million, and its territory is spread across more than 2,000 inhabited islands. It has great linguistic and ethnic fragmentation and many religions. Thus it is near the top in virtually all the categories associated with federalism. If Indonesia is to become a democracy, one would think that it would have to address the question of federalism or decentralization. Yet at a meeting of Indonesian political, military, religious, and intellectual leaders that I attended after the fall of Suharto, most of the participants (especially those from the military) rejected federalism out of hand because of secessionist conflicts at the end of Dutch colonial rule. Indonesia should at least consider what I call a *federacy* to deal with special jurisdictions like Aceh or Irian Jaya. A federacy is the only variation *between* unitary states and federal states. It is a political system in which an otherwise unitary state develops a federal relationship with a territorially, ethnically, or culturally distinct community while all the other parts of the state remain under unitary rule. Denmark has such a relationship with Greenland, and Finland with the Aaland Islands.

A Misleading Picture of Federalism

In seeking to understand why some countries are reluctant to adopt federal systems, it is helpful to examine what political science has had to say about federalism. Unfortunately, some of the most influential works in political science today offer incomplete or insufficiently broad definitions of federalism and thereby suggest that the range of choices facing newly democratizing states is narrower than it actually is. In large part, this stems from their focusing too exclusively on the model offered by the United States, the oldest and certainly one of the most successful federal democracies.

One of the most influential political scientists to write about federalism in the last half-century, the late William H. Riker, stresses three factors present in the U.S. form of federalism that he claims to be true for federalism in general.[1] First, Riker assumes that every longstanding federation, democratic or not, is the result of a bargain whereby previously sovereign polities agree to give up part of their sovereignty in order to pool their resources to increase their collective security and to achieve other goals, including economic ones. I call this type of federalism *coming-together federalism.* For Riker, it is the only type of federalism in the world.

Second, Riker and many other U.S. scholars assume that one of the goals of federalism is to protect individual rights against encroachments on the part of the central government (or even against the "tyranny of the majority") by a number of institutional devices, such as a bicameral legislature in which one house is elected on the basis of population, while in the other house the subunits are represented equally. In addition, many competences are permanently granted to the subunits instead of to the center. If we can call all of the citizens in the polity taken as a whole the *demos,* we may say that these devices, although democratic, are *"demos-constraining."*

Third, as a result of the federal bargain that created the United States, each of the states was accorded the *same* constitutional competences. U.S. federalism is thus considered to be constitutionally *symmetrical.* By contrast, *asymmetrical* arrangements that grant different competencies and group-specific rights to some states, which are not now part of the U.S. model of federalism, are seen as incompatible with the principled equality of the states and with equality of citizens' rights in the post-segregation era.

Yet although these three points are a reasonably accurate depiction of the political structures and normative values associated with U.S. federalism, most democratic countries that have adopted federal systems have chosen not to follow the U.S. model. Indeed, American-style federalism embodies some values that would be very inappropriate for many democratizing countries, especially multinational polities. To explain what I mean by this, let me review each of these three points in turn.

"Coming-Together" vs. "Holding-Together"

First of all, we need to ask: How are democratic federal systems actually formed? Riker has to engage in some "concept-stretching" to include all the federal systems in the world in one model. For example, he contends that the Soviet Union meets his definition of a federal system that came about as the result of a "federal bargain." Yet it is clearly a distortion of history, language, and theory to call what happened in Georgia, Azerbaijan, and Armenia, for example, a "federal bargain." These three previously independent countries were conquered by the 11th Red Army. In Azerbaijan, the former nationalist prime minister and the former head of the army were executed just one week after accepting the "bargain."

Many democratic federations, however, emerge from a completely different historical and political logic, which I call *holding-together federalism*. India in late 1948, Belgium in 1969, and Spain in 1975 were all political systems with strong unitary features. Nevertheless, political leaders in these three multicultural polities came to the decision that the best way—indeed, the only way—to hold their countries together in a democracy would be to devolve power constitutionally and turn their threatened polities into federations. The 1950 Indian Constitution, the 1978 Spanish Constitution, and the 1993 Belgian Constitution are all federal.

Let us briefly examine the "holding-together" characteristics of the creation of federalism in India to show how they differ from the "coming-together" characteristics correctly associated with the creation of American-style federalism. When he presented India's draft constitution for the consideration of the members of the constituent assembly, the chairman of the drafting committee, B.R. Ambedkar, said explicitly that it was designed to maintain the unity of India—in short, to hold it together. He argued that the constitution was guided by principles and mechanisms that were fundamentally different from those found in the United States, in that the Indian subunits had much less prior sovereignty than did the American states. Since they had less sovereignty, they therefore had much less bargaining power. Ambedkar told the assembly that although India was to be a federation, this federation was created not as the result of an agreement among the states, but by an act of the constituent assembly.[2] As Mohit Bhattacharya, in a careful review of the constituent assembly, points out, by the time Ambedkar had presented the draft in November 1948, both the partition between Pakistan and India and the somewhat reluctant and occasionally even coerced integration of virtually all of the 568 princely states had already occurred.[3] Therefore, bargaining conditions between relatively sovereign units, crucial to Riker's view of how and why enduring federations are created, in essence no longer existed.

Thus one may see the formation of democratic federal systems as fitting into a sort of continuum. On one end, closest to the pure model of a largely voluntary bargain, are the relatively autonomous units that "come together" to pool their sovereignty while retaining their individual identities. The United States, Switzerland, and Australia are examples of such states. At the other end of the democratic continuum, we have India, Belgium, and Spain as examples of "holding-together" federalism. And then there is what I call "putting-together" federalism, a heavily coercive effort by a nondemocratic centralizing power to put together a multi-national state, some of the components of which had previously been independent states. The USSR was an example of this type of federalism. Since federal systems have been formed for different reasons and to achieve different goals, it is no surprise that their founders created fundamentally different structures. This leads us to our next point.

"*Demos*-Constraining" vs. "*Demos*-Enabling"

Earlier, I described American-style federalism as "*demos*-constraining." In some respects, all democratic federations are more "*demos*-constraining" than unitary democracies. There are three reasons for this. First, unitary democracies have an open agenda, as Adam Przeworski points out, while in a federal democracy the agenda of the *demos* is somewhat restricted because many policy areas have been constitutionally assigned to the exclusive competence of the states.[4] Second, even at the center there are two legislative chambers, one (in theory) representing the one person–one vote principle, and the other representing the territorial principle. Third, because jurisdictional disputes are a more difficult and persistent issue in federal than in unitary systems, the judiciary, which is not responsible to the *demos,* is necessarily more salient and powerful.

Riker sees the *demos*-constraining aspect of federalism (and the weak politywide political parties normally associated with federalism) as basically good, because it can help protect individual rights from being infringed by the central government's potential for producing populist majorities.[5] But when examined from the point of view of equality and efficacy, both of which are as important to the consolidation of democracy as is liberty, the picture becomes more complicated. The deviation from the one citizen–one vote principle that federalism necessarily implies may be seen as a violation of the principle of equality. Overrepresentation in the upper house, combined with constitutional provisions requiring a supermajority to pass certain kinds of legislation, could, in certain extreme cases, lead to a situation in which legislators representing less than 10 percent of the electorate are able to thwart the wishes of the vast majority. This raises serious questions for the efficacious and legitimate functioning of democracy. If one were interested only in creating a system that best reflects the *demos* and that functions as an effective democracy, a case could be made that the democratic values of participation, decentralization, and equality would be better addressed in a unitary system that has decentralized participation than in a federal system. But if a polity has great linguistic diversity, is multinational, and is very large, its chances of being a democracy are much better if it adopts a federal system.

If federal systems were forced to adhere to the Rikerian model, multinational democracies would be faced with a stark choice: If they wished to adopt a federal system to reduce ethnic, religious, or linguistic tensions, they could do so only at the risk of severely constraining majority rule. But if we look at the federal systems that actually exist in the world, we see that not all federal systems are *demos*-constraining to the same degree. American-style federalism is *demos*-constraining, and Brazil is the most *demos*-constraining federation in the world. Yet the German federal system is much more *demos*-enabling than that of the United States, and India's is even more *demos*-enabling than Germany's. We can, in fact, construct a continuum, ranging from federal systems that are *demos*-constraining to those that are *demos*-enabling. Where a particular federal system lies on this continuum is largely determined by the nature of the party system, which I discuss elsewhere, and by three constitutionally embedded variables: 1) the degree of overrepresentation in the upper chamber; 2) the policy scope of the territorial chamber; and 3) the sorts of policy issues that are off the policy agenda of the *demos* because they have been allocated to the states or subunits.

1) Overrepresentation in the territorial chamber. I think it is fair to argue that the greater the representation of the less populous states (and therefore the underrepresentation of the more populous states), the greater the *demos*-constraining potential of the upper house will be. The United States and Brazil follow the same format: In both countries, each state gets the same number of senators. Since Wyoming had a population of 453,000 and California had a population of 30 million in 1990, this meant that one vote for a senator in Wyoming was worth 66 votes in California. In Brazil, the overrepresentation is even more extreme. One vote cast for senator in Roraima has 144 times as much weight as a vote for senator in São Paulo. Moreover, Brazil and Argentina are the only democratic federations in the world that replicate a version of this overrepresentation in the lower house. With perfect proportional representation, São Paulo should have 114 seats. It actually has 70. With perfect representation, Roraima should have one seat. It actually has eight. The Brazilian Constitution, inspired by the ideology of territorial representation, specifies that no state can have more than 70 seats in the lower house (thereby partially disenfranchising São Paulo) and that no state can have fewer than eight.

The principle of equal representation of each state in the upper house is not democratically necessary and may even prove to be a disincentive to multinational polities that contemplate adopting a federal system.

Yet the principle of equal representation of each state in the upper house is not democratically necessary and may even prove to be a disincentive to multinational polities that contemplate adopting a federal system. Many democratic federations have quite different formulas for constructing their upper houses. In Germany, the most populous states (or *Länder*) get six votes in the upper chamber, those of intermediate size get four, and the least populous get three. Austria, Belgium, and India are still closer to the one person–one vote end of the continuum. If multilingual India had followed the U.S. pattern, it would not have been able to do some things that were absolutely crucial for political stability. Between 1962 and 1987, India created six new culturally distinctive states in the northeast, mostly carved out of Assam, a conflict-ridden region bordering Burma and China. If India had followed the U.S. model, these new states, containing barely one percent of India's population, would have had to be given 25 percent of all the votes in the upper chamber. The other Indian states would never have allowed this. Thus something democratically useful—the creation of new states, some of which were demanding independence by violent means—would have been difficult or impossible under the U.S. principle of representing each state equally.

The range of variation among the world's federal democracies can be seen in Table 1 on the following page. This table also illustrates what I said above about most federal democracies choosing not to follow the U.S. model. The United States, along with Brazil and Argentina, which follow the same model, is an outlier on this continuum. The first line measures the degree of inequality of representation according to the Gini index. The values range from 0, which indicates perfect one person–one vote representation, to 1, which indicates that one subunit has all of the votes in the upper house. Belgium's upper house has a Gini-index value of close to 0. Austria's is not much higher. India's is .10. Spain's is .31. The U.S. Gini-index value is almost .50, and Brazil's is .52. This means that the best-represented decile in the United States has 39 percent of the votes in the Senate; in Brazil, the best-represented decile has 43

TABLE 1—A CONTINUUM OF THE DEGREE OF OVERREPRESENTATION IN THE UPPER HOUSES OF 12 MODERN FEDERAL DEMOCRACIES[1]

GINI INDEX OF INEQUALITY[2]	Belgium .015	Austria .05	India .10	Spain .31	Germany .32	Canada .34	Australia .36	Russia[3] .43	Switzerland .45	U.S.A. .49	Brazil .52	Argentina .61
RATIO OF BEST-REPRESENTED TO WORST-REPRESENTED FEDERAL UNIT (ON BASIS OF POPULATION)	Austria 1.5/1	Belgium 2/1	Spain 10/1	India 11/1	Germany 13/1	Australia 13/1	Canada 21/1	Switzerland 40/1	U.S.A. 66/1	Argentina 85/1	Brazil 144/1	Russia 370/1
PERCENTAGE OF SEATS OF BEST-REPRESENTED DECILE	Belgium 10.8	Austria 11.9	India 15.4	Spain 23.7	Germany 24.0	Australia 28.7	Canada 33.4	Russia 35.0	Switzerland 38.4	U.S.A. 39.7	Brazil 41.3	Argentina 44.8

1. Complete information on all federal countries is contained in the Alfred Stepan–Wilfrid Swenden federal data-bank. We are grateful to Cindy Skach and Jeff Kahn for having provided us with the data on India and Russia, respectively. Other data were taken from *Whitakers Almanac* (London: J. Whitaker, 1977); *The Europa World Year Book* (London: Europa, 1995); and Daniel J. Elazar, ed., *Federal Systems of the World*. For the constitutional provisions on second chambers, see S.E. Finer, Vernon Bogdanor, and Bernard Rudden, *Comparing Constitutions* and A.P. Blaustein and G.H. Flanz, *Constitutions of the Countries of the World* (Dobbs Ferry, New York: Oceana, 1991).

2. The Gini coefficient equals zero if the composition of the upper chamber is fully proportional and equals one if one subunit has all the votes in the second chamber. Arend Lijphart was among the first authors to use the Gini coefficient as a measure of inequality for the composition of second chambers. See Arend Lijphart, *Democracies: Patterns of Majoritarian and Consensus Government in Twenty-one Countries* (New Haven, Conn.: Yale University Press, 1984), 174.

3. The status of Russia as a democracy is the most questionable of the 12 countries in the table. The data are included for comparative purposes.

percent of the votes. In India, it only has 15 percent. The variations are immense. On this indicator, the United States is clearly on the *demos*-constraining end of the continuum.

2) Policy scope of the territorial chamber. Now let us turn to our second variable, the competences of the territorially based chamber. My proposition is that the greater the competences of the territorial house, the more the *demos*—which is represented on a one person–one vote basis in the lower house—is constrained. In the United States, the lower house has a somewhat more important role than the Senate in budget initiation, but if one takes into account the Senate's constitutionally exclusive prerogatives to advise and consent on judicial, ambassadorial, and major administrative appointments, the two houses come fairly close to policy-making parity. On this variable, Brazil has the most *demos*-constraining system in the world. There is no area that the Brazilian Senate does not vote on, and there are 12 areas where it has exclusive competence, including authority to set limits on how much states can borrow.

As we can see in Table 2 on the following page, however, other federal democracies do not give the upper house as much policy scope as they give the lower house. The German, Spanish, and Indian systems are less *demos*-constraining, because their upper houses are less unrepresentative and less powerful. While in Brazil senators representing 13 percent of the total electorate can block ordinary legislation (and in the United States, a committee chairman alone can at times block important nominations), in Germany important bills are seldom vetoed by the upper chamber. How can we account for such a difference? First of all, the upper chamber cannot participate in the two most important legislative votes, those for government formation and government termination. This power is the exclusive competence of the lower chamber. Second, the upper chamber can delay, but not veto, bills that do not directly involve the *Länder*. Third, on the approximately 50 percent of the bills that the upper chamber can theoretically veto because they do relate directly to the *Länder,* it seldom does so after closed-door reconciliation meetings are held in the joint committee representing both houses.

In Spain, Belgium, India, and Austria, as well as in Germany, only the lower house participates in no-confidence votes. In many countries, the upper house is largely a revisionary chamber, although it has a major role in anything having to do with federal intervention. In Spain, for example, if the government wishes to take action against a regional government that is in contempt of the constitution, the decision must be approved by two-thirds of the upper house. This, in my view, is entirely appropriate.

3) The degree to which policy-making authority is constitutionally allocated to subunits. The third constitutionally embedded variable on

TABLE 2—A CONTINUUM OF THE UPPER CHAMBER'S CONSTITUTIONAL PREROGATIVES TO CONSTRAIN A MAJORITY AT THE CENTER

Least Constraining				Most Constraining
INDIA	SPAIN	GERMANY	UNITED STATES	BRAZIL
The territorial chamber has no constitutional powers to protect subunit autonomy against a 60-day central intervention. Upper chamber has capacity to review or deny "President's Rule" only after 60 days.

Largely a revisionary chamber. | Major power is granted by Article 155 of the Constitution, which precludes intervention by the center unless it has received approval by an absolute majority of the upper house. Plays no role in constructive vote of no confidence or normal legislation.

Largely a revisionary chamber. | Plays no role in constructive vote of no confidence. Can play a potential veto role only in that part of the legislative agenda that directly relates to center-subunit issues. Power has grown somewhat over the last 20 years. Conflicts between the two chambers are resolved in closed-door meetings. | Extensive capacity to block a democratic majority. Senate has the same voting rights on all legislation as the "one person–one vote" chamber. Has exclusive competence to confirm or deny all major judicial and administrative appointments. A committee chairman alone can at times block important nominations. | Excessive for the efficacious and legitimate functioning of democratic government. The extremely disproportional upper chamber must approve all legislation. The Senate has 12 areas of exclusive lawmaking prerogatives. Senators representing 13 percent of the total electorate can block ordinary legislation supported by senators representing 87 percent of the population. |

which democratic federations differ greatly is the powers that are given to the *demos* at the center versus the powers that are constitutionally allocated to the states. The 1988 Brazilian Constitution is so extensively detailed that a great deal of ordinary legislation can be passed only by a supermajority. In Brazil, many specific provisions on state and municipal pensions, state banks (all the states have banks), and the right of states to tax exports were constitutionally embedded. This is extremely *demos*-constraining. When too many issues are constitutionally embedded, the result is profoundly undemocratic, because these issues cannot be decided by a normal majority. Almost everything of importance in Brazil is constitutionally embedded. In order to change the constitution, 60 percent of the members of both houses (both those present and those absent) must vote in favor of an amendment *twice*. In a country the size of a continent, with bad transportation, it is hard even to get 60 percent of the legislature to show up.

At the opposite end of the continuum (see Table 3 on the following page), India has a very *demos*-enabling constitution. At the time of its drafting, its authors were painfully aware that there were more than 15 languages spoken in the country that at least 20 million people could claim as their mother tongue. The boundaries of the states did not correspond with linguistic boundaries. To get the government closer to the people, the framers of the Indian Constitution had to respect the linguistic principle, so they decided (Article 3) that the lower house, by a simple majority vote, could eliminate any state, carve new states out of existing ones, or change their names. That is the sort of provision that a "holding-together" federation can write. In a "states'-rights" federation like the United States, such a provision would be absolutely impossible. But if it had not been possible in India, the failure to realize the "imagined communities" of the country's hundreds of millions of non-Hindi speakers might have led to secession in a number of places.

The U.S. Constitution is even more difficult to amend than the Brazilian Constitution, but it is parsimonious, so the vast majority of legislation can be passed by ordinary majorities. In Spain, the main constraint on the majority at the center derives from the statutes of autonomy, which deal primarily with questions of culture and language. In Germany, many federal programs are administered by the *Länder*, but lawmaking and policy oversight remain the prerogative of the center.

Constitutionally Symmetrical vs. Asymmetrical

Let us now turn to a final point concerning the U.S. model. The U.S. Constitution, as discussed above, establishes a form of symmetrical federalism, which is bolstered by a certain normative disinclination on the part of Americans to accept the concept of collective rights. With the exception of Switzerland (where none of the political parties strictly

TABLE 3—THE DEGREE TO WHICH POLICY MAKING IS CONSTITUTIONALLY ALLOCATED TO SUBUNITS OF THE FEDERATION

Least → *Most*

INDIA	GERMANY	SPAIN	UNITED STATES	BRAZIL
Does not constrain *demos*. Capacity to respond to minority desires by redrawing the boundaries of states. Probably should constrain the ease with which the majority can intervene in states. Since 1994 Supreme Court decisions give somewhat more protection to subunits from imposition of "President's Rule" from the center.	Federal Law explicitly given precedent over Land Law. Wide areas where lawmaking powers are either explicitly given to the center or are concurrent responsibilities. More tax money is spent by the *Länder* than by the center. Many federal programs are decentralized so as to be administered by the *Länder*, while lawmaking and policy oversight remains the prerogative of the center.	Major constraints on majority at the center derives from the statutes of autonomy. Occasional bargaining process if center needs votes of regional party during process of government formation.	Constitution is extremely difficult to amend but is parsimonious, so the vast majority of legislation can be passed as ordinary legislation. Power is horizontally shared at the center between three branches. Power is vertically devolved and shared in "marble-cake" federalism between the federal and the state governments.	1988 Constitution is so detailed about states' rights that much ordinary legislation can only be passed by exceptional majorities. States and municipalities had such extreme control over export taxes and banking that central government's fiscal and trade policy in 1989–96 was impeded. Some centralization of tax and bank policies in 1996–97 but extremely costly to the center.
Residual power with center.	Most powers are concurrent.	Residual power with center.	Residual power with states.	Residual power with states.

represents any one linguistic or religious group), all of the multinational democracies are constitutionally asymmetrical: In order to hold the multinational polity together, they assign different linguistic, cultural, and legal competences to different states. Under the symmetrical American model, many of the things that are most essential in a multinational context cannot be accomplished. With the possible exception of the special case of Switzerland, *all* federations that are constitutionally symmetrical—Austria, Germany, Australia, the United States, Argentina, and Brazil—are mononational. India, Belgium, Canada, and Spain are multinational and their federations are all asymmetrical. (The Russian Federation is also asymmetrical, but, constitutionally, it does not yet work as a democratic federation.)

The concept of collective rights is in tension with the traditional American way of thinking about such matters, which is based on individual rights. It is true that a polity cannot be a democracy unless the individual rights of all citizens are enshrined in the constitution and a countrywide system of horizontal and vertical controls is credibly established to support these rights. Whatever rights the national sub-units may possess, they cannot constitutionally or politically violate the rights of individual citizens. The enforcement of individual rights can be an obligation of both the center and the subunits, but the center cannot completely delegate responsibility for the establishment and maintenance of democratic rights and continue to be a democracy. Alexis de Tocqueville is very clear on this point. He admired the robust local associationalism of U.S. democracy but pointed out that the rule of law in the entire polity had to be guaranteed and enforced by the center.

In multinational polities, however, some groups may be able to participate fully as individual citizens only if they acquire, as a group, the right to have schooling, mass media, and religious or even legal structures that correspond to their language and culture. Some of these rights may be described as group-specific collective rights. Many thinkers in the liberal tradition assume that all rights are individual and universal and view any deviation from individualism and universalism with suspicion, but this assumption is open to question.

Let me conclude with four observations, partly drawn from studies of the historical development of democracy, about democratic group-specific rights (to use a term coined by the Canadian political philosopher Will Kymlicka).[6] First, individuals are indeed the primary bearers of rights, and no group rights should violate individual rights in a democratic polity. In democratic multinational federal states, this means that something like a bill of individual rights should be promulgated by the federal center, and any laws and social policies that violate it must fall outside the constitutionally guaranteed policy scope of the subunits.

Second, while individual rights are universal, it is simply bad history to argue that in actual democracies all rights have been universal.

Frequently, the struggle to reconcile the imperatives of political integration with the legitimate imperatives of cultural difference has led countries to award certain minorities group-specific rights, such as those given to French-speaking Quebec in Canada, to cultural councils in Belgium, and to Muslim family courts in India. The key point is that it is the obligation of the democratic state to ensure that no group-specific right violates individual or universal rights.

Third, while individuals are the bearers of rights, there may well be concrete circumstances in which individuals cannot develop or exercise their full rights unless they are active members of a group that struggles for some collective goods common to most of its members. If, for example, the Catalans had not been given certain group-specific rights involving the public status of their own language, I doubt whether as individuals they could have become full democratic citizens of Spain. Similarly, I do not think Kurds will become full democratic citizens of Turkey unless they are granted certain group-specific rights (such as the right to Kurdish newspapers and radio stations in the southeast of Turkey, where Kurds are a majority).

Finally, although such group-specific rights may not be consistent with some nineteenth-century tenets of Anglo-Saxon liberal democracy or with the French idea of citizenship in a nation-state, they are consistent with a polity in which group rights do not violate individual rights, and they permit effective democratic citizenship and loyalty to be extended throughout the polity. They offer, in fact, one of the few ways to craft democracy successfully in the difficult and populous world of multinational states.

The Limits of the U.S. Model

The U.S. model of federalism, in terms of the analytical categories developed in this article, is "coming-together" in its origin, "constitu-tionally symmetrical" in its structure, and "*demos*-constraining" in its political consequences. Despite the prestige of this U.S. model of federalism, it would seem to hold greater historical interest than contemporary attraction for other democracies.

Since the emergence of nation-states on the world stage in the aftermath of the French Revolution, *no* sovereign democratic nation-states have ever "come together" in an enduring federation. Three largely unitary states, however (Belgium, Spain, and India) have constructed "holding-together" federations. In contrast to the United States, these federations are constitutionally asymmetrical and more "*demos*-enabling" than "*demos*-constraining." Should the United Kingdom ever become a federation, it would also be "holding-together" in origin. Since it is extremely unlikely that Wales, Scotland, or Northern Ireland would have the same number of seats as England in the upper chamber of the new federation, or that the new upper chamber of the federation would be nearly equal in power to the lower chamber, the new federation would not be "*demos*-constraining" as I have defined that term. Finally, it would obviously defeat the purpose of such a new federation if it were constitutionally symmetrical. A U.K. federation, then, would not follow the U.S. model.

The fact that since the French Revolution no fully independent nation-states have come together to pool their sovereignty in a new and more powerful polity constructed in the form of a federation would seem to have implications for the future evolution of the European Union. The European Union is composed of independent states, most of which are nation-states. These states are indeed increasingly becoming "functionally federal." Were there to be a prolonged recession (or a depression), however, and were some EU member states to experience very high unemployment rates in comparison to others, member states could vote to dismantle some of the economic federal structures of the federation that were perceived as being "politically dysfunctional." Unlike most classic federations, such as the United States, the European Union will most likely continue to be marked by the presumption of freedom of exit.

Finally, many of the new federations that could emerge from the currently nondemocratic parts of the world would probably be territorially based, multilingual, and multinational. For the reasons spelled out in this article, very few, if any, such polities would attempt to consolidate democracy using the U.S. model of "coming-together," "*demos*-constraining," symmetrical federalism.[7]

NOTES

1. See William H. Riker, "Federalism," in Fred Greenstein and Nelson W. Polsby, eds., *Handbook of Political Science* (Reading, Mass.: Addison-Wesley, 1975) vol. 5: 93–172.

2. Ambedkar's speech is found in its entirety in: India. Constituent Assembly, *Debates: Official Report* (New Delhi: Manager of Publications, 1951) vol. II, 31–44.

3. Mohit Bhattacharya, "The Mind of the Founding Fathers," in Nirmal Mukarji and Balveer Arora, eds., *Federalism in India: Origins and Development* (New Delhi: Vikas, 1992), 81–102.

4. Adam Przeworski, "Some Problems in the Study of the Transition to Democracy," in Guillermo O'Donnell, Philippe C. Schmitter, and Laurence Whitehead, eds., *Transitions from Authoritarian Rule: Comparative Perspectives* (Baltimore: Johns Hopkins University Press, 1986), 47–63.

5. See William H. Riker, *Liberalism Against Populism: A Confrontation Between the Theory of Democracy and the Theory of Social Choice* (San Francisco: W.H. Freeman, 1982), 247–53. As Riker acknowledges, however, federalism may also give the majority in the subunits the power to limit the freedom of some of the citizens (as the history of the southern United States shows), making it difficult for the federal government to protect them.

6. See Will Kymlicka, *Multicultural Citizenship: A Liberal Theory of Minority-Rights* (Oxford: Clarendon, 1995). For a powerful argument by a distinguished legal theorist that group rights are often a precondition of individual rights, see Joseph Raz, *The Morality of Freedom* (Oxford: Clarendon, 1986), 193–216. For a political and philosophically acute discussion of these issues in India, see Rajeev Bhargava, "Secularism, Democracy, and Rights," in Mehdi Arslan and Jannaki Rajan, eds., *Communalism in India: Challenge and Response* (New Delhi: Manohar, 1994), 61–73.

7. The tentative arguments made in these concluding paragraphs will be developed analytically and empirically in much greater depth in *Federalism, Democracy and Nation,* a book being written by Juan J. Linz and myself.

17

MARKETS, LAW, AND DEMOCRACY

Charles Fried

Charles Fried *is Beneficial Professor of Law at Harvard University Law School. Born in Prague, he has served as Solicitor General of the United States (1985–89) and as an Associate Justice of the Supreme Judicial Court of Massachusetts (1995–99). His publications include* Contract as Promise *(1981) and* Order and Law: Arguing the Reagan Revolution *(1991). An earlier version of this essay was presented at a conference on property rights, markets, and the rule of law at Duxx, the Graduate School of Business Leadership, in Monterrey, Mexico, on 12 May 2000.*

What passes for a market economy in many of the countries that abandoned communism in the last decade has offered a sorry spectacle: In Russia, it has produced few material benefits for the majority of citizens. Their levels of health care, life expectancy, education, and economic security have all declined. In China, the transition to a freer economy has produced some striking material gains, in part because the starting point was so low and in part because a ruthless suppression of political liberties has underwritten a measure of social stability and order. Russia and China may be cited as models of bandit and tyrant capitalism, respectively. Of the smaller states that have emerged from the wreckage of the Soviet empire, few have been unqualified successes, and most have been plagued to some degree with the bandit mentality that afflicts Russia in a more extreme form. Undoubtedly, Václav Havel was correct to warn that a half-century or more of communism had degraded the human spirit so thoroughly that privatization, property rights, and even the recognition of basic political and personal liberties could not quickly reproduce in those ravaged lands the lineaments of a functioning liberal democracy.[1]

If we ask what is missing in either bandit or tyrant capitalist societies (in the way a physician studies the pathological in order to understand the healthy constitution), we will be led to those presuppositions of a healthy liberal market democracy so basic that they are almost invisible. The pathology that casual observers and critics of bandit economies have tended to emphasize is a crushing disparity between the situation of the many and the few. The focus on income inequality, however, obscures deeper truths, falsely suggesting that income equality is both necessary and sufficient to a well-ordered society. This fallacy leads many to treat the attainment and maintenance of income equality as the overriding virtue of the good society, and to be willing to sacrifice everything to its attainment and to suppress by all means anything that would disturb it.

This undue focus on equality deflects attention from the true goal of a good and well-ordered society: to offer every citizen a reasonable opportunity to define and attain his or her goals in life. This means a prosperous society. The few recent experiments in which societies have tried to create a good life for their citizens by deliberately suppressing prosperity (Pol Pot's Cambodia, Mao's Cultural Revolution) have been disasters. To be sure, they avoided prosperity, but they also crushed the human spirit with a brutality and totality unmatched by even the most corrupt, venal, and materialistic of regimes. The good society is also a prosperous society—not because material goods are an assurance of happiness, but because being productive for oneself, one's family, and one's fellow human beings is a natural expression of the active human spirit.

This definition of a good society may not seem, at first glance, to contradict the claims of tyrant capitalists. Their societies might permit infinitely varied opportunities for economic contracting (and thus engender economic prosperity), though without popular control over the mechanisms of government. Indeed, Hong Kong under Chinese rule may currently embody just such a compromise. Defenders of tyrant capitalism sometimes posit "Asian values" that are said to justify diminished individual political liberty in the name of increased collective wealth. Yet in the end, no matter what their geographic locale, tyrant capitalists defend their power-grabs by variants of the same slogan: The poor prefer bread to the ballot.

I believe that this general defense of tyrant capitalism fails for two interrelated reasons. First, as argued above, the true goal of society is to facilitate the independent choices of its constituent members. Even the desperately poor recognize that these choices cannot be restricted to the economic realm. Indeed the boundaries of the economic are not all that clear: Consumer choice is not free if it does not extend to the books and newspapers one may read, and labor freedoms are no less economic than they are political. The lack of political choice itself subtracts from a society's prosperity.

Second, tyrannies cannot remain both wealthy and stable indefinitely. We have seen in recent years how the erosion of the rule of law by tyrant capitalists soon undermined their economies. Because tyrant capitalism both enriches and insulates its political leaders, it leads to crony capitalism, which is itself unstable. Individuals living under such a system lose confidence in the honesty of their government, the impartiality of their judges, and the trustworthiness of their neighbors. Absent such trust, a free market cannot function. Thus tyrant capitalism tends to degenerate into bandit capitalism.

In contrast to tyranny, political liberty nourishes both polity and economy. Democracy supports the institutions on which it, in turn, depends: the rule of law and the free market. Moreover, as Amartya Sen has argued, democracy seems to be a vaccine against certain kinds of socially created disasters. Two such plagues have yet to affect a fully functioning democracy: war with another democracy and famine.[2] Much as in the economic market, free choice among competing "goods" is the most efficient way to produce good government.

Trust, Promise, and Markets

I begin with fundamentals. A society cannot prosper without stable institutions to elicit the thought and efforts of its members: stable entitlements (that is, property); regular, ready ways of engaging, transferring, and exchanging property (contracts); and transparent, dependable institutions to protect property and enforce contracts. None of this is possible without a community of trust and mutual respect. To work together, to trade, and to accept authority as an enabler rather than a hindrance to enterprise, people must trust each other, and trust requires and engenders respect. Gross inequalities are incompatible with relations of trust and respect. There can be no trust between citizens living in such radically different circumstances that they appear to inhabit different universes, to belong to different species, and not to share a common humanity. By the same token, a hungry, inarticulate citizen clothed in rags is likely to receive very different treatment from a person in authority than a citizen whose status more nearly approximates (or perhaps far surpasses) that of the official. Yet it is not inequality as such that is the hindrance. It is the destruction by inequality of relations of trust and respect. If we were all equal but did not trust and respect one another, there would be neither prosperity nor happiness.

Without trust there can be no freedom, no markets, and in the end, no prosperity. This is what the tyrant and bandit capitalists do not understand. I am afraid that people under such systems have been taken in by a combination of their propaganda and our clichés. The discourse of capitalism is replete with Darwinian metaphors: competition; survival of the fittest; bankruptcy as the death penalty of the market; ruthless selfishness as somehow leading, by the invisible hand of market economies, to the greatest good of the greatest number. A market economy is often seen as one in which the most violent, ruthless, cunning, deceitful, and fortunate prosper at the expense of everyone else. In such a jungle, there is no guarantee of prosperity, civilization, beauty, or even human survival. That is just what the old Marxist propagandists said about markets and what some of the new bandit and tyrant capitalists appear to believe.

The Darwinian jungle metaphor is worse than inapt; it entirely obscures the true nature of a market economy. The market is not a jungle. Rather, it is the convergence of free choices by free men and women in a context of mutual respect and the equal dignity of all. In the Darwinian struggle, the fittest do not prevail because they are antecedently identified as more fit; they are fit because they have survived. If circumstances favored the universal dominance of slime mold, then human beings, giraffes, whales, and orchids would have to bow to that edict. The market, by contrast, can be defended as a social, human, and moral institution that leads to the most effective fulfillment of human needs and desires. Competition in the market takes place on a platform of honesty, decency, and mutual respect. The way in which the bandit capitalists have understood the market may be likened to the reaction of a stranger who views the competition on a soccer field, tennis court, or even boxing ring, and does not understand that he is, in fact, seeing a game, a contest played according to rules, among athletes who respect, perhaps admire, and maybe even have affection for one another. To be sure, the end of these games is to amuse, but it is also to elicit a form of human excellence and to edify both players and audience by a demonstration not only of skill but also of faithfulness—faithfulness to the rules of the game and to the ethic of sportsmanship. That is why athletes are heroes, while thieves, poisoners, and arsonists are not.

Faithfulness and trust—these are the foundations of the market and of capitalism. Start with the basics. Even a single exchange requires the participants in that exchange to have a minimum of trust in each other: When we hand something over to another, we expect to receive in return roughly the thing we bargained for. A market is a locus of such exchanges. It deepens and complicates them along two axes: time and number. Take time. It is a great invention of the human spirit that the minimum of faithfulness implied in a transaction has been amplified into an institution that allows us to exchange things over time as if the exchange were instantaneous. This is called the institution of promise. It allows us to receive something now in exchange for something we will not be able to give until later. It allows us confidently to give up something now in return for something another person will give us later.

It is worth pondering for a moment what a remarkable thing this is. We live in time as a bird lives in the air. If we could not beat our wings against it, no coherent movement would be possible. Anything we do that has any complexity or importance, indeed all the things that make us alive and human, are spread out over time. Our most wonderful plans and our simplest gestures are extended in time as they are in space. Consider a dance step: It consists not only of the instantaneous deployment of limbs but also of the movement from one position to another, and the sequence makes a single unit just as much as an object in space is a distinct thing. Yet to accomplish the dance—or song, or story—we must carry through. Without this faithfulness to our project, this coherence over time, we would be incoherent not only to one another but to ourselves. Think of each moment during the performance as a promise to carry though to the end.

The regime of promise is a special case of this most general aspect of what makes us human, rational animals. It allows a kind of higher-order coherence, for just as our steadiness in our performance makes possible our own personal projects and thus makes us understandable to others, so promise is a way of coordinating our individual projects with those of others—and more. It makes possible higher-order, cooperative undertakings. We wish to act together: your shoes for my bread, but your shoes will not be ready for weeks and I want bread now. Moreover, the bread exchanged for shoes will be baked and eaten over several months. You might say that there is an immediate exchange here—bread for money and shoes for money. With that money, you can buy fresh bread every day over months, and I can buy my shoes when they are ready. But money is just a surrogate, the storehouse of our mutual promises to each other. And so performances are coordinated not only through time but also across space. It is almost a miracle. It is the conquest of time and space not by a machine but by another sort of human invention: mutual commitment.

We are not quite at the market. For coordination and coherence can also be found in armies and bureaucracies. This is top-down coherence, and it requires intelligence and coordination. And there is certainly an important element of reciprocity in this kind of coordination. An officer's orders must be understood by his soldiers, and that understanding requires a kind of minimum sympathetic response. No order can be completely explicit. The soldier must understand to some degree the purpose of the order, or he will fail to carry it out appropriately. In any complex organization, there is a degree of horizontal coordination as well. Each soldier must be able to count on his fellow soldiers having understood and being willing to carry out the orders given. Yet markets carry this intelligent coordination a step further. A market is the coordination of formal equality. It is pure horizontality, and it is the architecture of human liberty. It is the coordination of free choices by free persons.

There are many well-known efficiencies in organizing economies through markets, although they have not always been as celebrated as they are today. For my purpose, it is not necessary to add to this celebration. It is sufficient to take as a premise that markets are, in general, at least as efficient as other forms of economic organization in satisfying people's needs and wants. As I have said, the discourse of capitalism is highly misleading, and nowhere more so than in describing the functioning of markets. Comparing markets to a jungle emphasizes competition, but the competition is not the central aspect of a market; it is an epiphenomenon. The central aspect is the coordination of free choices. To be sure, this produces a kind of competition when the market attains any degree of complexity beyond the simplest uncoordinated system of barter. Competition ensues when people have choices—when they are free. When there is more than one person with whom I may deal, these persons may compete to deal with me. But this already gives the lie to the conception of the competitive market as a jungle, as a scene of force and fraud. Force and fraud are the antithesis of freedom: When people are tricked or bludgeoned, they have not exchanged freely; they have been cheated or robbed.

Market exchange, by contrast, must be free and honest. Thus each exchange not only satisfies the needs and wishes of the exchanging parties but also expresses respect between them and strengthens the bonds of community that make future exchange possible. When we move beyond the simple bilateral exchange to the multiparty, time-extended system of exchange that is the market (where I satisfy the wishes of unseen and unknown persons who may be distant from me not only in place but also, miraculously, in time), those bonds take on a depth and complexity that are truly wonderful. A particular exchange may satisfy the need of a person who has since died or who may not yet know that he has such a need. Such is the alchemy of money. The market binds together unknown persons and creates a practical community extending from the past into the future.

All this may seem hopelessly romantic, pollyannaish, and even ridiculous in light of the realities of any modern market economy—the vulgarity of commercialism, the manipulation of taste, the seduction of persons into imprudent and even destructive purchases, and the sometimes grotesque inequalities of wealth that make nonsense of the notion of free choice on the part of those struggling to meet basic needs. Yet my argument holds in spite—maybe even because—of these grim realities. For I am not saying that the market is a *sufficient* condition of human happiness and of a decent society, but rather a *necessary* condition. More importantly, a well-functioning market requires decency, community, and faithfulness, all of which not only make markets possible but also underwrite conditions of trust, mutual respect, and security that enrich many noneconomic aspects of life.

Sanctions and Their Limits

A well-functioning market depends on dependability. Moving beyond immediate barter requires people to be able to trust one another's word.

I have said that this is a matter of morality and mutual respect. A cynic might respond that, no, it is a matter of sanctions, both formal and informal. The formal sanctions of the law are exemplified, of course, in the enforcement of contract. The informal sanctions include social disapproval, exclusion from future opportunities, and violent, mafia-like reprisals. Yet to think in terms of sanctions is a big mistake. Sanctions cannot maintain a dependable system of exchange unless the occasions for their imposition are rare. No regime of exchange and mutual cooperation is possible when every exchange is the subject of sanctions. There could be no regime of promises if every promise had to be enforced in court. There could be no such regime even if every promise were enforced only by bringing to bear social or violent pressure. First, such a situation would be incredibly wasteful of time and resources. But more importantly, the dependability and the regularity that sanctions are intended to enforce themselves require that sanctions be dependably and regularly applied. A context in which we can trust the government (or the mafia, or our neighbors) to enforce agreements accurately and dependably is exactly the kind of context of trust and mutual regard that is necessary for successful mutual exchange *without* sanctions. Without trust and mutual regard *and* without sanctions, society becomes a jungle where robbery and fraud are rampant. A regime of sanctions without trust and regard is a regime of robbery and duress by those imposing the sanctions. So sanctions are no substitute for a regime of trust and respect.

In a society of men and women rather than angels, we need sanctions too. We need them for enforcement against the outliers. Honest, decent people must be made to feel that when they keep their word (which at any particular moment it may not be in their interest to do) they are not being taken for suckers. They must know that the few who steal or cheat will not profit. We see this in a tax regime. No system of enforcement and penalties can make an income-tax system work if everyone cheats. For the system to function, most people have to comply voluntarily, but they will do so only if they know that the few who do not are unlikely to wind up better off. Enforcement is society's collective debt to those who are willing to keep their word without being forced to do so. If society does not honor that debt, then fewer and fewer will be willing to keep their word. And if hardly any are willing to keep their word voluntarily, then enforcement can accomplish nothing. Moreover, enforcement itself depends on a higher-order agreement honestly meant and honestly kept: the agreement between those given (lent?) the power of enforcement and those on whom the enforcement eventually may be brought to bear. Just as there is a difference between a free exchange and a robbery, so there is a difference between a policeman and a thug who happens to wear a uniform. Trust and respect are that difference.

A complex society is not a family, or even a village. Like these, it functions best in an atmosphere of trust and respect, but its trust and respect are built into elaborate, abstract institutions: law, courts, and police. It is easy to think that because these institutions are elaborate, formal, and abstract, moral virtues like trust and respect are not relevant to them. That is a mistake. In a family, trust and respect work unmediated by institutions. In a complex society, the human nexus is maintained insofar as various levels of mediating institutions, beginning with the family, instantiate and foster trust and respect. A brutal father may hold his family together by fear, but his is a poisoned community. Instead of promoting the welfare of his wife and children, he inspires terror and desolation. If anything is created, it is despite, not because of, his regime. Moreover, brutality tends to replicate itself from generation to generation. A social regime based on force, fraud, and brutal inequality may also somehow survive, feed its people, and wring work and product out of them. But there is no joy there, no creativity, and at best only a mockery of prosperity. A healthy society has laws and courts and police, of course, but these are abstract, complex manifestations not of brutality and force but of trust and respect. When force is brought to bear—as it sometimes must be—it does no more than insist on the fulfillment of the duties of trust that are generally respected without the resort to force. Force is not the paradigm; it is the exception that maintains the paradigm.

Law and Civic Friendship

It is a mistake to focus too much on force and policemen for another reason. It is not just that force is exceptional even among the abstract, formal institutions of the society. Force is—and in a well-ordered society, must be—the last resort. Laws and courts, by contrast, are not a last resort. They do not represent what is anomalous and must be brought into line. Law is intrinsic to a free, complex society of persons who trust and respect one another. In a perfect world, there would not have to be policemen, but there would still be law and courts. Law is the nexus of the reasonable expectations that free persons entertain of one another. Citizens of a well-ordered society cannot know all their fellow citizens personally. Indeed, it is the virtue of a complex society that it can bind together by bonds of trust and mutual respect people who have never met. The laws are those bonds. To the extent that they are good laws, my willingness to abide by them expresses my respect for my fellow citizens. When I come together in an abstract relationship with a citizen-stranger—say, in buying goods from him online or in paying taxes for our common civic amenities—I perform an act of trust, and thereby I express my respect for him. We prosper and also strengthen the bonds of civic friendship between us. When I cheat or betray him, I weaken those bonds. In each case, the impact is infinitesimal. When I pass a counterfeit bill, I loosen those bonds and degrade the utility of the currency by an infinitesimal amount, but degrade it I do. And if too many others follow my example, we will be reduced to the penury of barter. That much is obvious. It is less obvious, but no less true, that each time I keep my bargain, pay my bill, pay my taxes, I strengthen those bonds. It is not too much to say that every honest dealing is an act of civic friendship that, on its cooler and more abstract level, is analogous to an act of kindness to a friend or family member.

The law binds us together and makes possible our civic friendship. Yet not all law does that, but only law that expresses and facilitates our dealings with one another on a basis of trust and equality. I come back to my description of the market: a nexus of free citizens, most of whom are unknown to one another. The nexus of the market is like the nexus of the law. Of course, the relation is more intimate than that. Citizens deal with one another in the market according to the rules of law, and citizens' mutual contacts according to the law are in fact a kind of market, or an aspect of the market, or the market itself. This suggests what the law must be like. It must encourage citizens to deal with one another by reaffirming their reasonable expectations and facilitating their exchanges. In other words, it must establish stable rules of property and reasonable rules of exchange.

If law fails to establish stable rules of property and reasonable rules of exchange, it hinders growth. A 1995 World Bank study found that red tape imposed a 50 percent tax on the cost of new housing in Kuala Lumpur,[3] while researchers in Peru trying to set up a textile factory found that the process took 289 days, 11 permits, two bribes, and 32 times the minimum monthly living wage.[4] In Peru and Malaysia, these examples suggest, the law plainly does not exist to facilitate the activities of the countries' citizens. It is an impediment, not a framework. This is an insult to the citizenry and a violation of equality, because the law in these cases is clearly not a servant of the people. It is, to a greater or lesser extent, part of an organized protection racket of those who already make or import certain products, or simply of the officials who would have less to do if their permission were not needed. The people are subordinated to the interests of the officials; the law becomes a racket and the bureaucrats become racketeers. This is the misuse of law. Its proper use is to define and protect expectations so that people may deal securely with one another, so that they can plan and invest in schemes of cooperation. That means that the law must define a stable regime of property rights and offer a regular framework for the exchange and combination of those rights. The details may vary; it is the stability, completeness, and transparency of the definitions and framework that matter.

However clear the definitions and however transparent the rules of cooperation and exchange, they will not establish a regime of confident and fair dealing unless they establish *in fact* the terms of the citizens' common life. This means that rules must not only be written and known;

they must also be enforced. Even if men were angels—that is, willing always to act according to the law—there would still be a need for authoritative exposition at the cognitive level. Even among men of perfect good will there will be divergences about where property lines are drawn and how engagements are to be understood in concrete circumstances not fully anticipated when they were made. The need for enforcement exists at the borders of men's willingness to act in good faith and at the borders of their understanding. It exists only at the borders because if reluctance and lack of mutual understanding were to characterize the entire terrain, the law would be swamped and powerless. As I have said, we must expect most people in most circumstances to know what they have to do and to do it without any prodding. Understanding and fidelity must be the rule, disputes and defaults, the exception. That is why the law—its definitions and its framework— must be transparent. If the law were not transparent and if persons outside the exchange had to step in to order (or reorder) it every time, it would not be—or be experienced as—the free ordering of free men. It would be an order imposed from outside by whoever had the power of interpretation and enforcement. Yet the borderland exists, and it must be policed. Otherwise, the desert on the other side of the border will encroach more and more on the heartland until no voluntary system and no order is left. Thus the need for judges and policemen.

The Duty of Judges

Judges are even more essential than policemen. Even men of the greatest good will need judges to settle disputes and misunderstandings. More fundamentally still, just as there can be no contracts and no schemes of mutual cooperation without a settled and secure scheme of property rights and a settled and certain way of transferring, exchanging, and coordinating them, so neither of these can exist without institutions to interpret and apply the rules of property and the rules by which it is transferred and exchanged. All of these require both will and mind: the will to respect property and to keep your word, but also the intellect to understand what your property rights are when I have indeed given you my word—in short, the intellect to know the law. A system of laws must be transparent and perspicuous (close enough to ordinary understanding for ordinary men and women to be able to abide by it in most cases just by being members of the same community, in the way that ordinary men and women who are educated native speakers do not need professional grammarians to help them speak their language correctly and understandably). It is also important for courts to apply the rules in close cases and to keep them serviceable for new situations. Honest men know what it means to shake hands after a long negotiation to signal that they have come to terms. Currency traders know that the slightest hesitation after being given a bid over the phone is inadmissible and means that the bid is withdrawn.[5] But what are the understandings on the Internet?

The application of the rules and their adaptation to new circumstances require knowledge, imagination, and steadiness: *knowledge* of the rules and of the world to which the rules apply; the *imagination* to conceive of the possible arrangements that might solve difficult puzzles and to recognize how the inappropriate application of old rules to new situations disappoints rather than fulfills expectations; and *steadiness,* because the rules can be very intricate and because their application to new situations may be controversial. Trust and respect, prerequisites for a good society, must apply to judges in particular. In every dispute, one side is likely to be disappointed. They must have grounds to believe that their arguments were heard and considered on their merits, that who they were had nothing to with the decision, and that the decision was according to law and not according to anything else. Only in this way can the steadiness and regularity of a regime of rules be transmitted to concrete individuals in a particular case. Without trust and mutual respect, you cannot have a society that elicits the best, most imaginative contributions from its members. And without law, you cannot move from a primitive society to a complex society of trust and respect.

Yet laws are only as good as the judges who interpret and apply them. So how does one get steadiness and regularity in judges? Article 29 of the Declaration of Rights of the Constitution of the Commonwealth of Massachusetts, drafted by John Adams in 1780, put it this way:

It is *essential to the preservation* of the rights of every individual, his life, liberty, property, and character, that there be an impartial interpretation of the laws, and administration of justice. It is the right of every citizen to be tried by judges as free, impartial and independent as the lot of humanity will admit. It is, therefore, not only the best policy, but essential for the security of the rights of the people, and of every citizen, that the judges of the supreme judicial court should hold their offices as long as they behave themselves well; and that they should have honorable salaries ascertained and established by standing laws.

The language may be a bit archaic, but the meaning is clear: Those who interpret and apply the law must be altogether independent of the political pressures that inevitably—and even properly—attend the process by which the rules are made and the ordinary business of government is administered. Democracy makes law, but after that it must yield to reason in the law's application. It is a little like the old children's system for distributing cake: One side divides, the other chooses. Democracy makes the rules and cuts up the cake, but independent judges, ruled by the reason of the law, distribute the pieces. What in legislation is politics in judging becomes corruption.

The duty of judging according to the rules is often put in terms of favoring neither the rich nor the poor. Mindlessly, this is taken to mean merely that judges should not seek personal advantage by currying favor with the rich and powerful. But the maxim speaks of favoring neither the rich *nor the poor*. This requires more thought than it usually gets. In general, it seems a virtue to be especially solicitous of those whose lot in life is hard. This is human kindness, but in a judge it is as much corruption as is seeking the favor of the rich. For once a judge respects persons and not the law, all regularity is gone. It takes a particular kind of fortitude to be a good judge. Without that fortitude, the rule of law collapses. And in its collapse, the poor suffer most of all. A well-ordered society is a regime of trust and respect. If a judge favors the rich man because he is rich, then the poor man has been despised. But if the judge favors the poor man in a way that the law does not, then he insults the poor man's standing as an equal citizen. And the bond of civic friendship that should bind the two together is replaced by a poisonous web of envy and condescension.

It is not an easy job to be a judge. According to an Islamic saying: "Judges are three: two in Fire, and one in Paradise. A man who has knowledge, and judges by what he knows—he is in Paradise. A man who is ignorant, and judges according to his ignorance—he is in the Fire. A man who has knowledge and judges by something other than his knowledge—he is in the Fire."[6] And this is what Jethro said to Moses: "Moreover thou shalt provide out of all the people able men, such as fear God, men of truth, hating covetousness."[7]

Who is "a man of truth"? Is it not a man who judges according to the facts and according to the law? A judgment that ignores the one or the other is a false judgment. Who is "an able man"? He is one who knows the law and is worldly enough to know the ways of men. Yet despite his worldliness, he is neither a cynic nor a relativist, but rather a man of truth who fears God. Pontius Pilate is the archetype of a judge who is not "a man of truth"—not because he was a liar or corrupt, but because in his worldliness, his world-weariness, he acted expediently and bureaucratically. "What is truth?" he shrugged and carelessly gave the most famous unjust judgment in history. The man of truth is not a bureaucrat, and neither is a good judge.

Where does one find such men (and women)? In practical terms, a society seeks its judges from among its most respected members—"able men," "men of truth," learned men. Then, following John Adams's advice, it makes them "as free, impartial and independent as the lot of humanity will admit." That means paying them well, say at the level of the governor of a state or a senior executive. It means giving them long tenure, preferably for life or until they retire. And it means offering them a retirement pension dignified enough so that society may reasonably ask them not to seek to earn more, thus avoiding the appearance that later employment was in fact the postponed payment of a bribe for services rendered while in office. A system in which judges serve only for the term of the political officials who appoint them seems designed to make these judges not as "free, impartial and independent as the lot of humanity will admit," but as subservient and partial as the will to power can bend them to be. A man must be a hero indeed to resist that kind of pressure. Although it is a cynical and self-defeating stance to deny that ordinary men and women will behave decently and reasonably unless strongly coerced to do so, it is a first principle in designing institutions not to rely on moral heroism as a necessary condition of their proper functioning.

Forming Virtuous Individuals

So we must have citizens who trust and respect each other, laws of property and exchange that assume such trust (allowing citizens to deal with one another in all confidence and security), and magistrates who will interpret and enforce the laws in a spirit of impartiality. Where does one find such magistrates, and how does one produce citizens who trust and respect one another? Well-functioning institutions, including the rule of law, foster and sustain such qualities among citizens, but those qualities, in turn, seem to be a necessary precondition of such institutions. I return to Václav Havel, who saw that merely importing Western institutions into the blasted moral landscape of postcommunism would not be sufficient to create a society of law. Trust and mutual respect are moral virtues of individuals, and we must ask what will form such individuals. It seems like a circle into which we cannot break: Either men and women are virtuous and they sustain the institutions that sustain their virtues; or men and women lack these virtues, and then no institutions capable of sustaining them can arise or flourish.

There is a way, however, to cut into the circle—through the most fundamental social institution, the family. Because the family is held together by ties more primitive and basic than the abstract ties on which civic friendship rests, it can serve as the school for human affection and mutual forbearance which, when abstracted and generalized, can become the habits of mind and heart from which trust and mutual respect may grow. It seems altogether obvious that civic friendship is not just a metaphor; it is an abstraction from personal friendship, and it assumes a capacity for human sympathy. But surely the family is the school of human sympathy (as it is also the school for many of society's pathologies). There are few, if any, autodidacts in the subject of human fellowship. So here is a ground for hope: Mothers and fathers can show the way. Learning from how they treat one another, mothers, fathers, and children may begin the extrapolation to civic friendship, trust, and respect. There is no guarantee—but there are surely more loving families than there are just and prosperous societies. The former will always provide the soil from which, from time to time, the latter arise.

NOTES

The author wishes to acknowledge helpful suggestions from Stephen G. Breyer, Mary Ann Glendon, and David Hoffman.

1. Václav Havel, "The State of the Republic," Paul Wilson, trans., *New York Review of Books,* 5 March 1998, 42; Václav Havel, "The Post-Communist Nightmare," Paul Wilson, trans., *New York Review of Books,* 27 May 1993, 8.

2. Amartya Sen, *Development as Freedom,* (New York: Random House, 1999), 152.

3. "Citadels of Power," *The Economist,* 29 July 1995, 14.

4. Hernando de Soto, *The Other Path: The Invisible Revolution in the Third World* (New York: Harper and Row, 1989).

5. The reason: A hesitation allows the recipient of the bid to check a screen or other phone to see if a better bid is available and thus to turn what is intended as a firm offer into the start of a negotiation. The only control against this is just that the bidder may treat as ineffective an acceptance that is not immediate. Instead, it becomes a counter offer that the former bidder may accept or decline.

6. A saying attributed to the Prophet, Ibn Hanbal, 6:75; al-Bayhaqi, 10:96. Quoted in Frank E. Vogel, *Islamic Law and Legal System: Studies of Saudi Arabia,* unpubl. ms., 24, n. 41.

7. Exod. 18:21.

18

FREE POLITICS AND FREE MARKETS IN LATIN AMERICA

Jorge I. Domínguez

Jorge I. Domínguez is Clarence Dillon Professor of International Affairs and director of the Weatherhead Center for International Affairs at Harvard University. Among his recent books are Democratic Politics in Latin America and the Caribbean *(1998) and* Toward Mexico's Democratization: Parties, Elections, and Public Opinion *(1999). This chapter is drawn from a longer essay, coauthored with Susan Kaufman Purcell, that appeared in the 1999 volume* The United States and the Americas: A Twenty-First-Century View.

Never before in the history of Latin America have so many countries had constitutional governments, elected in free and competitive elections under effective universal suffrage, that also pursue market-based economic policies. Early in the twentieth century, many Latin American governments favored open economies, but rulers were chosen either by narrow oligarchies or by military officers. By the middle of the century, many Latin American governments were democratically chosen, but pursued statist policies that sought, as far as possible, to sever the links between their nations' economies and the world market. Thus the combination of the 1990s—an era of free politics and free markets—is truly without precedent.

This may explain why scholars, policy makers, and many ordinary citizens have found it hard to believe that democracy and open markets can even coexist, much less thrive jointly. The 1970s were pervaded by a seemingly well-grounded pessimism about the ability of Latin American democracies to implement sound, growth-friendly economic policies. There seemed to be an elective affinity between sensible economic policies and bureaucratic-authoritarian regimes, and also between economic malperformance and the demagogic populism of civilian politicians.[1]

In the late 1980s and early 1990s, democratic rule returned to Latin America at about the same time that it was making its dramatic entrance in Eastern Europe. During those years, the democratic pessimists argued that "democracy in the political realm works against economic reforms."[2] They predicted that populist demagogues would bar or wreck market-oriented policies, or else that such reforms as might make headway under democratic conditions would prove politically destabilizing, as rent-seeking firms and labor union bosses worked to get the reformers voted out of office.[3] The least pessimistic of these observers allowed that democracies might enact reforms and survive, but only if strong presidents or prime ministers could force their peoples to be free.[4]

The record does not bear out these arguments. Latin American authoritarians proved no better than democratic populists at making sound economic policy.[5] Indeed, the authoritarian governments that had taken over in country after country by the late 1970s were principally responsible for the catastrophic regionwide economic collapse of 1982–83.

Consider the allegedly sterling economic performance of General Augusto Pinochet's dictatorship in Chile (1973–90). His government deserves credit for inaugurating several valuable structural economic reforms, yet its overall record hardly bespeaks economic wizardry. According to the UN Economic Commission for Latin America and the Caribbean (UNECLAC), in 1982, at the birth of the international debt crisis, Pinochet's Chile experienced the worst one-year per-capita GDP decline (a 14.5 percent drop) of any country in the Western Hemisphere. Behind the debacle lay the arrogance and blundering of Pinochet's economic advisors. Moreover, according to the Inter-American Development Bank, from 1981 to 1990 Chile's per-capita GDP (as measured in 1988 dollars) grew at an average annual rate of just 1 percent—a miracle, yes, but only in public relations.[6]

Even if they were mistaken about the larger picture, the democratic pessimists did offer an important insight. The truth was that freely elected governments in Latin America had not put together a good record of sound, sustained macroeconomic policies and performance. Whether one looks at Brazil in the early 1960s under President João Goulart, or Chile in the early 1970s under President Salvador Allende, or Argentina in the mid-1970s under President Isabel Perón, or any number of other cases, one sees a depressing parade of constitutional regimes hewing to stunningly irresponsible economic policies that brought poverty and hardship to millions and contributed to the breakdown of democracy.

And yet even in these countries, democratic governments had once done much better. Examples would include Brazil in the late 1950s under President Juscelino Kubitschek, Argentina in the mid-1960s under President Arturo Illia, and Chile in the middle and late 1960s under President Eduardo Frei.[7] A key question, therefore, was whether democrats could learn from their mistakes and change their economic preferences and policies. Another was whether democrats could win the support of many of those who, at one time or another, had supported authoritarian rule.

The Critical Junctures for Change

If the great Latin American depression of the 1980s had any good result, it was that it did wonders for the prospects of democracy and markets. The severity and duration of the downturn forced many to reassess their basic assumptions about the statist, import-substitution policy framework that had prevailed for decades. When the crisis hit, authoritarian governments still ruled most countries, and even in the fledgling democracies recently discredited authoritarians came in for much of the blame. The crisis itself contributed to the further opening of political systems, but did not produce instant learning. When constitutional governments under presidents José Sarney of Brazil and Raúl Alfonsín of Argentina chose to resist fundamental reform and thereby suffered eventual political defeat, their cautionary example convinced politicians across Latin America to embrace the need for further changes.

During the crisis, there was available an international pool of theoretical and empirical ideas that emphasized the utility of markets. These ideas had become dominant in the governments of the industrialized countries in the 1970s and 1980s, and enjoyed important bases of support in private foundations, universities, and international financial institutions. They were learned by young "technopols"—politically involved, adept, and technically qualified people—and brought home for application. In the 1990s, earned social-science doctorates graced the resumés of the Brazilian and Mexican presidents as well as a number of finance ministers across the region. Most important reformist technopols had spent much time in the opposition; some had been political exiles. While the economic crisis did not "cause" the political opening, the former did ease the way for the latter by giving technically expert opposition leaders an occasion to criticize authoritarian technocrats on their own terms. Bolstered by the legitimacy they derived from the support of the international community, opposition technopols challenged their governments and, in so doing, built their own constituencies at home.

Beginning in the 1970s, another international pool of ideas became available. It asserted the centrality of democracy as the way to govern and the importance of respect for human rights in the relationship between state and society. The international federations of Christian democratic, social democratic, and liberal parties, present worldwide but especially prominent in Western Europe, contributed mightily to this international change. Especially pertinent for Latin America was Spain's experience under President Felipe González and his social democratic government. Spain's Socialists demonstrated that market-oriented policies fostered the consolidation of democracy and, just as importantly, that voters would reward politicians who dropped past statist commitments in favor of promarket policies.

The international community began to demand democracy in politics and competence in economics just as a new generation of Latin American elites was at last able and willing to supply them. In this way, the governments of the major industrial democracies, the international financial institutions, and the major private foundations made a powerful contribution to Latin America's simultaneous double transition toward democracy and markets. Although one must look at each country separately to explain the particulars of these developments, the synchronic hemispheric sweep of the change can only be understood as part of a common international process. Latin America's transformation is a dramatic example of the power of ideas and international action to foster change within a number of different countries at more or less the same time.

The Logic of Democracy and Markets

Market reforms (especially deregulation, privatization, and the ending of business subsidies) can serve democratic goals. Under statism, broader participation and fair contestation tend to suffer as economic and political elites become bedfellows. The leading business groups are often those whose profits depend more on political connections than on efficiency or quality. Market reforms can break the ties between political and economic elites, reduce the opportunities for corruption and rent-seeking, and create a more level playing field for economic actors. Involvement in international markets, especially if guaranteed by free-trade agreements, increases the leverage that external actors can apply in defense of constitutional government, should the need arise.

While not an absolute guarantee against authoritarianism, freer markets can be an important check on the abuse of state power. They would, for instance, have left less room for arbitrary state actions of the sort that were prevalent across much of Latin America from the mid-1960s to the late 1980s. Markets may not disperse power sufficiently for all purposes (in Latin America's small economies market power is often highly concentrated), yet they do disperse power more than if it were centralized in the hands of state decision makers.

Democracy can help to consolidate a market economy. In countries with traditionally high levels of societal contestation and political instability and strong, well-organized opposition forces, democracy can reduce "transaction costs." Grievances and energies that might otherwise fuel strikes or insurgencies can take the form of peaceful, democratic political activism instead. In addition, democratic regimes can involve the political opposition in support of a market economy more effectively than can authoritarian regimes.

Most importantly, a democratic polity informed by a genuine and practical commitment to markets is in the long run the best political response to the problems posed by the rational expectations of economic actors. Presidents, ministers, and cabinets can and do change; rational economic actors look for rules and institutions that endure. Authoritarian regimes can provide certain assurances to economic actors for some time, but democratic regimes can also provide long-run assurances, provided that both government and opposition are committed to the same broad framework of a market economy. In this sense, the opposition gives a market economy its most effective long-term guarantee. When the opposition supports the basics of a market economy, actors can rationally expect that the end of a particular administration will not spell the reversal of all their economic expectations. And only a democratic polity can embody the compromises and commitments that are needed freely to bind government and opposition to a consensus on a market-oriented framework.

Nor are these all the advantages that democracy can offer. Competitive elections provide a regular means for making "a clean sweep." Voters get the chance peacefully to retire failed policies and politicians and start afresh, something that is not so easy to arrange under authoritarian conditions. Democracy's stress on the consent of the governed gives leaders an incentive to consolidate efficient economic reforms for the long run, setting and signaling the sorts of clear, lasting political and economic policy rules that create stable expectations and promote productive economic life. Experience has long borne out this lesson in Western Europe, North America, and Japan. In the 1990s, it finally became Latin America's experience as well.

No democratic regime has ever survived in the absence of a market economy. To add the claim that democracy can be good for markets, as I have done, is more controversial, especially if Latin America is the region under discussion. Hence we turn to some Latin American case studies.

Internalizing New Policies and Practices

In many Latin American countries in the 1990s, democratic institutions and procedures have worked to set the long-term rules that enable rational economic actors to believe that the open market economy is here to stay. To be sure, democracy means civil contestation, and conflicts may take a long time to settle, often with a compromise that leaves neither side fully satisfied. Yet the harder and longer the struggle, the more credible the bargained outcome often is. In none of the cases discussed below was the process simple. In many instances, citizens and politicians had to give up cherished hopes. But once an agreement was reached, time and again it helped to set and then to begin consolidating the foundations for Latin America's comprehensive economic turnaround in the 1990s.

Chile. By the late 1990s, Chile featured Latin America's most clearly consolidated open-market economy. The birth of that consolidation can be marked precisely. In March 1989, Chile's broad-based democratic opposition coalition, the Concertación (comprising principally the Christian Democrats, the Socialists, and the Party for Democracy), adopted a detailed social and economic program for government. After spirited and contentious debate, the coalition agreed to support the broad framework of a market economy and to pursue policies consistent with it. Only when the opposition so agreed could rational economic actors believe that the market framework would endure. (The outgoing dictator could guarantee his policies only during his own tenure.) Once in power, the Concertación delivered. Economic actors could count on the long-term endurance of open economic policies precisely because all the major political parties had endorsed them. Democracy's capacity to fulfill the rational expectations of economic actors was superior to that of the Pinochet dictatorship.[8]

Equally important was the new democratic government's commitment, right from the start, to seek a consensus on economic policy that was often broader than the share of votes it commanded in Congress. That government's first significant measure, for example, was a tax increase earmarked for social spending to address needs long neglected by the dictatorship. The new government negotiated the key details of the tax package with the center-right opposition, securing a congressional supermajority. In this instance, it was the center-right National Renovation party that successfully addressed the problem of rational expectations: Chileans from both the right and the left were ready to invest in the health and education of their people.[9]

Argentina. A prosperous country at the beginning of this century, Argentina had to work hard to achieve underdevelopment. At least since the 1930s, its economic history has been a sad study in persistent policy incompetence and decline. Argentina turned around in the 1990s, however, and its story illustrates the utility of democracy for the transition toward a more open market economy.

In May 1989, Carlos Menem was elected president, returning the Peronist party to power for the first time since the 1976 military coup. Bucking his party's old and deep attachment to economic statism, Menem endorsed orthodox macroeconomic policies and a turn toward more open markets. Yet in keeping with another aspect of Peronist tradition, he sought to enact these changes through an assertion of presidential power.

He issued decrees, in effect trying to command markets to be free. In his first two years in office, he issued three times more presidential decrees with the force of law than all other Argentine presidents combined since the adoption of the 1853 Constitution. Menem's mania for decrees proved counterproductive. Argentines had no reason to take him at his word; in their lifetimes, no president had deserved that much trust. They took it for granted, for instance, that no government would ever tame inflation, which in the 1980s had reached dizzying heights.

Economic recession and yet another bout of hyperinflation forced Menem to reconsider his approach. In early 1991, he appointed Domingo Cavallo his economy minister. Cavallo's key contribution was to grasp: 1) that Argentina's basic macroeconomic problems could only be addressed through politics; and 2) that the procedures of democracy were especially well-suited to this task. At first, Cavallo's credibility and prospects in this area seemed as shaky as his boss's. He was Menem's fourth economy minister in less than two years, and his earlier brief stint at the head of the Central Bank under military rule had been a fiasco.

What was needed for the new anti-inflation policy, therefore, was a self-binding strategy. The 1991 "convertibility law" established the free convertibility of the national currency into dollars at a fixed rate of exchange. The Central Bank was prohibited from printing paper money to cover budget deficits unless new currency issues were backed by gold or foreign reserves. Most importantly, this policy was adopted not by decree but through an act of Congress. Henceforth, only Congress could authorize either a change in the value of the currency or the issuance of paper money under other rules. The purpose of the law was to bind the president, the economy minister, and Congress (and through the latter the Peronist party) to the anti-inflation policy. The law was an immediate, stunning, and lasting success. It has become the anchor of Argentina's impressive macroeconomic performance in the 1990s. Only through democratic procedures could Argentina's economy finally achieve a turnaround. The executive and legislative branches jointly enacted most of the significant measures to promote an open-market economy (including detailed approval of privatization decisions), thereby contributing to make the new rules credible for the long term.[10]

Several subsequent democratic steps helped. Before the 1995 presidential election, leading opposition contender José Octavio Bordón of the FREPASO party ran to the left of Menem but nonetheless endorsed the fundamentals of the new economic framework. Then in July 1996, Menem replaced Cavallo as economy minister with no change of policy, signaling a continuity that transcended personnel. In preparation for the October 1997 congressional elections, the new opposition alliance of the Radical party and FREPASO, the country's second and third largest parties, endorsed the new economic framework, not as a candidate's personal decision but as a program adopted by these parties. Heading toward the presidential balloting slated for late 1999, all the major contenders continue to voice public support for the fundamental framework of a market economy.[11]

It was not, in short, the president's decree authority, or the talent and boldness of his economy minister, or even the skill of his entire governing team that ensured the inauguration and later the consolidation of Argentina's shift to an open-market economy. Indeed, the "strong" presidency at first actually impeded the installation of market reforms.[12] And consolidation began only when the opposition endorsed the change in framework and the policy survived the departure of its key architect. Only democracy can commit the future.

El Salvador. In the early 1980s, no one would have predicted that the late 1990s would see El Salvador with its brutal civil war ended, fair and competitive elections the norm, and one-time blood enemies sitting side-by-side in Congress. Peace came to El Salvador because the lesson of Thomas Hobbes' *Leviathan* proved true once again: After years of watching the hard hand of war make so many lives "poor, nasty, brutish, and short," citizens thirsting for order found it through a complex and far-reaching political contract. Peace, not surprisingly, became the cornerstone of prosperity. According to UNECLAC's 1997 *Preliminary Overview,* El Salvador has been Central America's top economic performer in the 1990s.

Democratic procedures helped to build the peace. El Salvador's democratic left played a crucial role in constructing the bases for a peace settlement prior to the formal agreement. For example, in the 1980s Rubén Zamora had been allied with the revolutionary insurgency and served as its international civilian spokesman. Eventually, his Democratic Convergence (CD) party chose to participate in the 1989 and 1991 national elections. After the latter, the ruling conservative party (best known by its acronym, ARENA) and the CD agreed to organize the legislature, voting for each other's respective candidates for leadership posts. Thus the democratic left reassured the military and conservative elites that it could be trusted to be law-abiding and to govern, and it signaled to the insurgents that much could be gained through elections.[13]

Democratic procedures have also improved the prospects for economic growth. In May 1995, economic exigencies forced President Armando Calderón Sol's ARENA government to hike the value-added tax. Deserted by his normal legislative allies, who feared the political repercussions of the vastly unpopular increase, Calderón Sol cut a deal with the new Democratic Party, led by the leading former revolutionary commander, Joaquín Villalobos. In what turned out to be a very costly decision for himself and his party, Villalobos agreed to push the tax increase through Congress.[14]

In June 1997, a new opposition majority in the legislature repealed the law governing the privatization of the state-owned telephone company. With its other hand, however, the opposition held out to the administration an offer of detailed negotiations (indeed, the government's lack of consultation and resort to presidential decree had been at the heart of the opposition's objections to the way in which phone-company privatization was being handled). The talks succeeded, and in July 1997 a legislative supermajority approved a privatization plan that increased the probability of more competition and more effective regulation.[15]

El Salvador is at an earlier stage than Chile or Argentina in learning how to use democratic procedures to consolidate a market economy. Yet Salvadoran politicians from both the right and left are slowly learning that democracy and the market can be mutually enhanced if each supports the other, and that in the long run only a democratic opposition can ensure the future of market-oriented economic reforms.

Brazil. For decades, Fernando Henrique Cardoso was Brazil's internationally best-known social scientist. He was also a man of the left and a political exile during the military government. Cardoso intellectually observed, and personally suffered, the arbitrariness of Brazil's oversized state under military rule. He also learned firsthand the volatility, indiscipline, and unreliability of Brazil's political parties. As a member of Congress, finance minister, and eventually president, he set for himself the goal of democratizing Brazil. That required shrinking the bloated state, making it subject to law, and reinventing parties and parliaments to make democratic procedures work.[16]

Cardoso has acted in the persistent belief that laws enacted by Congress are by far the best means available to reorder Brazil's economy for the twenty-first century. He has had good empirical (as well as normative) reasons for such beliefs. In the decade before his election, three presidents had tried and failed to stabilize the economy and enact economic reforms by decree. To be sure, steering reform through Congress is a maddeningly slow business. Cardoso's party is in the minority, and coalition and party discipline are so feeble that each vote must be negotiated afresh. But an act of Congress offers more assurance than a mere presidential decree that today's economic rules will endure tomorrow.

By the late 1990s, Congress had approved key proposals on the privatization of telecommunications and the oil industry. The fixed-line telephone sector became open to private capital, which also gained access to an oil sector that had long been a state monopoly. Important privatizations have also occurred in iron mining, electricity, and railroads, among other sectors. Congress has enacted some administrative reforms and even crept toward meaningful social security reform. Each success has depended on the laborious cobbling together of a multiparty coalition, yet this makes it more likely that today's policies will be supported by many parties tomorrow. Laws are superior to decrees, and coalition governments and supermajorities are often superior to simple one-party majorities in increasing the likelihood that new rules will be credible and enduring.[17]

All was not rosy, to be sure. In order to enact these reforms, Cardoso and his lieutenants have had to engage in the pork-barreling and horse-trading that have long been congressional specialties. "One vote, one side payment per pivotal deputy" seems to be the standard operating procedure. Nonetheless, Cardoso's program has gathered behind it a large majority whose occasional volatility has not eclipsed its usual reliability. It has been strengthened by public opinion, and by the growth of the president's own party, the Brazilian Social Democratic Party (PSDB), whose internal coherence and discipline are among the highest in Brazilian politics.

In late 1997, the Asian financial crisis that had broken out in the second half of the year threatened to overwhelm Brazil, whose stock market tumbled badly. In November, the Cardoso government announced a combination of tax increases, payroll cuts, and other spending reductions intended to slash the budget deficit. By this time, international investors, too, had begun to learn the lesson of democracy and markets: Praise for the measures was accompanied by a plan to wait and see whether Congress would support them. It did, and the crisis eased.[18] Democratic procedures played an important role in this success.

Brazil's economy in the 1990s did not perform as well as that of Chile, Argentina, or El Salvador, but Brazil's economic restructuring moved forward through democratic procedures, making it more likely that its economic growth rate will improve.

Nicaragua. Throughout most of the last quarter of the twentieth century, Nicaragua has been an economic "basket case." According to UNECLAC's 1995 Overview, Cuba and Nicaragua are the only two Spanish-speaking countries in the hemisphere whose per-capita GDP fell substantially during the first half of the 1990s. The legacy of civil and international war made it virtually impossible for Nicaraguans to address their country's fundamental economic problems. Their national legislature barely functioned. One of the most enduringly divisive issues was the dispute over property seized by the Sandinista government of 1979–90. Success in sorting out property disputes eluded the 1990–96 government of President Violeta Chamorro. The lack of credible property rules was one important reason for Nicaragua's poor economic performance.

Arnoldo Alemán took office as president in January 1997, trumpeting his intention to step on toes, recover properties "usurped" by the revolutionaries, and bring order to property relations. His stance was reminiscent of President Menem's belief that he could right economic wrongs on his own. Alemán failed in his quest until he turned toward democratic compromise. In November 1997, a legislative supermajority comprising Alemán's Liberal Party and the Sandinistas enacted a new property law to settle disputes and open a new chapter in the country's political and economic history.[19] The law was just a beginning; much detailed conflict resolution must follow. But Nicaragua's story shows yet again how useful democratic procedures can be in sealing a political and economic peace and reopening the possibility of economic growth.

Answering the Critics

Some might object that, in important respects, democratic procedures in Latin America are superficial or even a sham, and that at heart the problem is that democracy and the market have been forced together in a kind of "shotgun marriage." Democracy requires, theorists would insist, that the majority's duly voted-on preferences regarding economic policy be translated into government policy. Yet there have often been yawning gaps between campaign promises and eventual policy, as typified, for instance, in the 1982 election of Salvador Jorge Blanco in the Dominican Republic, the 1989 election of Carlos Menem in Argentina, and the 1990 election of Alberto Fujimori in Peru. The gap was also considerable in the 1985 election of Víctor Paz Estenssoro in Bolivia, the 1989 election of Carlos Andrés Pérez in Venezuela, and the 1989 election of Michael Manley in Jamaica. In each case, the winner, once elected, proved to be much more economically orthodox and market-friendly than his campaign rhetoric had suggested. Many voters understandably felt deceived. The connection between the preferences of voters and the actions of elected officials had been severed, at democracy's peril.[20] And if such politicians would lie to voters, might they not lie to investors as well?

Voters later had opportunities to pass judgment on the liars and the relative merits of the programs eventually adopted. In the Dominican Republic and Venezuela, they punished the liar's party in the next presidential elections. In both Argentina and Peru, however, voters approved a change in the constitution to permit the incumbent president's immediate reelection, and then reelected him. In Jamaica, the liar's party was also rewarded with the electoral ratification of its incumbency. In the round of elections after the politicians had sinned, voters discerned differently in various countries according to the economic results. Democracy malfunctions when politicians lie, but democracy is self-correcting: It allows the voters to render judgments iteratively. So too in the case of markets: Investors could judge the results and, in most cases, they joined in the judgment of the voters.

In many other cases, campaign promises all along have been closer

to the actual programs of government. This has been the case in all
Chilean elections since the restoration of democracy and in El Salvador
since the late 1980s. The connection between promises and policies was
also quite close in the 1994 elections in Brazil and in Mexico.

Three broad trends, in brief, were evident in the relationship between
economies and elections in Latin America in the 1980s and 1990s. First,
amid economic crisis in the 1980s, voters tended to vote against the incumbent party in virtually every country where competitive elections
were held (Colombia was the main exception). Second, in a number of
these elections, key politicians lied, but voters retained the opportunity
to pass judgment on them or their parties at the next election. Third, by
the mid-1990s, "sincere" campaigning had become more common.
Incumbents had little choice but to run on their record. More importantly, challengers in many countries—including countries as different
as Brazil and El Salvador—chose to run on transparent platforms. Blatant
lying on the campaign trail—troubling and damnable as it is—may have
turned out to be just a regrettable transitional phenomenon.

Another worry is that democracies will endure only as long as prosperity does, and that economic setbacks will lure democracies back to
their old statist and populist habits. The 1990s provided at least one
modest test of this proposition. In December 1994, a financial panic hit
Mexico. It affected the entire region to some degree, hurting Mexico,
Argentina, and Uruguay quite badly. Yet no Latin American government was overthrown by the armed forces in 1995, nor did any backtrack
on its commitment to markets. Most impressively, Argentine voters
reelected Menem despite a deep recession with very high unemployment.
Statism and populism, these voters understood, were not the answer to a
business-cycle downswing, even a severe one. And neither Menem nor
his principal opponent advocated statist or populist policies.

Other grounds exist for doubting that the connection between democracy and the market is wholly benign. Do not many of the devices
designed to maintain fiscal discipline barely meet the test of democracy?
Closed and technical styles of decision making reinforce state unrespon-
siveness to societal demands. Elected presidents sometimes rule by
decree, deliberately bypassing the legislature. This has been the case in
virtually every country discussed in this essay. The turn toward markets
has coincided with spectacular corruption scandals, two of which brought
down the presidents of Brazil and Venezuela through Congressional
impeachment. Concern about corruption looms large in nearly every
country. The early stages of privatization, for example, bring many
opportunities for officials to favor certain groups. And the courts are
always slow, and often inept or corrupt. All of this, and more, is true. In
every instance, however, the performance of authoritarian regimes was
either no better or actually worse.[21]

Democracy means pork-barreling, of course, and so exacts a cost in terms of reduced economic efficiency and transparency. This cost no doubt remains high across Latin America. President Fujimori used pork-barrel expenditures in order to build himself a bastion of popularity among Peru's poor and rural voters, for instance.[22] Pork still greases the wheels of the Brazilian Congress, as it lurches forward toward reforms that will one day make the pork barrel smaller. In Mexico, President Ernesto Zedillo pacified near-rebellious state governors from his own party by handing major revenue-sharing schemes over to their control. In the Dominican Republic, former president Joaquín Balaguer built his highly successful political career on pork. These costs are difficult to purge from democratic politics. Most Latin American countries have yet to accomplish this—and prospects do not look good.

Moreover, there remain tragic cases of systematic political and economic malpractice where the ills of Latin America's democratic past remain very much alive. Ecuador is a case in point. Until 1998, no successful presidential candidate since the return of civilian rule in 1979 had been both a supporter of sound market-oriented macroeconomic policies *and* "sincere" about it during the presidential campaign. Each successful Ecuadoran presidential candidate during the past two decades had been deceitful during the campaign, albeit to varying degrees. Ecuadoran political parties remain both fragmented and undisciplined. Coalitions are formed for transient tactical advantage; they have not been governing coalitions of the type that has worked so effectively at various times in Chile, Bolivia, or Colombia, for example. Presidents have lacked congressional majorities and, consequently, have relied on decrees. Congress notoriously retaliated by impeaching the most hyperactive president, Abdalá Bucaram, in 1997. Most parties are clientelistic and rent-providing in their approach to politics; most of these parties are regionally based and lack a national scope. Yet whereas Ecuador might have been the "poster boy" for Latin American populist democracies decades ago, in the late 1990s it is noteworthy precisely because it has become an exception. No other Ibero-American country is so badly governed.[23]

Democracy is not a cure-all. But in Latin America in the 1990s democracy is serving people's needs far better than it ever has before, or than other types of regimes could. In none of the cases considered here did presidential caesarism ever manage to launch economic reform. Rather, reform took off *only* when constitutional procedures were followed to create credible economic-policy commitments based on reliable assurances about respecting and honoring the role of opposition political parties. Prospects for the consolidation of democratic politics and economic reforms depend on the use of democratic procedures to construct stable majorities in support of freer markets and freer politics. Democracy, in sum, is more likely to represent citizens' preferences, to build the structures and rules that will credibly address the rational expectations of economic actors, and to enact the wise laws that make us free.

NOTES

1. The classic statement appears in Guillermo O'Donnell, *Modernization and Bureaucratic-Authoritarianism: Studies in South American Politics* (Berkeley: Institute of International Studies, University of California, 1973), ch. 2.

2. Adam Przeworski, *Democracy and the Market: Political and Economic Reforms in Eastern Europe and Latin America* (Cambridge: Cambridge University Press, 1991), 161.

3. Ibid., 180.

4. In democratic transitions, "centralized executive authority plays a pivotal role in overcoming the collective action problems and distributive conflicts associated with the initiation of comprehensive economic reforms." Stephan Haggard and Robert R. Kaufman, *The Political Economy of Democratic Transitions* (Princeton: Princeton University Press, 1995), 163.

5. An examination of the data for Latin America during the 1970s and 1980s reveals no significant statistical relationship between regime type and economic performance. See, among others, Karen L. Remmer, "Democracy and Economic Crisis: The Latin American Experience," *World Politics* 42 (April 1990): 315–35.

6. United Nations Economic Commission for Latin America and the Caribbean, *Preliminary Overview of the Economy of Latin America and the Caribbean, 1989* (Santiago, Chile, 1989), 19; Inter-American Development Bank, *Economic and Social Progress in Latin America: 1991 Report* (Baltimore: Johns Hopkins University Press, 1991), 273. For an analysis, see Sebastian Edwards, "Stabilization with Liberalization: An Evaluation of Ten Years of Chile's Experiment with Free-Market Policies, 1973–1983," *Economic Development and Cultural Change* 33 (January 1985): 223–49.

7. For a comparison, see William Ascher, *Scheming for the Poor: The Politics of Redistribution in Latin America* (Cambridge, Mass.: Harvard University Press, 1984).

8. Jeanne Kinney Giraldo, "Development and Democracy in Chile: Finance Minister Alejandro Foxley and the Concertación Project for the 1990s," in Jorge I. Domínguez, ed., *Technopols: Freeing Politics and Markets in Latin America in the 1990s* (University Park: Pennsylvania State University Press, 1997), 229–75.

9. Delia M. Boylan, "Taxation and Transition: The Politics of the 1990 Chilean Tax Reform," *Latin American Research Review* 31 (1996): 7–31.

10. Javier Corrales, "Why Argentines Followed Cavallo: A Technopol Between Democracy and Economic Reform," in Jorge I. Domínguez, ed., *Technopols*, 49–93.

11. Interviews conducted in Buenos Aires, 21–24 July 1998, with former president Raúl Alfonsín, candidate Eduardo Duhalde, leading opposition economic advisor José Luis Machinea, candidate Graciela Fernández Meijide, candidate Ramón Ortega, Economy Minister Roque Fernández, and President Carlos Menem.

12. In his influential article, "Delegative Democracy," *Journal of Democracy* 5 (January 1994): 55–69, Guillermo O'Donnell drew heavily from Argentina under Menem to reflect upon cases of highly Caesarist presidential behavior, and to criticize the consequences of such behavior for democracy. It should also be remembered that O'Donnell argued that "delegative democracy" might at first give the illusion of

economic achievement, but that it would produce few if any meaningful reforms. My analysis agrees with O'Donnell's on this key point, although I also suggest that even that initial illusion is particularly fleeting.

13. Rubén Zamora, "Democratic Transition or Modernization? The Case of El Salvador Since 1979," in Jorge I. Domínguez and Marc Lindenberg, eds., *Democratic Transitions in Central America* (Gainesville: University of Florida Press, 1997), 165–79.

14. Jack Spence, David Dye, Mike Lanchin, Geoff Thale, with George Vickers, *Chapúltepec, Five Years Later: El Salvador's Political Reality and Uncertain Future* (Cambridge, Mass.: Hemisphere Initiatives, 1997), 26.

15. For details, see "El Salvador: Compromise Reached on Sale of ANTEL," *Lagniappe* (New York), 25 July 1997, 9; "Asamblea Legislativa frena venta de ANTEL," *Nacional* (San Salvador), 30 May 1997.

16. João Resende-Santos, "Fernando Henrique Cardoso: Social and Institutional Rebuilding in Brazil," in Jorge I. Domínguez, ed., *Technopols,* 145–94.

17. Riordan Roett, "Brazilian Politics at Century's End," in Susan Kaufman Purcell and Riordan Roett, eds., *Brazil Under Cardoso* (Boulder, Colo.: Lynne Rienner, 1997).

18. On the response to the Asian crisis, see *Lagniappe,* 12 December 1997, 3. On the general role of Congress in the process of economic reform, see page 3 of each of the following issues of *Lagniappe:* 25 July 1997, 17 October 1997, 14 November 1997, and 28 November 1997.

19. "Nicaragua: Law Aims to Solve Property Mess," *Lagniappe,* 12 December 1997, 9.

20. Susan Stokes, "Democracy and the Limits of Popular Sovereignty in South America," in Joseph S. Tulchin and Bernice Romero, eds., *The Consolidation of Democracy in Latin America* (Boulder, Colo.: Lynne Rienner, 1995), 59–81.

21. See the detailed case studies in Jorge I. Domínguez and Abraham F. Lowenthal, *Constructing Democratic Governance: Latin America and the Caribbean in the 1990s* (Baltimore: Johns Hopkins University Press, 1996).

22. Carol Graham and Cheikh Kane, "Opportunistic Government or Sustaining Reform? Electoral Trends and Public Expenditure Patterns in Peru, 1990–1995," *Latin American Research Review* 33 (1998): 67–104.

23. Anita Isaacs, "Ecuador: Democracy Standing the Test of Time?" in Jorge I. Domínguez and Abraham F. Lowenthal, eds., *Constructing Democratic Governance: South America in the 1990s* (Baltimore: Johns Hopkins University Press, 1996), 42–57.

19

A NEW JURISPRUDENCE FOR AFRICA

H. Kwasi Prempeh

H. Kwasi Prempeh, a Ghanaian national, studied at Yale University and was, until recently, an associate at a Washington, D.C. law firm. He is currently a legal policy and governance specialist with the Centre for Democracy and Development (CDD-Ghana), an independent think-tank based in Accra, Ghana. He also serves on the governing board of CDD-Ghana and is the author of numerous articles on various aspects of democratization.

Africa's judiciaries are emerging at last from decades of powerlessness and marginalization at the hands of omnipotent executives and strongmen. Constitutional reforms that have accompanied democratic transitions in countries like Benin, Ghana, Malawi, Namibia, South Africa, Tanzania, Zambia, and Zimbabwe are helping to redefine the role and enhance the stature of the judiciary in the contemporary African state. While past judiciaries served primarily as passive instruments of legitimation for authoritarian regimes, today's African courts, like their counterparts in emerging democracies elsewhere, must enforce constitutional limitations on the exercise of governmental power, as well as protect the rights of citizens, the media, and civil society. The idea of judicial review is now enthusiastically embraced in a growing number of African countries.

Establishing judicial review is, of course, the easy part; a clause or two in the national constitution is generally all that is required to bestow such awesome power on the courts. The challenge is to ensure that judges in newly democratizing states exercise their new power so as to advance and deepen the transition to constitutional democracy. This is indeed a matter of genuine concern, because judicial review, though widely celebrated by democrats and constitutional architects in transitional democracies, is not quite the unmitigated virtue it is frequently made out to be. As Alexander Bickel has reminded us, "judicial review means not only that the Court may strike down a legislative [or executive] action

as unconstitutional but also that it may validate it as within constitutionally granted powers and as not violating constitutional limitations."[1]
Because judicial review "performs not only a checking function but also a
legitimating function,"[2] it is a double-edged sword. If exercised courage-
ously (but prudently) to defend rights or hold the line against abuses of
power, it could enhance constitutionalism in transitional democracies.
In the hands of weak, insecure, or illiberal judges, however, judicial
review could easily become an even more formidable instrument for
legitimating authoritarianism.

Thus Africa's newly democratizing states must seek to minimize the
risk that judicial review will become a curse rather than the blessing it
was meant to be. Because it has generally been assumed that the African
judiciary's primary problem to date has been the lack of institutional
autonomy and career security for judges, Africa's contemporary constitutional architects have adopted the standard Hamiltonian solution:
judicial independence. Thus Africa's new constitutions all carry the standard provisions designed to secure judges in their jobs, salaries, jurisdiction, and judgments. Judges no longer hold their offices at the suf-
ferance of the executive; judicial salaries and other benefits may not be
varied to the judges' detriment; the jurisdiction of the courts may not be
diminished at the pleasure of the executive or legislature; and, in general,
at least two independent institutions must cooperate in making judicial
appointments. In some cases, as in Ghana, the new constitution goes
even further by giving the judiciary autonomy in the preparation,
administration, and control of its own budget.

Except in South Africa and Benin, where newly created "constitutional
courts" have been laid over the preexisting judiciary, Africa's newly
refurbished judiciaries have generally consisted entirely of holdovers
from the *ancien régime* "grandfathered" into the new constitutional
arrangement in the name of institutional continuity. The assumption
seems to have been that, given a new constitution with a host of rights-
friendly provisions, limitations on governmental power, and guarantees
of judicial independence, judicial review will lead to a liberal-democratic
jurisprudence almost as a matter of course. Yet the evidence that is
emerging, especially from the common-law jurisdictions, suggests that
there is a significant risk that an *asymmetrical jurisprudence* will take
hold, with the constitutional text contemplating a rights-friendly, liberal-
democratic jurisprudence while the actual decisions and reasoning of
the courts take a different course. Ghana's experience under its new
constitution is a case in point.

Liberal Constitution, Illiberal Jurisprudence

On 7 January 1993, Ghana's fourth republican constitution went into
effect. The constitution, adopted by referendum in April 1992 (hence

the "1992 Constitution"), promises a new beginning in the life of the country. In contrast to the political and legal order that immediately preceded it, the new constitution proclaims the people of Ghana collectively as "sovereign" and guards against a resurgence of absolutist rule by providing for a set of "fundamental human rights and freedoms"; a system of checks and balances involving the sharing of power among three separate but coordinate branches of government; an independent commissioner with power to investigate and remedy citizen complaints of human rights violations and abuse of administrative power; a prohibition against a de jure one-party system; a two-term limitation on the tenure of the president; and an independent judiciary headed by a Supreme Court that has exclusive power to determine the constitutionality of disputed legislative and executive acts.

Although Ghana has experimented with similar liberal-democratic constitutions in the past (notably, the 1969 and 1979 constitutions), there is exceptional optimism that the 1992 Constitution is here to stay. Significantly, Ghana has already achieved an unprecedented feat under the new constitution. General elections held in December 1996 marked the first time in the country's postcolonial history that an elected government had successfully served out its constitutional term of office (and, in this case, been reelected to a second term) without the intervention of a coup d'état. This breaking of the jinx, coupled with discernible public antipathy toward military rule and with the "conditioned" investment made by the international donor and investor community in Ghana's ongoing transition, has given Ghanaians renewed hope and confidence that their country's latest attempt at constitutional democracy, though fraught with challenges, is irreversible.[3]

Much of the burden of this expectation has come to rest on the shoulders of the Ghanaian judiciary, in its new role as the final arbiter of interinstitutional disputes and guardian of the Bill of Rights. Already, however, public faith in the courts has been dampened by a string of rulings that bespeak a lack of judicial solicitude for freedom of expression and of the press.

The Supreme Court of Ghana has ruled, for instance, that a seditious libel statute, first enacted during the colonial period and later reenacted without much modification during the one-party era of the 1960s, does not violate the media-friendly provisions of the 1992 Constitution. This ruling, together with another upholding a related criminal libel law, has paved the way for the criminal prosecution of journalists for alleged defamation of the government and of certain influential public figures. In addition, despite language in Article 162 of the Constitution stating that "editors and publishers shall not . . . be penalized or harassed for their editorial opinions and views, or the content of their publications," a number of courts have imposed "perpetual" injunctions and financially crippling damages on certain publishers and editors in a barrage of civil libel lawsuits brought by leading members of the government and their allies. As justification for these rulings, a justice of the Supreme Court has asserted that the laws criminalizing defamation of public officials are "necessary to protect the dignity of public office," while another has defended such laws, despite their English common-law and colonial antecedents, as reflecting "the customs and traditions" of Ghanaian society.

To date, no fewer than three newspaper editors have been summarily imprisoned and fined for criminal contempt of court for violating court-imposed "prior restraints." In another case, a columnist for an independent newspaper was sentenced by the Supreme Court to a 30-day term of imprisonment and a fine for committing a nonstatutory crime called "scandalizing the court." The writer's offense was accusing a justice (now Chief Justice) of the Supreme Court of "judicial chicanery" for committing, and then surreptitiously retracting after the fact (that is, after he had delivered his written judgment in the case), an error of attribution in a politically charged case. In sentencing the defendant, the Supreme Court refused to accept "truth" as a defense or mitigating factor, reaffirming instead an old common-law maxim ("Truth is no defense") that harkens back to the days of the infamous English Court of the Star Chamber.

These rulings, directed at Ghana's popular private media, have caused considerable alarm among significant sections of the Ghanaian public. In reaction to the latest "anti-press" rulings, various groups and individuals have joined hands under the banner of "Friends of Freedom of Expression" to protest what they perceive as an unwarranted judicial assault on a right that is, for Ghanaians, as hard-earned as the right to vote.

What is important for our purposes is not the politically interesting question of who the losers and winners have been in the cases ruled upon by the Ghanaian courts. In fact, were that the primary concern, one would have to acknowledge that the Supreme Court has ruled against the government in some high-profile constitutional cases, especially during the very early years of the transition. Even so, except for one highly controversial ruling in which the Court enjoined the government from celebrating with public funds the anniversary of the coup d'état of 31 December 1981, most of the rulings that have been adverse to the government have involved provisions of the constitution that did not leave much room in the text for ambiguity or fudging.

What *is* problematic about the decisions of the Ghanaian courts is the dominant jurisprudence—or set of values, beliefs, and assumptions—that seems to be informing the reasoning and the result in the "hard" cases. Do the Ghanaian courts continue to draw largely upon the assumptions, practices, and precedents of the past, or do they project a transformative vision? Do they resolve textual ambiguity in favor of constitutionalism or in favor of the status quo ante? Do the courts appear willing to consult the liberal-democratic spirit of the constitution in expounding upon its letter, or are they given, instead, to literalism? Do they, when they deem it necessary to lean on precedents from other jurisdictions, select those persuasive authorities that tend to advance liberal-democratic values, or do they selectively avoid such precedents? The picture that emerges from a close study of appellate court opinions and rulings since the new constitution went into effect suggests that the Ghanaian judiciary remains attached to a jurisprudence that is far more authoritarian than liberal.

The case of Ghana indicates that reliance on judicial review and formal guarantees of judicial independence as the exclusive mechanisms for liberating African courts from their authoritarian past may be futile, unless such reforms are considered as incidental to the more fundamental question of how to produce a paradigm shift in the jurisprudence of the judges. If the constitutions of Africa's transitional democracies can be said to compel a new *jurisprudence of constitutionalism,* it also appears that recourse to tradition and longstanding common-law doctrine, an ingrained deference to executive *diktat,* and the force of *stare decisis* all propel Africa's judges back toward a *jurisprudence of executive supremacy.* The trajectory of Africa's democratic transitions will be adversely altered if Africa's judiciaries fail to make a contemporaneous transition from the jurisprudence of executive supremacy to the jurisprudence of constitutionalism.

The Old Order and the New

A *jurisprudence of executive supremacy* regards the "state" (personified in an omnipotent chief executive), not a supervening constitution, as the source, juridically speaking, of all "rights" and "freedoms." The state is thus subject to only such restraint as it chooses to place upon itself, while the citizen has only such rights as the state may allow. Consequently, judges operating on the basis of a jurisprudence of executive supremacy lean heavily on those "claw-back" or derogation clauses that typically appear in the nominal constitution and allow the state essentially to take back whatever "rights" it may have granted previously, leaving citizens with only such protection as might remain after the state has had its "due." In short, under a jurisprudence of executive supremacy, the state walks into the courthouse with an almost irrefutable presumption of lawfulness as to its conduct.

A judiciary habituated by custom, training, or experience to this way of thinking learns, quite naturally, to be excessively deferential to the state and all manner of public authority. Such a judiciary reckons its institutional role primarily as one of maintaining "law and order," and not as protecting freedom or restraining government.

For the better part of its life, the African state—and for that matter, the African judiciary—has paid homage to a jurisprudence of executive supremacy, with regrettable consequences for civil liberties and personal freedom across the continent. It has been observed, for example, that the Kenyan courts' longstanding fidelity to this brand of jurisprudence is partly to blame for how Kenya's once potentially promising Bill of *Rights* ended up as a "Bill of *Exceptions*."[4] The Kenyan courts consistently allowed the limited exceptions tagged on to the Bill of Rights to trump the rights themselves. If current efforts at reconstituting the social compact in Africa along liberal-democratic lines are to stand a chance of succeeding, the jurisprudence of executive supremacy must give way to what we might call a *jurisprudence of constitutionalism.*

A jurisprudence of constitutionalism differs in fundamental respects from a jurisprudence of executive supremacy. In general, judges who follow the latter disclaim any exercise of discretion on their part in matters of interpretation. In practice, too, they tend to follow strictly the dictates of past precedents and usually give literal effect to the plain meaning of legal texts. As a result, their methods of interpretation tend to be narrow, rule-driven, and text-bound. A jurisprudence of constitutionalism, on the other hand, invites more active judicial intermediation and interpretation. In particular, it demands that judges interpreting a constitutional text not only consult the spirit of the law but also endeavor to harmonize the letter with the spirit. To do so, judges must bring to their reasoning and decisions a clear understanding of the overarching values and philosophical foundations of a liberal democracy; of the social, economic, and political evolution of their country; and of the historical antecedents and contemporary purposes of the particular provision in dispute.

A jurisprudence of constitutionalism is also less doctrinaire in its insistence on *stare decisis* and does not regard the "common law" as either cast in stone or beyond judicial review. Instead, it invites judges to weigh the value of keeping the law certain and settled against the imperative to do right in the particular case at hand. The rationale is that, in a legal dispute concerning human rights, civil liberties or the scope of governmental power, as opposed to, say, a dispute over the meaning of a clause in a commercial contract, it is deemed far more important that the result be right than that it follow some precedent from a bygone era.

Interpretive methods aside, the primary substantive difference between a jurisprudence of executive supremacy and a jurisprudence of constitutionalism lies in their different conceptions of the relationship of the individual to the state and vice versa. In general, liberal-democratic constitutions address the state in a language of obligation ("shall") or of restraint ("shall not"), but speak to the individual in a voice connoting entitlement or autonomy. Thus a jurisprudence of constitutionalism is more solicitous of individual rights and civil liberties and less deferential to state assertions of power. This is in sharp contrast to a jurisprudence of executive supremacy, which accords disproportionate deference to the state and shows less solicitude for individual assertions of right.

Perhaps no issue better highlights the distinction between these two competing brands of jurisprudence than the different ways in which they each deal with "limitation clauses." Limitation clauses, in the context of a liberal-democratic constitution, are those "subject to" caveats that typically follow a statement of rights in the constitution. Courts accustomed to a jurisprudence of executive supremacy are inclined to interpret such limitation clauses as nothing more than contemporary restatements of the clawback clauses of old. Because such clawback clauses effectively allow statutory exceptions to swallow constitutional rights, to treat limitation clauses as though they were functionally equivalent to clawback clauses would practically eviscerate the bundle of rights secured under a liberal-democratic constitution. Yet this is a fairly common course taken by transitional judiciaries.

> *A jurisprudence of constitutionalism imposes on state actors a heavy burden of proof and persuasion before a constitutional right may be lawfully restricted.*

Once again, Ghana's case is illustrative. In addition to naming the right to freedom of the press among the "fundamental human rights and freedoms," Ghana's present constitution devotes an entire chapter of the 26-chapter document to the "freedom and independence of the media." One provision in this chapter outlaws censorship by prior restraint; another immunizes publishers, editors, and other journalists against punishment or harassment based on "the content of their publications." The chapter goes on to state, in language connoting obligation, that the media "shall uphold the responsibility and accountability of the Government to the people of Ghana." After this strong statement of media rights comes the limitation clause of Article 164: "The [foregoing] provisions . . . are subject to laws that are reasonably required in the interest of national security, public order, public morality and for the purpose of protecting the reputations, rights and freedoms of other persons."[5] It was on the basis of this clause that Ghana's Supreme Court upheld the country's decades-old sedition and criminal libel statutes as constitutionally valid.

At first blush, the Court's rulings might seem justified, even compelled, by the terms of the limitation clause. Yet in other constitutional democracies, some of them transitional democracies like Ghana, where courts have had occasion to consider the import and effect of substantially similar limitation clauses, they have reached conclusions far more protective of the rights at stake and far less deferential to the government's assertion of the power to restrict.[6]

This divergence of judicial opinion is explained not so much by substantive differences in the relevant constitutional texts as by the different strands of jurisprudence at play. In general, courts that lean toward a jurisprudence of constitutionalism treat clauses like Article 164 of Ghana's Constitution not as clawback clauses, but as clauses that state, in somewhat general terms, the threshold criteria against which any purported restriction of a constitutionally protected right must be measured. A jurisprudence of constitutionalism would have any such restriction pass the tests of necessity, proportionality, and compatibility with widely accepted democratic practice. Thus while the liberal-democratic state may limit the scope of a constitutional right, it may not do so by a means that is disproportionate to its intended purpose and its effect on the right at stake, or at variance with the liberal-democratic spirit of the constitution. Simply put, the constitutional state may not crack a nut with a sledgehammer.

For instance, where a defamed public figure can have recourse to compensatory civil damages, a right to a rejoinder, or a public retraction and apology, a resort to criminal prosecution or to punitive damages will not be a "justifiable" or "reasonable" response to the media's abuse of the right to freedom of expression. Indeed the offense of seditious libel itself, which criminalizes speech that is injurious to the "reputation of the government," and which traces its doctrinal roots to such medieval notions as the divine right of kings and royal infallibility ("The King can do no wrong"), is fundamentally at odds with a jurisprudence of constitutionalism. For the latter proceeds on the assumption that government and the holders of public office are paid agents and servants of the people and, as such, must be open to wide-ranging criticism and robust commentary by the public and the media.[7]

In sum, a jurisprudence of constitutionalism imposes on state actors a heavy burden of proof and persuasion before a constitutional right may be lawfully restricted. In this regard, it compels the state to move away from the habit of coercion and self-assertion and to cultivate instead an ethic of restraint and justification. It is this rights-respecting jurisprudence, and not the might-justifying jurisprudence of the past, that must now guide the exercise of judicial review by Africa's courts.

Promoting a Jurisprudence of Constitutionalism

A jurisprudence of constitutionalism cannot, of course, be decreed into existence. Nor is it bound to emerge naturally once a liberal constitution, an independent judiciary, and judicial review have formally been established. This does not mean, however, that the evolution of a jurisprudence that would complement and advance a transition to constitutional democracy must be left to the vagaries of chance. At least some steps can be taken, beyond judicial review and formal guarantees of judicial independence, to minimize significantly the risk of an illiberal jurisprudence taking hold. And the place and time to start is at the beginning, when the new constitution is being put together.

Clarity and Interpretive Guidance in the Constitutional Text. Constitutional drafters in newly democratizing states are often urged to keep the final document "short and vague." Advocates of brevity in this matter usually point to the example of the "pocket-size U.S. Constitution," which nonetheless has generated a strong jurisprudence in the area of civil liberties and governmental restraint. By the standards of its time, however, the U.S. Constitution was far from short or vague. Indeed, in comparison to the unwritten constitution of its former colonizer, the U.S. Constitution was rather detailed. Informed by their political past and eager not to leave doubts about the different path they wished to chart for themselves, the Americans reduced their notions of government and liberty to paper, beginning with the Articles of Confederation, which were later superseded by what survives today as the U.S. Constitution.

Placed in proper historical perspective then, the American example is not one of brevity over detail, but rather one of explicitness over silence or ambiguity. Therefore, if transitional democracies must look to the example of the United States in this regard, the lesson to be learned is that the constitutional text must be made to reflect, as clearly but as concisely as possible, the institutional and doctrinal discontinuities between the old order and the new and the juridical import and meanings of such discontinuities. Transitional democracies that leave such matters open-ended and inexplicit, for the sake of keeping the constitutional document short and vague, leave too much to chance and risk a retrogressive judicial interpretation sometime in the future.

In particular, the prospects for a jurisprudence of constitutionalism are significantly enhanced if the constitutional text includes clear guideposts for interpreting and applying limitation clauses. Rather than state simply, as Ghana's constitution does, that certain delineated rights are "subject to" lawful restrictions "reasonably required" to achieve some undefined public purposes, the constitutional text could further explain that such restrictions are to be construed narrowly; that only the least restrictive of means may be adopted; that there must be proportionality between means and ends; and, above all, that such restrictions must conform with contemporary democratic practice.

A good example in this regard is Section 36 of the South African Constitution, which states: "The rights in the Bill of Rights may be limited only in terms of law of general application to the extent that the limitation is reasonable and justifiable in an open and democratic society based on human dignity, equality, and freedom, taking into account all relevant factors, including the nature of the right; the importance of the purpose of the limitation; the nature and extent of the limitation; the relation between the limitation and its purpose; and less restrictive means to achieve the purpose." Similarly, the new Constitution of Malawi provides that "no restrictions or limitations may be placed on the exercise of any rights and freedoms provided in this Constitution other than those prescribed by law, which are reasonable, recognized by international human rights standards, and necessary in an open and democratic society." It adds that a restriction "shall not negate the essential content of the right or freedom in question." Such provisions, by providing clear, albeit general, interpretive guideposts and standards for the judicial review of governmental restrictions, should incline judges toward a more rights-friendly jurisprudence, or at least impel them to apply a heightened degree of scrutiny in determining the constitutionality of a particular restriction.

Democracy advocates can also greatly facilitate the transition to a constitutional jurisprudence by insisting that the key legislative legacies of the authoritarian era (such as laws on "preventive detention," newspaper licensing, sedition, and criminal libel) be repealed *ex ante* by express provision in the new constitution. Otherwise such laws will remain on the books until their constitutionality is tested through *ex post* constitutional litigation and judicial review or until a future legislature decides to repeal them. If the constitutional repeal approach is taken, the repeal provision must make clear that the list of repealed laws is not intended as an exhaustive list of the preexisting laws rendered invalid under the new constitution. The approach of repeal by constitutional fiat has the advantage of settling forthrightly and in advance the unconstitutionality of some of the most obnoxious laws on the books, thereby eliminating the risk that the courts will fail to rule such laws unconstitutional or that the legislature will refuse to repeal them.

Creation of Constitutional Courts. The risk of a reversion to an authoritarian jurisprudence might also be minimized through constitutional design, specifically by the establishment of a "constitutional court." There is nothing talismanic, of course, about a constitutional court. Its virtue lies in the opportunity it provides to chart a new course of constitutional jurisprudence by superimposing on the holdover judiciary a new body whose preeminent function is to exercise final jurisdiction over constitutional cases. Because such a court is laid over the preexisting judiciary, it owes little, if any, institutional allegiance to the preexisting jurisprudence crafted by courts now subordinate to it. And because it has no past precedent or preexisting case law of its own to which it might feel bound by the force of *stare decisis,* it is also, generally speaking, institutionally free to begin writing a new jurisprudence on a tabula rasa. Moreover, establishing a constitutional court, as opposed to merely bestowing formal independence on a holdover judiciary, signals to the citizenry, politicians, and judges alike that a new era has dawned and that the rules of the game have changed accordingly—as, indeed, has the referee.

The majority of Africa's transitional democracies, however, have not followed the lead of Benin and South Africa in establishing constitutional courts. In South Africa and Benin, constitutional architects and political actors were fully cognizant early on that a new constitution, however liberal-democratic its text, could not be entrusted to a judiciary that was entirely a holdover from an illiberal and antidemocratic regime without risking a reversion to the jurisprudence of the past. The evidence so far, from both South Africa and Benin, indicates that the virtues claimed on behalf of constitutional courts are far from merely theoretical.

Since its inception in 1993, the Constitutional Court of Benin has led the way in redefining the contours of the horizontal relationship that the country's new constitution envisions among the various branches of government. The Court has also held the line against government attempts to restrict the right to freedom of association in a manner that would stymie the growth of an autonomous civil society.[8] South Africa's Constitutional Court has been even more activist in articulating a decidedly liberal jurisprudence. Its record to date includes rulings declaring the death penalty unconstitutional; recognizing the right of criminal defendants to have access to exculpatory police evidence and witnesses; and affirming the right of convicted prisoners and pretrial detainees to vote.

Of course, a constitutional court is only as good as the members who constitute it. Thus such questions as who sits on the court and how its members are selected are of the utmost importance. While constitutional courts generally have included some holdover judges (usually those known for their progressive attitudes), a significant portion of their membership has tended to come from outside the bench and bar. For example, both the Benin and South African constitutional courts include as member-judges constitutional scholars with no previous judicial or advocacy experience. In fact, South Africa leaves the door open for non-lawyers to be appointed to the constitutional court, as long as they possess the requisite "expertise in the area of constitutional law." Extending the membership of constitutional courts beyond the judicial establishment to include academic lawyers, human rights advocates and other such persons enriches the jurisprudence of the court with perspectives and insights that have not been shaped unduly by the prevailing judicial culture and mindset.

The mode of appointment to the court must also ensure that the court's membership reflects broad agreement among the main parties or factions of the political elite represented in national politics. In the context of Africa's newly democratizing states, where transitional elections typically result in single-party dominance of both the legislature and the executive, such judicial appointments should require, at least, the approval of a supermajority of the legislative chamber. Granting the dominant party free rein in the selection of judges undermines the prospects for a jurisprudence of constitutionalism, because a court that is cut almost exclusively from a single political cloth (that of the incumbent party) is less likely to hold the line against breaches of the constitution by its benefactors in the government.

Extraterritorial Learning and Borrowing. Africa's newly democratizing states, like transitional democracies generally, start off with an impoverished stock of homegrown constitutional case law. The absence in their past of a tradition of judicial review preordains such an outcome. This dearth of domestic constitutional case law necessitates some reliance, if only during the early stages of the transition, on relevant constitutional precedents and doctrine developed elsewhere. While wholesale borrowing from any one foreign source is plainly unwise and must be avoided, there is much that Africa's transitional democracies can gain by looking to the experiences of other jurisdictions.

National courts generally have discretion to borrow persuasive and relevant case law from other jurisdictions. Transitional judiciaries, however, may require more than an implicit grant of discretion to induce them to abandon their longstanding insularity and inertia in matters of jurisprudential innovation and borrowing. One approach, adopted by South Africa's constitutional drafters, is to insert in the constitutional text a provision explicitly affirming the authority of the national courts (or at least, the court of last resort) to consult and rely on extraterritorial and international sources of law in their interpretation of the constitution. Thus Section 39 of the South African Constitution provides that "when interpreting the Bill of Rights" the courts of South Africa "must consider international law" and "may consider foreign law." Malawi's Constitution also compels judicial recourse to "international human rights standards" in reviewing the validity of legislative restrictions on rights. Provisions of this kind can benefit other transitional judiciaries in Africa by providing both firm authority and affirmative encouragement in the constitutional text for relying on persuasive precedents from abroad.

Although Africa's transitional judiciaries have yet to produce a substantial corpus of constitutional case law, a few, notably South Africa's, Namibia's, and Benin's, have produced some important precedents in an assortment of areas. So too, to some extent, has the African continent's most consistent constitutional democracy, Botswana. Thus, other transitional African judiciaries that prefer first to consult an African precedent might be able to find help just across the border. If they are unable to find such precedents, Africa's new courts, especially those that belong to the common-law tradition, should have little difficulty finding adaptable constitutional precedents from countries like Canada, India, and the United States. In cases involving individual rights and civil liberties, the judgments of the European Court of Human Rights (interpreting the European Convention on Human Rights), which themselves lean heavily on precedents from many different national jurisdictions, could also provide valuable persuasive authority and guidance.

Continuing Legal Education for Judges. The jurisprudence of Africa's transitional courts might also be influenced through continuing education. Programs of continuing judicial education indeed have become an institutionalized part of the process of judicial recruitment and training in a growing number of countries. Some mature democracies and an increasing number of emerging democracies have even established formal judicial training schools.

In view of the jurisprudential challenge that confronts Africa's judges, continuing judicial education in Africa's transitional democracies must accord priority to a comparative study of contemporary constitutional law, administrative law, human rights law, and public law jurisprudence in general. Judges' appreciation of the jurisprudence of constitutionalism could also be enhanced by learning gained from cognate disciplines like political theory, legal history, and ethics. Ideally, programs of continuing judicial education should be initiated and administered from the highest levels of the judiciary.

Continuing judicial education need not be limited to seminars or classroom-type instruction. Judicial exchange programs, improved library and research facilities (including regular subscriptions to professional journals), and Internet access would not only provide Africa's judges with additional opportunities to share experiences and perspectives with their professional peers from other jurisdictions, but also help to improve their morale and productivity.

Reform of Formal Legal Education. Sustained and lasting change in constitutional jurisprudence cannot occur without appropriate reform in the content of formal legal education. Thus Africa's academic lawyers, upon whose shoulders rests the task of training future generations of lawyers and judges, must themselves reevaluate their jurisprudence and make their own necessary transition from the old order to the new.

Promoting a jurisprudence of constitutionalism through reform of legal education entails not merely the introduction of new course titles but also appropriate changes in the emphasis and content of legal instruction. The prestige and profile of public law courses like constitutional law (both national and comparative), administrative law, and human rights law must be enhanced within the academy through the allocation of more resources for research, teaching, and publishing in these areas. Simultaneously, some ingrained theoretical biases in the content of legal education must be redressed. In Africa's common-law jurisdictions, for example, the historical dominance of John Austin's command theory of law (or Austinian positivism) has led to a marked avoidance in the law curriculum both of a critical or "outsider" perspective and of discussions of legal policy or the social consequences of legal rules.[9] But policy and normative critiques of the law (the "prudence" half of jurisprudence, so to speak) cannot so easily be ignored in a jurisprudence of constitution-alism, concerned, as that is, with not only the letter but also the spirit or aspiration of the law.

Furthermore, Africa's legal scholars and jurists will have to reevaluate, in the light of contemporary sociopolitical developments and trends, the assumptions and beliefs underlying certain longstanding common-law doctrines and maxims that have been passed on like folklore to succeeding generations of lawyers. For example, archaic maxims like "Truth is no defense" that make public officials into tin gods have no contemporary value in a liberal democracy and must be consigned to the past. For a jurisprudence of constitutionalism to become firmly rooted in Africa's legal culture and discourse, the legal academy must view and teach the law through more critical and contemporary lenses. In short, Africa's academic lawyers must serve the law without becoming intellectually subservient to it.

Jurisprudence Matters

In the current transition to constitutional democracy taking place in various parts of Africa, courts and judges have generally not been regarded as part of the old authoritarian order that needs to be transformed. Somehow it has been assumed that, once the power of judicial review and constitutional guarantees of independence are bestowed on them, Africa's holdover judiciaries will simply begin to assert themselves and give meaning to the new liberal-democratic constitutions entrusted to their care. But a judiciary that has become habituated to an illiberal jurisprudence through prolonged service in an authoritarian political and legal culture does not simply emerge the morning after espousing a new and unfamiliar liberal-democratic jurisprudence. Africa's transitional democracies risk reverting to the jurisprudence of the past unless they contemporaneously attend to the critical issue of how to create and nurture a new constitutional jurisprudence to complement the process of democratic and constitutional change. Like the democratic journey itself, the complementary transition in jurisprudence will take time, effort and commitment. Still, it is a transition that cannot wait if the promise of Africa's new liberal democratic constitutions is to become a reality.

NOTES

1. Alexander M. Bickel, *The Least Dangerous Branch: The Supreme Court at the Bar of Politics* 2nd. ed. (New Haven: Yale University Press, 1986), 29.

2. Ibid.

3. For an insightful assessment of the progress of Ghana's democratic transition, see E. Gyimah-Boadi, "Ghana's Encouraging Elections: The Challenges Ahead," *Journal of Democracy* 8 (April 1997): 78–91.

4. Kathurima M'inoti, "Why The Kenyan Bill of Rights Has Failed," *Expression Today* (November 1998).

5. Article 165 of the Ghanaian constitution requires that this clause be read in conjunction with Article 21(4)(e), which mandates that a restriction of a fundamental right be "reasonably justifiable in terms of the spirit of [the] constitution."

6. Examples are the Namibian Supreme Court in *Kausea v. Minister of Home Affairs* (1995); the Supreme Court of Canada in *R. v. Zundel* (1992); and the European Court of Human Rights in *Bowman v. United Kingdom* (1998).

7. See, for example, the judgment of the Supreme Court of India in *Rajagopal v. State of Tamil Nadu* (1994) and of the U.S. Supreme Court in *New York Times Co. v. Sullivan* (1964).

8. This and other leading cases decided by Benin's Constitutional Court are discussed in Bruce Magnusson, "Testing Democracy in Benin: Experiments in Institutional Reform," in Richard Joseph, ed., *State, Conflict, and Democracy in Africa* (Boulder, Colo.: Lynne Rienner, 1998), 217–37.

9. See Muna Ndulo, "Legal Education in Zambia: Pedagogical Issues," *Commonwealth Legal Association Newsletter* 42 (July 1985).

20

HOW DEMOCRACIES CONTROL THE MILITARY

Richard H. Kohn

Richard H. Kohn *is professor of history and chairman of the Curriculum in Peace, War, and Defense at the University of North Carolina at Chapel Hill. A specialist in American military history and civil-military relations, he has taught at CCNY and Rutgers University–New Brunswick, and was Chief of Air Force History for the United States Air Force from 1981 to 1991. He also codirected the Triangle Institute for Security Studies project on the gap between military and civilian society in the United States. He is currently at work on a study of presidential war leadership in American history.*

Among the oldest problems of human governance has been that of securing the subordination of military forces to political authority. In the twentieth century alone, civilian control of the military has been a concern of democracies like the United States and France, of communist tyrannies such as the Soviet Union and China, of fascist dictatorships in Germany and Italy, and since 1945, of many smaller states in Africa, Asia, and Latin America. Whether—and how—a society controls those who possess the ultimate power of physical coercion, and ensures their loyalty both to the particular government in power and to the regime in general, is basic to democratic governance.

Civilian control has special significance today. Throughout the post-communist world, societies are struggling to build democratic institutions. The North Atlantic Treaty Organization has declared civilian control a prerequisite for membership. In encouraging democratization, the United States and other Western powers use civilian control as a measure of progress toward democracy. While democracy is spreading in South and Central America, and in Europe, Asia, and Africa, there exists no set of standards by which to evaluate whether civilian control exists, how well it functions, and what the prognosis is for its continued success.

Control by civilians presents two challenges. For mature democracies, where civilian control has historically been strong and military establishments have focused on external defense, the test is whether civilians can exercise supremacy in military policy and decision making—that is, frame the alternatives and define the discussion, as well as make the final choice. When the military enjoys great prestige, possesses advanced bureaucratic skills, believes that its ability to fulfill its mission may be at risk, or comes to doubt the civilian leadership, civilians can face great obstacles in exercising their authority.

Fledgling democracies, with scant experience in combining popular government and civilian control, face a tougher challenge. They must ensure that the military will not attempt a coup d'état, or otherwise defy civilian authority. In many former autocracies, the military has concentrated on internal order or been deeply involved in politics, sometimes preying on society rather than protecting it. There the chief requirement is to establish a tradition of civilian control, to make the military establishment politically neutral, and to prevent or preclude any possibility of military intervention in political life. The task will still remain to establish civilian control over national security policy and decision making. But in the new democracies, civilian efforts to gain supremacy over military affairs risk provoking military defiance, or, if public opinion does not support the civilians, perhaps even military intervention.

What are the common characteristics or experiences that have, historically, fostered civilian control under democracy? While this essay is based mostly on Western and particularly Anglo-American experience, the analysis applies to any society that practices, or is making the transition to practicing, government based upon the sovereignty and will of the people.

For democracy, civilian control—that is, control of the military by civilian officials elected by the people—is fundamental. Civilian control allows a nation to base its values, institutions, and practices on the popular will rather than on the choices of military leaders, whose outlook by definition focuses on the need for internal order and external security. The military is, by necessity, among the least democratic institutions in human experience; martial customs and procedures clash by nature with individual freedom and civil liberty, the highest values in democratic societies.

Because their basic purpose is to wage armed conflict, military institutions are designed for violence and coercion, and over the centuries have developed the organizational structure, operating procedures, and individual values needed to succeed in war. Authority in the military emphasizes hierarchy so that individuals and units act according to the intentions of commanders, and can succeed under the very worst of physical circumstances and mental stresses.

While many of the military's professional values—courage, honesty, sacrifice, integrity, loyalty, service—are among the most respected in human experience, the norms and processes intrinsic to military institutions diverge so far from the premises of democratic society that the relationship is inherently adversarial and sometimes unstable. Military behaviors are functional imperatives. If society were to be governed by the personal ideals or institutional perspectives of the military, developed over centuries to support service to the state and sacrifice in war, then each individual citizen (and the national purpose) would become subservient to national security—to the exclusion, or at least the devaluation, of other needs and concerns.

The point of civilian control is to make security subordinate to the larger purposes of a nation, rather than the other way around. The purpose of the military is to defend society, not to define it. While a country may have civilian control of the military without democracy, it cannot have democracy without civilian control.

Defining Civilian Control

In theory, civilian control is simple: All decisions of government, including national security, are to be made or approved by officials outside the professional armed forces, in democracy, by popularly elected officeholders or their appointees. In principle, civilian control is absolute and all-encompassing: No decision or responsibility falls to the military unless expressly or implicitly delegated to it by civilian leaders. Even the decisions of command—the selection of strategy, of what operations to mount and when, what tactics to employ, the internal management of the military—derive from civilian authority. They are delegated to uniformed personnel only for reasons of convenience, tradition, effectiveness, or military experience and expertise. Civilians make all the rules, and they can change them at any time.[1]

The reality is quite different. For a variety of reasons, military establishments have gained significant power and achieved considerable autonomy, even in those democracies that have long practiced civilian control. In some countries, the military has by custom kept control over much of military life; in others, governments have never managed to develop the tools, the procedures, the influence with elites, or the prestige with the public needed to establish supremacy over their armed forces. For the most part, however, a degree of military autonomy has grown out of the need to professionalize the management of war. In the last two centuries, war has become too complex—the preparations too elaborate, the weapons too sophisticated, command too arduous, operations too intricate—to leave the waging of combat to amateurs or part-time practitioners. As a result, the influence of the professional military has grown, and it has sometimes used democratic processes to further its own professional and institutional independence.

Forty years ago, the great theorist of civilian control Samuel P. Huntington argued in *The Soldier and the State* that the way to optimize civilian supremacy was to recognize such "autonomous military professionalism." In arguing for what he called "objective civilian control," Huntington asserted that the state should encourage "an independent military sphere" so that "multifarious civilian groups" would not "maximize their power in military affairs" by involving the military in political activity. Such interference, he believed, not only diminished the effectiveness of military forces and thus a nation's security, but actually invited the military to involve itself in governance beyond national security affairs. An officer corps focused on its own profession—and granted sufficient independence to organize itself and practice the art of war without interference in those areas requiring technical expertise— would be politically neutral and less likely to intervene in politics.[2] The paradox of Huntington's formulation is that while "objective" civilian control might minimize military involvement in politics, it also decreases civilian control over military affairs.

The critical issue is where, and how, to distinguish between military and civilian responsibility. With war increasingly dangerous, civilians want more control to ensure congruence with political purpose; with weapons and operations becoming ever more technical and complex, military officers want more independence to achieve success with the least cost in blood and treasure. Where to divide authority and responsibility has become increasingly situational, and uncertain.

The truth of the matter is that, fundamentally, *civilian control is not a fact but a process.* It exists along a continuum, running from the extreme of countries that are ruled by military establishments or experience frequent direct or indirect military intervention in politics, to those that do not even possess standing military forces. *The best way to understand civilian control, to measure its existence and evaluate its effectiveness, is to weigh the relative influence of military officers and civilian officials in decisions of state concerning war, internal security, external defense, and military policy (that is, the shape, size, and operating procedures of the military establishment).*

Sometimes, where civilian control is weak or nonexistent, military influence laps over into other areas of public policy and social life. Even in mature democracies that have long practiced civilian control, the balance between military and civilian varies with time and place, with the personalities involved, with the personal or political ambitions of senior military officers and leading politicians, and with the circumstances that give the military prestige and weight in public opinion. Even in those democracies with rich traditions of unbroken civilian dominance, war and security can (and have) become so important in national life and so central to the definition of the state that the military, particularly during or after a crisis or war, can use its expertise or public standing to limit civilian influence in military affairs. But even beyond such circumstances, civilian control depends frequently on the individuals involved: how each side views its role and function; the public respect or popularity possessed by a particular politician or political institution or military officer or armed force; the bureaucratic or political skill of the various officials.

If civilian control of the military is a process defined by the relative influence of civilian and military officials, then the central issue confronting scholars and policy makers today is how to judge the extent to which civilian control exists, how well it functions, and whether it is sufficient for democratic governance. Ultimately, civilian control rests upon a set of ideas, institutions, and behaviors that has developed over time in democratic societies. Together, these practices check the likelihood that the military will interfere in political life; they form a system that provides civilian officials with both the authority and the machinery to exercise supremacy in military affairs. Civilian control contains inherent tensions and still suffers periodic strains and lapses, but the system can be introduced and made to function in almost any country where democracy begins to take root.

The Foundations for Civilian Control

The first requirement for civilian control in democracy is democratic governance itself: the rule of law, civil liberty, a stable method for peaceful succession in power, workable practices for electing officials, and a government and governing process (perhaps spelled out in a written constitution) that are legitimate in the eyes of both key elites and the general public. Civilian control can reinforce democracy, but civilian control is only one aspect—necessary but not sufficient—of democratic rule. Without a stable and legitimate governmental system and process, the military may interfere in order to protect society from chaos, internal challenge, or external attack—even when intervention may itself perpetuate instability and destroy legitimacy in government. The tradition of legitimacy in government acts on the one hand to deter military interference in politics, and on the other to counteract intervention should it threaten or occur.

Furthermore, the state must, as a matter of standing national policy, clearly specify the role of the military. Certainly uniformed leaders can and should be consulted in this process as the mission of the military changes to suit new conditions. But the military cannot define its own function or purpose. Additionally, every effort must be made to limit the military to external defense so that it functions as a representative of the whole society, acting in the best interest of the entire nation. Only in the direst of emergencies should military forces be used to secure internal order; they must see themselves, and be seen, as the guardians and not the oppressors of the people. The courts, the police, the militia, or border guards should keep order and execute the laws. Tasking the military with everyday law enforcement, as opposed to maintaining order as a last resort, pits the military against the people, with a loss of trust and confidence, eventual alienation on both sides, and a diminishing of civilian control.

A second foundation for civilian control lies in the operating mechanisms of government—the methods by which civilian authority rules military forces. If they are to function as an expression of the whole society's will, their subordination must be to the entire governmental structure, not simply to the incumbent president or prime minister. Divided control does contain dangers. The military can become adept at boosting its own influence by playing civilian authorities against one another. But separation of authority reduces the possibility that the executive could use the army to overturn the constitution or coerce the legislature. Accountability to the legislature implies accountability to the people, forcing public discussion and scrutiny of defense policy, budgets, and cases of military mistakes or malfeasance. Active parliamentary oversight makes military affairs more transparent, and should actually strengthen national defense by reinforcing military identification with the people and popular identification with the military. The judiciary plays a supporting but indispensable role, holding members of the military personally accountable to law.

A third element that fosters civilian control is countervailing power. The military can be blocked from even considering interference in two ways. The first is through force brought to bear by other armed bodies in society (such as the militia, the police, or an armed populace). The second is by the knowledge that illegal acts will lead to personal disgrace, retirement, relief, fine, arrest, trial, conviction, prison—whatever legal punishment fits the crime and can be made to stick. The more likely it is that violations of civilian control will be resisted and punished, the less likely they are to occur. Historically a most effective counterweight has been a reliance on citizen-soldiers as opposed to full-time professionals. Knowledge that revolt would lead to crisis and be opposed by an armed populace, or that citizen forces might not heed illegal orders, has been an effective deterrent. Standing forces should also be kept as small as security permits: so that the populace will consent to provide the resources, the military will be devoted solely to external defense, and civil-military friction will be reduced.

Finally, a critical underpinning of civilian control must be the military itself. The essential assumption behind civilian supremacy is the abstinence by the military from intervention in political life. While coups have diminished worldwide over the last decade, in many places the threat lingers. In still others, the military has the power to make or break governments, or to impose or block policies wholly outside the realm of national security. Civilian control is, by its very nature, weak or non-existent if the armed forces can use force or influence to turn a government out of power, or to dictate the character of a government or policy. Even the hint of such extortion, if unpunished, inhibits civilian officials from exercising their authority, particularly in military affairs. Thus civilian control requires a military establishment dedicated to political neutrality: one that shuns under all circumstances any interference with the constitutional functioning or legitimate process of government, that identifies itself as the embodiment of the people and the nation (and not a particular party, agenda, or ideology), and that counts unhesitating loyalty to lawful authorities and the system of government as crucial aspects of its professionalism.

In mature democracies, where military intervention in politics is no longer an ongoing concern, the same professional ethos is crucial if civilian control is to function properly. The military must possess a sophisticated understanding of civilian control and actively promote it, for in the process of policy and decision making, senior officers must abstain from insinuating their own preferred policy outcomes or outmaneuvering civilian authority even when they can get away with it. Because of their expertise and role as the nation's guardians, military leaders in democracies can possess great public credibility, and can use it to limit or undermine civilian control, particularly during and after successful wars. The difficulty is to define their proper role and to confine their activity within proper (even if often indistinct) bounds. The Israeli scholar of civil-military relations Yehuda Ben Meir contends that the military should *advise* civilians and *represent* the needs of the military inside the government, but *should not advocate* military interests or perspectives publicly in such a way as to undermine or circumscribe civilian authority. And the military must never become an advocate, public or private, for a particular policy or decisions that extends beyond its professional sphere.[3]

Helpful to this ethos is an officer corps that is, in every respect possible, representative of the larger society. While some countries have enjoyed civilian control with officers drawn only from particular races, religions, classes, or ethnic backgrounds, it seems wiser to build an officer corps that equates itself with the national population and identifies its first loyalty as being owed to the country rather than to the profession of arms. To draw officers from a single segment is to risk creating a group that sees itself as separate from and superior to society. If they see their own values as being at variance with those of the population and their loyalties to their group of origin and to the military as primary, they may delude themselves into thinking that their purpose is to preserve or reform society's values and norms, rather than safeguard the nation's physical security.

Nor should serving military personnel participate in any fashion in politics, not as members of parties, in elected office, or even in appointive office as members of a political administration at the local or national level. If officers belong to a political party, run for office, represent a particular group or constituency, publicly express their views (or even say how they voted), attack or defend the executive leadership—in short, behave like politicians—they cannot be trusted by voters or by other politicians to be neutral servants of the state and guardians of society. Even personal identification with a political program or party can compromise an officer in the performance of his or her duty.

In theory, nothing prevents armies from interfering in politics or even attempting to overturn their government. But where civilian control has succeeded over a long period, military professionals have internalized civilian control to an extraordinary degree. In those countries, the people and civilian leaders expect, because of law or tradition, military subordination to civil authority. The organs of public opinion, in the press and among elites, accept the principle, and in times of stress in civil-military relations declare it as an axiom of government. Some countervailing power to the military force may exist, but military personnel understand that any step toward insubordination would immediately provoke a crisis that by consensus they would lose, with the possibility of legal sanctions against them personally.

Yet ultimately, it is the military's own professionalism and restraint that on a daily basis maintains civilian control. Whether or not they would face dismissal or prison, they *choose* to submit, to define their duty as advice to civilian bosses rather than advocacy, and to carry out all lawful orders effectively and without complaint. But because civilians frequently lack knowledge and understanding of military affairs, and the apportioning of military and civilian responsibility depends so often on circumstances, the relationship even in the most stable governments has been messy, uncertain, and periodically tense. And thus, historically, the *degree of civilian control,* that is, *the relative weight of the civilian and the military,* has depended on the people and the issues involved.

Civilian Control Day to Day

Because civilian control is a process, it depends heavily on the organization and functioning of a government. The military cannot perform its duty, nor can civilians exercise their authority, unless the machinery of government allows military and civilian perspectives to mix in the formulation of policy, enabling the two sides to understand each other and work together. Military establishments tend naturally to try to maximize their autonomy in order to gain the resources that they believe necessary to organize, arm, and recruit most effectively for their tasks. Armed forces in democracies instinctively strive to accomplish their tasks with the fewest casualties and the smallest risk of failure. So strong are those impulses that commanders and staffs sometimes try to control the definition of the mission or to stipulate the rules of engagement, to the point of circumventing or evading the direction of their civilian superiors. The challenge in democratic government is to exercise civilian authority while satisfying the legitimate needs of the military in its pursuit of national security.

The first and most important feature of organization is a clear chain of command under all conceivable circumstances, with the head of the government atop that chain. Even before democracy developed, command defined civilian control—all the way back into biblical times when kings and tribal leaders directed battles personally. If the executive power in government cannot always control where, when, and how military forces are used, then civilian control cannot be said to exist. And because of the nature of military command, this power must reside in a single individual; there must be no opportunity for confusion, which could excuse disobedience. In governments that have both a president and a prime minister, final authority and operational control must reside in one office or the other. Furthermore, any disobedience must be treated as mutiny or revolt, with the attendant harsh penalties.

The second critical need is to ensure that the decision to begin or end warfare lies in civilian hands, and that in the transition from peace to war, even when indistinct, the military can respond unhesitatingly to proper orders. Such decisions often determine the fate of whole societies. Democracy cannot function if people other than the elected leadership decide issues of such magnitude; war causes the military to expand, the power and importance of government to grow, and its intrusions into people's lives to increase—including more taxes, limits on freedoms, and perhaps compulsory military service.

The third critical area is military policy, meaning broadly all decisions affecting the size, shape, organization, character, weaponry, and internal operating procedures of the military establishment. Other than strategy and operations in wartime, peacetime military policy excites the most friction between civilian and military officials, and offers the greatest opportunities for the military to exercise its influence. If in peacetime military officers instead of elected officials make such choices—particularly regarding who can and cannot serve and how much money goes into defense—then the military controls the shape and character of a society.

These three broad but basic areas where civilians must rule cover nearly every conceivable aspect of national security. Theoretically every detail lies in the hands of civilians. Yet the reality, once again, is quite different. While civilians may possess the legal authority and may have the opportunity to exercise their influence even to the point of irresponsibility, there are definite practical limits to the exercise of these powers. In all three categories, civilians would be quite unwise and very much open to criticism if they made decisions without consulting the professionals who study war and defense full-time, possess actual experience, and carry considerable prestige with elites and the public. Military advice and cooperation are crucial to the quality and effectiveness of policy, and uniformed opposition, whether public or mounted behind the scenes, can, given the right circumstances, destroy the policy and devastate civilians' standing, and even their careers. The public expects that "the experts" will be involved and that their judgment, depending on the situation and personalities, will receive proper weight. Political opponents of the party in power will use military opinions, especially those that vary with a decision or policy, in the give-and-take of public debate. Thus in the process of civilian control, both civilian officialdom and the military are bound within limits and enmeshed in a reciprocal relationship; how each behaves depends upon a complex mix of factors, some unique to the situation and some the products of the broader institutions, practices, and traditions of civilian control. Critical to both process and outcome are the ways in which a government makes military policy and administers the military establishment.

Checks and Balances

In the waging of war and the management of military forces, civilian control operates most effectively when exercised by the executive branch of government or the ministry. But broader decisions regarding the size and character of the forces must come from the legislature, the body of government representing the people as a whole, which must possess its own machinery for investigation and review. The two branches must cooperate if the military is to function. Such divided but shared rule— the system of checks and balances—benefits civilians and the military alike. Civilian control grows stronger because no civilian can alone use the military to abuse power, and the military possesses both the efficiency of unitary command and the legitimacy of sanction by the people's representatives.

Historically, the executive, in addition to commanding the forces and conducting war, proposes military policy, including the budget and initiatives relating to the very existence and functioning of the armed forces. The executive commissions officers, recruits and trains troops, promotes and assigns individuals, formulates (or at least oversees) strategy and operations, buys weapons, issues orders, and makes decisions about virtually every aspect of military life. Every chief executive relies on a ministry or department of defense; civilian control requires a civilian minister or secretary, supported by a civilian bureaucracy of sufficient experience and technical expertise to gain the confidence of politicians and voters on the one hand, and of the military on the other. This can be a tense relationship in democracies, one marked by continual bargaining, negotiation, and conflict as well as cooperation. Neither side wholly trusts the other, nor can it. Some problems—for example, strategy, the rules of engagement for forces at risk, the operational authority of commanders, the types of weapons, the roles and missions of the services, and the size of the defense budget—are continually at issue or regularly renegotiated. But it is imperative that the president and prime minister be advised and served by civilians; the bonds of trust and loyalty, the self-identification, and the shared experiences and perspectives of the professional military are so strong that politicians cannot afford to rely exclusively upon military officers, whether serving or retired. At a minimum, a "second opinion" from outside (as in medicine), is necessary.

Especially in nations new to democracy, where the military carries the burden of loyalty to previously autocratic governments, the public should insist that a civilian serve as defense minister. This official, in turn, will require an expert staff from outside of the military to gather information and provide independent advice. Judgments about the size and character of the risks a nation faces, whether to institute or practice conscription, what weapons to purchase, and a variety of other choices invariably possess social, economic, and political implications that go beyond narrow security considerations. Nearly every society faces conflict between domestic needs and defense, choices which in the end are political in the purest sense of that word. In a democracy, by definition, elected rather than uniformed leaders must make those choices.

The role of the legislature is to approve the existence of the military (usually by appropriating money), make policy on the size and character of the armed forces, oversee their activities (including formal investigation of any issue or incident), and approve actions taken by the executive. Crucial to this process are hearings to air publicly all matters that can be discussed without breaching military secrecy. It is critically important to civilian control that the parliament exercise these powers independently of the executive (though the two branches may sometimes share authority). In testimony under oath before the legislative branch, the military is held publicly accountable, and officers can be required to express their personal as well as professional views if asked. Thus the legislature can get the military expertise it needs in order to exercise intelligent oversight.

Because civilian control rests ultimately on the behavior of individuals, armed forces personnel policy is critical. Typically, the executive and legislature share authority here. Civilians must decide who serves and whether or not there is to be compulsory military service, the ultimate intrusion of government into the private lives of individuals in democratic societies. The decision must be the result of some consensus in society, and not be imposed by the military. Equally important are the policies relating to the commissioning, education, promotion, assignment, and retirement of officers. It is the officer corps that historically has defined military establishments. Officers provide not only the leadership in war and in peace, but continuity over time to the military profession. Like every profession, the military strives to limit outside jurisdiction over its domain, to define its own requirements for membership, its own standards of behavior, the scope of its expertise, the principles for advancement and assignments, the character of its relationship with clients and society generally, and virtually every other aspect of its professional world, including the limits on membership and power within the group. Because of the unique responsibilities of battle, the military must possess a large measure of autonomy. Civilians recognize the legitimacy of much of this self-definition, to the point even of permitting a separate system of justice, with different categories of crimes and punishments for members of the armed forces. Civilians recognize that both civilian control and military effectiveness require that the officer corps be insulated from partisan politics, particularly from the promotion and assignment of officers on the basis of partisan affiliation. But civilian authority must restrict autonomy to what is necessary and functional.

To the extent that the military is a self-defining and self-perpetuating elite, it is less subordinate to the rest of society. The executive and legislature must control officer promotions; there must be mandatory retirements so that no one person can come to control the military forces indefinitely. In countries where civilian control is weak, support for military subordination to civilian authority should be an essential criterion for promotion and assignment. But the partisan leanings of an officer, if they exist, should never enter the equation, or the officer corps will be politicized and corrupted.

The exercise of civilian control by parliament occurs through legislation, much of which must rely on open hearings and a process of oversight that holds the military and the civilian defense bureaucracy accountable. Lawmakers must have access to, yet safeguard, the information necessary for policy making and for investigating malfeasance and failure. Information must be demanded and provided, which in turn puts parliament under the obligation to ask only for that classified information that is necessary for oversight, legislation, and policy, and never to release classified information. The legislative branch must be able to compel testimony from officials, punish false statements, and require military officers to express their professional opinions independent of policy on all matters before, during, and after decisions are made. The process is inherently contentious. For the military, it is especially awkward, for it frequently squeezes them between two bosses. It can also be politically explosive. Parliament must hold the ministry accountable or legislative power will cease to have effect. Parliament's most potent weapon is financial; by withholding money or directing its uses (hence the importance of limited-term budgets), parliament wields a mighty club over the rest of government. But budgets are also a clumsy weapon. By approving officer promotions and assignments, especially at the senior levels, parliaments can negotiate compliance to policy and demand obedience from individual military leaders.

Finally must come arrangements to ensure that, as a matter of course, individual members of the military are held accountable to the law for their actions. While most countries recognize the necessity for a separate legal system for the military to ensure obedience in battle and enforce discipline, the system must function under the jurisdiction, even if rarely exercised, of the civilian judiciary. Military personnel must be held accountable to society for their individual behavior, although not necessarily in exactly the same ways as civilian officials. Military service imposes a harsher, more demanding set of requirements and responsibilities. Yet the soldier's essential citizenship, with all of its obligations, cannot be abolished or suspended, because in a democracy no one can be above the law or beyond the reach of its sanctions.

A Difficult Transition

The widespread practice of democracy has emerged only in the last two centuries. In formerly communist countries, and in others where military dictatorship or intervention has occurred, the transition to civilian control is likely to be difficult. To devise wise and workable procedures and policies will require not only patience, but courage on the part of civilians, acquiescence on the part of the military, and public support that will encourage both sides to reach a stable relationship characterized by cooperation and mutual respect.

If civilian control is a process, and its measure is the relative influence of the military over policy, then civilians and military personnel have to work together day after day, week after week, year after year. Competent, effective, and courageous civilian officials are indispensable to civilian control: men and women who understand the military ethos, treat those who wear the uniform with courtesy, contest them when necessary, and protect their professionalism when others in the political arena attempt to gain partisan advantage by using or abusing the military leadership. Senior officers fear being stuck with the blame for policies or operations that fail not because of military mistakes, but because of decisions by politicians. Some degree of confidence must be built up on both sides; that, too, is highly situational, and rests in the hands of individual officials and officers when they begin their working relationships. Military leaders need direct access to the highest authority in the land; they need to be respected and their counsel must be sought. Civilian leaders, whatever their background, must come to know enough about military affairs to gain sympathy for the military's professional needs, obligations, requirements, and perspectives. But they must be tough enough to oppose military judgments when necessary and make their authority felt in spite of the political risk. They will need the backing of the voters. Civilian control must be accepted as axiomatic by the military, the political leader-ship, and the populace. Military subordination to civilian authority must be supported actively and vocally by the organs of opinion: the media, the universities, political parties, commercial and professional associa-tions, and others. Without a vigilant press and a widespread public under-standing of the nature and importance of civilian control, it can appear to be functioning properly but in actuality be quite weak.

As the next millennium approaches, newly emerging democracies, with long-established armed forces accustomed to a large degree of auto-nomy, face the challenge of reaching the point where they can say with confidence that they have civilian control over their military. Military establishments unaccustomed to having their judgment or authority ques-tioned, especially by the cacophony of groups and individuals (many of whom conspicuously do not subscribe to the values and behaviors tradi-tional to military groups) typical of democratic governance, will experi-ence an equally uncomfortable challenge. How that transition is managed will be crucial in determining the fate of democracy around the world.

NOTES

1. It could be argued that in constitutional systems, the "rules" are fixed in the written charter. Constitutions can be amended, however, and in democratic societies civilian courts interpret the laws and apply the constitution to specific cases and general situa-tions. Constitutional practice changes over time.

2. Samuel P. Huntington, *The Soldier and the State: The Theory and Politics of Civil-Military Relations* (Cambridge: Belknap Press of Harvard University Press, 1957).

3. Yehuda Ben Meir, *Civil-Military Relations in Israel* (New York: Columbia University Press, 1995), 25.

IV

Prospects and Challenges for Democracy in the New Century

21

A QUARTER-CENTURY
OF DECLINING CONFIDENCE

Susan J. Pharr, Robert D. Putnam, and Russell J. Dalton

Susan J. Pharr, *Edwin O. Reischauer Professor of Japanese Politics at Harvard University, is the author of* Losing Face: Status Politics in Japan *(1990) and* Media and Politics in Japan *(1996).* **Robert D. Putnam,** *Peter and Isabel Malkin Professor of Public Policy at Harvard University, is the author of* Making Democracy Work: Civic Traditions in Modern Italy *(1993) and* Bowling Alone: The Collapse and Revival of the American Community *(2000).* **Russell J. Dalton,** *director of the Center for the Study of Democracy at the University of California at Irvine, is author of* Critical Masses *(1999) and* The Green Rainbow *(1994). This essay is adapted from the introductory chapter to Pharr and Putnam's edited volume* Disaffected Democracies: What's Troubling the Trilateral Countries? *(2000).*

A quarter-century ago, Michel J. Crozier, Samuel P. Huntington, and Joji Watanuki argued that the nations of Europe, North America, and Japan confronted a "crisis of democracy."[1] Their starting point was a vision, widespread during the 1960s and 1970s, of "a bleak future for democratic government," an image of "the disintegration of civil order, the breakdown of social discipline, the debility of leaders, and the alienation of citizens."

The central thesis of the subtle, nuanced, and wide-ranging analysis by Crozier, Huntington, and Watanuki (hereafter CH&W) was that the Trilateral democracies were becoming overloaded by increasingly insistent demands from an ever-expanding array of participants, raising fundamental issues of governability. Within that common framework, the three authors offered somewhat distinct diagnoses of the problems facing their respective regions. In Europe, Crozier emphasized the upwelling of social mobilization, the collapse of traditional institutions and values, the resulting loss of social control, and governments' limited room for maneuver. Huntington asserted that America was swamped by a "democratic surge" that had produced political polarization, demands for more equality and participation, and less effective political parties and government. His provocative therapy was to "restore the balance" between democracy and governability. By contrast, Watanuki argued that Japan did not (yet?) face problems of "excessive" democracy, thanks in part to rapid economic growth and in part to its larger reservoir of traditional values. Whatever the regional and national nuances, however, the authors sketched a grim outlook for democracy in the Trilateral countries: delegitimated leadership, expanded demands, overloaded government, political competition that was both intensified and fragmented, and public pressures leading to nationalistic parochialism.

In historical perspective, the sense of crisis that permeated *The Crisis of Democracy* may have reflected the confluence of two factors: first, the surge of radical political activism that swept the advanced industrial democracies in the 1960s, which began with the civil rights and antiwar movements in United States and was then echoed in the events of May 1968 in France, Italy's "Hot Autumn" later that year, and student upheavals in Japan; and second, the economic upheavals triggered by the oil crisis of 1973–74 that were to result in more than a decade of higher inflation, slower growth, and, in many countries, worsening unemployment. The Trilateral governments were thus trapped between rising demands from citizens and declining resources to meet those demands. Moreover, the legitimacy of governments was suspect in the eyes of a generation whose motto was: "Question Authority." CH&W warned that these ominous developments posed a threat to democracy itself.

A quarter-century is an opportune interval after which to revisit the issue of the performance of our democratic institutions. The intervening years have witnessed many important developments in our domestic societies, economies, and polities, as well as in the international setting.

Most dramatic of all, of course, was the end of the Cold War, symbolized by the fall of the Berlin Wall in 1989. If it did not signal the end of history, the removal of the communist threat surely did mark the end of a historical epoch. It transformed the fundamental underpinnings of security alliances and eliminated the principal philosophical and geopolitical challenge to liberal democracy and the market economy. In some of the Trilateral countries it also coincided with, and to some extent triggered, an intellectual and ideological revolution. In each country it transformed domestic political calculations and alignments in ways that are still being played out.

Economically, the decades that followed the appearance of the CH&W volume were distinctly less happy than those that preceded it. The oil shocks of 1973–74 and 1979–80 drew the curtain on that fortunate early-postwar combination of high growth, low inflation, and low unemployment. Although economists differ on the origins of the pervasive slowdown, virtually all econometric analyses confirm the view of the man and woman in the street: Western economies took a turn for the worse around 1973–74, and recovery was a slow and uncertain process. The immediate inflationary effects of the oil crises were overcome by means of stringent monetary policies, but the economic malaise continued. In subsequent years, Europe had unprecedentedly high structural unemployment, the United States endured sharply reduced rates of real wage growth, and after 1992 Japan experienced the longest recession in the country's postwar history.

"Interdependence" was already widely discussed in the early 1970s, and integration of the world economy has continued at a rapid pace in the years since then. International trade has grown faster than gross domestic products, and foreign investment more rapidly than either of them. Western economies are even more porous internationally now than when CH&W wrote, and our economic fates are even more intertwined. Nowhere is this more true, of course, than in Europe: The European Union has taken shape and extended its reach to an increasing number of policy domains with stunning speed. Moreover, the rise of newly industrializing economies challenges the competitiveness of all the Trilateral countries. Finally, immigration from the less-developed to the more-developed nations of the world has accelerated, creating new difficulties and social tensions.

Socially and culturally, these decades have witnessed significant change. Increased mobility and growing individuation have eroded traditional family and community ties. Some observers believe that the decline in respect for authority that CH&W underscored has continued apace in all sectors of society; others see evidence of increased tolerance of diversity. The role of women in economic life (and to some extent in public life more generally) has grown. The expansion of higher education during the 1950s and 1960s continues to boost the university-educated share of the electorate. The electronic media have transformed how we spend our leisure time as well as how we follow public affairs. In many of our cities, the problems of drugs, crime, homelessness, and blight are even more visible now than a quarter-century ago. Finally, older people occupy a growing share of the population in all Trilateral countries, which is certain to have major consequences for both social and economic policy in the decades to come.

The Trilateral Democracies Today

When *The Crisis of Democracy* appeared, citizens in the Trilateral world were still primarily concerned about market failure in sectors as diverse as social services, culture, and the environment. Demands for government intervention to redress those failures were ascendant. This ideological climate fed the preoccupation of CH&W with governability. As symbolized by the advent of Thatcher, Reagan, Nakasone, Kohl, and similar figures elsewhere, however, public concern had shifted by the early 1980s from *market* failure to *government* failure. Responding to and in part encouraging this sea change in public opinion, conservative leaders proposed a reduced role for government, and this ideological shift to the right was accelerated everywhere by the discrediting of state socialism after 1989. Facing an altered electoral marketplace, political leaders everywhere now call for less government—less bureaucracy, less regulation, less public spending—although policy has yet to catch up with rhetoric. Even a relatively liberal Democratic president in the United States has proclaimed that "the era of big government is over." In one sense, the problem of "overload" identified by CH&W appears to have solved itself: Many people seem to have concluded that government action is not the answer to all their problems.[2] Yet citizens still hold government responsible for their social and economic well-being, and cutting "entitlement" programs remains difficult everywhere.

Against this backdrop of geopolitical, economic, social, and ideological change, how should we assess the current status of the advanced industrial democracies of North America, Western Europe, and Japan? At the outset we want to emphasize a distinction that CH&W felt less need to stress: the distinction between the effectiveness of specific democratic governments and the durability of democratic institutions per se. On the one hand, we see no evidence in any of these countries that democracy itself is at risk of being supplanted by an undemocratic political regime or by social or political anarchy. On the other hand, we do see substantial evidence throughout the Trilateral world of mounting public unhappiness with government and the institutions of representative democracy.

Earlier alarm about the stability of democracy itself—which CH&W were in part responding to and in part amplifying—now seems exaggerated. The happy contrast between political developments in the advanced industrial democracies after World Wars I and II is indeed dramatic. Within two decades after the end of World War I, fledgling democracies had collapsed in Italy, Germany, Spain, and Japan, and more established democracies elsewhere were under siege. Now, more than half a century after the end of World War II, democratic regimes are deeply rooted throughout the Trilateral world and have multiplied in other parts of the world as well. Bearing in mind the tragic failures of democracy in the interwar period, it was entirely natural in the first decades after World War II for observers of Western politics to ask whether the same thing could happen again. Political science has a poor record of prognostication, especially with respect to radical change, and we should not be too presumptuous in writing about such fundamental issues, but with half a century of democratic stability under our collective belts, the answer is almost certainly no.

The case for this optimism does not simply rest on the passage of time. Decades of surveys in North America, Western Europe, and Japan yield little evidence of diminished support for liberal democracy among either mass publics or elites. If anything, the opposite is true: Commitment to democratic values is higher than ever.[3] In sharp contrast to the period after World War I, no serious intellectual or ideological challenge to democracy has emerged. Whether tracked over the more than five decades since the end of World War II or over the decade since the fall of the Berlin Wall, opponents of democracy have lost support. Even where public discontent with the performance of particular democratic governments has become so acute as to overturn the party system (as in Japan and Italy in 1993–95), these changes have not included any serious threat to fundamental democratic principles and institutions. In this sense we see no significant evidence of a crisis of democracy.

Nevertheless, to say that democracy per se is not at risk is far from saying that all is well with the Trilateral democracies. In fact, public confidence in the performance of representative institutions in Western Europe, North America, and Japan has declined since the original Trilateral Commission report was issued, and in that sense most of these democracies are troubled.

Symptoms of Distress

Public attitudes toward democracy can be assessed at various levels of abstraction. We find no evidence of declining commitment to the principles of democratic government or to the democratic regimes in our countries. On the contrary, if anything, public commitment to democracy per se has risen in the last half century. At the other extreme, we are not concerned with day-to-day evaluations of specific leaders, policies, and governments (in the European sense of the word); we assume that evaluations of this kind of governmental performance will rise and fall in any well-functioning democracy. Rather, our concern is with popular confidence in the performance of representative institutions. Among the specific indicators we focus on are trends in: 1) attachment to, and judgments of, political parties; 2) approval of parliaments and other political institutions; and 3) assessment of the "political class" (politicians and political leaders) and evaluations of political trust. Whatever the "normal" background level of public cynicism and censure of politics, citizens in most of the Trilateral democracies are less satisfied—often much less satisfied—with the performance of their representative political institutions than they were a quarter-century ago.

North America. The onset and depth of this disillusionment vary from country to country, but the downtrend is longest and clearest in the United States, where polling has produced the most abundant and systematic evidence.[4] (The evidence from Canada, if less abundant and dramatic, conforms to this general picture.) When Americans were asked in the late 1950s and early 1960s, "How much of the time can you trust the government in Washington to do what is right?" three-quarters of them said "most of the time" or "just about always." Such a response would sound unbelievably quaint to most people today. This decline in confidence followed a decade or more of exceptionally turbulent political conflict—the civil rights movement, Vietnam, and Watergate and its successor scandals—that transformed American politics. Third-party challengers for the presidency, divided government, a term-limits movement, and other political developments signaled the public's increasing disenchantment with the political status quo.[5] Public confidence in the ability and benevolence of government has fallen steadily over this period. The decline was briefly interrupted by the "It's Morning in America" prosperity of the Reagan administration, and even more briefly by victory in the Gulf War, but confidence in government ended up lower after 12 years of Republican rule. Indeed, of the total decline, roughly half occurred under Republican administrations and half under Democratic ones. The economic prosperity of the late 1990s has seen an uptick in confidence in government, but the figures still remain well below those of the 1970s, not to mention those of the halcyon days of the late 1950s and early 1960s.

> *In the 1960s, two-thirds of Americans rejected the statement "Most elected officials don't care what people like me think"; in 1998, nearly two-thirds of Americans agreed with it.*

Public-opinion data tell the story of this decline. For example, whereas three-quarters of the American public once trusted the government to do what is right, only 39 percent felt this way in 1998. In 1964, only 29 percent of the American electorate agreed that "the government is pretty much run by a few big interests looking out for themselves." By 1984, that figure had risen to 55 percent, and by 1998, fully 63 percent of voters concurred. In the 1960s, two-thirds of Americans rejected the statement "Most elected officials don't care what people like me think"; in 1998, nearly two-thirds of Americans agreed with it. This negative assessment applies to virtually all parts of government. Those people expressing "a great deal" of confidence in the executive branch fell from 42 percent in 1966 to only 12 percent in 1997, and equivalent trust in Congress fell from 42 percent in 1966 to 11 percent in 1997.[6]

Almost every year since 1966, the Harris Poll has presented a set of five statements to national samples of Americans to measure their political alienation: 1) "The people running the country don't really care what happens to you." 2) "Most people with power try to take advantage of people like yourself." 3) "You're left out of things going on around you." 4) "The rich get richer and the poor get poorer." 5) "What you think doesn't count very much anymore." Every item on this list has won increasing assent from Americans since the opinion series began. In the late 1960s—at the very height of the Vietnam protests—barely one-third of Americans endorsed these cynical views; by the early 1990s fully two-thirds of all Americans concurred. By almost any measure, political alienation has soared over the last three decades.[7] A single comparison captures the transformation: In April 1966, with the Vietnam War raging and race riots in Cleveland, Chicago, and Atlanta, 66 percent of Americans *rejected* the view that "the people running the country don't really care what happens to you." In December 1997, in the midst of the longest period of peace and prosperity in more than two generations, 57 percent of Americans *endorsed* that same view.[8]

Europe. Comparable public-opinion trends in Europe are more variegated, but there, too, the basic picture is one of spreading disillusionment with established political leaders and institutions. Trust in politicians and major political institutions has fallen over the last quarter-century in countries as diverse as Britain, Italy, France, and Sweden.

Britons' traditional deference to elites has been replaced by growing skepticism. In 1987, for example, fewer than half of Britons believed that either civil servants, the national government, or local councils could be trusted to serve the public interest.[9] And while 48 percent of the British public expressed quite a lot of confidence in the House of Commons in 1985, that figure had been halved by 1995. Public protests over government decisions had become a common feature of politics in a nation once known for popular deference to political elites. As a symbol of this spreading skepticism, a series of high-profile Parliamentary committees in the 1990s studied issues of government corruption, ethical standards in politics, and campaign-finance abuses. Sweden, which invented the consummate welfare state and was once widely considered to have found a happy "middle way" between the free-for-all of market capitalism and the oppression of state socialism, is emblematic of Europe's troubled mood. The proportion of Swedes who rejected the statement that "parties are only interested in people's votes, not in their opinions" decreased from 51 percent in 1968 to 28 percent in 1994.[10] In 1986, even after the onset of the trend of decreasing political trust, a majority (51 percent) of Swedes still expressed confidence in the Riksdag; by 1996, however, only 19 percent did.

Especially striking are the patterns for the postwar democracies of Germany and Italy. Political support grew in these nations during the postwar decades, but the trends reversed at some point, and support has now eroded significantly from postwar highs. For instance, the percentage of Germans who said they trusted their Bundestag deputy to represent their interests rose from 25 percent in 1951 to 55 percent in

1978; by 1992, it had declined to 34 percent.[11] Other survey responses point to a general erosion of Germans' trust in government since the early 1980s. Similarly, student unrest and extremist violence in the 1970s strained Italians' postwar democratic agreement, and public skepticism broadened and deepened with the political scandals of the past decade. This was signaled most dramatically by the radical restructuring of the party system in the mid-1990s. The percentage of Italians who say that politicians "don't care what people like me think" increased from 68 percent in 1968 to 84 percent in 1997.

At least until recently, such trends have been less visible in some of the smaller European democracies. Still, patterns of growing political cynicism have become more common in Austria, Norway, Finland, and other small states during the past decade. Almost everywhere, it seems, people are less deferential to political leaders and more skeptical of their motives. Across Europe the pattern of declining political support has apparently accelerated in the past decade. A recent evaluation of all the relevant long-term evidence found "clear evidence of a general erosion in support for politicians in most advanced industrial countries."[12]

Japan. Public evaluations of politics and government in Japan reveal similarly disturbing trends. While *The Crisis of Democracy* portrayed Japan as an outlier, buffered from travails the authors saw looming elsewhere by a deferential political culture in which state authority was accepted,[13] Japanese citizens' disillusionment with government and political institutions has, if anything, proven to be more persistent than elsewhere in the Trilateral world. Japan began the postwar era with confidence levels at a low point. With a generation of leaders discredited by wartime defeat and with the new democratic institutions imposed by the Occupation as yet untested, it is little wonder that political uncertainty prevailed, as attested to by extremely high proportions of Japanese responding "Don't know" to survey questions. By the 1960s, confidence in democracy per se was well established, and people's evaluations of government and politics had improved somewhat from these abysmal beginnings, but they nevertheless remained low relative to those in most other advanced industrial democracies.[14] Although the mid-1980s witnessed a brief upturn, confidence levels declined noticeably in the politically turbulent and economically distressed 1990s. The long-term trends toward less deference to political leaders, diminished loyalty to established political parties (including the long-dominant Liberal Democratic Party, or LDP), and increased political dissatisfaction all predate the scandals that finally brought down the LDP in 1993 after 38 years of uninterrupted rule.

The proportion of Japanese voters who agree with the deferential view that "in order to make Japan better, it is best to rely on talented politicians, rather than to let the citizens argue among themselves" has fallen steadily for 40 years. Although this is probably a good indicator of the *strengthening* of the cultural and sociological foundations of Japanese democracy, the proportion of voters who feel that they exert at least "some influence" on national politics through elections, demonstrations, or expressions of public opinion also fell steadily between 1973 and 1993. In other words, Japanese voters have become less and less satisfied over the last 20 years with their limited role in politics, and less content to leave public affairs in the hands of political leaders. This is the backdrop against which a series of political corruption scandals broke prior to 1993, discrediting the LDP and causing public esteem for political leadership to decline still further. In yet another sign of a downturn in confidence, trust in the country's once-esteemed elite civil servants has also plummeted over the past decade.

Trends in Political Confidence

When we step back from surveying the Trilateral landscape region by region, the overall picture that emerges is disturbing. Long series of national-election studies and reputable commercial public-opinion surveys provide extensive evidence of how public sentiments have changed over time. Evidence of the decline in political support has been especially apparent in three areas: disillusionment with politicians, with political parties, and with political institutions.

Politicians. If public doubts about the polity surfaced only in evaluations of politicians or the government in power at any particular point in time, there would be little cause for worry. After all, citizens' dissatisfaction with an incumbent government routinely spurs voters to seek a change in administration at the next election and then extend support to the new incumbents. In that case, disaffection is a healthy part of the democratic process. Because citizens have the power to "throw the rascals out," democracy has a potential for renewal and responsiveness that is its ultimate strength. If dissatisfaction is generalized to the point where citizens lose faith in the entire political class, however, then the chances for democratic renewal are seriously diminished.

The patterns we have described separately, region by region, appear to be common to most Trilateral democracies. When the data for recent decades are assembled, the picture that emerges is stark (see Figure 1 on pp. 300–1). Overall, *there is evidence of some decline in confidence in politicians in 12 out of 13 countries for which systematic data are available.* The convergence of results across Trilateral democracies is striking, because each has experienced its own unique political events over the past quarter-century. Although the decline is not universal,[15] there is a general pattern of spreading public distrust of politicians and government among the citizens of Trilateral democracies. The political

FIGURE 1—CONFIDENCE IN POLITICIANS

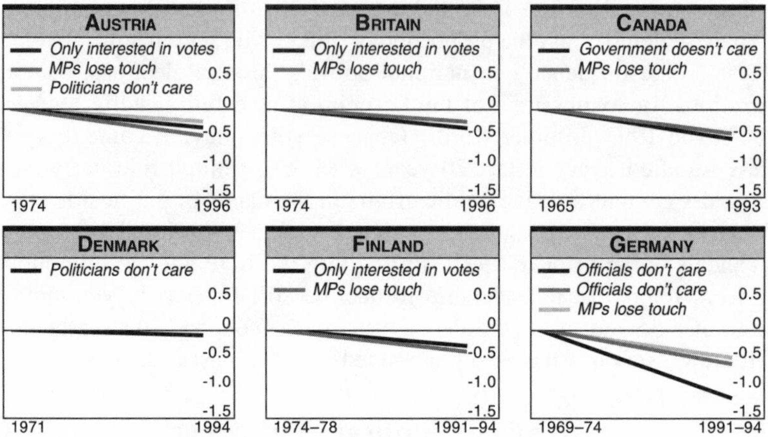

process undoubtedly faces strains when an increasing number of people distrust those individuals who are running the institutions of democratic governance.

Political Parties. For more than a century, political parties have played a central role in the theory and practice of democratic government. To be sure, classical philosophers conceived of democracy as a kind of unmediated popular sovereignty in which "the people" rule directly, but they had in mind the context of a small city-state and never imagined that democratic government could function in societies as large and complex as today's Trilateral nations. This hurdle of scale was overcome by the greatest modern political innovation—representative democracy—which required intermediary institutions to link citizens to their government, to aggregate the increasingly diverse universe of conflicting social and economic interests into coherent public policies, and to ensure the accountability of rulers to the ruled. With the advent of universal suffrage, these functions came to be performed by political parties throughout the democratic world.

Although parties have long been the target of vociferous criticism, without them, the eminent scholar E.E. Schattschneider once asserted,[16] democracy would be unthinkable. One need not be blind to the deficiencies of partisanship nor romanticize the internal workings of party organizations to recognize the importance of parties to representative government. Joseph Schumpeter once defined democracy as "that institutional arrangement for arriving at political decisions in which individuals acquire the power to decide by means of a competitive struggle for the people's votes."[17] Although Schumpeter did not specifically emphasize the role of parties in this competition, his theory did clarify how parties

FIGURE 1—CONFIDENCE IN POLITICIANS *(cont'd)*

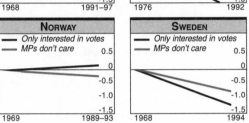

Notes: Table entries are per-annum change coefficients estimated by unstandardized regression coefficients of time on each variable. The original variables are coded so that negative regression coefficients indicate a decrease in trust over time.
Sources: The respective National Election Study series in each nation.

contribute to democracy. Just as firms in a free market are led to innovate and to satisfy consumers by a combination of self-interest and the rules of open competition, party competition provides the linchpin between voters and public policy and the mechanism for turning disparate "special interests" into some version of "the public interest." Just as brand names allow consumers to choose on the basis of past experience and to penalize shoddy performance, party labels ensure that voters can reward the successful stewardship of public affairs and punish incompetence or dishonesty. Partisan "brand loyalty" gives political leaders the right incentives: They are free to innovate and make difficult decisions that may be painful in the short run, while they remain accountable to their constituents in the long run. Parties, in short, make the political marketplace orderly. Parties offer other advantages as well. They allow the voters to rise above their feelings about individual politicians; party supporters can be dissatisfied with a set of candidates, yet remain committed to the party's goals and the principle of representative democracy.

Because of the centrality of parties to democracy, people's feelings of attachment to or identification with political parties are one of the most widely studied of political attitudes. Fine-tuned efforts have been made to measure both affinities toward specific parties and acceptance of the general system of party-based democracy.[18]

Signs of waning public attachment to political parties first emerged in several Trilateral democracies during the 1970s.[19] The collapse in citizen engagement with political parties over the subsequent decades is as close to a universal generalization as one can find in political science.

Card-carrying membership has always been less important for American than for European parties, but the proportion of Americans who reported that they engaged in party work at least once during the previous year fell by 56 percent between 1973 and 1993, and the proportion who reported attending a campaign rally or speech fell by 36 percent over the same period. Comparably massive declines in party membership have been registered in most Trilateral countries over the last 25 years.[20] As attachments to political parties have eroded, electorates have become more volatile and skeptical. A comprehensive look at this pattern of weakening party ties, or "dealignment," reveals that popular identification with political parties has fallen in almost all the advanced industrial democracies. *The percent of the public expressing a partisan attachment has declined in 17 of the 19 Trilateral nations for which time-series data are available.* The strength of party attachments was separately measured in 18 nations: All show a downward trend.[21]

Seldom does such a diverse group of nations reveal so consistent a trend. The only major variation is in the timing of the decline. Dealignment in the United States, Great Britain, and Sweden has been a long-term and relatively steady process that moved partisanship to a lower baseline level. For example, 65 percent of the Swedish public claimed party ties in 1968, compared to only 48 percent in 1994. In other countries, the change has been more recent. French and Irish partisanship has eroded over the past two decades. German partisanship, which had grown during the early postwar decades, began to weaken in the late 1980s and dropped off markedly in the 1990s. In Canada, the collapse of the Progressive Conservative and New Democratic Parties in the 1993 elections accentuated a similar trend toward dealignment. In Japan and Austria, too, detachment from parties accelerated in the 1990s, in response to a breakdown of political consensus in both nations. Specific variations aside, the overall pattern is consistent and striking. If party attachments represent the most fundamental type of citizen support for representative democracy, as many scholars assert, then their decline in nearly all advanced industrial democracies offers strong and disturbing evidence of the public's disengagement from political life.

Beyond reflecting dissatisfaction with politicians and current party leaders, weakening partisan ties also signal a growing disenchantment with partisan politics in general. For example, responses to several questions from the American National Election Study indicate a trend of declining faith that parties and elections are responsive to the public's interests.[22] A variety of other evidence points to Americans' growing disillusionment with political parties as agents of democratic representation.[23] Along with other factors, disenchantment with political parties fueled public demand for major electoral reforms in Japan, Italy, and New Zealand. Across most of the Trilateral democracies, more citizens are now maintaining their independence from political parties

and the institutions of representative democracy that they
represent.

Political Institutions. In the
Trilateral democracies, citizens'
skepticism about politicians and
political parties extends to the
formal institutions of democratic
government. It is one thing for
citizens to be skeptical of the
president or the prime minister
(or even the group of politicians
in parliament); it is quite different if this cynicism broadens to
include the institutions of the
presidency and the legislature.

Because of its abundance of
long-running,   high-quality
public-opinion surveys, the best
evidence once again comes from
the United States. One question
gauges confidence in the officials
running the three branches of
American government.[24] In the
mid-1960s, a large proportion of
Americans expressed a great deal
of confidence in the Supreme
Court, the executive branch, and
Congress, but that confidence
dropped dramatically by the early
1970s, and slid even further for
the executive and Congress over
the following two decades.
Significantly, it is the Supreme
Court, the least partisan and

FIGURE 2—CONFIDENCE IN PARLIAMENT IN 14 TRILATERAL COUNTRIES

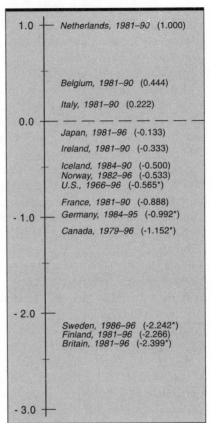

Notes: Table entries are the per-annum change in the percentage expressing a great deal or quite a lot of confidence in par-liament (*$p < 0.05$).

Sources: World Value Surveys (WVS) data are from the 1981–83, 1990–94, and 1995–98 surveys; other data are from individual national-survey series.

political institution, that has best retained the public's confidence. By the
mid-1990s, barely a tenth of the American public had a great deal of
confidence in the people running the executive branch or Congress—
dramatic evidence of Americans' dissatisfaction with government.

Figure 2 presents data on trends in confidence in parliament for 14
Trilateral democracies.[25] Parliament is the prime institution of representative democracy, the link between citizens and elites. Thus we focus
on public images of parliament as a key institution in the structure of
democratic politics.

The time coverage and the extensiveness of the evidence varies considerably across nations, but the overall pattern is quite apparent. *In 11 out of 14 countries, confidence in parliament has declined.* Although in a number of cases the evidence does not rise to the level of statistical significance (largely because of the limited number of time points), in the five countries (Britain, Canada, Germany, Sweden, and the United States) for which the most extensive data are available, the drop in confidence in the national legislature is both pronounced and statistically significant.

Citizens' declining confidence in the institutions of democratic government extends beyond parliament. A separate analysis, using the 1981 and 1990 World Values Surveys, evaluated confidence in the armed services, judiciary, police, and civil service, as well as parliament. Although some institutions have scored gains in public trust over time, the general downward trajectory is clear. On average, confidence in these five institutions decreased by 6 percent over this single decade.[26] In fact, only Denmark and Iceland displayed absolute increases in institutional confidence during the 1980s, and those increases were small.

The trends described here are not homogeneous across all the Trilateral countries. The degree and timing of growing distrust of political leaders, dissatisfaction with government performance, and estrangement from established parties vary greatly, depending on national traditions, specific political events, the effectiveness of individual leaders, and so on. Generally speaking, the trends are clearer in the larger countries (and clearest of all in the largest of all) and less visible (or, in a few cases, almost wholly absent) in some of the smallest countries.

Quite apart from any temporary disenchantment with the present government or dissatisfaction with particular leaders, most citizens in the Trilateral world have become more distrustful of politicians, more skeptical about political parties, and significantly less confident in their parliament and other political institutions. Compared to the state of public opinion at the time that CH&W wrote, the political mood in most of our countries today is not just grumpy, but much grumpier.

Why Worry?

Although public concern over these trends is widespread, it is nevertheless reasonable to step back and ask whether we should be worried about the many signs of erosion in popular confidence in government and the institutions of representative democracy. Some observers would reply with a resounding "No," offering three main arguments. The first holds that a critical citizenry signals not illness in the body politic but rather the health of democracy, and that the real challenge is to explain not the long-term decline in confidence, but why it was as high as it was in the 1950s and early 1960s, especially in the United States. A variation on that same view sees changes in values, driven by prosperity, technology, and other factors, as having created a more critical citizenry that rejects the political status quo and is also forcing new issues such as environmentalism and women's rights onto the political agenda, thus reforming and revitalizing democracy.

A second objection holds that new forms of political participation (such as referenda and "town-hall"–style fora) and an upsurge in certain types of grassroots activism (including social movements that are more broad-based than in the past) have supplanted previous forms of political engagement. A third objection proceeds from a particular perspective on the appropriate relation between government and citizens. The task of government, this view holds, is to give citizens not necessarily what they want, but what they need. Thus sound and appropriate policies are the best measure of governmental performance. Confidence levels are immaterial as long as the public supports the government enough to comply with its laws, pay taxes, and accept conscription.

Although each of these arguments has merit, we see reason to worry in the fact that voters' "report cards" on their representative institutions in the Trilateral democracies have generally become more critical—and often much more critical—in recent decades. Although we do not believe that this sour mood is a precursor of the collapse of Western democracy, a decent respect for our fellow citizens' views compels us to consider why they are increasingly distrustful of, and discontented with, their political institutions. If the decline in public confidence is justified (because of growing corruption, for example), then we might applaud citizens' ire but not its cause, just as we would be glad to have discovered a child's fever without being glad that her temperature was high.

If citizens are less satisfied with their representative institutions, this is a politically relevant and important fact. Yet few would argue that popularity is the sole measure of democratic performance, and most of us would admit that governments often must (or should) take actions that might reduce their popularity in the short run. Opinions differ on whether public satisfaction per se is a relevant measure of democratic performance. Some believe that democracy is not (just) about making citizens happy, and that it is also supposed to facilitate "good government," whether or not citizens are pleased with government actions. Others endorse the more populist view that what is distinctive about democracy is that the ultimate criterion of performance is citizens' collective judgment, so if public confidence declines over the long run, that is prima facie (though not irrefutable) evidence that the performance of representative institutions has declined.

A Model for Explaining the Decline

For disaffection in particular countries, explanations have been offered that are studded with proper nouns: Vietnam, Nixon, Craxi, Mulroney,

Thatcher, Recruit, and so on. Such interpretations offer important insights into the national catalysts for democratic distress, but it seems surprising that so many independent democracies just happened to encounter rough water or careless captains simultaneously. Although we do not discount the importance of specific national factors, we seek more generalizable explanations.

Unraveling the question of why confidence in government has declined to varying degrees across the Trilateral world is a complex task. In our view, public satisfaction with representative institutions is a function of the information to which citizens are exposed, the criteria by which the public evaluates government and politics, and the actual performance of those institutions (see Figure 3 on the facing page). Thus a decline in satisfaction might be due to a change in any of these variables.

First, the accuracy and comprehensiveness of publicly available *information* about democratic performance might have changed. Logically, this might be due to either deterioration (worse information about good performance) or improvement (better information about bad performance), but the most common interpretation is that voters have over time become better informed about their governments' performance, particularly about leaders' conduct in office (for example, corruption), even though malfeasance per se might not have worsened. Here, the role of the media is clearly central.

Second, the public's *criteria for evaluation* of politics and government might have changed in ways that make it harder for representative institutions to meet those standards. This in turn might be due to either rising or diverging expectations (or both). If public demands on government spiral insatiably upward, satisfaction could fall even if performance remains unchanged. In part, this was the interpretation offered by CH&W. If the heterogeneity of public desires increases, either by polarization along a single dimension or by divergence across multiple dimensions, then it becomes more difficult for government to identify any feasible set of policies that would satisfy its constituents.

Third, the *performance of representative institutions* might have deteriorated. Measuring performance objectively is a challenging task, of course. Because it is reasonably well established in most of the Trilateral countries that cyclical fluctuations in citizens' evaluations of incumbents correlate with macroeconomic indicators, one obvious approach is to measure macroeconomic outcomes (inflation, unemployment, growth, and the like). A growing body of work, however, generally discounts this as the primary explanation for the decline in public confidence in political institutions.[27] As Nye and his colleagues[28] note with regard to the United States, for example, the largest decline in confidence occurred over the high-growth decade between 1964 and 1974; confidence actually increased during the recession of the early 1980s.

Once these economic measures are set aside, there is little agreement

FIGURE 3—EXPLAINING CONFIDENCE IN GOVERNMENT
AND POLITICAL INSTITUTIONS: A MODEL

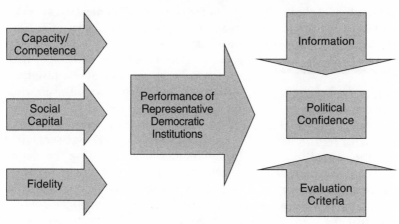

over which dimensions of performance are relevant across countries, time, and individual citizens. One obvious measure might be gains or losses in social welfare. One might argue that levels of confidence have remained high in countries in which social-welfare guarantees are secure while they have dropped elsewhere as a result of rollbacks of the welfare state. Yet testing such a hypothesis runs into the problem of how to measure governmental performance on social welfare. If we use government outlays, we run up against the fact that, despite the rhetoric hailing "small government," governmental transfers (which are heavily skewed toward social programs) as a percentage of GNP have increased strikingly in the Trilateral countries precisely over those decades in which confidence has decreased. Alternatively, to measure results like increased longevity and improved health would fail to take into account the many factors other than government policies (diet and economic prosperity, for example) that produce them. Another problem is choosing a point in time at which policy success or failure can be judged. For example, some people believe that the American war in Vietnam or the process of German reunification constituted massive policy failures that contributed powerfully to declining political confidence; other observers might argue that, in the long run, these policy "failures" represent historic successes.

Thus objective measures of policy performance have obvious limits. When searching for why citizens feel the way they do about their government, their subjective appraisal of governmental performance is what ultimately matters. The fact that public confidence has declined can be taken to mean that governmental performance is less satisfactory than it once was. We consider citizens' falling confidence in government to be focused specifically on political institutions and to have principally political roots and therefore seek to identify broad explanations for the deterioration of governmental performance. These can be collected under two rubrics.

The first of these is declines in the *capacity* of political agents to act on behalf of citizens' interests and desires (see Figure 3 on p. 307). Thus we seek to identify forces that may have undermined the ability of national governments to implement their chosen policies and to respond to citizen demands in a satisfactory way. The principal such force is internationalization, which creates a growing incongruence between the scope of territorial units and the issues raised by interdependence, reducing the output effectiveness of democratic nation-states.

> *Some commentators may tell their fellow citizens that the problem is "just in your head" . . . but we are inclined to think that our political systems are not, in fact, performing well.*

The second broad explanation concerns declines in the *fidelity* with which political agents act on citizens' interests and desires. Within this category fall arguments about failures of political leadership, failures of political judgment on the part of voters, and deterioration of the civic infrastructure (or social capital) by means of which interests are articulated and aggregated.

A final problem relating to the issue of fidelity arises from the complex relationship among three sets of variables: confidence in government; governmental performance; and civic engagement, social capital,[29] and social trust. A key issue is precisely how an erosion of social capital and social trust may affect citizens' confidence in government. Much evidence to date suggests low levels overall of social capital and social trust in any given society do indeed contribute to poor governmental performance, which, in turn, adversely affects all citizens to varying degrees; as a consequence, they will give the government low marks. Metaphorically speaking, no citizen (no matter how high his or her *own* social trust or civic engagement) can escape the rain precipitated by poor governmental performance, perhaps produced in part by the social disaffection or civic disengagement of his or her neighbors.

Over the quarter-century since CH&W issued their report, citizens' confidence in governments, political parties, and political leaders has declined significantly in most of the Trilateral democracies, even though the depth and timing of this decline have varied considerably from country to country. Some commentators may tell their fellow citizens that the problem is "just in your head"—a function of unrealistic expectations rather than deteriorating performance—but we are inclined to think that our political systems are not, in fact, performing well, although perhaps for reasons beyond their immediate control. These criticisms of governments and leaders do not necessarily translate into a "crisis of democracy" that threatens constitutional and representative government.

Nevertheless, the fact that representative democracy per se is not at risk does not imply that all is well with our political systems. Indeed, most of our fellow citizens believe that all is *not* well. Due regard for their views, as well as a prudent concern for the future, suggests that we should explore the sources of this democratic discontent.

NOTES

1. Michel Crozier, Samuel P. Huntington, and Joji Watanuki, *The Crisis of Democracy* (New York: New York University Press, 1975), 2.

2. Polls do not, in fact, generally confirm the thesis that ordinary citizens' views about the proper role of government have shifted nearly as much as has the climate of elite opinion. Equally important, however, there is little survey evidence that citizens have become more insistent on government action in recent decades.

3. Pippa Norris, ed., *Critical Citizens: Global Support for Democratic Government* (Oxford: Oxford University Press, 1999); Hans-Dieter Klingemann and Dieter Fuchs, eds., *Citizens and the State,* vol. 1 of Kenneth Newton, ed., *Beliefs in Government* (Oxford: Oxford University Press, 1995); Max Kaase and Kenneth Newton, eds., *Beliefs in Government,* vol. 5 of Kenneth Newton, ed., *Beliefs in Government.*

4. The most comprehensive assessment of the evidence for declining confidence in government in the United States, as well as initial evaluations of alternative explanations, is Joseph S. Nye, Philip D. Zelikow, and David C. King, eds., *Why People Don't Trust Government* (Cambridge, Mass.: Harvard University Press, 1997).

5. Martin Wattenberg, *The Decline of American Political Parties* (Cambridge, Mass.: Harvard University Press, 1996); Joseph S. Nye, Philip D. Zelikow, and David C. King, eds., *Why People Don't Trust Government.*

6. Seymour Martin Lipset, "American Democracy in Comparative Perspective," in Robert S. Leiken, ed., *A New Moment in the Americas* (New Brunswick, N.J.: Transaction Publishers, 1994); Seymour Martin Lipset and William Schneider, *The Confidence Gap* (New York: Free Press, 1983).

7. Harris Poll, February 1994. Although systematic data on political alienation in America before the advent of regular national surveys in the 1950s are sketchy, some evidence suggests that alienation had declined from the mid-1930s to the mid-1960s. See Robert E. Lane, "The Politics of Consensus in an Age of Affluence," *American Political Science Review* 59 (December 1965): 874–95.

8. Harris Poll, February 1994.

9. Roger Jowell and Richard Topf, "Trust in the Establishment," in Roger Jowell, Sharon Witherspoon, and Lindsay Brook, eds., *British Social Attitudes: The 5th Report* (Brookfield, Vt.: Gower Publishing, 1988). A longer time series asking about the honesty and ethics of members of Parliament is available from British Gallup. In 1982, only 26 percent of the British public gave MPs a low or very low score on this scale, but this increased to 43 percent in 1993. A similar question asked by Canadian Gallup shows an increase in negative sentiments from 39 percent in 1982 to 49 percent in 1992 (Hastings and Hastings, eds., *Index to International Public Opinion* [Westport, Conn.: Greenwood Press, 1994], 312).

10. Ola Listhaug, "The Dynamics of Trust in Politicians," in Hans-Dieter Klingemann and Dieter Fuchs, eds., *Citizens and the State.*

11. Elisabeth Noelle-Neumann and Renate Koecher, *Allensbacher Jahrbuch fuer Demoskopie* (Allensbach, Germany: Allensbach Institute, 1993), 657.

12. Russell J. Dalton, "Political Support in Advanced Industrial Democracies," in Pippa Norris, ed., *Critical Citizens: Global Support for Democratic Government,* 63.

13. Michel Crozier, Samuel P. Huntington, and Joji Watanuki, *The Crisis of Democracy,* 3–9, 161–70.

14. Scott C. Flanagan, Shinsaku Kohei, Ichiro Miyake, Bradley M. Richardson, and Joji Watanuki, *The Japanese Voter* (New Haven: Yale University Press, 1991); Bradley M. Richardson, *The Political Culture of Japan* (Berkeley: University of California Press, 1974).

15. The sharpest deviation from the pattern of declining trust is the Netherlands: The two longest Dutch opinion series show statistically significant improvements between 1971 and 1994. These are the only two statistically significant positive coefficients in the table. We suspect that the Dutch time series begins too late to capture the stable period of Dutch politics before the end of pillarization and the realignment of the party system in the late 1960s (which would be equivalent to U.S. opinion levels before the drop in trust in the late 1960s). For example, in his study of Dutch electoral behavior, Rudy Andeweg maintains that the Provo violence of 1965–66 damaged the legitimacy not just of government authorities but also of authority more generally, and that these patterns continued into the 1970s. Rudy Andeweg, *Dutch Voters Adrift* (Leiden, the Netherlands: University of Leiden, 1982).

16. Elmer Eric Schattschneider, *The Semi-Sovereign People* (New York: Holt, Rinehart and Winston, 1960).

17. Joseph A. Schumpeter, *Capitalism, Socialism, and Democracy,* 4th ed. (London: Allen and Unwin, 1952), 269.

18. Herbert Weisberg, "A Multidimensional Conceptualization of Party Identification," *Political Behavior* 2 (March 1980): 33–60.

19. Russell J. Dalton, Scott C. Flanagan, and Paul Beck, *Electoral Change in Advanced Industrial Democracies* (Princeton, N.J.: Princeton University Press, 1984).

20. Robert D. Putnam, "Bowling Alone: America's Declining Social Capital," *Journal of Democracy* 6 (January 1995): 65–78; Susan Scarrow, "Parties Without Members? Party Organization in a Changing Electoral Environment," in Russell J. Dalton and Martin Wattenberg, eds., *Parties Without Partisans: Political Change in Advanced Industrial Democracies* (Oxford: Oxford University Press, 2000).

21. "The Decline of Party Identifications," in Russell J. Dalton and Martin Wattenberg, eds., *Parties Without Partisans.*

22. Russell J. Dalton, *Citizen Politics: Public Opinion and Political Parties in Advanced Industrial Democracies* (Chatham, N.J.: Chatham House, 1996), 271.

23. Martin Wattenberg, *The Decline of American Political Parties.*

24. Robert Blendon, John M. Benson, Richard Morin, Drew E. Altman, Mollyann Brodie, Mario Brossard, and Matt James, "Changing Attitudes in America," in Joseph S. Nye, Philip D. Zelikow, and David C. King, eds., *Why People Con't Trust Government.*

25. Where possible, we use separate national-survey series because these tend to have a longer time span and more frequent measurements. When such data are not available, we track confidence in parliament on the basis of the 1981 and 1990 World Values Surveys.

26.Russell J. Dalton, "Political Support in Advanced Industrial Democracies" and Ronald Inglehart, "Postmodernization, Authority and Democracy," in Pippa Norris, ed., *Critical Citizens: Global Support for Democratic Government.*

27. Joseph S. Nye, Philip D. Zelikow, and David C. King, eds., *Why People Don't Trust Government;* Pippa Norris, ed., *Critical Citizens: Global Support for Democratic Government.*

28. Joseph S. Nye, Philip D. Zelikow, and David C. King, eds., *Why People Don't Trust Government,* 10–11.

29. By analogy to physical and human capital, some scholars have introduced the term "social capital" to refer to the norms and networks of civil society that enable citizens and their institutions to perform more productively. Without adequate supplies of social capital—that is, without civic engagement, healthy community institutions, norms of mutual reciprocity, and trust—democracies and market economies may begin to falter.

22

LATIN AMERICA AT THE CENTURY'S TURN

Abraham F. Lowenthal

Abraham F. Lowenthal *is the founding president of the Pacific Council on International Policy, an independent, nonpartisan international leadership forum. A professor of international relations at the University of Southern California and a vice president of the Council on Foreign Relations in New York, he was also the founding director of the Inter-American Dialogue, and before that, of the Latin American Program at the Woodrow Wilson Center in Washington, D.C.*

A skeptical, even pessimistic mood has been gathering in and about Latin America. Only two or three years ago, many observers were trumpeting the region's determined march toward free-market economics and constitutional democratic politics. As the new century begins, however, one must recognize the region's lackluster overall economic performance, the reversion toward authoritarian practices in some countries, and the pervasive limits on both free markets and effective democratic governance. It is hard to be upbeat about Latin America and the Caribbean at the century's turn.

This discouraged mood reflects some unpleasant realities: the past year's bleak economic indicators; the concentration of personal authority by presidents Hugo Chávez and Alberto Fujimori in Venezuela and Peru, respectively; the growing strength of insurgent movements in Colombia; and the galloping economic and political deterioration in Ecuador. Yet the disconcerting gap between yesterday's rosy projections and today's gloomy appraisals also derives from three other sources: unrealistic expectations about the pace of economic reform and democratization, unexpected exogenous forces beyond the region's control, and a failure to draw the proper distinctions among countries and subregions whose differences are as great as those among the nations of Europe or Asia. Many of the negative comments being made about Latin America today would carry much-diminished force if observers started with a more appropriate framework, discounted temporary external setbacks, and distinguished more sharply among subregions with extremely diverse experiences.

Taken as a whole, Latin America has experienced a very difficult couple of years, especially by contrast with the previous optimistic projections. After achieving a 5.2 percent expansion in GDP in 1997, the second highest rate of overall annual growth in 20 years, Latin America's economies fell to 2.3 percent growth in 1998—only half a percent above the rate of population increase. The next year was considerably worse for most countries. Latin America and the Caribbean registered no overall growth for 1999.

Ecuador's economy shrank about 7 percent during 1999. Venezuela's dropped 9 percent during the first half of the year, although increases in world petroleum prices then halted the country's free fall. Colombia suffered its worst recession in 60 years, with GDP down 5 percent and unemployment reaching 20 percent. Argentina's economy declined about 3.5 percent, with unemployment at nearly 15 percent. Brazil, once considered South America's economic locomotive, struggled to register any growth for the year. In Chile, for so long a top performer, GDP actually declined by more than 1 percent.

Of the major Latin American economies, only Mexico—closely linked to the United States and benefiting from the U.S. boom as well as from the North American Free Trade Agreement (NAFTA)—had growth above 3 percent in 1999. The Dominican Republic, Costa Rica, Nicaragua, and Trinidad and Tobago also had good years, but their success, too, was largely a consequence of close integration with the U.S. economy.

Several South American countries began to recover in the second half of the year, and there are consensus projections of renewed growth for the whole region this year. The UN Economic Commission for Latin America and the Caribbean and other international agencies predict that overall growth in Latin America during the year 2000 could be as high as 3.6 percent if the U.S. economy remains strong; a hard landing of the U.S. economy, on the other hand, would be very damaging for much of Latin America.

Even if Latin America does rebound, however, the region's overall economic performance has been disappointing by contrast with the expectations aroused in the early 1990s. Despite the much-touted economic reforms in Latin America and the Caribbean, the average annual economic growth rate for the region as a whole during the 1990s was less than 3 percent, or about half what it was in the 1960s and 1970s and well below the 5–6 percent rate needed to reduce poverty. Although the share of Latin Americans officially regarded as in poverty (according to United Nations statistics) declined from 41 percent in 1990 to 36 percent in 1997, even that percentage is as high as it was in 1980. Some 200 million Latin Americans still live in poverty.

Income distribution, long more unequal in Latin America than in any other region, has become even more skewed. The richest 10 percent of Latin America's population receive 40 percent of the region's income, while the poorest 30 percent receive just 7.5 percent. The gap has grown between the "fast caste"—with their cellular phones, Internet connections, walled homes, and private security guards—and those mired in deprivation.

The social and political ramifications of this economic record are alarming. Unemployment and underemployment are up and real wages are falling. Labor conflicts and social protests are expanding. Street crime, kidnapping for profit, and the sale of children are rising. Rejection of established authorities and institutions is growing, and the approval ratings of many incumbent democratic leaders have plummeted. Pressures to emigrate are swelling, even in countries such as Brazil and Colombia, where this has not heretofore been the case.

A particularly troubling repercussion has been the undermining of democratic governance, especially in the Andean region. In Venezuela, Hugo Chávez, a retired army lieutenant colonel who led a bloody failed coup attempt in 1992 and won popular election as president in 1998, has rapidly consolidated enormous personal power by intimidating Congress, restructuring and purging the judiciary in the name of fighting corruption and cronyism, and installing former colleagues from the military in key posts. He convened a Constituent Assembly, popularly elected but hand-picked and with only one representative of the country's two traditional political parties, which put forward a populist draft constitution approved by national plebiscite.

In Peru, Alberto Fujimori, an ethnic outsider, won wide popular backing nearly a decade ago, in part by attacking the traditional elite. He continues to strengthen his grip by repressing dissent, allying himself with a murky military-intelligence network, and keeping the opposition divided and off balance, and he seems determined to override the constitutional barriers to continuing his rule.

In Colombia, Andrés Pastrana, who was elected president in 1998 with strong support, is now widely disparaged, while Marxist insurgent movements and paramilitary counterinsurgency forces are gaining strength. A recent poll shows that 94 percent of Colombians think conditions are deteriorating in their country, and an astounding 60 percent say they would favor a U.S. military intervention to turn things around.

Ecuador has endured a period of economic disarray and partisan political destructiveness, reinforced by mismanagement, that forced the country to default on its Brady Bond debt-repayment obligations. The financial community's stern response has had disastrous consequences for the country's medium-term growth prospects and for its political stability. The military's ouster of President Jamil Mahuad has not ended Ecuador's trauma.

Latin America is indeed lagging—as East Asia begins to recover, Europe gains momentum, and the United States continues to grow. Credit ratings for several major Latin American countries have recently been downgraded, and the cost of capital has consequently risen. Although elected presidents rule in almost every Latin American country, effective democratic governance is unambiguously strong only in Costa Rica and Uruguay (where it was well established 40 years ago), and it is much closer to reality in the Southern Cone than in the Andean region or in most of Central America and the Caribbean. Personal insecurity, pervasive corruption, and tenuous civilian control of the armed forces are grim realities in much of the region.

Cyclical Exaggerations

This sobering précis of Latin America's situation is accurate, as far as it goes, but it may also be somewhat misleading, particularly in its sharp contrast with the glowing depictions circulating just a short time ago. Latin America's external image changes more rapidly and extensively than is warranted, and this volatility adds to the region's difficulties. The widespread international impression that Latin America oscillates between boom and bust (and between dictatorship and democracy) is more an artifact of how both markets and the media work than of underlying realities. Beneath the temporary ups and downs that capture world attention, the significant underlying changes that have occurred in Latin America during the past few years are often underestimated.

Twenty years ago—even ten years ago, at the end of the "lost decade" of the 1980s—Latin America was still widely discussed internationally as a series of "basket cases," of perennial failures supposedly trapped in culture-bound backwardness; the occasional exceptions were either overlooked or explained away. Latin America was frequently (and unflatteringly) compared with North America and East Asia. Latin America's development prospects seemed to be doomed to await a *mañana* that would never come, while Asia's tigers and tiger cubs were ever on the prowl.

Then Latin America, beginning with Chile, turned toward market-oriented economic reforms and greater integration into the world economy. Substantial foreign capital (some $40 billion per year, on average) started to enter the region in the 1990s. Latin America became a favorite for investors specializing in "emerging markets" and for direct investment by a number of multinational firms in agriculture, banking, consumer products, energy, health care, mining, telecommunications, and tourism. Latin America began to be promoted as a region of solid growth and potential boom.

A similar shift could be seen in the external discussion of Latin America's political climate, which had been sharply critical during the

military dictatorships of the late 1970s and early 1980s but then became
highly favorable in the late 1980s and 1990s, as the region turned from
authoritarian rule toward democratic governance. The U.S. government,
in both Republican and Democratic administrations, talked of "the
world's first democratic hemisphere" (with the significant exception of
Fidel Castro's Cuba). Other observers heralded what they saw as a
regional wave of democratization that would create a more uniform and
congenial hemispheric environment.

These flattering portrayals of Latin America oversold what was
actually happening in the region, however, by glossing over major
difficulties and differences. Latin America's immense challenges were
often downplayed in the glow of satisfaction about the region's turn
toward economic reform and democracy.

The Limits of Reform

Latin America's moves toward free-market economics and integration
into the world economy were indeed important paradigm shifts, but
they were not panaceas. After two generations of import-substitution
industrialization and an ever larger state role in economic activity—in
many ways quite successful in promoting the region's growth until the
late 1970s—most Latin American economic policy makers by the mid-
to-late 1980s came to share the view that, to grow further, Latin America
would need to prune the state's economic activities, privatize production
and distribution, attract foreign investment, emphasize exports, and
open itself to international competition. These were major conceptual
changes with considerable practical implications, but they could not,
and did not, all have an immediate positive impact.

To be sure, Latin America has made noteworthy economic progress
in the 1990s, especially in contrast to the 1980s. Growth, although not
robust by Asian standards, was substantial until the region was hit by
the contagion effect of the 1997 Asian economic crisis. In most Latin
American countries, the crippling problem of inflation was confronted
and mainly resolved. Public-sector deficits were dramatically slashed
in many cases, though not in all. Tariffs, subsidies, and other protectionist
devices were cut back sharply. Intraregional trade greatly expanded,
especially in the Mercosur region encompassing Brazil, Argentina, and
their closest neighbors. Many major privatizations occurred, though
some merely replaced public monopolies with private ones or let favored
groups gain great wealth with little risk. Important institutional
reforms—particularly the establishment of autonomous central banks—
were adopted in several countries.

These changes are indeed significant, but it is important to avoid
either exaggerating their immediate effects or ignoring the problems
that remain, some of which are by-products of the reforms themselves.

The regionwide promulgation of the first generation of market-oriented economic reforms—trade liberalization, privatization, deregulation, and the opening to foreign capital—was in a sense deceptively easy. It was stunning that such similar measures could be undertaken in such short order in extremely different countries, often by politicians who had actually campaigned against such reforms. Yet in most cases this convergence owed much more to prevailing international currents, the pressure of international financial institutions, and virtual consensus among international technocrats than to broad-based national accord or unshakable conviction by political leaders. In many countries, these reforms do not yet have solid mass (or even broad middle-class) support. They are still opposed by tenacious vested interests in the bureaucracy, economic sectors that have benefited from protection, and entrenched trade unions—forces that together have succeeded in slowing the implementation of reforms.

It is difficult, if not impossible, for governments to sustain popular backing for programs that may only slowly strengthen the aggregate economy and that seem to enrich a privileged few without providing a credible promise of broad prosperity. Some of the potential constituency for the reform programs has been alienated: Millions of Latin Americans who earlier thought they had entered the middle class have found their real incomes ground down by recession and austerity measures. The first-generation structural reforms might be made more broadly palatable by strong social safety nets and improved public services, yet these are hard to achieve because the reforms themselves—along with years of low growth and fiscal crisis—have eroded the state's capacity to deliver social services. Measures to restore fiscal balance in the late 1980s and early 1990s required cuts in social programs that are only now being rebuilt.

As a result, changes in policy (or at least in pace and emphasis) are beginning to be promoted in several countries where it is generally perceived that income distribution has grown more inequitable, that unemployment is rising, and that social, economic, and ethnic divisions are widening. Parties and leaders critical of the "Washington Consensus" on market-oriented macroeconomic reforms and pledging to alleviate poverty and expand social services won election in Argentina and Chile and came close to winning in Uruguay, although it should also be emphasized that all major contenders in these recent elections endorsed the mainstream thrust of reliance on market capitalism. In Mexico, even if the long-reigning Institutional Revolutionary Party retains the presidency in the July 2000 election, its candidate will, in effect, have run against recent neoliberal economic policies. In Brazil, President Fernando Henrique Cardoso's congressional coalition has weakened, and his cabinet has been divided over how to respond to economic pressures. Brazil's capacity to maintain even its modest pace of economic reform has been cast into doubt.

Although what its critics call "savage capitalism" is under attack in many countries, no broad agreement has been reached on an alternative policy framework. A wholesale reversion to statist approaches, demagogic populism, and fiscal irresponsibility is unlikely, but so is the unrelieved application of neoliberal orthodoxy. Instead, new approaches are beginning to emerge, rooted in market economics but including a stronger state role in improving and extending education, public health, and social services, as well as in alleviating poverty and reducing inequality.

It remains to be seen, however, whether detailed and coherent "third way" programs that foster improved equity together with economic expansion can be designed and successfully implemented, and where the resources will come from to undertake what is promised. Populist appeals and programs may yet emerge in some countries, with likely negative consequences for both foreign and domestic investment.

Latin America's transition to international competitiveness is far from complete or irreversible. The reforms that have been undertaken are still tentative and vulnerable in many settings, and the needed "second generation" of complementary reforms—dealing with such institutional, political, and social issues as the justice system, transparency, the professionalization of independent regulatory agencies, and education—have been hard to initiate, particularly within the context of anemic growth.

The regional turn to democracy, though real, has also been oversold. The emergence of broad regional accord on the goal of constitutional democracy has certainly been striking. It is now widely accepted in Latin America that, to be legitimate, government authority must derive from the uncoerced consent of the majority, tested regularly through fair, competitive, and broadly participatory elections. Elections have become the rule in Latin America, and attempted military coups are now rare (and successful coups even more so); multilateral pressure to maintain constitutional procedures has been legitimized. Those with authoritarian impulses in Latin America today must pay lip service to democracy as an established norm.

Beyond the explicit acceptance of constitutional democracy as the goal and the repeated conduct of reasonably free and fair elections, there have been other undeniably positive changes in Latin America's politics since the early 1980s. The press and nongovernmental organizations play more important roles. There are considerably greater scope and representation for indigenous peoples, and the space for diversity of various kinds has grown. Women have substantially expanded their participation and influence in politics. The protection of human rights, both civil and social, has been strongly enhanced, albeit unevenly. Central America has turned away from civil wars toward peaceful political competition. "Effective suffrage," so long an empty slogan, is finally becoming a reality in Mexico.

Rather than riding a great and inexorable wave of democratization, however, many Latin American countries are still battling a strong undertow that threatens to halt, or even reverse, democratic advance. In a number of Latin American countries—especially in the Andean region—authoritarian practices today coexist with democratic forms or threaten to overturn democratic rule.

In country after country, polls show that most people, although they still say they favor "democracy," are increasingly critical of the performance of democratic governmments and deeply skeptical of all democratic political institutions. This is especially true in countries where the narcotics trade and other lucrative criminal enterprises corrupt and undermine government, where guerilla violence challenges state authority, where public order and personal security are flagrantly lacking, and where the rule of law is often flouted. Sustained political stability based on valued democratic institutions cannot be achieved where there is no accountability. The hard truth is that constitutional democracy is not yet truly being consolidated in most of Latin America, in many cases because it is yet to be constructed, in others because it has proven painfully inadequate. Peru, Ecuador, Haiti, and Paraguay are examples of the first class of countries; Colombia and Venezuela, of the second.

Although Latin America has moved a long way from statist economies and authoritarian politics, it will take many more years of strenuous effort and sustained institution-building if efficient market economies and robust democratic governance are ever to be achieved. It should not be surprising that most of Latin America is still far from these goals. Even in the advanced industrial nations where market capitalism and constitutional democracy function best, it took many decades to build successful institutions, and constant vigilance is still required to protect them from abuse or manipulation. And in Latin America, unlike most of the successful industrial democracies, highly stratified social structures with vast disparities of power and wealth make it all the harder to build both democracy and markets.

External Forces

Latin America's disappointing pace in achieving economic progress and democratic governance also reflects the impact of strong and unexpected external forces beyond the region's control.

Because the globalization of finance and trade, combined with the communications revolution, makes it possible for market uncertainties to provoke financial turbulence far from the initial crisis, Latin America's growing integration into the world economy has ironically made the region more vulnerable to external shocks. Thailand's inability to protect the baht in mid-1997 detonated a series of currency destabilizations, later reinforced by Russia's meltdown in mid-1998. These had strong negative repercussions, direct and indirect, for most of Latin America: skittishness about portfolio investments in emerging markets; pressures to sell Latin American securities to cover losses elsewhere; shrinking markets for Latin American exports, especially in hard-hit Asia, which had only recently become a growing market for the most competitive Latin American producers; and declining commodity prices, due mainly to the general international recession. A steep drop in oil prices hit Venezuela, Ecuador, Mexico, and Colombia with particular force in 1998 and the first half of 1999. Prices for virtually all Latin American primary exports—copper, iron, tin, coffee, bananas, soybeans, and various other agricultural commodities—have also dropped, some to their lowest value in real terms in a century. Latin America has been hurt both by economic slowdown in many of its export markets and by renewed protectionism in developed countries.

A second exogenous strain on Latin America's recent development has come from horrific weather: a particularly nasty *El Niño* that lashed Ecuador and Peru; Mitch, the century's worst hurricane, which devastated much of Central America; Hurricane Georges, which caused heavy damage in the Dominican Republic; a major earthquake in the main coffee-producing region of Colombia; and devastating floods in Venezuela.

A third external constraint, less immediate in its impact but nonetheless significant, has been the failure of the U.S. government to deliver on its promises (made at the Miami Summit of the Americas in December 1994) to incorporate Chile into NAFTA, to secure NAFTA parity for the Caribbean and Central American economies, and to encourage brisk progress toward a Free Trade Area of the Americas (FTAA) that would create an integrated market from Alaska to Patagonia. Despite dozens of conferences, working groups, studies, and reports, little concrete progress has been made on these three points. This is largely because the U.S. Congress, reflecting American public opinion, has been skeptical about the advantages of NAFTA and of FTAA for the United States, and the Clinton administration has been unwilling to invest its dwindling political capital in this cause. Those in Latin America who based their arguments for reforms on the premise of a hemispheric common market have been set back, and the prospect that the FTAA will help to "lock in" these reforms is waning.

Regional Differences

Perhaps most important, the contrast between recent triumphalism and current concerns about Latin America also arises from the tendency to generalize too broadly about the region, drawing on evidence from one country to interpret another. Latin American and Caribbean nations range from ministates to a mega-country. They include states whose inhabitants are almost exclusively of European origin, others with a strong African presence, and still others with large and not yet fully integrated indigenous populations. Some Latin American countries have abundant natural resources, while others have few. Some developed strong civilian political institutions decades ago, while others did not. Such differences have made Argentina as different from Haiti, or Peru as different from Panama, as Sweden is from Turkey, or Australia from Indonesia. Latin American and Caribbean countries are not alike, and they are not simply evolving at different rates, ineluctably going through the same stages of development in a prescribed order. Their paths have diverged and may diverge still further in the future.

This growing differentiation is particularly true along four dimensions: 1) the nature and degree of economic and demographic interdependence with the United States; 2) the extent to which they have committed their economies to international competition; 3) the relative capacity of the state; and 4) the strength of democratic institutions.

1) Interdependence with the United States. The differences that have long existed between the Caribbean Basin region and South America have been very strongly reinforced in the past 15 years. Although Ronald Reagan's Caribbean Basin Initiative and NAFTA have been partly responsible for this reinforced bifurcation, these measures were actually more consequences than causes of a long-term process of functional integration—economic, demographic, social, cultural, and to some extent, even political—between the United States and its nearest neighbors.

The ongoing "silent integration" between Mexico and the United States has now become boisterous and irreversible. Eighty-five percent of Mexico's trade is now with the United States, which is the market for 88 percent of Mexico's exports. The U.S. dollar is the unofficial currency for substantial parts of the country. Remittances from Mexicans in the United States amount to some $7–8 billion a year, nearly as much as foreign direct investment (FDI) in a period when FDI has been at record levels. The burgeoning flow of Mexican migrants, documented and undocumented, into the United States continues. During the past 30 years, the border between Mexico and the United States has blurred, particularly in California. Today, for example, two-thirds of the students in the public schools of Los Angeles County are Latino, most of them of Mexican origin.

The integration of the Caribbean and Central American nations with the United States is less widely noted, but equally dramatic. U.S. exports to the Caribbean Basin Initiative countries rose by more than 200 percent from 1983 to 1997, reaching $19 billion in that year, almost $6 billion more than exports to China—and this is all before NAFTA parity legislation, which will significantly further expand Caribbean Basin trade.

The demographic aspect of Caribbean Basin interdependence with the United States is also striking. It is well known that some 10 percent of Cuba's population has come to the United States since Fidel Castro took over, but immigration from the Dominican Republic, Haiti, and Jamaica account for 12, 14, and 15 percent of those countries' populations, respectively. Los Angeles has become as linked to Central America as is Miami, which in many ways is the capital of the whole Caribbean Basin region. Central American and Caribbean immigrants in the United States provide the largest source of foreign exchange to their home countries through remittances, but they also bring home crime and gang warfare. The politics and culture of the home countries and the U.S. mainland are increasingly intertwined.

During the next 25 years, the Caribbean and Central American nations are likely to become even more fully absorbed into the U.S. orbit: using the dollar as their currencies; sending almost all their exports to the United States; relying largely on U.S. tourists, investment, imports, and technology; absorbing U.S. popular culture and fashions; sending migrants northward; and developing baseball players for the North American major leagues (and perhaps eventually fielding major-league teams of their own). All these statements will probably also apply to Cuba in time, perhaps sooner rather than later.

Mexico, Central America, and most of the Caribbean countries are by now so closely tied to the United States on so many fronts that their futures are to a very large degree conditioned by what happens on the mainland and by U.S. policies. Generalizations about the Caribbean Basin frequently do not apply to South America, and vice versa, because of the former's extraordinary degree of interdependence with the United States.

The countries of South America, and especially of the Mercosur region, by contrast, have much more diverse regional and international relationships, both political and economic. Some of these are as significant as their links with the United States, or indeed, more so. While the closest neighbors of the United States have accelerated their functional integration with North America, the countries of the Southern Cone have been cultivating closer commercial, financial, and political relationships in Europe and Asia—and especially among themselves. The past few years have seen an extraordinary increase in the linkages among Southern Cone nations: private sector investments in one another's countries, educational exchanges, the growth of transnational associations of various kinds, and physical integration through hydroelectric projects, highways, and other infrastructure.

In the Andean countries, by contrast, there has been much less regional integration with the United States, less success in developing international ties in Europe and Asia, and less subregional integration. Although Venezuela continues to be closely tied to the United States by petroleum exports, U.S. commercial, financial, and investment links with Peru, Colombia, Ecuador, and Bolivia have slowed compared with those involving the Caribbean Basin, Brazil, and the Southern Cone.

Peru, Bolivia, and Colombia, however, are most salient for the United States in one unfortunate dimension—narcotics.

2) Integration into the world economy. A second key distinction among Latin American countries lies in their degree of commitment to the process of international integration. Chile, Bolivia, Argentina, and Peru have moved the farthest toward international competitiveness; Venezuela and Ecuador, the least. Brazil and Mexico have both traveled some distance, but quite unevenly. Mexico has no viable policy option other than to proceed toward an open economy because of its high level of interdependence with the United States, but Brazil still faces unresolved policy choices that will continue to be fought out between contending parties, regions, and policy elites in the coming months and years. Brazil alone accounts for about 40 percent of Latin America's total economic production, so its course is crucially important both for its immediate neighbors and for Latin America as a whole.

3) The capacity of the state. A third important variation concerns the strength of the state, and particularly whether public authorities are powerful enough to combat crime effectively. In Colombia, Panama, Paraguay, parts of the Caribbean, and some regions of Mexico and Brazil, a desperate struggle is underway between the state and criminal elements, particularly in the narcotics trade. High financial stakes are often involved, overwhelming the integrity of fragile institutions, including the police and the judiciary. The increasing involvement of armed forces in trying to redress the balance introduces new elements of strain and new sources of danger to democratic political institutions, and the specter of expanding U.S. involvement raises yet another troubling dimension. Generalizations about Latin America that ignore these unpleasant realities are badly misleading.

4) The strength of democratic institutions. The countries of Latin America and the Caribbean also vary enormously with regard to the autonomy and efficacy of their political institutions. Apart from the special case of Costa Rica, political institutions are most highly developed in the countries of the Southern Cone, as has been amply demonstrated by the recent elections in Argentina, Chile, and Uruguay.[1] In each of those countries, long-established political parties and an enduring political culture have combined to consolidate political democracy. The electoral process has reinforced public confidence in democratic governance and has pushed both political discourse and proposed economic and social policies toward the center. Politics has become less exciting but far more constructive in countries that only a generation ago were bitterly and brutally divided.

Brazil, historically less well endowed with established political parties and institutions, has also made significant strides toward effective democratic governance in recent years. The Congress has become a strong branch of government, the judiciary has been strengthened, and presidential authority has both grown and been more effectively constrained. Party discipline and political accountability are still limited, but the makings of a viable presidential system are emerging, encouraged in part by the important roles played by the media and other organizations of civil society.

Mexico, long subject to an entrenched authoritarian system, has changed remarkably in the past decade. At the beginning of a new century, Mexico has competitive political parties, increasingly fair electoral procedures, more independent media and public opinion, stronger civic institutions, a clearer separation of powers among different branches of government, and considerable decentralization and devolution of public authority. But while Mexico's past politics has been shattered, the shape of the new Mexico is not yet determined, especially because the rule of law is still spotty and uneven, the judicial system remains weak, and impunity is stronger than accountability.

The Caribbean and Central American countries vary enormously with regard to the strength of their democratic institutions, but most are struggling—with varying degrees of success—to increase the autonomy of legislatures and judiciaries, to encourage the building of political parties and independent associations, and to secure civilian control of the armed forces.

The Andean countries—particularly Colombia, Venezuela, Peru, and Ecuador—all are facing grave crises of governance, as manifested in the discrediting of established institutions, parties, and ruling elites, public distrust of virtually all sources of authority, and an accelerating deterioration of civic life. The rise of authoritarian leaders in Peru and Venezuela has been a response to turbulent conditions also evident in Colombia and Ecuador, where similar turns toward authoritarianism cannot be ruled out.

Given all this variety, along so many different dimensions, discussions of Latin America's medium-term prospects must be more specific and precise than is usually the case in the international media and even among investment analysts. Business decisions must be made country by country, sector by sector, and firm by firm. Public policy decisions, too, need to be much more specifically calibrated than familiar discussions of "Latin America" permit. The very term "Latin America" probably obscures as much as it illuminates at this point.

Common Challenges

In spite of its enormous and in some ways increasing diversity, Latin America as a whole faces several broadly shared challenges and dilemmas. First is the central problem of equity—the vast imbalances of wealth, income, and power that have long characterized most of Latin America and the Caribbean and, at least for the time being, have been exacerbated, not alleviated, by the market reforms of the 1990s. Just when it has become unfashionable to talk about class, the divisions in Latin America have widened. Even if the most optimistic projections by international agencies about the region's growth in the next decade turn out to be correct, income distribution may become even more inequitable. If unaddressed, this polarization could become social and political dynamite, especially where resentment about gross inequalities is heightened by rampant corruption, crime, and personal insecurity. Programs to alleviate extreme poverty, improve tax collection, facilitate credit for microenterprises, and provide broader access to social services are thus all crucial for Latin America's future.

A second and closely linked problem is that of achieving improved accountability and a more consistent implementation of the rule of law. Neither political democracy nor market capitalism can develop well without independent judiciaries, civilian control of the armed forces and police, broad access to information, autonomous and effective regulatory agencies, and other institutional constraints on executive power. Even more than economic policies, investment, or physical infrastructure, the "software" of effective governance is key.

Third, there is a growing consensus in Latin America that expanded political participation, stronger growth, and improved equity all depend upon major improvements in education. Substantially increased and well-targeted investments are needed to assure that the changing technologies shaping the world economy do not leave an underclass of the uneducated further and further behind. It is crucial to improve basic education; to upgrade teaching and standards; to make secondary education more widely available, especially for girls; to train and retrain workers for a more technological economy; and to redirect resources from upper-class entitlement programs to those with broader benefits.

Fourth, all Latin American and Caribbean nations—coming from different starting points and at different speeds—are groping to fashion ways to combine market instruments and the requirements of investment capital with greater attention to the grave social problems that markets do not resolve by themselves. Those Latin American nations most devoted to market reforms need to confront this issue—but so does Cuba, which is turning by fits and starts toward capitalist mechanisms after 40 years of emphasizing social welfare and equity.

Latin Americans today have painful choices to make. It is not easy to balance the gains from interdependence with the costs to autonomy and sovereignty. It is hard to reconcile the advantages of global economic and political integration with the risks of vulnerability. The requirements of capital accumulation (and investment) and those of equity do sometimes conflict. So do the imperatives of political and economic liberalization, for the demands of economic elites and the claims of an impatient populace may be contradictory, at least in the short and medium term. Building and maintaining the coalitions necessary to manage all these tensions successfully requires statesmanship, and that skill remains in short supply everywhere.

A Sense of Perspective

It is by no means clear at the century's turn whether or when the various Latin American and Caribbean countries will be able to turn the many corners that must be successfully negotiated to achieve sustainable economic development together with effective and enduring democratic governance. The euphoria about Latin America sometimes propagated in recent years by emerging-market funds, investment-promotion boards, and a number of prominent editorial pages was as unjustified as the earlier and often indiscriminate tendency to dismiss Latin America as hopelessly behind.

Yet thoughtless pessimism should also be avoided. Latin America's current difficulties need not touch off a new cycle of decline. If they do, it will be in part because understandable frustration within the region, together with exaggerated and excessively broad-brush concerns abroad (in the United States, Canada, Europe, and Japan), produce self-fulfilling prophecies by drastically slowing capital inflows.

The effects on Latin America of financial crises detonated elsewhere in the world need not always be dire. Indeed, they could ultimately turn out to be positive for those Latin American countries that can show that they are better prepared than Asia's tigers or the postcommunist nations to ride out the next set of storms because they have built sounder financial and political institutions.

In a world of rude surprises, many Latin American nations have made enormous headway in recent years. International recognition of both Latin America's extraordinary diversity and its substantial progress, along with a better sense of perspective about its periodic setbacks, would improve the region's chances for further success. So would a sharper and more committed focus, both within and outside the region, on equity, education, and governance as the next century's indispensable agenda. These tough challenges must be confronted effectively if Latin America is to resume its forward momentum.

NOTE

1. See Steven Levitsky, "The 'Normalization' of Argentine Politics," *Journal of Democracy* 11 (April 2000): 56–69; Arturo Fontaine Talavera, "Chile's Elections: The New Face of the Right," *Journal of Democracy* 11 (April 2000): 70–77; Manuel Antonio Garretón, "Chile's Elections: Change and Continuity," *Journal of Democracy* 11 (April 2000): 78–84; and Jeffrey Cason, "Electoral Reform and Stability in Uruguay," *Journal of Democracy* 11 (April 2000): 85–98.

23

THE POSTCOMMUNIST DIVIDE

Jacques Rupnik

Jacques Rupnik is director of research at the Centre d'Etudes et de Recherches Internationales in Paris. He is the author of Les Balkans: Paysage après la bataille *(1996) and* Le Déchirement des nations *(1995) and the editor with François Fejtö of* Le printemps tchécoslovaque 1968 *(1998).*

Ten years after the collapse of the Soviet empire, one thing is clear: The word "postcommunism" has lost its relevance. The fact that Hungary and Albania, or the Czech Republic and Belarus, or Poland and Kazakhstan shared a communist past explains very little about the paths that they have taken since. Indeed, it is striking how vastly different the outcomes of the democratic transitions have been in Central and Eastern Europe. Nonetheless, certain patterns do emerge. A new tripartite political geography of formerly communist Europe is emerging: a new Central Europe (the so-called Visegrád group, the Baltic countries, and Slovenia) as a clear "success story"; the Balkans, where the democratic transition has often been derailed by the priorities of nation-state building or undermined by the legacies of communism and economic backwardness; and Russia, in search of a postimperial identity and teetering on the brink of economic disaster. (The fate of democratizaton in Ukraine, Belarus, and Moldova will to a large extent depend on what happens in Russia.)

Shortly after the collapse of the communist system, Ralf Dahrendorf identified three interrelated areas of change with different "timetables": political democracy and the rule of law (six months), the conversion to a market economy (six years), and the emergence of a civil society (six decades). Almost a decade later, it appears that so far the new political elites in Central Europe have successfully met the challenge posed by the disjunctive time spans of these three processes of change. They have established parliamentary democracy as the only game in town, creating a constitutional framework and political institutions that are seen as legitimate by all political actors; moreover, the formation of a relatively stable party system, allowing for smooth alternation in power, by now has taken place everywhere in Central Europe. A market economy has been established, with more than half of GNP produced in the private sector and over three quarters of trade now conducted with the OECD countries. A civil society is developing, with both its economic dimension (emerging new strata of entrepreneurs) and its networks of nongovernmental organizations (NGOs).

This picture contrasts not only with the former Soviet Union (the Baltic states excepted) but also with the Balkans. The most extreme case of a "derailed" transition, of course, is former the Yugoslavia, because of the war and the breakup of the Federation into several successor states whose legitimacy and viability are still being questioned. The legitimacy of the territorial framework clearly remains the first prerequisite for a democratic transition.

To be sure, the situation in the Balkans should not be seen solely through the prism of the Yugoslav war and ethnonationalist conflict. There have been encouraging developments in both Bulgaria and Romania. In the former, the winter of discontent (1996–97), culminating in the ransacking of Parliament, forced the incompetent and corrupt ex-communist government to step down and call for an early election, opening the way for much delayed economic reforms. In Romania, a belated alternation in power ("We have lost seven years," said President Constantinescu when taking over from Iliescu) saw the ex-communists replaced by a right-wing coalition, although after two years in power it has produced little or no reform. If the contrast between the Central European and Balkan models can be summed up as that between democratic consolidation and the rise of "illiberal democracies," then Romania and Bulgaria (as well as Slovakia) are in an intermediate position.

There is, of course, no single factor that accounts for this process of differentiation. One can only point to a combination of factors, explanations, or hypotheses that can help make sense of the uneven progress of the democratic transition in the region.

1) The legacies of communism. More important than the manner of the changeover in 1989–91 (gradual or sudden, negotiated from above or imposed from below) in influencing the longer-term prospects for democratic success are the nature of the old communist regime and the depth of its imprint on society. The harshest totalitarian domination in the postwar period tended to be in the Balkans (Albania, Romania, Bulgaria), whereas a greater degree of reform and accommodation was characteristic of the post-1956 regimes in Poland and Hungary. Of course, the contrasting cases of relatively liberal Yugoslavia (since the 1960s) and of "normalized" Czechoslovakia after 1968 show the limits of such a generalization.

Nonetheless, it is instructive to examine the nature of the pre-1989 crises of communism in the two regions. In Central Europe, communism experienced three major crises (the 1956 Hungarian revolution, the Prague Spring in 1968, and the rise of Poland's Solidarity movement in 1980–81) that posed primarily the issue of democracy and civil society, and only in a second phase (under growing external constraint) that of national independence. By contrast, the three major crises of communism in the Balkans (Tito's 1948 break with Stalin, Hoxha's 1961 switch of allegiance from Moscow to Peking, and Ceauşescu's 1968 bid for foreign policy independence) all stressed the autonomy of the national communist apparatus vis-à-vis Moscow, while reinforcing the totalitarian features of the regime. The origins of the rebirth of civil society in Central Europe go back to the region's three major crises, as well as to the dissident movements of the 1970s and 1980s. The origins of "nationalism as the final stage of communism" (Adam Michnik's phrase) in the Balkans owe a great deal to the legacies of Tito, Hoxha, and Ceauşescu. Similarly, the emergence of alternative political elites during and in the immediate aftermath of 1989 in Central Europe owes a great deal to the existence of organized democratic opposition movements. These were largely lacking in Southeastern Europe, where the first free elections were all won by the ex-communist parties.

2) Market and civil society. "No bourgeoisie, no democracy." Barrington Moore's famous phrase provides a second clue for a comparative assessment of the democratic transitions in Central and Eastern Europe. There were, of course, differences due to the uneven level of economic development dating back to the precommunist period or the degree of economic reform pursued in the decaying phase of communism (here Hungary and Poland were the frontrunners, while Romania and Bulgaria lagged behind). The most striking contrast, however, is between those who after 1989 embarked on radical market reforms and those who chose gradualism or simply the postponement of market reforms and privatization.

The results are fairly clear, not only in terms of the relative size of the private sector, but also in foreign trade, growth rates, and the level of foreign investment (nearly half of direct investment in Central and Eastern Europe went to Hungary alone). There are one million registered private entrepreneurs in the Czech Republic and over 800,000 in Hungary. The emergence of new middle classes is also related to the progress of the "information revolution" and the formidable expansion of the service sector, areas where "human capital" is rewarded. (Before 1989, less than a third of Czechs believed that education was related to success; today almost two-thirds do.) The development of these middle strata, along with the conversion (through the privatization process) of part of the old *nomenklatura* into the new bourgeoisie, provides the backbone of the new market.

As for civil society, a term that emerged within the dissident movement in the late 1970s, it was originally understood as a self-organizing alternative society (a "parallel polis," as Václav Benda put it in 1978) in opposition to totalitarian rule. After the collapse of the latter, the concept acquired two new meanings relevant to the democratic transition. The first, prevalent in Central Europe among "liberals on the right," tended to identify it with the above described economic revolution. This is civil society as *Bürgergesellschaft,* secured by the market economy.

The second definition of civil society, prevalent among "liberals on the left," divorced the term almost completely from the market economy and identified it with the so-called third sector, that is, NGOs. According to this view, civil society is distinct from both state and market. The NGO is doubly pure, corrupted neither by power (that is, politics) nor by money (that is, the market). Civil society understood in terms of the first definition is more developed in Central Europe, while the NGO sector has been relatively more important to the transition in Southeastern Europe, where it can help compensate for the weakness of both the middle class and of political opposition to semi-authoritarian rule (Romania under Iliescu, ex-Yugoslavia). In the 1998 elections in Slovakia, which after 1993 seemed to be drifting away from the Central European model, the "third sector" demonstrated how effective it can be in mobilizing society and helping the opposition to overcome the "democratic deficit."

3) The rule of law and the "Habsburg factor." The recent debate about "illiberal democracies" has usefully reemphasized the crucial importance of the rule of law for democratic consolidation, a relationship that is underscored by the experience of the past decade. Although all generalizations are also exaggerations, one can say that the rule of law, constitutionalism, and the existence of an independent judiciary are undoubtedly more developed in Central Europe than in the Balkans. Explanations for this fact can be sought in specific political circumstances and in the degree of receptivity of the new elites to Western models of the separation of powers.

There is another factor, however, that warrants mention in this connection: the legacy of the Austrian as opposed to the Ottoman empire. It may be going too far to call the Habsburg Empire liberal, but neither was it an autocracy like Czarist Russia. It was a *Rechtsstaat,* that is, a state run by the rule of law. Indeed Austrian turn-of-the-century literature (from Musil and Roth to Broch and Kafka) is dominated by the question of the law, the tension between legitimacy and legality. That Habsburg legacy of the rule of law has influenced several of its Central European successor states, as reflected in their legal scholarship, public administration, and political culture more generally. It was already being rediscovered in the last phase of communism, as the rulers began to accept some limitations on their powers and the opposition began to challenge their rule in the name of accepted domestic and international legal commitments. The 1990s have confirmed the trend. The weakness of the rule of law in the former Habsburg domains of Slovakia and Croatia qualifies but does not invalidate the general argument.

4) Nation-state building and "homogeneity." The return of democracy in 1989 was inseparable from the return of the nation: Popular sovereignty and national sovereignty became indistinguishable. In this respect, 1989 followed in the footsteps of 1848 and 1918, reaffirming the idea that the nation-state is the natural and most favorable framework for democracy. The demise of federalism inherited from communism in the Soviet Union, Yugoslavia, and Czechoslovakia seemed to validate this conviction. But a preoccupation with building the nation-state can also work against democracy and the rule of law, as we have seen in the former Yugoslavia. This classic dilemma was described by the Hungarian thinker István Bibo at the end of World War II in his essay on *The Misery of the Small Nations of Eastern Europe:* "Fascism exists in germ everywhere where, following a cataclysm or an illusion, the cause of the nation separates from that of freedom." The fear that freedom and democracy will "threaten the cause of the nation" was a major impediment to democracy during the interwar period and has no doubt been an important factor in the sidetracking of the democratic transition after 1989 in the Balkans.

One reason why Central Europe has been less troubled by the national question than Southeastern Europe is that today its populations are more homogeneous (and where they are not, as in Slovakia, is precisely where the transition has been least successful). Poland, where minorities once comprised a third of the population, today is a homogeneous state; this dream of Poland's old nationalist right was realized with the help of Hitler and Stalin. Similarly, the Czech Republic today is without Jews, Germans, and now even Slovaks. Alone at last! Slovenia, the only Yugoslav successor state where the democratic transition fits the Central European pattern, also does not have a significant minority population. In short, in Central Europe "ethnic cleansing" was completed half a century ago, whereas in the Balkans the process of "homogeneous" nation-state building is still under way. This, as Ernest Gellner once put it, is purely a description, not a prescription. It would be absurd to suggest that ethnic "homogeneity" is a prerequisite for democracy. Yet the contrasting situation in this respect of Central Europe and the Balkans accounts at least in part for the different fates of their democratic transitions.

5) Culture. This is one of the oldest arguments about the development of democracy, going back to Max Weber's classic thesis about the Protestant ethic and the spirit of capitalism. In looking at the balance sheet of the democratic transition in Central and Eastern Europe, is there a case for pushing the Weberian thesis one notch further and suggesting a correlation between Western Christianity and democratic success (Central Europe), or between Orthodox Christianity and difficulty in achieving democratic and market-oriented change? The argument revolves around the issue of whether the subordination of the Church to the State and the close identification between religion and ethnicity in Orthodox Christianity poses a significant obstacle to the emergence of a democratic public space and a civil society.

This whole subject has become politically loaded since the publication of Samuel Huntington's thesis about the "clash of civilizations," which has many ardent disciples in the Balkans and has been widely used and abused in analyzing not only the war in Bosnia but the goals of Western policy. Fortunately, democratic difficulties in Catholic Slovakia and Croatia (as well as encouraging developments in Orthodox Romania and Bulgaria) tend to disprove Huntington's thesis. My response to this controversy is both to reject cultural determinism (especially when reduced to its religious dimension) as misleading or politically dangerous, but also to avoid the kind of political correctness that would make Max Weber's classic sociological question taboo.

6) The international environment. The international environment, at least so far, has been exceptionally favorable to the democratic transition in Central Europe: Russia is weak and its sphere of influence shrinking; Germany is powerful but democratic and integrated in both the EU and NATO; and there are no significant regional conflicts. This favorable combination of factors, unprecedented in Central European history, contrasts with the instability in the Balkans—not merely the wars in the former Yugoslavia, but the collapse of the Albanian state at the very moment that the Kosovo issue is intensifying, and the latent Greek-Turkish rivalry.

This divergence is reinforced by the prospects of "Euro-Atlantic" integration, the Central European code word for the double enlargement of NATO and the EU. Both institutions insist on democracy as a condition for membership (and, as the case of Slovakia showed, they mean it). On the whole, it can be argued that both these institutions embodying democratic Western values have been preoccupied primarily with the integration of Central Europe. No Balkan country is high on the list of candidates for either NATO or the EU. It remains to be seen what impact the noninclusion of Romania and Bulgaria will have on the democratic process in those countries. Thus far the differentiation in the enlargement process between the "ins" and the "outs" has largely been a consequence of the relative success of their democratic transitions. In the future, however, the enlargement process itself could help to undermine the democratic transition precisely where it is most fragile.

24

PUTIN'S RUSSIA: ONE STEP FORWARD, TWO STEPS BACK

Michael McFaul

Michael McFaul *is a senior associate at the Carnegie Endowment for International Peace and an assistant professor of political science at Stanford University. His latest book is* Russia's Unfinished Revolution: Political Change From Gorbachev to Putin *(2001).*

Russia's March 2000 presidential election represents one step forward and two steps back for Russian democracy. For the first time in Russia's history, power within the Kremlin has changed hands through an electoral process. The election not only took place but was conducted as constitutionally prescribed, no small achievement for a country with Russia's authoritarian history. More than two-thirds of the eligible voters participated, and they appeared to make informed choices among a range of candidates who offered competing platforms, policies, and leadership styles. The election, however, was not contested on a level playing field. The winner, acting president Vladimir Putin, enjoyed tremendous advantages that tainted the process. Although weak in some arenas, the Russian state still enjoys too much power with respect to the electoral process, while nongovernmental forces—political parties, civic organizations, trade unions, and independent business groups—remain too weak to shape the outcomes of elections.

Does this latest election represent a fundamental turn away from democratic practices or merely a temporary setback for democratic consolidation in Russia? It is too early to tell. Putin may turn out to be Russia's Milošević. Or he may develop into a weak leader presiding over a feudal order, dominated by oligarchs and regional barons, in which the people have little say. Yet it is also possible that he will lead Russia out of its chaotic, revolutionary, and anarchic recent past into a more stable decade of economic growth and political stability—and economic growth and political stability can help consolidate democratic institutions. Thus far, Putin has provided mixed signals about the direction in which he wants to take Russia and has demonstrated a real indifference to democracy. Consequently, the only honest assessment to be made at this stage is that democracy in Russia is not lost, but its future remains uncertain.

Why Putin Won

The first step in coming to grips with post-Yeltsin Russia is to understand why Putin won. The election reveals much about the evolution of Russia's political system and the mood of Russian society.

The simple explanation goes like this: Putin was chosen by Yeltsin and his band of oligarchs as a loyal successor who would keep them out of jail and preserve the existing system of oligarchic capitalism, in which oligarchs make money not by producing or selling goods and services but by stealing from the state. To boost Putin's popularity in order to get him elected, they had to provoke a war with Chechnya. Some assert that this cabal was even responsible for blowing up apartment buildings in Moscow and elsewhere last fall—crimes that were attributed to Chechen terrorists—as a way to bolster support for the war and Putin. This "popular" war, however, could sustain Putin only for so long. Therefore Yeltsin resigned on 31 December 1999 to allow the presidential election to take place three months earlier. As acting president, Putin had at his disposal all the resources of the Russian state, which he wielded to win a convincing election victory.

There is much truth to this simple account, but it is only part of the story. To see the fuller picture, one must reexamine the role of the war in Chechnya and bring other actors into the analysis, including the voters and the other presidential candidates.

1) The Chechen war. Why do we always think that the people in the Kremlin are so smart and everyone else in Russia is so dumb? In the summer of 1999, no one believed that a quick little war with the Chechens would be the formula for delivering electoral success the following year. On the contrary, when Yeltsin ordered the Russian military to respond to the Chechen incursion into Dagestan in August 1999, most electoral analysts in Russia thought that the counteroffensive would result in another unpopular military debacle.[1] If the entire event was staged to assist Putin's electoral prospects, then Shamil Basaev—the Chechen commander who led the military intervention in Dagestan aimed at freeing the people there from Russian imperialism—must be either a traitor to his people or a fool. Basaev, it should be remembered, is the same Chechen commander who in August 1995 led the raid on Budennovsk in southern Russia, killed hundreds of Russian citizens, seized a Russian hospital, and then escaped. His record in the field suggests that he is neither a traitor nor a fool.

Basaev did, however, overestimate the anti-imperial sentiment in

Dagestan and underestimate the determination of the Russian state to respond. Putin, then prime minister, acted decisively, with the blessing of Boris Yeltsin. Everyone who has discussed the Chechen war with Putin personally will tell you that he expresses real passion only about his resolve to "destroy the Chechen terrorists." In the summer of 1999, for the first time since 1941, a military force invaded Russia. It is excessively cynical to argue that the Russian military response to this incursion was motivated solely by electoral calculations. Terrorist attacks on apartment buildings in Moscow and elsewhere shortly after the invasion made the Russian people feel like a nation under siege. Society demanded a response from its leaders, and Putin responded.

What was different about this particular response was its apparent "success." In the first Chechen war, the Russian forces appeared to be losing the war from the outset, in part because they performed so miserably and in part because the rationale for the war was not embraced by either the Russian army or the population as a whole. Independent media, led by NTV, a nationwide television network owned by Media-Most, reported on military setbacks and questioned Russia's war aims. After several months of fighting, a solid majority in Russia did not support the war.[2] Compelled by electoral concerns, Yeltsin called for a ceasefire in April 1996 and then allowed his envoy, Aleksandr Lebed, to broker a temporary settlement with the Chechen government. The second war started under very different circumstances. First, the Russian military and the Russian people believed that the rationale for this war was self-defense. A majority of Russian citizens supported the counter-offensive from the very beginning and have continued to support the invasion of Chechnya throughout the military campaign. Second, the Russian army used different tactics in this campaign, relying on air power to a much greater extent than in the first war. The complete demolition of Grozny is the gruesome result of this change in tactics. Third, coverage of the war in the Russian media has been much less critical. The Russian state has exercised a greater degree of control over media coverage of this war; at the same time, it has learned the value of conducting its own propaganda war on the airwaves to help sustain the military offensive on the ground. Over time, NTV has become more critical of Russia's war aims and the means deployed, but not nearly to the same degree as in the last war. All other major media outlets supported the Kremlin's position in the months leading up to the presidential vote.

Consequently, this second Chechen war has been a popular one in Russia. During the 2000 presidential campaign, public support remained steady at roughly 60 percent; it did not waver, as many had predicted, when Russian casualties increased.[3] Popular support for the war translated into positive approval ratings for Putin. Opinion polls conducted in the fall of 1999 demonstrated that people were grateful to Putin for accepting responsibility for the security of the Russian people.

He looked like a leader who had taken charge during an uncertain, insecure time and had delivered on his promise to provide stability and security. By the end of 1999, he enjoyed an astonishing 72 percent approval rating.[4]

2) A vote for the future. Putin's decisive response to the sense of insecurity that prevailed in Russia in the fall of 1999 is the reason why he initially rose in the polls. Yet his Chechnya policy is not the only factor that enabled Putin to maintain a positive approval rating throughout the spring of 2000. In fact, our polls of Russian voters in December 1999–January 2000 showed that 28 percent of those planning to vote for Putin believed that Chechnya should be allowed to leave the Russian Federation—almost as large as the proportion of Putin voters (35 percent) who believed that Russia should keep Chechnya at all costs.[5] This distribution of opinions roughly reflects the distribution of opinion on this question among *all* Russians. Thus other factors—more psychological than material in nature—also must have come into play. First, Putin symbolized for voters the end of revolution. For the first several years of the past decade, Russian politics was polarized by the struggle between communists and anticommunists. In contrast with the more successful transitions from communist rule in Poland or Hungary, in Russia the debate about communism as a political and economic system continued for many years after the Soviet collapse. A period of volatile and unpredictable politics resulted. In his last years of power, Yeltsin further fueled political instability by constantly changing prime ministers. Putin's coming to power signaled for many an end to this volatile period and the advent of the "Thermidor" of Russia's current revolution.

Putin's youth and energy also provided a striking contrast to his old and sick predecessor. Voters welcomed this generational change. In focus groups that we commissioned in December 1999 and March 2000, Russian voters uniformly stated that Putin's youth was a positive attribute. Ironically, Putin's rise to power reminds many Russians of that of Mikhail Gorbachev.

Second, Putin's lack of a record as a public leader allowed voters to project onto him their wishes and desires for the future. With the exception of his policy toward Chechnya, he was a *tabula rasa* on which voters could write what they wanted. In focus groups that we commissioned on the eve of the presidential election, participants had a long and diverse list of expectations about Russia's future under Putin's leadership, which included everything from order in Chechnya, respect for Russia on the international stage, and a crackdown on crime to higher pensions, a better educational system, and more job opportunities for young people. In other words, his supporters were casting their votes for Putin as a future leader, not supporting him for his past achievements, ideological beliefs, or policy positions. Understanding this mood in the Russian electorate, Putin and his campaign managers deliberately refrained from articulating a program or set of policies before the election.[6]

This motivation on the part of Putin voters was radically different from what we had witnessed among Yeltsin supporters in 1996. In that election, voters knew exactly what they were getting with Yeltsin and had no illusions about a more promising future. Yeltsin won 54 percent of the vote in the second round of the 1996 election, even though his approval rating was only 29 percent at the time. In 1996, people were voting against communism, supporting the lesser of two evils. In the spring of 2000, Putin supporters had a much more positive assessment of their leader and were much more optimistic about the future. They were motivated more by this emotional feeling about the future than by individual material interests, ideological beliefs, or party identification. For instance, when asked in a January 2000 poll about their attitudes concerning Russia's political future, 41 percent of respondents believed that the new year would be an improvement over the previous year, while only 9 percent believed that the political situation would worsen. Similarly, 39 percent of respondents believed that the economy would improve in 2000, while only 12 percent believed that it would worsen.[7] The last time that Russians were so optimistic about the future was the fall of 1991.

Strikingly, Putin's support was national in scope and not influenced by age or even by income level. He did just as well in rural areas as in urban areas and won as many votes from the poor as the rich. Amazingly, he carried 84 out of Russia's 89 regions. His chief opponent, communist leader Gennady Zyuganov, won in only four regions, and Aman Tuleev received the highest number of votes in the region where he is governor, Kemerovo Oblast. By contrast, Zyuganov had carried 25 regions in the second round of the 1996 presidential vote.

3) The lack of an effective opposition. A third important reason why Putin won was the weak competition he faced. Though often forgotten in analyses of Russian politics, the real story of the 1990s is not the Kremlin's cleverness but the ineptitude of its opponents. The Communist Party of the Russian Federation (KPRF) continues to dominate the space of opposition parties in Russian electoral politics, yet it has not generated new leaders or a new image. To be sure, the KPRF's economic platform in the 1999 parliamentary election and 2000 presidential election was considerably more market-friendly than the communist ideas the party had advocated in 1995 and 1996. Zyuganov tried to look and sound more modern, and even appeared on a campaign poster with young people. So far, however, the makeover has had only limited success. The contrast between the modern, Western-oriented, and young leader of the left in Poland, Aleksander Kwasniewski, and his traditional, anti-Western, and elderly Russian counterpart could not be more striking.

Years ago, well before anyone had even heard of Vladimir Putin, all experts on Russian electoral dynamics knew that whoever emerged as the candidate of the "party of power" would win the 2000 election. The reasoning is simple when one keeps in mind the solid and consistent electoral support for Zyuganov and Russia's two-ballot electoral system. Zyuganov was virtually assured of a second-place showing—and possibly a first-place showing—in the first round no matter who ran against him. His voters have supported him and his party consistently for the last decade. There was no reason to doubt that they would do so in 2000. At the same time, however, polls have also shown for years that Zyuganov would lose to almost anyone in a runoff. The only presidential contender he could beat would be Vladimir Zhirinovsky. Consequently, Putin and his associates were eager to see the KPRF do well in the parliamentary vote to ensure that Zyuganov would decide to run in the presidential election.

We also knew that Grigory Yavlinsky, the leader of the liberal Yabloko party, would run for president in 2000. Yet no serious analyst ever believed that Yavlinsky stood a chance of making it into a second round. Yavlinsky also has his loyal core of supporters, but his share of the vote has never exceeded ten percent.

The only real question, then, was who would emerge from the so-called party of power. In 1998, Moscow mayor Yuri Luzhkov looked poised to assume this mantle, but in 1999, former prime minister Yevgeny Primakov emerged as a more likely candidate. When Yeltsin fired him as prime minister, Primakov's popularity soared. Many regional leaders and part of the Moscow elite rallied to his cause. As a symbol of stability in a time of uncertainty, Primakov skyrocketed in the polls. Having navigated Russia out of a financial crisis that began in August 1998, Primakov earned a reputation as a pragmatist who would chart a slow, "centrist" reform course, somewhere between radical reform and communist restoration. He originally joined the Fatherland-All Russia electoral bloc as a means to jump-start his presidential bid and as a strategy for building parliamentary support for his presidency.

These plans proved premature. In fact, Primakov's participation in the December parliamentary elections actually damaged his prospects as a presidential candidate. During the runup to the parliamentary elections, the Kremlin's media empire launched a full-scale negative campaign against Primakov and his bloc. With varying degrees of truth and evidence, the Kremlin's media accused the former prime minister of being a feeble invalid, a lackey of NATO, a Chechen sympathiser, a closet communist, and a destabilizing force in international affairs who had ordered the assassination attempt against Georgian president Eduard

Shevardnadze. This smear campaign, in combination with Putin's spectacular rise in popularity, helped to undermine popular support for Fatherland-All Russia, which won only 12 percent of the popular vote, while the Putin-endorsed Unity bloc won 24 percent.

In effect, the parliamentary vote served as a presidential primary for the party of power. Primakov lost this primary and pulled out of the presidential contest. With Primakov out of the race, there was never any doubt that Putin would win the presidential election. The only real question was whether Putin could win more than 50 percent in the first round and thus avoid a runoff. He did, capturing 52.9 percent of the vote in the first round, compared to Zyuganov's 29.2 percent.

4) The early election. By resigning on 31 December 1999 and thereby moving the electoral calendar forward three months, Yeltsin gave Putin the most important campaign present of all. According to Putin's own advisors, his popularity peaked in mid-January, when 55 million eligible voters were prepared to vote for him. On election day on 26 March 2000, only 40 million voters cast their ballot for the acting president. In other words, between January and March, Putin lost the support of five million voters each month. Putin's "no-campaign" campaign strategy was viable only in a short campaign season. If the vote had not been held until June, Putin most certainly would have faced a runoff.

Winners and Losers

Putin was the clear winner of this election. He will now serve for a fixed four-year term, and the ebbs and flows of his approval rating will matter very little for the next three years. The fact that he managed to escape a runoff by only a few percentage points will also fade in importance over time. Instead, he is now enjoying a honeymoon period in which everyone—oligarchs, governors, parties, the Duma, and the people—is supporting him and seeking his favor. No one in postcommunist Russia has ever enjoyed this level of support.

Putin's small majority, however, does have a few immediate political implications. Because Putin just squeaked by in the first round, he and his team are much less likely to dissolve the Duma and call for new parliamentary elections anytime soon. In the wake of the pro-Putin Unity bloc's strong showing in the December 1999 parliamentary vote and Putin's skyrocketing support in the polls in early 2000, some of his allies, including Unity's new leaders, had called for new Duma elections immediately after the presidential vote, believing that Unity could win an even larger share of the parliamentary seats. Such a move became very unlikely after Putin's weaker-than-expected showing, since most observers concluded that a new parliamentary vote would yield basically the same result as last December. This is a positive outcome that should result in stable relations between the president and the legislature for the foreseeable future.

Putin's narrow majority is also likely to make him more cautious in taking steps against his election allies. Before the election, for instance, Putin's advisors spoke brashly about removing "difficult" governors from office. With a smaller mandate, however, Putin is now less likely to move aggressively against regional leaders. He must tread especially lightly in those places where regional leaders may have falsified the results to help push Putin over the 50-percent threshold. For the same reasons, Putin will now be reluctant to take action against the oligarchs who helped him win election. He is also less likely to pursue constitutional amendments, such as extending the presidential term to seven years.

Gennady Zyuganov and the KPRF must be satisfied with their performance in the first round, even if they were unable to force a second round. Citing the results of their own parallel vote count, KPRF officials claim that the results were falsified and that Putin did not win 50 percent in the first round. They did not pursue this issue vigorously, however, perhaps because Zyuganov believes that the KPRF can cooperate with Putin. On election night, Putin made very conciliatory comments about Zyuganov and the communists, remarking that their strong showing demonstrates that many Russian citizens are dissatisfied with the status quo. Boris Yeltsin would have never made such a comment.

Putin did not include communists in major positions in his new government. He understands the importance of creating an ideologically unified team. At the same time, however, he is likely to continue to consult and cooperate with the communists on a long list of issues where they hold similar positions, including the war in Chechnya, greater support for the military-industrial complex and intelligence services, and the building of a stronger state. Unlike Yeltsin, Putin has never seen Russian politics in bipolar terms. More generally, Putin is much more of a nationalist than Yeltsin and therefore shares the worldview of many prominent KPRF leaders.

For Zyuganov personally, his strong showing—five percentage points above his party's total just three months earlier in the parliamentary vote—ensures that he will remain the leader of the KPRF for the foreseeable future. Compared to 1996, he increased his vote totals in many large cities and even outpolled Yavlinsky in both Moscow and St. Petersburg. This new strength in urban regions, combined with a drop in support in traditionally communist rural areas, suggests that the KPRF's electorate may be gradually changing. Although it is dangerous to generalize based on one election, economic concerns and the resentment over hardships associated with market reforms may be replacing age and nostalgia for the Soviet Union as the most important motivators for KPRF supporters. With the threat of a communist restoration having faded, protest voters may believe it is now safe to vote for Zyuganov.

Russia's liberals suffered a major setback in this presidential election. The Union of Right Forces (SPS)—a coalition of liberals headed by former prime ministers Sergei Kirienko and Yegor Gaidar, former deputy prime ministers Anatoly Chubais and Boris Nemtsov, and a handful of other prominent figures such as Samara governor Konstantin Titov and businesswoman Irina Khakamada—emerged from the December 1999 parliamentary vote with real momentum. To everyone's surprise, they placed fourth in that election, winning 8.5 percent of the popular vote and outpolling their liberal rival Yabloko by more than two percentage points. Many thought their strong electoral showing marked the rebirth of Russian liberalism. Yet SPS squandered this momentum through their indecision regarding the presidential election. They failed to endorse a presidential candidate, even though one of their founding members, Governor Titov, was on the ballot. Some SPS leaders, such as Kirienko and Chubais, backed Putin while others wavered. In the end, SPS had no impact on the presidential vote.

Yavlinsky, however, fared no better, despite the fact that his campaign was flush with money.[8] Without question, he spent more on campaign advertising than any other candidate. In contrast to previous elections, he also enjoyed access to all the major television networks. He did endure some slanderous attacks from ORT, the largest television network, only days before the vote,[9] but few experts believed that these attacks had any effect. Yavlinsky ran a very professional campaign, his best performance to date. Yet despite an excellent and well-funded campaign, very little harassment from the state authorities, and the absence of serious competitors for the liberal vote, Yavlinsky finished with only 5.8 percent, well below his 7.4 percent showing in 1996 and only a fraction above Yabloko's share of the December 1999 parliamentary vote. This constituted a major defeat for Yavlinsky personally and for Russian liberals as a whole. In the mid-1990s, running as a "third-way" alternative to both the retrograde communists and the extremely unpopular Yeltsin and his "radical" reformist allies, Yavlinsky seemed to have real electoral potential. In 2000, however, running against a popular prime minister who was not firmly identified with "shock therapy" (or even with Yeltsin himself) and a communist candidate who no longer advocated a Soviet restoration, Yavlinsky's "third way" seemed less attractive, even stale.

The election was also a setback for nationalist leaders and parties independent of the Kremlin. Vladimir Zhirinovsky, the head of the Liberal Democratic Party of Russia, fared very poorly, winning a paltry 2.7 percent. None of the other nationalist hopefuls won more than 1 percent of the vote. This is in marked contrast to 1996, when General Aleksandr Lebed took third place a strong double-digit showing, which enabled him to deliver a critical endorsement to Yeltsin in the second round.

In several respects, the first round of the 2000 vote resembled the runoff in the 1996 presidential race. Third-party candidates played a much smaller role in 2000 than in the first round in 1996. In fact, the biggest losers in 2000 were liberal and nationalist parties, whose candidates performed so poorly that one has to wonder if they will be able to survive as political movements in Russia in the future.

Implications for Russian Policy

Because Putin ran an issue-free campaign, we learned very little about what he intends to do as president. Putin himself probably is still forming views on the thousands of issues that he now must address. This is not a man who spent decades preparing to become president. After all, this was the first time he had ever run for political office! Yet we do have some clues regarding his priorities.

We know that Putin is committed to preserving Russia's territorial integrity at any cost. In addition to continuing to support a military solution to the Chechen crisis, Putin will attempt to strengthen the center's control over the regions more generally. In his first weeks in office, Putin moved aggressively to weaken the powers of the governors by creating seven new supraregional district administrators who will report directly to the president. He also announced plans to introduce direct elections to the Federation Council, the upper house of parliament. (Currently all oblast governors and republic presidents hold seats in this body.) The battle to reign in the regions and change the composition of the Federation Council will be a protracted one. Proposals for change are not the same as real changes. Nonetheless, it is clear that Putin has assigned the highest priority to the task of strengthening the authority of the federal government.

Regarding economic reform, Putin's initial signals have been clear and positive. Putin called upon a young team of economists, many of whom formerly worked for former prime minister Yegor Gaidar, to draft a comprehensive reform program.[10] In his first major new appointment to his economic team, he invited Andrei Illarionov, Russia's most ardent and principled proponent of radical market reforms, to be his economic advisor.[11] Putin's new program, still in draft at the time of this writing, covers all the right subjects, including tax reform, a new land code, deregulation, social-policy restructuring, and new bankruptcy procedures. Yet his new government, under the leadership of Prime Minister Mikhail Kasyanov, is not composed entirely of people dedicated to this radical program. The new finance minister, Aleksei Kudrin, and the new minister of the economy and trade, German Gref, are dedicated liberals, but the rest are not. It remains to be seen if Putin has the will and the political skill to execute far-reaching reforms. Paradoxically, short-term economic growth fueled by devaluation and rising oil prices might make the new government complacent about undertaking the painful structural reforms necessary for sustained long-term economic expansion.

Regarding foreign policy, the initial signals have been less clear, but mostly positive. Putin does not speak fondly of "multipolarity" or use the tired language of balance-of-power politics. Instead, he claims to want to make Russia a normal Western power. During the presidential campaign, he even entertained the possibility that Russia might someday join NATO. His international heroes come not from the East or the South, but from the West.[12] In his short time in office, he has devoted particular attention to England, meeting twice with Prime Minister Tony Blair before holding his first summit with President Clinton in June 2000. He appears to want to put greater emphasis on Europe and less on Russia's relations with the United States. Yet Putin appears ready to cooperate with the United States on key issues. Even before his inauguration, he pushed the new Duma to ratify START II and the Comprehensive Test Ban Treaty and urged his diplomats to begin negotiations on START III and modification of the Anti–Ballistic Missile treaty. At the same time, Putin has emphasized the need to expand Russian arms exports and trade more generally with all comers, a new initiative that could include the transfer of nuclear technologies to countries like Iran and renewed trade ties (in violation of UN sanctions) with Yugoslavia and Iraq.

Putin's views on democracy are less clear. Although he has expressed his admiration for past Soviet dictators such as Yuri Andropov, Putin has expressed no desire to restore authoritarian rule in Russia. He has pledged his loyalty to the constitution and has not (yet) supported calls for the creation of new authoritarian regime like that of General Augusto Pinochet in Chile as a means for jump-starting market reform. Yet neither is he a passionate defender of democracy. In his first several months in office, Putin has demonstrated a willingness to use the power of the state and to ignore the democratic rights of society in pursuit of his objectives. For Putin, the ends justify the means.

In the realm of electoral politics, Putin wielded the power of the Russian state in ways that have caused considerable damage to democratic institutions. After Putin and his allies created the Unity party out of thin air in October 1999, state television incessantly promoted it and destroyed its opponents with a barrage of negative advertising never before seen in Russian politics. As a result, Unity won nearly a quarter of the vote in December. Putin then used national television to broadcast his "anti-campaign" for the presidency.

More gruesome has been Putin's indifference to the human rights of his country's own citizens in Chechnya. Russia has a right to defend its borders, but the egregious violations of human rights in his pursuit of this cause reveal the low priority that Putin assigns to democratic principles. Independent journalists, leaders of nongovernmental organizations, and academics also have felt the heavy hand of the Russian state under Putin. Reporters like Radio Liberty's Andrei Babitsky and national television networks like NTV have suffered the consequences of reporting news from Chechnya that inconveniences the Kremlin. Babitsky was arrested and then handed over to the Chechens; the offices of Media-Most, the owner of NTV, were raided by the Federal Security Service (FSB). Commentators and columnists critical of Putin report that many newspapers are unwilling to carry their articles. Self-censorship has returned to Russia. Environmental groups and human rights organizations also have reported increased monitoring of their activities by the FSB in the Putin era.

Many of Putin's proposed political reforms also sound antidemocratic. His advisers speak openly about changing the electoral law to eliminate the requirement that half of the Duma's deputies be elected by proportional representation—a revision that would virtually keep Russia's prodemocratic political parties out of parliament. Putin and his aides also have expressed support for the highly antidemocratic idea of appointing governors rather than electing them. Putin has even hinted that he would like to extend the term of the Russian presidency to seven years. None of these innovations alone would spell the end of democracy. In combination, however, they could resurrect a system dominated by a single "party of power," the Kremlin.

Despite all of these ominous signs, it would be wrong to conclude that Putin is an "antidemocrat." He is simply too modern and too Western-oriented to believe in dictatorship. Rather, Putin is indifferent to democratic principles and practices, perhaps believing that Russia might have to sacrifice democracy in the short run to achieve "more important" economic and state-building goals. He will continue to allow an independent press, elections, and individual liberties as long as they do not conflict with his agenda of securing Russia's borders, strengthening the Russian state, and promoting market reform. What will happen, however, when democracy becomes inconvenient for him?

Implications for Russian Democracy

The fate of democracy in Russia does not depend solely on Putin's views on the subject; if it did, Russia could not be considered a democracy. In fact, it has now become fashionable both in Russia and the West to assert that Russia is not a democracy, and the rise of Putin is cited as the latest confirming evidence. Some assert that Russia has never been a democracy, contending that the current regime in Russia is at best comparable to that of the late Soviet period, with a small group of people at the top making all the political decisions. Others have even likened contemporary Russia to feudal Europe, a system in which a handful of nobles—now called oligarchs and regional barons—decide everything.[13]

Such historical analogies, however, are dangerously distorted. They suggest that no change has occurred in Russia over the last decade or the last 400 years. They imply cultural continuity in Russia. Russian leaders are authoritarian and the Russian people support them because Russian leaders and Russian society have always favored dictatorship. This line of argument suggests that there is no threat to Russian democracy today because there is no democracy to be threatened.

To be sure, Russian democracy is weak and unconsolidated. Russia is not a liberal democracy. Pluralist institutions of interest intermediation are weak, mass-based interest groups are marginal, and the institutions that could help to redress this imbalance—parliament, the party system, and the judiciary—lack strength and independence.[14] The weakness of these institutions means that Russia's electoral democracy is more fragile than a liberal democracy would be.[15] In addition, a deeper attribute of democratic stability—a normative commitment to the democratic process on the part of both the elite and society—is still not present in Russia. Although all major political actors and Russian society as a whole recognize elections as "the only game in town" and behave accordingly, antidemocratic attitudes persist. A 1999 public-opinion survey revealed that solid majorities think it "impermissible" to ban meetings and demonstrations (66 percent), cancel elections (62 percent), or censor the mass media (53 percent),[16] but these numbers should be much higher ten years after the collapse of communism. Qualitative elite surveys show stronger support for democratic institutions and values.[17] Yet the marks given for the practice of Russian democracy to date are very low. Only 2 percent believe that Russia has achieved a democracy, while 46 percent believe that Russia has failed to do so.

Finally, the rise of a leader with Putin's background and the process by which he was elected are not positive signs for democratic consolidation. No one who welcomed the destruction of the Soviet police state can be happy that a former KGB officer has now become the president of Russia. And what does it mean for democratic consolidation when the electorate supports antidemocratic policies such as the slaughter of innocent people in Chechnya?

When assessing Russian democracy and its prospects, however, the real question is: Compared to what? Compared to American or even Polish democracy, Russian democracy has a long way to go. Yet compared to other states that emerged from the Soviet Union or to Russia's own authoritarian past, Russia does appear to have made progress in building a democratic political order. Czarist-era peasants did not vote, did not read independent newspapers, and did not travel freely. Neither did Soviet citizens. Princes and Communist Party secretaries were not removed from power by the ballot box, as were four out of nine regional leaders and hundreds of Duma deputies in the December 1999 election. Moreover, two-thirds of an extremely well-educated population freely opted to participate in presidential and parliamentary elections. If these elections were meaningless, then why did these people bother to show up? Even societal reaction to some of Putin's early antidemocratic moves has been encouraging. For instance, in response to the FSB raid on Media-Most, the Communist Party, the Union of Right Forces, Yabloko, human rights groups and media monitoring organizations, and even several business tycoons united to denounce the intimidation.

The more interesting question is not whether or not today's Russia is a democracy, but what its future trajectory will be. Putin's victory and the way that victory was achieved are not positive steps. Yet it would be premature to generalize about the long-term future of Russian democracy from this one election. Even in established democracies, the same party can remain in power for decades. Only time will tell if Putin's election is the beginning of the creation of a one-party state or just a rather accidental consequence of a popular war and a weak opposition.

The fact that a man like Putin, whose credentials and proclivities are not prodemocratic, could be elected president of Russia nearly ten years after the collapse of the Soviet Union suggests that the future of democracy in Russia is highly uncertain. At this moment in history, after years of revolutionary turmoil, the Russian people clearly want a leader with a strong hand who promises to build a stronger state. But neither popular desires for stability and security nor Putin's lack of commitment to democracy need necessarily translate into authoritarianism. Russia today is a large, divided, and multilayered society. Consequently, reestablishing dictatorship would be difficult and costly, especially if Putin and his team are serious about wanting to integrate Russia into the Western world. But if their new government does try to move toward dictatorship, would the Russian people be willing to sacrifice their democratic freedoms for more order? Or would they be willing to fight for these freedoms? After a decade of transition, these unfortunately are still open questions.

NOTES

1. The author convened a seminar of Russian electoral analysts at the Moscow Carnegie Center shortly after the counteroffensive, and this was the consensus at the time.

2. Fond "Obshchestvennoe mnenie" (FOM), "Klyuchevye problemy predvybornoi kampanii v zerkale obshchestvennogo mneniya," *Rezul'taty sotsiologicheskikh issledovannii* 29 (10 May 1996): 4–5.

3. See the tracking polls conducted by the Russian Center for Public Opinion and Market Research (VCIOM) at *www.russiavotes.org*.

4. Agentstvo regional'nykh politcheskikh issledovanii (ARPI), *Regional'nyi Sotsiologicheskii Monitoring* 49 (10–12 December 1999), 39. Sample size: 3,000 respondents in 52 Federation subjects.

5. This survey project of 1,900 Russian respondents, directed by Timothy Colton and Michael McFaul and executed by Polina Kozyreva and Mikhail Kosolapov of DEMOSCOPE, was conducted shortly before the parliamentary vote.

6. Author's interview with Mikhail Margelov, Putin's campaign manager (February 2000).

7. FOM, *Soobshcheniya fonda "Obshchestvennoe mnenie,"* 536 (12 January 2000), 30.

8. Author's interviews with senior Yabloko leaders (March 2000).

9. ORT commentators asserted that Yavlinsky and Yabloko were funded by German and Jewish organizations. They also showed clips of homosexuals announcing that they planned to vote for Yavlinsky and intimated that Yavlinsky himself was gay.

10. This team of economists and lawyers, under the direction of German Gref at the Strategy Center formed by Putin last year, in many ways represents the most liberal thinkers in Russia. The list of specialists includes Vladimir Mau, Aleksei Ulukaev, Sergei Sinelnikov (all former Gaidar aides and deputies), Oleg Vyugin, Andrei Illarionov, Mikhail Dmitriev, and their chief mentor, Yevgeny Yasin.

11. For a snapshot of his views, see Andrei Illarionov, "The Roots of the Economic Crisis," *Journal of Democracy* 10 (April 1999): 68–82.

12. See *Ot pervogo litsa: razgovory s Vladimirom Putinym* (Moscow: Vagrius Books, 2000).

13. See the comments by Thomas Graham in "A New Era in Russian Politics," *Meeting Report* 2 (Washington, D.C.: Carnegie Endowment for International Peace, 30 March 2000).

14. For the author's own assessment of these institutions and the causes of their weakness, see Michael McFaul, "The Perils of Protracted Transition," *Journal of Democracy* 10 (April 1999): 4–18; "Party Formation and Deformation in Russia," working paper, Carnegie Endowment for International Peace (May 2000); "Russia's 'Privatized' State as an Impediment to Democratic Consolidation: Part I," *Security Dialogue* 29 (June 1998): 191–200; and "Russia's 'Privatized' State as an Impediment to Democratic Consolidation: Part II," *Security Dialogue* 29 (September 1998): 315–32.

15. On the differences between electoral and liberal democracies, see Larry Diamond, *Developing Democracy: Toward Consolidation* (Baltimore: Johns Hopkins University Press, 1999).

16. The survey was conducted by ROMIR in July 1999.

17. See Sharon Werning Rivera, "Explaining Elite Commitments to Democracy in Post-Communist Russia," unpubl. ms., September 1999; Arthur Miller, Vicki Hesli, and William Reisinger, "Conceptions of Democracy among Mass and Elite in Post-Soviet Societies," *British Journal of Political Science* 27 (April 1997): 157–90; and Judith Kullberg and William Zimmerman, "Liberal Elites, Socialist Masses, and Problems of Russian Democracy," *World Politics* 51 (April 1999): 323–58. Kullberg and Zimmerman, however, find a real gap between elite and mass values, with the latter exhibiting more illiberal ideologies.

25

WILL CHINA DEMOCRATIZE?

Michel Oksenberg

Michel Oksenberg, *until his death in 2001, was a senior fellow of the Asia/Pacific Research Center at Stanford University. He served as president of the East-West Center in Honolulu, Hawaii, from 1992 to 1995, and taught at the University of Michigan from 1973 to 1992. His publications include* The Chinese Future *(1997) and* China Joins the World: Progress and Prospects *(1999).*

Since the brutal suppression of student demonstrations in June 1989, China scholars have waged a vigorous debate about the prospects for a democratic transition in the People's Republic of China (PRC). Roughly speaking, three views exist. The first stresses the strengths and resiliency of the existing authoritarian arrangements. The second emphasizes their weaknesses. The third focuses less on the toughness or fragility of the current political system, and looks instead at the long-term democratizing implications of economic and social change.

The first school argues that China's institutional arrangements are deeply embedded in society, and are yielding sufficient economic resources and coercive capabilities to keep the communist elite in power indefinitely. This elite is determined to maintain its power through authoritarian rule. The regime's performance, as reflected in high economic growth and the avoidance of a Soviet-style social and political collapse, garners it a required minimum of support from relevant sectors of society. Institutional developments such as village elections and the strengthening of the National People's Congress, which are often cited as evidence of democratization, are still in an incipient stage. They face considerable opposition and an uncertain future, and it is too early to say whether they will lead to democracy.

Moreover, these promising developments have not prevented the regime from increasing its capacity to suppress dissent and quell unrest through expanded surveillance and the strengthening of the People's Armed Police.

The trends of the past two decades point less toward democracy than toward the rise of a corrupt "soft" authoritarianism not unlike that found in Suharto's Indonesia or Park Chung Hee's South Korea. Only a calamity severe enough to divide and paralyze the top leadership and rouse widespread social unrest could fundamentally threaten the regime. And any such collapse would more likely unleash widespread violence and chaos, followed by the reimposition of authoritarian rule, than bring about democracy.

Adherents of this first view also find little support for democracy in Chinese political thought, whether traditional or contemporary. They typically believe that the 1989 demonstrations were not fundamentally democratic in nature, and furnished little evidence of an emerging civil society. Finally, these analysts tend to think that the Chinese dissident community will have little influence over China's future.

The second opinion claims that: 1) the Chinese Communist Party (CCP) is moribund; 2) the central state is losing power relative to provincial and local political units; 3) the regime is losing popular support; 4) the armed forces may no longer be willing to carry out a crackdown like that of 1989; and 5) growing corruption is corroding the regime's legitimacy and effectiveness. Proponents of this view find evidence of some of the same dynamics that destroyed communism in the former Soviet bloc. They also look upon the 1989 demonstrations as indicating a popular yearning for democracy and a potential for the formation of a civil society. They find support for democracy in traditional Chinese political thought, and even more so in the recent work of Chinese political thinkers who hail from Hong Kong and Taiwan but have influence on the mainland as well. Such analysts usually believe that political dissidents, whether living abroad or imprisoned in China, are likely to play an important role in the years ahead.

The third set of analysts finds encouragement in China's openness to the outside world and the country's dramatic move away from socialist planning and the command economy. These analysts point to the inevitable political consequences of economic growth, the communications revolution, and the emergence of a more diverse society and an urban middle class. They tend to see in China the same economic and sociological processes that have led to democracy elsewhere in East and Southeast Asia. They stress the importance of a range of recent reforms, including village elections; the strengthening of people's assemblies at all levels of the hierarchy; the formation of government-licensed nongovernmental organizations; the development of a legal system; the expansion of the media and the beginnings of investigative journalism; and the leadership's acceptance of a species of interest-based politics (even if most interests are pursued by and through agencies of the state). Some claim that the market economy toward which China is supposedly moving will give the individual more power vis-à-vis the state and necessitate the adoption of democracy and the rule of law.

While these analysts caution that change may well occur slowly (perhaps taking as many as 15 or 20 years), they remain confident that the process of China's transformation is inevitable and under way.

The best analysts of the contemporary scene weave these seemingly conflicting perspectives into a coherent whole. They recognize that all these perspectives yield cogent insights. China's political structures do indeed seem firm and deeply rooted. At the same time, certain key aspects of the system do appear vulnerable to rapid disintegration. Finally, profound underlying economic, technological, and social changes are clearly propelling China into a new political era.

New Factors at Work

As the debate has unfolded, China itself has changed. The prospects of a speedy regime collapse, which seemed sizeable in 1989, have since diminished. Yet incremental changes continue. In particular, the growing autonomy of Chinese society vis-à-vis the state and the rapid pace of economic transformation are making it increasingly likely that the current political system will not be able to persist unaltered. The question increasingly seems to be about the scope of the transition. Will it be limited, producing a more durable, predictable, and humane authoritarian regime that rules through law yet excludes real democracy? Or will it go farther, to the point where leaders are selected through competitive, universal-suffrage elections and officials operate not merely *through* but *under* law? And can a transition from "soft" authoritarianism to some form of democracy occur gradually and peacefully, as it did in Taiwan or South Korea, or will there be widespread violence and economic hardship, as we have seen in Yugoslavia or the former Soviet Union? Finally, one might even ask if some other, unanticipated type of political transformation will be the one that actually occurs.

Such questions are being debated not only by China specialists outside of China, but even (if very quietly) by nondissident intellectuals within China—in itself evidence both of the uncertainty that haunts China's political future and of the serious possibility that a democratic transition might be in store. Several developments in the past two years have not only increased the likelihood of the latter, but also hint that it might occur more rapidly than most observers expect. These developments include an important evolution in the thinking of the leaders; an increased probability of social unrest that will demand a high-level strategic (rather than tactical) response; the influence of Hong Kong and Taiwan on mainland politics; and the consequences of the Chinese leadership's involvement in world affairs.

Most important, the nature of political discourse is changing. China's leaders are mentioning political participation and democracy in more serious fashion than at any time since the mid-1950s. Mao Zedong wrote about China's "New Democracy," but that was before he proclaimed the founding of the People's Republic. Following his ascent to power, he spoke primarily in Leninist terms about "the dictatorship of the proletariat" or "democratic centralism." Deng Xiaoping did not even tolerate explorations of democratic theory, much less reveal any interest in it.

More recently, however, China's leaders have begun to talk about their country's eventual evolution into a democracy. At the Fifteenth Congress of the CCP in September 1997, General Secretary Jiang Zemin stated explicitly that by the middle of the twenty-first century, "China will have become a prosperous, strong, democratic, and culturally advanced socialist country." Jiang avoided specifics, gave no explanation of what he meant by "democratic," and made clear elsewhere in the same speech that he was committed to preserving the supremacy of the CCP at all costs. In his many meetings with visiting Americans, Jiang has not denigrated democracy as a form of government, but rather avers that China, still plagued by poverty and a poorly educated populace, currently lacks the capacity to sustain it. To some Americans, Jiang has explicitly stated that nations pursue different paths of development due to their diverse cultures and historical experiences, but will converge in their social and organizational forms.

Let there be no illusion: Jiang gives no evidence of being a closet liberal democrat, and has shown himself willing and able to suppress dissent. Yet whatever his intentions, Jiang has helped to make "democracy" a word of acceptable currency among China's leaders and its populace. Nor is this rhetoric limited to Jiang. Officials of the CCP, especially at the lower levels, often admit that they must move in the direction of increased political participation, although it is not clear that their understanding of the term "democracy" resembles the meaning cherished by most Americans. In short, in the 1990s, China's elite political culture has begun to change. Democracy has begun to be enshrined as an ultimate goal for China, and it is just a matter of time before discussions begin over the features of "socialist democracy with Chinese characteristics" and the methods that the nation should use to move toward this goal. Once such a debate begins, it will assume a life of its own and accelerate the process of change.

The second major development accelerating the pace of political change will be the consequences of the reform of state-owned enterprises (SOEs). The pressure to embark upon this very difficult reform has become intense. Subsidies for inefficient SOEs are absorbing large shares of both the government budget and available bank credit, draining the state's coffers and plaguing the financial system with bad debt. This misallocation of investment retards national economic development. Yet letting these firms go under, in the absence of an effective social security system, will spark worker discontent and protest. As Elizabeth Perry has shown, the Chinese working classes have long exhibited a considerable propensity for various forms of labor unrest. Perry persuasively contends that worker movements have had a much more significant impact on the evolution of Chinese politics than most observers realize. Already there have been signs of spontaneous unrest and organization in response to wage cuts and job losses at SOEs around the country.[1]

In the past, such activity usually would have led to crackdowns, possibly accompanied by tactical efforts to redress some worker grievances. But an alternative response to an increasingly restive society could be for the leaders in Beijing to increase the number of democratically elected local officials, with the idea of letting them bear the brunt of popular discontent. Thus responsibility for managing SOE reform would be shifted away from the center, while opportunities for local-level political participation would increase. There are three indications that the top leaders are thinking precisely along these lines. First, Jiang's Fifteenth Party Congress report explicitly mentioned the need to make officials at the grassroots more accountable through elections. Second, the SOEs slated for privatization are the ones run not by the central government, but rather by local governments. Finally, plans are under way to experiment with extending direct, competitive elections to county-level people's assemblies as well as urban wards and neighborhoods.

The likely increase in social unrest will confront China's leaders with the classic dilemma that other authoritarian regimes have faced: whether to repress dissent, or to seek to bolster the regime's legitimacy and support by broadening opportunities for political participation. Following Robert Dahl, we may anticipate that the leaders' calculations will be governed by an assessment of the relative costs, benefits, and risks to them of each course of action. If the unrest is widespread but not so massive as to threaten communist rule, the leaders might opt for an orderly and accelerated expansion of democratizing reform, especially if such changes also come to be seen as offering one way to curtail corruption, which now concerns rulers and public alike. Such an admittedly difficult decision would be eased by some confidence that a more open political system would not challenge the dominance of the CCP, and a recognition that suppression would be costly. That is, the leaders would calculate that communist rule, political stability, and honest government would be enhanced rather than weakened by a process of democratization. One can now envision circumstances in which a majority of the Politburo would support such a conclusion.

In a development that most analysts have not yet taken into account, Hong Kong's reversion to PRC sovereignty and Taiwan's transition to democracy will accelerate the process of change. No longer can it be claimed that Chinese culture is somehow incompatible with democracy. Taiwan's March 1996 presidential election, in which incumbent Lee Teng-hui triumphed over vigorous opponents and won majority support in an electorate of 14 million people, was without precedent in 4,000 years of Chinese history. Taiwan's experience shows that a Chinese populace can indeed participate effectively in electoral politics extended well beyond the local community. Moreover, Hong Kong will be under pressure to achieve the stated goal of directly electing, through universal suffrage, all 60 members of its Legislative Council. If that city continues to thrive under freedom and democracy, many Chinese will naturally conclude that these principles can enhance the quality of rule on the mainland as well.

Furthermore, the tens of thousands of Hong Kong and Taiwan citizens working throughout the mainland, and the many PRC citizens temporarily residing in Hong Kong will affect the mainland's political culture. The massive flow of people among these three parts of China will probably increase the yearnings on the mainland for greater freedom and political participation. In addition, a firm and credible commitment to democratization on the part of the PRC leadership would facilitate a peaceful resolution of the Taiwan issue.

Finally, the involvement of China's leaders in world affairs will have a cumulative effect on their approach to governance at home. Paradoxes now abound. Chinese leaders traveling abroad will take questions from foreign audiences, but will not allow any such thing in China. They give speeches at foreign universities and nongovernmental organizations, while protestors demonstrate outside, but are unwilling to subject themselves to such discipline at home. They go to international gatherings where they are among the few (or sometimes even the only) leaders who have not had to win the votes of their citizens. How does this anomalous situation affect the self-perception of China's leaders? Will they begin to pay an unacceptable political, economic, or psychological price for it? Will they eventually feel impelled to seek the same kind of mandate that leaders of other countries enjoy? In short, will their craving for stature, respect, and equality in international affairs become an increasing consideration in the years ahead?

Obstacles to Democratization

Naturally, enormous political obstacles deter China's leaders from explicitly embarking upon the process of democratization. An acknowledgment that major mistakes were made in the crushing of the 1989 demonstrations is probably a prerequisite for the adoption of such a bold political course, and the current leaders—many of whom were at least indirectly involved in the crackdown—are reluctant to revisit that event. A reappraisal of the June 1989 tragedy would necessitate finding a scapegoat for it, and none is readily available. And a reappraisal would vindicate and thereby rehabilitate deposed General Secretary Zhao Ziyang and his supporters, a very divisive move. Moreover, powerful conservatives among the leaders, including officials of the military and security apparatus, would no doubt oppose an explicit commitment to democratization, fearing political instability and a loss of power by the CCP. The strength of these conservative forces is evident in the leaders' reluctance to resurrect the slogan of a decade ago—"separate the Party and government"—which falls far short of democratization but which would entail constraints on the CCP's authority. In addition, the party would surely face stiff competition at the ballot box in Tibet and Xinjiang, complicating Han Chinese rule in those regions. An openly competitive political system could also invite efforts by Taiwan and the United States to intervene in Chinese domestic politics. It might produce the same chaotic consequences as in Russia. Finally, the organization and conduct of fair elections would be a gargantuan undertaking. China has roughly 2,000 counties, each with a population ranging from a third of a million to a million or more. Many are comparable in size to small republics such as Haiti, Nicaragua, or El Salvador—to name three countries where the difficulties surrounding the introduction of elections proved to be considerable.

To conclude, several factors are propelling China toward a speedier democratic transition than most analysts think likely. Yet cautious forecasts seem realistic in light of the obstacles to a swift transformation. Nonetheless, for the reasons already noted, China's leaders are likely to find introducing democracy at lower levels of the system and firmly committing themselves to the attainment of full democracy over a protracted period to be an increasingly attractive option. The commitment would have to be accompanied by a realistic plan for maintaining Communist Party dominance, and by a strategy for ensuring that the use of elections expands only gradually, while the ancillary institutions necessary to the maintenance of a vibrant democracy are put in place.

The logic of the situation is compelling. Such a course would contribute to China's stability, increase the international respect accorded to China's leaders, enhance their power, and improve the governance of China. China's leaders may come to the same conclusion—provided they are not pressured to do so—at an earlier date than most outside observers now think possible. On the other hand, history is replete with authoritarian rulers who, out of fear or habit, proved unwilling to adjust to new realities and then lost power; with leaders who bravely sought to undertake democratic reforms and then failed; and with dictators who hung on for years or even decades, often bringing their societies stability and growth while confounding outside observers' predictions of the early demise of their system.

NOTE

1. Elizabeth Perry, *Shanghai on Strike: The Politics of Chinese Labor* (Stanford, Calif.: Stanford University Press, 1993); "Shanghai's Strike Wave of 1957," *China Quarterly* 137 (March 1994): 1–27; "Labor's Battle for Political Space," in Deborah Davis et al., eds., *Urban Spaces in Contemporary China* (New York: Cambridge University Press, 1995), 302–26; and (with Li Xun), *Proletarian Power: Shanghai in the Cultural Revolution* (Boulder, Colo.: Westview, 1997).

26

IS PAKISTAN THE (REVERSE) WAVE OF THE FUTURE?

Larry Diamond

Larry Diamond *is coeditor of the* Journal of Democracy, *codirector of the National Endowment for Democracy's International Forum for Democratic Studies, and a senior research fellow at the Hoover Institution. He is the author of* Developing Democracy: Toward Consolidation *(1999).*

At the dawn of the twenty-first century, democracy is at high tide in the world. By the count of Freedom House, the number of democracies in the world (120) and the proportion of states that are democratic (63 percent) are higher in 1999 than ever before.[1] It is tempting to see this ongoing expansion as indicative of a historic universalizing trend—the global triumph of democracy as a moral imperative and form of government. The U.S. State Department's *1999 Country Reports on Human Rights Practices* termed democracy and human rights a third "universal language" (along with money and the Internet).[2]

The current "third wave" of democratization (which began in 1974 but gathered particular momentum after 1989) stands in sharp contrast in both duration and scope to the second wave, which began around the end of the Second World War and expired in less than 20 years. That movement gave way to a "second reverse wave," in which democracy broke down in more than 20 developing countries.[3] Remarkably, a quarter-century after the inception of the third wave, there is no sign that the world has entered a "third reverse wave." During the first 25 years of the third wave, there were only three blatant reversals of democracy in countries with more than 20 million people: the 1983 military coup in Nigeria, the 1989 military coup in Sudan, and the 1991 military coup in Thailand. The first two occurred before the third wave of democratization reached Africa in 1991. The Thai coup was a major setback for democracy in Southeast Asia, but it did not last. Within 17 months, popular mobilization against the military's project to perpetuate its rule in a civilian electoral guise brought new elections and the return of a genuine democracy.

Before October 1999, there had been three other types of democratic reversals during the third wave. First, there were democratic breakdowns during the 1990s in such small, relatively marginal states as Congo (Brazzaville), the Gambia, Lesotho, Niger, and Sierra Leone. Second, democratic openings were aborted in such countries as Cambodia, Lebanon, Kenya, Nigeria, and several post-Soviet states. Finally, democracy was mangled by elected presidents themselves in Peru and Zambia, but in ways that preserved the framework of competitive multiparty politics.

With the exception of the Nigerian military's outrageous voiding of Moshood Abiola's landslide election to the presidency in June 1993, none of these other democratic reversals threatened to spark a wave of democratic breakdowns. Either they took place in countries that were too small to capture wide attention or the events were too ambiguous to provide a clear-cut model that could be emulated or denounced. Even in Nigeria, the impact of the military's 1993 cancellation of the final step in its own democratic transition plan was somewhat blunted by the cynicism that had accumulated through several previous manipulations of the transition process. The resilience of the third wave was dealt a much more serious challenge, however, on 12 October 1999, when the military seized power in Pakistan.

Pakistan's Descent

The Pakistani coup is the single most serious reversal of democracy during the third wave. With a population of 130 million, Pakistan is not only the largest but by far the most strategically influential country to have suffered a democratic breakdown. It now possesses nuclear weapons, and it has become a major source of terrorist training and financing. It could soon fight a major (even nuclear) war with a powerful neighbor, and its ruling military leaders are less inclined than the elected civilians they displaced to seek a negotiated solution to the problem of Kashmir.

While democratic Pakistani governments were manifestly corrupt and abusive, the country did witness repeated alternation in power between two political parties that had each mobilized substantial (albeit declining) popular support. Finally, Pakistan will not follow Thailand's path of rapid democratic restoration. The damage done to democratic institutions and norms, state capacity, public services, and civil society—first by successive authoritarian regimes and then by 11 years of venal misrule under the alternating elected governments of Benazir Bhutto and Nawaz Sharif—has been too great. Even under an enlightened and reform-minded leadership (which is far from assured under the current military regime), it will take several years to restore the minimal foundations for effective governance. Until these foundations are restored, Pakistan will continue its ugly slide toward a failed state. And unless state disintegration can be reversed, no democracy can succeed.

Although General Pervez Musharraf's seizure of power was precipitated by personal and institutional interests, the causes of Pakistan's democratic breakdown involve three more fundamental factors. Each of these eroded the legitimacy of the civilian constitutional regime and its capacity to manage political conflict peacefully.[4]

The first factor was the deterioration of the justice system and the rule of law. Never very strong or autonomous, Pakistan's judicial system became increasingly corrupt and politicized under the alternating governments of Bhutto and Sharif. Executive power was personalized (undermining other political institutions, such as parties and parliament) and criminal prosecutions were politicized, as relations between the ruling and opposition parties fell victim to "a depressing cycle of persecution and resistance."[5] Under the second administration of Nawaz Sharif, who swept into office in February 1997 determined to consolidate a firm grip on power, the political subjugation of the judiciary reached a new low, the justice system was mobilized to destroy Bhutto and her party, and press freedoms were curbed. In the name of fighting "terrorism," civil liberties were flagrantly abused and summary military courts were established to try acts of political violence in Sindh Province. Ironically, Sharif increasingly relied on the military to maintain order and administer the country, but there was less and less order to maintain, as political and sectarian violence escalated. Meanwhile, the police became increasingly brutal, corrupt, and ineffectual.

Second, Pakistan was increasingly polarized along ethnic and especially religious sectarian lines, as diverse groups felt or feared marginalization, and as Bhutto and Sharif fell back upon their bases of support in their respective home provinces of Sindh and Punjab. In response to Sharif's centralization of power, exclusion of regional rivals, and suppression of political opposition, political parties representing ethnic minorities felt more and more alienated, and both they and extremist religious movements increasingly turned to political violence and intimidation. "In the view of many Pakistanis," the brutal tactics of groups like the MQM (Muttahida Qawmi Movement, representing many of the *muhajirs*, or descendants of the refugees from India after the 1947 partition) "legitimized the use of violence by the state to curb their demands."[6] (State repression, in turn, further radicalized these groups.) Religious violence between militant Shi'ite and Sunni Muslim groups, each with external backers, dealt an additional blow to political stability, escalating the overall levels of violence, terrorism, and insecurity and reflecting their passionate rejection of the legitimacy of the democratic system.

These problems were fed and compounded by economic failure and injustice, made worse by the relentless political penetration and enervation of the state bureaucracy, which was increasingly unable to deliver such basic services as water, gas, and electricity. Under civilian rule, Pakistan was unable to achieve the economic growth necessary to reduce widespread poverty (Pakistan ranks 169th of 210 countries in per-capita income). During the 1990s, economic growth (4 percent annually) barely kept ahead of population growth (2.8 percent).[7] Human capital stagnated, with half of the adult males and three-quarters of the females still illiterate. Unable to tax its major sources of national income (licit or illicit), Pakistan borrowed to the point where it now spends 40 percent of the government budget on debt servicing. With another quarter of the budget going to the military and more leaking out in corruption, little remains for development.[8] The successive civilian administrations were unable to implement the administrative and economic reforms—such as controlling corruption and smuggling, taxing agriculture (and thus the feudal landlords), and liberalizing state controls—necessary to build the confidence of domestic and foreign investors. As a result, capital has fled, unemployment has risen for want of new investment, and legitimate economic activity has increasingly given way to the smuggling of drugs, weapons, and consumer goods and to other forms of predatory profiteering.

Pakistan's travails of governance viciously reinforce one another. Deepening poverty heightens the tensions between different ethnic and religious groups. Violent ethnic and religious strife further deters investment. Corruption, capital flight, smuggling, gun running, drug trafficking, and the evaporation of international donor and investor confidence, in turn, all further undermine state capacity.

Pakistan's descent—first into an increasingly illiberal and dysfunctional democracy, then into an authoritarian and potentially failed state—merits close study, for it starkly depicts the problems of governance and state capacity that threaten many third-wave democracies, including many of the largest and most influential ones.[9] Unless these three core problems of governance are seriously addressed elsewhere in the coming years, Pakistan will not be the last high-profile country to suffer a breakdown of democracy. Indeed, if there is a "third reverse wave," its origin may well be dated to 12 October 1999, when the Pakistani military seized power.

The Strategic "Swing" States

To assess the current state of democracy worldwide, we need to disaggregate global trends. The 120 democracies of the world (as classified by Freedom House) are not all equally influential, nor are they equally democratic and stable. Indeed, one may even question whether some of them—where recent national elections were deeply flawed—even meet the minimal definition of democracy.[10] We must also distinguish between electoral democracy and liberal democracy. The latter encompasses not only electoral competition for power but (inter alia) basic civil liberties, a rule of law under which all citizens are treated equally, an independent judiciary, other institutions of "horizontal accountability" that check the abuse of power, an open and pluralistic civil society, and civilian control over the military.[11]

These various dimensions of democratic quality constitute a continuum, and it is hard to say exactly when a regime has sufficient freedom, pluralism, lawfulness, accountability, and institutional strength to be considered a liberal democracy. I believe the most reasonable empirical standard is an average score of 2.0 or better (lower) on the parallel Freedom House scales of political rights and civil liberties (each of which ranges from 1, "most free," to 7, "least free"). For some years, I took as an indicator of liberal democracy the Freedom House designation of a country as "Free" (an average score of 2.5 or better). Yet countries with average scores of 2.5 almost always have civil-liberties scores of 3 on a 7-point scale, indicating serious deficiencies in the rule of law and the protection of individual rights. Typically in such countries (for example, the Philippines, El Salvador, and of late, India), the judiciary is weak and ineffectual, corruption is widespread, and police and other security forces abuse the rights of citizens with considerable impunity. Such countries are only "semiliberal," while those with average freedom scores of 3.5 or higher (and typically, civil-liberties scores of 4 or worse) are illiberal.

We also need to determine how stable and firmly rooted democracies are. For political scientists, democracies are considered to be "consolidated" when all significant political elites, parties, and organizations, as well as an overwhelming majority of the mass public, are firmly committed to the democratic constitutional system and regularly comply with its rules and constraints. What is striking about the third wave of democratization that began in 1974 is how slow the progress toward consolidation has been. Outside of the new democracies of Southern Europe and a few scattered others (see below), the third-wave democracies have not taken firm root.

Democracy is most firmly established in the core of the global system: the wealthiest, most technologically advanced countries. Thirty countries comprise this core: the 24 countries of Western Europe, the four other rich Anglophone countries (the United States, Canada, Australia, and New Zealand), and Japan and Israel. All of these are consolidated and liberal democracies.

Of the remaining 162 countries, 41 have populations of less than one million, and many of the others are marginal in power and influence. We should not write off any country, however; even small countries (like Botswana in southern Africa) have the potential to serve as models. Nevertheless, the global prospects for democracy depend more heavily on the richer, more resourceful, and more populous countries—in part because the way they are governed affects a much greater proportion of the world's population, and in part because bigger and richer countries are more likely to exert "demonstration" effects on other states in their regions.

TABLE 1—THE STRATEGIC "SWING" STATES

	GNP (in billions of U.S. $)	POPULATION (millions)	1999 AVERAGE FREEDOM SCORE	REGIME TYPE
THE TOP TWENTY				
COUNTRY	GNP (in billions of U.S. $)	POPULATION (millions)	1999 AVERAGE FREEDOM SCORE	REGIME TYPE
CHINA	928.9	1,239	6.5	Authoritarian
BRAZIL	758.0	166	3.5	Democracy (illiberal)
INDIA	421.3	980	2.5	Democracy (semiliberal)
MEXICO	380.9	96	3.5	Electoral authoritarian
SOUTH KOREA	369.9	46	2.0	Liberal democracy
RUSSIA	337.9	147	4.5	Democracy? (illiberal)
ARGENTINA	324.1	36	2.5	Democracy (semiliberal)
TAIWAN	284.8[1]	22	2.0	Liberal democracy
TURKEY	200.5	63	4.5	Democracy (illiberal)
POLAND	150.8	39	1.5	Liberal democracy
INDONESIA	138.5	204	4.0	Democracy? (illiberal)
THAILAND	134.4	61	2.5	Democracy (semiliberal)
SAUDI ARABIA	128.9[1]	21	7.0	Authoritarian
SOUTH AFRICA	119.0	41	1.5	Liberal democracy
IRAN	109.6	62	6.0	Electoral authoritarian
COLOMBIA	106.1	41	4.0	Democracy (illiberal)
SINGAPORE	95.1	3	5.0	Electoral authoritarian
PAKISTAN	63.2	132	6.0	Authoritarian (military)
BANGLADESH	63.2	126	3.5	Democracy (illiberal)
NIGERIA	36.4	121	3.5	Democracy? (illiberal)
THE ADDITIONAL TEN				
VENEZUELA	81.3	23	4.0	Democracy (illiberal)
MALAYSIA	79.8	22	5.0	Electoral authoritarian
EGYPT	79.2	61	5.5	Electoral authoritarian
PHILIPPINES	78.9	78	2.5	Democracy (semiliberal)
CHILE	71.3	15	2.0	Liberal democracy
PERU	61.1	25	4.5	Electoral authoritarian
CZECH REP.	51.8	10	1.5	Liberal democracy
UKRAINE	42.7	50	3.5	Democracy? (illiberal)
VIETNAM	25.6	78	7.0	Authoritarian
ETHIOPIA	6.1	61	5.0	Electoral authoritarian

Sources: World Bank, *World Development Report 1999–2000* (New York: Oxford University Press, 2000), and Freedom House, *1999–2000 Survey of Freedom in the World.*
[1] Figures are for 1997. Taiwan figure is from *The Republic of China Yearbook: 1999* (Republic of China Government Information Office); Saudi Arabia and Kuwait are from *World Development Report 1998–99.*
? A question mark indicates a dubious quality to the freedom and fairness of national elections.

Of the 162 countries outside the very rich, (post)industrial, liberal democratic core, which are the largest, most resourceful, and most powerful? Only 19 of these 162 have gross national products (GNPs) of over $100 billion annually or populations larger than 100 million people. To these can be added Singapore, which, despite its small population, has a GNP of nearly $100 billion and is one of the ten richest countries in the world in per-capita income. Never before in history has there been an authoritarian regime whose population is anywhere near as rich and well-educated as Singapore's.

These 20 countries are the most politically influential ones outside the core. Together, they account for 62 percent of total world population and 18 percent of world income. One could enlarge this list by adding the ten countries that have populations of 50 to 100 million or GNPs of $50–100 billion. These 30 influential countries and their key properties are listed in Table 1 on the previous page. I call them "strategic swing states" because how they evolve will heavily determine the future of democracy in the world.[12]

Freedom House states that today, "58.2 percent of the world's population lives under democratically elected leadership."[13] More than 60 percent of the states in the world are democracies, and 44 percent are "Free." How do our 30 "swing" states compare with the global picture? They have the same proportion of democracies as the world overall, but they are significantly less liberal and free. Globally, more than a third of all states are liberal democracies but only one-fifth of the swing states are. Well over two-fifths of all the world's democracies but only a third of the 30 swing states are rated "Free" (see Table 2 below). While nearly three-fifths of all the world's democracies are liberal, only a third of the democracies among the swing states are liberal democracies. Nearly half of the swing states are decidedly illiberal, compared to just an eighth of democracies overall. In fact, of the 16 illiberal democracies in the world, nine are clustered among the strategic swing states (see Table 3 on the following page).

In most of the swing states, democratic institutions are in play but far from firmly rooted. Only five of them (China, Vietnam, Saudi Arabia, Egypt, and Singapore) have stable and longstanding authoritarian regimes (and the latter two have contested elections). Pakistan has just returned to military rule. Another five swing states have electoral regimes that fall short of democracy; they may be quite repressive, but pressure for democratization is significant and growing (Mexico, Peru, Malaysia, Iran, and Ethiopia; see Table 1 on the previous page). Six swing states

TABLE 2—DEMOCRACY AND FREEDOM, BY TYPE OF STATE, 1999–2000

	ALL COUNTRIES (n=192)	CORE COUNTRIES (n=30)	SWING STATES (n=30)	COUNTRIES UNDER 1 MIL. POPULATION (n=41)
PERCENT DEMOCRACIES*	63% (120)	100% (30)	63% (19)	78% (32)
PERCENT LIBERAL DEMOCRACIES**	37% (71)	100% (30)	20% (6)	68% (28)
PERCENT FREE STATES*	44% (85)	100% (30)	33% (10)	71% (29)
AVERAGE FREEDOM SCORE	3.49	1.18	3.87	2.41

* As identified by Freedom House in its 1999 Survey of "Freedom in the World."
** As indicated by an average freedom score for 1999 of 2.0 or lower.

TABLE 3—COMPOSITION OF DEMOCRACIES, BY TYPE OF COUNTRY

	ALL DEMOCRACIES (n=120)	CORE COUNTRIES (n=30)	SWING STATES (n=19)
LIBERAL DEMOCRACY (average freedom score of 1.0 – 2.0)	59% (71)	100% (30)	32% (6)
SEMILIBERAL DEMOCRACY (average freedom score of 2.5 – 3.0)	19% (23)	0	21% (4)
ILLIBERAL DEMOCRACY (average freedom score of 3.5 – 5.0)	13% (16)	0	47% (9)

are liberal democracies (South Korea, Taiwan, Poland, South Africa, Chile, and the Czech Republic) in which democracy has either been moving toward consolidation or at least (South Africa) is not in immediate danger. In the other 13 states (almost half the group), democracy functions illiberally, with extensive corruption, abuse of executive authority, judicial inefficacy, and violations of human rights.

Varied Progress Toward Consolidation

If we set aside the core states and the microstates (states under one million population, which are overwhelmingly democratic and liberal; see Table 2 on the previous page), strikingly few other democracies in the world are clearly "consolidated." Among the longer-standing democracies in the developing world, one could count India (even with all its troubles), Costa Rica, Mauritius, and Botswana as consolidated. Venezuela and Colombia were both considered consolidated democracies in the 1970s and 1980s but have become destabilized and seriously threatened during the 1990s through economic mismanagement, corruption, and state decay. Indeed, the entire Andean region now suffers from a deep crisis of governance that is sharply eroding the authority and capacity of the state and public confidence in democratic institutions. Like Colombia, Sri Lanka's long-established democracy has sunk into illiberality and instability as a result of protracted internal violence— in this case, an ethnic civil war. In South America, only Uruguay shows the levels of elite and popular commitment to democracy that mark consolidation, though the recent presidential elections in both Argentina and Chile (as well as the growing readiness of Chile to confront the crimes of its authoritarian past) indicate progress toward consolidation.[14]

Significantly, the region where the most rapid and visible strides toward democratic consolidation are being made is the other half of Europe. In Central and Eastern Europe, formerly communist countries are slowly entrenching democratic practices and norms. Electoral returns, elite behavior, and mass attitudes and values (as revealed in public-opinion surveys) show a deepening commitment to democracy in Po-

land, Hungary, Slovenia, Estonia, Latvia, Lithuania, and (with some recent erosion) the Czech Republic. Slovakia, Bulgaria, and Romania have
also made progress in this regard. In a number of postcommunist states,
democratic orientations are especially strong among younger people;
hence, the political culture and party system figure to become more democratic as voters who have come of age in the postcommunist era become
more numerous.[15] Within a decade (or two at most), almost all of Europe
from the Atlantic to the former Soviet border is likely to consist of
consolidated liberal democracies, as integration into the European
Union and NATO helps to lock the new democracies into place.

Levels of freedom, democratic quality, and mass support for democracy are all considerably weaker in the former Soviet republics (excluding
the Baltic countries). In 1998, for example, Richard Rose found that 37
percent of Russians and 45 percent of Ukrainians said that they would
approve the suspension of parliament, while only 25 percent of
respondents from Central and Eastern Europe said that they would do
so.[16] In Russia, Ukraine, and other post-Soviet states, power is wielded
much more roughly, elections are much less democratic, corruption is
rife, state capacity is crippled, and the rule of law is routinely abused.

Civic Decay and the Triple Crisis of Governance

The travails of democracy in the post-Soviet states and in the Andean
countries mirror the three broad elements of political decay that led to
democratic breakdown in Pakistan: 1) the lack of accountability and a rule
of law, as evidenced in massive corruption, smuggling, drug-trafficking,
criminal violence, personalization of power, and human rights abuses; 2)
the inability to manage regional and ethnic divisions peacefully, in a way
that gives all groups of citizens a stake in the system; and 3) economic
crisis or stagnation, deepened by the failure to implement reforms to liberalize the economy and to rationalize and strengthen a corrupt bureaucracy.

These problems feed on one another, undermining confidence in all
public institutions and in the future. Fearful and distrustful, citizens shirk
their legal obligations, give up on civic life, and retreat into informal
institutions; some seek to emigrate or to send their children and money
abroad. Foreign investors shy away, unless they can make a quick killing
or find a secure niche in an economic enclave like oil.

As they gather momentum, these pathologies of governance choke
off the horizontal relations of trust, cooperation, honesty, reciprocity,
and public-spiritedness that constitute the social capital of a vigorous,
prosperous democratic society—what Robert Putnam calls the "civic
community." Unless these grave institutional weaknesses can be
remedied, the vicious cycles of the "uncivic community" take hold.
Lacking any faith in institutions or in one another, people fall into
hierarchical chains of dependence, seeking short-term gain or protection.

The civic engagement that could constrain the abuse of power and breed accountability and responsiveness wilts. In its place come unmediated conflict, opportunism, corruption, the ready resort to violence, populist mobilization of the masses, and the steady depletion of truly collective enterprises—the state, the nation, the legitimate economy. People are left feeling cheated, exploited, cynical, and dependent, becoming all the more ready to engage in behavior—and reward the type of leadership—that undermines democracy and effective governance, which renders them still more cynical and bereft of social capital.[17]

The disintegration of social capital and the bankruptcy of governance are alarmingly advanced in Pakistan and Nigeria. It is precisely the fierce interaction of these two dynamics—one cultural, the other institutional—that now propels these two immensely important and influential states toward collapse. None of the other swing states is in such grave and imminent danger. Yet the three broad crises of governance (legal, ethnic, and economic or administrative) afflict not only Latin America and the former Soviet Union but Africa and parts of Asia as well. In fact, they bear particularly heavily on the "swing-state" democracies, in part because many of them are large in population and territory and suffer acute regional and ethnic divisions. These divisions particularly diminish or endanger democracy in India, Turkey, Nigeria, Indonesia, Ethiopia, and, as we have seen, in Pakistan.

In 17 of the 30 swing states, the emergence or survival of democracy is threatened, or the consolidation of democracy is obstructed, by the three crises of governance.[18] These problems of governance—particularly corruption, crime, and the partisanship or weakness of the justice system—also plague most of the liberal democracies in this group, such as Korea, Taiwan, and the Czech Republic. They also loom as major obstacles to the development of democracy in most of the authoritarian swing states, such as China, Vietnam, and Egypt. In Iran, the blatant partisanship of the judicial system, controlled by the hard-line Islamic clergy, represents one of the most tenacious barriers to a genuine democratic transition. In short, among the strategic swing states, even more than among developing political systems in general, *democratic development and consolidation confront fundamental problems, even crises, of governance.* These must be urgently addressed if Pakistan is not to herald the reverse wave of the future.

Improving Governance

Every state is unique, but just as there are generic disorders of governance, there are also generic remedies. The crises of governance in the swing states are multidimensional; so must be the policy responses. Most of these emerging democracies suffer serious institutional deficits. Correcting these deficits will require building or revitalizing institutions.

1) Strengthening horizontal accountability. To be effective and
stable, a democratic state must be legitimate; to sustain popular legitimacy, it must be a "self-restraining state."[19] Common to all the troubled
democracies is the need for more (and more powerful) state institutions
to check the abuse of power by other state institutions and actors and to
ensure that state officials comply with the law, the constitution, and
norms of good governance.

The most important institution in this regard is the judicial system.
With a few exceptions, the legal systems of the swing-state democracies
are understaffed, underpaid, underfunded, ill-equipped, inefficient, and
much too susceptible to political direction and constraint. In the most
troubled cases, including Russia, Ukraine, Turkey, Brazil, Mexico,
Colombia, and Nigeria, corruption warps the administration of justice,
despite the presence of some courageous individual judges. As a result,
judiciaries lack public confidence. In Brazil, 70 percent of the public
distrusts the justice system; in the former communist countries, on
average 83 percent are skeptical of or distrust the courts.[20]

Comprehensive reforms are needed to modernize and professionalize
the judiciary and to insulate its appointment, remuneration, administration, and supervision from political influence. This requires giving
judges long terms (even life tenure), decent salaries, and autonomous
means for the financing of the judicial branch (administered by the supreme court or by an independent judicial council). Moreover, it means
giving judicial councils—made up of judges, retired judges, lawyers,
law professors, the bar association, and other nonpolitical (or less political) actors in civil society—primary say over appointing new judges,
elevating them to higher courts, and disciplining the profession. Judges
must be held accountable to high standards of ethics and performance.

Reform of the legal system must go beyond the judiciary to be effective. Standards for entry into the legal profession must be established
and regulated through impartial examinations. Prosecutors must be
insulated from partisan politics so that the personal interests of elected
officials cannot motivate or squelch prosecutions (as has happened even
in the "liberal" democracies of Korea and Taiwan). Systems for recording
and reporting court decisions need to be improved so that judges can be
held accountable and court rulings and proceedings can become standardized, transparent, and predictable. Legal codes need extensive revision,
particularly in Latin America and the postcommunist states.[21] In short,
the quest for more effective and independent judicial systems requires
reinforcement from complementary institutions, demand from below,
and support from the outside.

A genuine rule of law requires an overlapping, reinforcing system of
agencies of horizontal accountability. This involves the creation or empowerment of a number of other complementary institutions that are
truly independent of partisan politics: a counter-corruption commission,

human rights commission, ombudsman, auditor-general, and national electoral commission. A counter-corruption commission should be responsible for recovering annually declarations of assets from all elected officials and other high officeholders; making those declarations publicly available and scrutinizing and investigating them; bringing charges for bribery, embezzlement, influence-peddling, and other wrongdoing; and prosecuting violations before a court or special tribunal. A human rights commission should receive citizen complaints about violations of rights that are guaranteed under the constitution and international and regional covenants. It must have the legal authority and obligation to investigate those complaints, make its reports public, compensate victims, and recommend the removal or punishment of offending officials. Citizens should have the opportunity to register complaints about ill treatment and abuse of power by various state agencies with an ombudsman's commission that will investigate wrongdoing, report publicly, and recommend redress. An auditor general should have the authority to audit the accounts of any state agency periodically and on suspicion of any wrongdoing, and its findings must be made available to parliament and the public. The national electoral administration must see to it that vertical accountability can work by enabling voters to turn rotten incumbents out of office. It must ensure that opposing parties and candidates can campaign freely and with reasonable access to the media, and that citizens can vote freely and have their ballots counted fairly and accurately.

> *A genuine rule of law requires an overlapping, reinforcing system of agencies of horizontal accountability.*

Many emerging democracies have some or all of these institutions of horizontal accountability, but typically they do not function very effectively. Like the judicial systems in these countries, they are politically influenced or constrained and lack the resources and authority to do a serious job. All of these institutions need to be empowered. They need a huge infusion of human capital—training for judges, lawyers, prosecutors, paralegals, accountants, and technical and research support staff. And they need other, "harder" infusions of capital: more money for higher salaries, computers, and other equipment. Most of all, they need the political incentive and authority to exercise their functions. As with the judiciary, they must be institutionally isolated from political interference in appointments, supervision, administration, and funding. Countries need to design new bodies to oversee these agencies of horizontal accountability, drawn perhaps from the senior ranks of the judiciary or respected actors in civil society who are at least somewhat removed from partisan politics.

2) Empowering civil society. Strengthening state institutions alone will not ensure the rule of law or control corruption. An effective reform strategy also requires strengthening the capacity of professional and civic associations, think tanks, the mass media, and independent interest groups (including trade unions and business chambers). These actors in civil society must mobilize vigorously to generate broad societal demand for institutional reforms. They also can provide an additional and independent arena for monitoring government performance, thus both checking and reinforcing the conduct of the relevant formal agencies of horizontal accountability (investigative media are vitally important in this regard). In addition, civil-society organizations and mass media need to educate citizens so that they can defend their rights and support the institutions of horizontal accountability. And legal-aid organizations and human rights groups can help citizens, particularly the poor and marginalized, to make use of these institutions of accountability. In these direct ways and through their own internal functioning, civil-society organizations and independent media can help stop the descent into the fragmented, cynical world of the uncivic community by generating a different set of expectations based on cooperation and respect for law and properly exercised state authority.

3) Mediating conflict and reframing the national bargain. The challenges to the peace and integrity of the nation-state are diverse, but all derive in one way or another from the feeling of some groups that they are excluded from a fair share of power and resources or are otherwise victimized by the groups that control the central state. Big and diverse countries such as India, Nigeria, Indonesia, Russia, Turkey, and Brazil cannot be held together democratically unless aggrieved groups and regions feel they have a stake—and a safe, dignified place— in the nation-state. The challenge of constructing this is far too complex to survey even briefly here, but everywhere there are at least two requirements. First, every group deserves the right to use its culture and language and to have its group identity respected and protected in the larger system. Turkey's historic reluctance to acknowledge these rights for the Kurdish people has played a large role in that country's long, debilitating civil violence. Second, territorially based groups—the Kurds of southeastern Turkey, the Chechens in Russia, the Acehnese (and numerous others) in Indonesia, the besieged Kashmiris in India, the indigenous people of Chiapas in Mexico, or the long-exploited minority peoples of Nigeria's oil-rich delta—need real political autonomy if they are to surrender their aspirations for total independence. This need not always mean a fully federal system (in Turkey, Indonesia, and South Africa, federalism is so culturally or historically tainted that it may never be politically acceptable), but it must grant aggrieved regions a constitutionally embedded right to some meaningful self-government, including the ability to mobilize and use a good share of their resources for their own development. None of the affected countries can achieve stable, liberal democracy until it resolves its ethnic and regional insurgencies through negotiations along these lines.

4) Economic and state reform. Creating the foundations for sustained, vigorous economic growth involves streamlining and strengthening the state while restructuring and liberalizing the economy. Liberalization (to reduce state distortion and obstruction of the market) and privatization of inefficient industries cannot succeed unless state capacity is reformed and enhanced. State bureaucracies need both training and comprehensive regulatory reform to become more professional and efficient at collecting taxes, guaranteeing property rights, registering new enterprises, approving new construction, and exercising prudential regulation of banking, finance, insurance, and securities markets. Liberalization and privatization cannot succeed or gain public legitimacy unless the legal institutions of horizontal accountability function effectively to deter, expose, and punish the corruption and brazen insider dealings that have broadly discredited structural economic reforms in countries such as Russia, Mexico, Nigeria, and of late, the Czech Republic.

5) Rooting and strengthening political parties. The problems afflicting the troubled democracies can be solved only with more skillful, responsive, transparent governance. In a good half of the strategic swing states today, democracy hangs in the balance. It may not yet be hanging from a thread (as, in retrospect, it clearly was in Pakistan), but it is very far from secure. Better governance means improving the performance and integrity of the state, but in a democracy that cannot be accomplished without politics. Many of the needed reforms require legislative action. In a country plagued with multiple crises of governance, mobilizing a sustainable coalition for reform is a maddeningly difficult but quintessentially political task—as President Fernando Henrique Cardoso has discovered in Brazil.

In a democracy, crafting such a coalition must involve political parties. It is political parties that in the end must bargain, coalesce, and produce the votes for reform in parliament. Political parties must be involved in mobilizing popular support in society and in linking the grievances of citizens and the demands of interest groups to an agenda for institutional reform. In all of the troubled democracies, and even in such liberal ones as Korea and the Czech Republic, parties are in disrepute and have yet to sink (or reestablish) deep and enduring roots in the society. The crises of governance cannot be resolved democratically without reforming and rebuilding political parties. This means enhancing their organizational coherence and capacity, democratizing

and making more transparent their own internal governance, and forti-
fying their autonomy through (at least partial) public financing of parties
and election campaigns.

Forward or Backward?

The global democratic prospect is less rosy than the aggregate
numbers imply. Beneath the high tide of freedom in the world lurk
multiple, interrelated crises of governance that could cause democracy to recede dramatically by inducing breakdowns in influential
swing states, whose failures would lower the threshold for the overthrow
of democracy in neighboring countries. The future of democracy
globally will depend on a vigorous, coordinated, and timely response
to the crises of governance, directed in particular at the troubled swing
states.

The situation is not without hope. From Thailand to Brazil, from
Korea to Argentina, reform is at least on the agenda. And the crises of
governance also threaten authoritarian regimes, as in China, Iran, and
Egypt. As Indonesia is discovering, however, regime transition driven
by a breakdown of governance does not leave a very favorable legacy
for a new democracy.

The necessary reform agenda is expensive and politically difficult to
swallow. International actors have a crucial role to play in pressing
these reforms, in supporting civil society actors who see the need for
them, and in providing the financial and technical resources needed to
help construct or strengthen the necessary institutions. An international
commitment to reform, with distinct institution-building targets and
country priorities, could transform an increasingly precarious global
situation. Alternatively, a failure of will or a lack of clear vision could
squander an unparalleled opportunity to build a truly democratic world.

NOTES

1. Adrian Karatnycky, "The 1999 Freedom House Survey: A Century of Progress,"
Journal of Democracy 11 (January 2000): 187–200.

2. U.S. Department of State, *1999 Country Reports on Human Rights Practices*
(Washington, D.C.: U.S. Government Printing Office, 1999). Available online at
www.state.gov/www/global/human_rights/1999_hrp_report/overview.html.

3. Samuel P. Huntington, *The Third Wave: Democratization in the Late Twentieth
Century* (Norman: University of Oklahoma Press, 1991), 14, 18–21.

4. The following account draws from: Ameen Jan, "Pakistan on a Precipice," *Asian
Survey* 39 (September–October 1999): 699–719; Leo Rose and D. Hugh Evans, "Pakistan's
Enduring Experiment," *Journal of Democracy* 8 (January 1997): 83–94; and U.S.
Department of State, *1999 Country Reports on Human Rights Practices,
www.state.gov/www/global/human_rights/1999_hrp_report/pakistan.html.* I also
thank Ameen Jan and Erik Jensen for their comments.

5. Leo Rose and D. Hugh Evans, "Pakistan's Enduring Experiment," 89.

6. Ameen Jan, "Pakistan on a Precipice," 702.

7. World Bank, *World Development Report 1999/2000* (New York: Oxford University Press, 2000), 235, 251.

8. Ameen Jan, "Pakistan on a Precipice," 708.

9. On the relationship between state capacity and the viability of democracy, see Juan J. Linz and Alfred Stepan, *Problems of Democratic Transition and Consolidation: Southern Europe, South America, and Post-Communist Europe* (Baltimore: Johns Hopkins University Press, 1996).

10. Djibouti, the Kyrgyz Republic, Liberia, Niger, and Sierra Leone had levels of coercion and fraud that made their recent national elections less than free and fair. Other countries rated as electoral democracies by Freedom House had national elections sufficiently dubious to put them on the margin of "electoral democracy." These include Russia, Ukraine, Nigeria, and Indonesia.

11. For a fuller description, see Larry Diamond, *Developing Democracy: Toward Consolidation* (Baltimore: Johns Hopkins University Press, 1999), 10–12.

12. As medium-sized countries such as Romania grow economically, they will become more consequential and may already merit inclusion in the second tier of swing states. In fact, Central and Eastern Europe can be considered a "swing region" whose movement toward liberal and consolidated democracy will have a significant global impact.

13. Adrian Karatnycky, "The 1999 Freedom House Survey," 189.

14. Steven Levitsky, "The 'Normalization' of Argentine Politics," Arturo Fontaine Talavera, "Chile's Elections: The New Face of the Right," and Manuel Antonio Garretón, "Chile's Elections: Change and Continuity," all in *Journal of Democracy* 11 (April 2000): 56–84.

15. Marta Lagos and Richard Rose, *Young People in Politics: A Multi-Continental Survey* (Glasgow: University of Strathclyde Studies in Public Policy No. 316, 1999), 33 and Table A2.

16. Richard Rose, *New Russia Barometer Trends Since 1992* (Glasgow: University of Strathclyde, Studies in Public Policy No. 320, 1999), 48.

17. Robert D. Putnam, *Making Democracy Work: Civic Traditions in Modern Italy* (Princeton, N.J.: Princeton University Press, 1993).

18. The affected states are Russia, Ukraine, Turkey, Brazil, Argentina, Venezuela, Colombia, Peru, Mexico, India, Bangladesh, the Philippines, Thailand, Indonesia, Nigeria, South Africa, and Ethiopia.

19. Andreas Schedler, Larry Diamond, and Marc F. Plattner, eds., *The Self-Restraining State: Power and Accountability in New Democracies* (Boulder, Colo.: Lynne Rienner, 1999).

20. Pilar Domingo, "Judicial Independence and Judicial Reform in Latin America," in Andreas Schedler et al., eds., *The Self-Restraining State,* 156; Richard Rose, William Mishler, and Christian Haerpfer, *Democracy and Its Alternatives: Understanding Post-Communist Societies* (Baltimore: Johns Hopkins University Press, 1999), 154.

21. For an excellent regional overview of the challenges, see Pilar Domingo, "Judicial Independence and Judicial Reform in Latin America," 151–75.

INDEX

Abiola, Mashood, 356
Aceh, 216
Adams, John, 241–42
Africa: constitutional case law in, 271; crises of governance in, 364; establishment of constitutional courts in, 269–71; judicial independence in, 261; judicial reform and review in, 260; legal education in, 272; postcolonial democracies in, 135; use of legal precedents in judiciary of, 272
Ahimsa, 20
Al-Afghani, Jamal-Eddin, 38
Albania, 327–28; 1996 elections in, 209; collapse of the state in, 332
Alemán, Arnoldo, 254
Alfonsin, Raul, 247
Alianza Popular (Spain), 136
Allende, Salvador, 246
Ambedkar, B.R., 218
American colonies, 81
American Council of Learned Societies, 131
American National Election Study, 302
American Revolution, 4
American Sociological Review, 180
Amnesty International, 32
Andean region: crisis of government in, 362; integration with the

United States, 322–23
Andropov, Yuri, 343
Angola, 201
Anti–Ballistic Missile Treaty, 343
APRA (Peru), 192
Aquino, Corazon, 24
ARENA (El Salvador), 252
Argentina, 115, 143, 145, 159, 169, 177, 227, 246, 250, 255; "convertibility law" in, 251
Armenia: "federal bargain" in, 218
Ashoka, 14
Asia Watch, 32
"Asian values," 16, 20, 23, 26, 33, 35
Assembly of Tibetan Peoples' Deputies, 20
Australia, 219, 227, 359
Austria, 195, 227
Authoritarian regimes: downfall of, 78
Authoritarianism, 23, 27
Authority: group-oriented attitudes toward, 32
Azerbaijan: "federal bargain" in, 218

Bagehot, Walter, 173
Balaguer, Joaquin, 257
Balkans: three crises of communism in, 329
Bangladesh, 13, 181
Banks, Arthur S., 176

Barro, Robert, 7
Basaev, Shammil, 334
Basque National Party, 137
Basque region, 135, 142
Batasuna, Henri, 137
Belarus, 327
Belgium: constitution of, 218;
    group-specific rights in, 228;
    holding-together federalism in,
    218; as a multinational
    democracy, 216
Benda, Vaclav, 330
Benin, 145
Bentham, Jeremy, 82
Berlin Wall: fall of, 292
Bhattacharya, Mohit, 218
Bhutto, Benazir, 356
Bibo, Istvan, 331
Bickel, Alexander, 260
Binder, Leonard, 41
Blair, Tony, 343
Bobitsky, Andrei, 344
Bolívar, Simon, 175
Bolivia, 115, 143, 145, 179, 192,
    196–97
Bollen, Kenneth A., 180
Bordón, José Octavio, 251
Bosnia-Herzegovina: 1996 elections
    in, 212; war in, 332
Bosnian Federation, 212
Botswana, 8, 359, 362
Brazil, 99, 143, 145, 146, 181, 192,
    195, 196, 227, 246, 317, 253–
    54; Congress of, 196;
    constitution of, 221, 225;
    economic performance of, 254;
    effect of Asian financial crisis
    on, 254; federal system in, 220;
    need for conflict mediation in,
    367; presidential impeachment
    in, 256; referendum in, 176;
    upper-house representation in,
    220
Brazil Party of National
    Reconstruction, 188

Brazilian Social Democratic Party,
    254
Britain, 81; declining political
    confidence in, 304
Brizola, Leonel, 146
Brubaker, Rogers, 102
Bucaram, Abdala, 257
Buddhism, 18–19, 28
Budennocsk: Chechen raid on, 334
Bulgaria, 332; economic reform in,
    328, 329, 363
"Burgeresellschaft," 330
Burma, 13, 20

Cairo, 15
Cambio 90 (Peru), 188
Cambodia, 201, 356
Canada, 187, 359; declining
    political confidence in, 304;
    group-specific rights in, 228;
    as a multinational democracy,
    216
Cardoso, Fernando Henrique, 253,
    317, 368
Caribbean: economic integration
    with the United States, 321
Carnegie Council on Ethics and
    International Affairs, 13
Catalonia, 105
Cavallo, Domingo, 251
Ceauşescu, Nicolae, 329
Central America: economic
    integration with the United
    States, 321
Central Asia: Russians in, 105
Central Europe: democratic
    transitions in, 327
Chamorro, Violeta, 254
Charfi, Mohamed, 40, 43, 48
Charter of Tibetans in Exile, 20
Chávez, Hugo, 312, 314
Chechnya: human rights in, 343;
    war in, 334
Checks and balances: importance of
    within government, 284

Chile, 93, 99, 114, 115, 117, 137, 145, 156, 169, 171, 187, 246; GDP of, 246

China, 7, 20, 28, 30, 31, 348, 361; adoption of democracy in, 349; bandit capitalism in, 231; citizenship and, 30; communist leadership of, 31; MFN status and, 23; National People's Congress of, 348; "New Democracy," 351; People's Armed Police of, 348; state-owned enterprises (SOEs) in, 351; transition to a free economy in, 231; village elections in, 348

Chinese Communist Party (CCP), 349; 15th Congress of, 351

Christianity, 28, 32; Orthodox, 332; Western, 332

Chubais, Anatoly, 341

Citizenship: inclusive and equal, 105–6

Civil society, 31; conditions for, 96–99; definition of, 96

Civilian control: challenges of, 275–76; characteristics of, 276; measurements of, 278; requirements for, 279–82

Cold War: end of, 292

Collier, David, 151

Colombia, 115, 362; drop in oil prices in, 320; earthquake in, 320; inadequate constitutional democracy in, 319; insurgent movements in, 312; judicial corruption in, 365

Comprehensive Test Ban Treaty, 343

"Concept-stretching," 218

Concertación (Chile), 250

Confucianism, 27; Chinese, 29, 31; personal ethic of, 28; political, 28

Confucius, 14

Congo (Brazzaville), 356

Congo (Kinshasa), 181

Consolidated democracy:

characteristics of, 94; definition of, 95; types of, 95–96

Consolidation: democratic, 150, 185; full, 133; positive, 133; stages of, 144

Consolidology, 150, 159

Constatinescu, Emil, 328

Constitutional courts: membership of, 270

Constructive importance, 10

Coppedge-Reinecke scale, 181

Costa Rica, 115, 143, 313, 315, 362

Country Reports on Human Rights Practices, 1999, 355

Crisis of Democracy, The, 292, 293

Croatia, 332

Crozier, Michel J., 291, 304, 308

"Cultural relativists," 26

Cultural Revolution, 232

Czech Republic, 20, 143, 145, 195, 327, 329, 331, 363; party identification in, 191

Czechoslovakia, 328; demise of federalism in, 331

Dagestan: Chechen incursion into, 334

Dahl, Robert A., 93, 113, 132, 145, 150, 167, 171, 202–3

Dalai Lama, 20

de Mello, Fernando Collar, 188, 192

Declaration of Independence, 80

Declaration of the Constitution of the Commonwealth of Massachusetts, 241

Declaration of the Rights of Man and Citizen, 80

Democracies: advanced, 151; civilian control as a measure of progress toward, 275; classifications of, 144; Confucian, 27; Confucianism and, 23, 31; "consociational," 105; economic growth and, 170;

Democracies *(cont'd)*
electoral, 150; illiberal, 157;
incomplete, 113; Indian, 106;
Italian, 142; limited, 138;
multinational, 216; poverty and,
177; presidential, 99; pseudo-,
138; rate of investment in poor,
168; rise of, 3; Spanish, 142;
stabilization of, 154; survival of,
171, 178; third-wave, 185;
unconsolidated, 145
Democracy in America, 84
Democradura, 155
Democratic Convergence (El
Salvador), 252
Democratic development: UN
support for, 201; Western
support for, 201
Democratic regimes: public support
for, 136
Democratic transition, 103
Democratization, 355
Demos, 103
Deng Xiaoping, 351
Denmark, 217
Diamond, Larry, 169, 170
Diamondouros, P. Nikiforos, 140
Dictatorships: rate of investment in,
168
Disraeli, Benjamin, 85
*Dissertation on the First Principles
of Government,* 82
Dominican Republic, 114, 179, 257,
313; immigration to the United
States from, 322
Dreyfuss, Ruth, 4
Drèze, Jean, 8
Duma (Russian Parliament), 339;
1995 election of, 196

ETA (Basque separatist movement),
137
Euro-Atlantic integration, 332
East Asia, 35
East-Central European countries:

economic well-being in, 108–9
Eastern Europe: democratic
transitions in, 327
Economic society, 100–1;
institutionalized, 99
Ecuador, 115, 192, 196, 197, 245,
257; lack of constitutional
democracy in, 319; oil prices in,
320
Education: Confucian emphasis on,
28
Egypt, 361
El Niño, 320
El Salvador, 25, 114, 252–53, 369
Elections: defining free and fair, 202
England, 26; party identification in,
191; Putin's attention to, 343
Eritrea, 201
Essay on Government, 83
Estenssoro, Víctor Paz, 255
Estonia, 104, 363
Ethiopia, 8, 361; regional and ethnic
divisions in, 364
Eurobarometer survey, 136
Europe, 12; postcommunist
countries of, 108; trust of
politicians in, 297
European Union (EU), 229, 293,
332

Fatherland-All Russia electoral bloc,
338, 339
Fay, Michael, 23, 34
Federal Security Service (FSB), 344
Federalism, American-style, 218;
goals of, 217; risks and benefits
of, 215
Federation Council (Russia), 342
Filmer, Sir Robert, 80
Finland, 192, 217
First Treatise on Government, 80
Foreign Affairs, 78
France, 102, 175, 177; 1968 student
riots in, 292
Franco, Francisco, 136

Free trade agreements, 248–49
Free Trade Area of the Americas
    (FTAA), 320
Freedom House, 355, 358
Frei, Eduardo, 246
French Revolution, 4, 81
FREPASO (Argentina), 251
Fujimori, Alberto, 114, 188, 192,
    255, 312, 314

Gaidar, Yegor, 341–42
Gambia, The, 356
Gandhi, Mahatma, 12, 20
Gastil scale, 181
Gellner, Ernest, 37, 104, 331
Georgia, "federal bargain" in, 218
Germany, 102, 175, 332;
    Bundestag, 297; declining
    political confidence in, 304;
    federal system in, 220; as
    symmetrical federation, 227
Ghana, 181; Bill of Rights in, 262;
    Constitution of, 261-262;
    freedom of expression in, 262,
    266; "Friends of Freedom of
    Expression," 263; judicial
    autonomy in, 261; Supreme
    Court in, 262
Gini index, 221
Gladstone, William Ewart, 85
Glendon, Mary Ann, 34
González, Felipe, 247
Goodwin-Gill, Guy, 211
Gorbachev, Mikhail, 336
Goulart, João, 246
Government performance:
    measuring political satisfaction
    in, 306–08
Great Britain: partisanship in, 302
Great Leap Forward, 8
Greece, 102, 131, 133, 141, 145,
    147, 185, 191
Greek-Turkish rivalry, 195
Gref, German, 342
Grozny: demolition of, 335

Guidelines for Future Tibet's
    Policy, 21
Gulf War, 296
Gunther, Richard P., 140
Gurr scales, 181

Haiti, 114, 201; immigration to the
    United States from, 322; lack
    of constitutional democracy in,
    319
Hapsburg Empire, 106
Havel, Václav, 231, 243
Hegemonic-party systems, 156
Himmelfarb, Gertrude, 85
Hirschman, Albert, 170
Hitler, Adolf, 331
Hobbes, Thomas, 252
Hodgson, Marshall G.S., 41
Holding-together federalism, 218
Honduras, 114
Hong Kong, 79, 350, 352–353;
    Chinese rule in, 232
Hoxha, Enver, 329
Hungary, 143, 145, 327–28, 363;
    1956 Revolution, 329; economic
    reform in, 329; party
    identification in, 191
Huntington, Samuel P., 16, 27, 30,
    32, 33, 145, 155, 169, 170, 187,
    291, 304, 308, 332
Hurricane Georges, 320
Hurricane Mitch, 320

Illia, Arturo, 246
Illiberal democracies: debate about,
    330
India, 5, 20, 106, 359, 362;
    consociational practices in, 216;
    constitution of, 218, 225; federal
    system in, 220; group-specific
    rights in, 228; Hindu nationalists
    in, 106; "holding-together"
    federalism in, 218; Kashmiris in,
    367; as multinational democracy,
    106; need for conflict mediation

India *(cont'd)*
     in, 367; regional and ethnic
     divisions in, 364
Indonesia, 9, 13, 20, 216; Acehnese
     in, 367; need for conflict
     mediation in, 367; regional and
     ethnic divisions in, 364; tainted
     federalism in, 367
Institutionalism: definition of, 187
International Covenant on
     Economic, Social and Cultural
     Rights, 87
Iran, 343, 365
Irian Jaya, 216
Israel, 359
Italy, 141, 142, 187, 195; demands
     for electoral reform in, 302; "Hot
     Autumn" in, 292; party systems
     in, 161

Jabri, Mohamed Abed, 45, 46
Jackman, Robert W., 180
Jamaica, 255; immigration to the
     United States from, 322
Japan, 24, 27, 33, 35, 102, 146,
     298, 359; "bubble economy" in,
     25; culture of, 25; demand for
     electoral reforms in, 302
Jiang Zemin, 351
Judicial review, 88
Jurisprudence: asymmetrical, 261;
     of constitutionalism, 264, 265,
     267, 271; of executive
     supremacy, 264; illiberal, 268
Justicialist Party (Argentina), 188

Kashmir, 356
Kasyanov, Mikhail, 342
Kazakhstan, 327
Kenya, 356; 1992 presidential
     elections in, 208; Bill of Rights
     in, 265
Kenya African National Unity party,
     208
Kerala, Indian state of, 11

Khakamada, Irina, 341
"Khalifa rachida," 42
Kirienko, Sergei, 341
Kohl, Helmut, 293
Korea, 27
Kosovo, 332
Kotowski, Christoph, 159
KPRF (Communist Party of the
     Russian Federation), 337, 340
Kubitschek, Juscelino, 246
Kudrin, Aleksei, 342
Kwaniewski, Aleksander, 338

Laitin, David, 105
Latin America, 31, 113, 138, 143,
     145, 156, 176, 181; authoritarian
     regimes in, 153–54; credit
     ratings in, 315; crises of
     governance in, 364; democratic
     rule in, 245; economic progress
     in, 316; economies of, 313; lack
     of basic entitlements in, 99;
     Mercosur region of, 316; moves
     toward free-market economies
     in, 316; political and economic
     malpractice in, 257; primary
     exports from, 320; shared
     challenges and dilemmas in,
     324–26; Southern Cone
     countries of, 169; "technopols"
     in, 247
Latinobarómetro survey, 191, 195
Latvia, 104, 363
Lebanon, 356
Lebed, Aleksandr, 6, 192, 335
"Lee Hypothesis" the, 6, 341
Lee Kuan Yew, 6, 23, 27
Lesotho, 356
Leviathan, 252
Levitsky, Steven, 151
Liberal democracy, 25
Liberal Democratic Party (Japan),
     25, 35, 298
Liberal Democratic Party of Russia,
     341

Liberal-democratic constitutions: language of obligation in, 265; language of restraint in, 265; limitation clauses in, 266
Liberal Party (Nicaragua), 255
Liberalism: democratization of, 81
Liberalization, 179
Liberalized nondemocratic regimes, 94
Liberty, Equality, Fraternity, 85
Lijphart, Arend, 105
Linz, Juan J., 116, 132, 145, 156, 170–73, 179
Lipset, Seymour Martin, 24, 169, 169–70, 177
Lithuania, 363
Locke, John, 80–81
Lowe, Robert, 85
Luzhkov, Yuri, 338
MacAllister, Ian, 191, 194
MacArthur, Douglas, 25
Macaulay, Thomas Babington, 83–84
Magna Carta, 4
Mahuad, Jamil, 257, 314
Maimonides, 15
Mainwaring, Scott, 174
Maitreyee, 11
Majoritarianism: political, 86
Malawi, 145, 201; constitution of, 269
Malaysia, 239, 361
Malthusian doctrine, 84
Manley, Michael, 255
Mao Zedong, 350–51
Market autonomy, 100
Market economics, 87
Market reform, 107
Mauritius, 362
Media-Most, 335, 344
Meir, Yehuda Ben, 281
Menem, Carlos, 250, 255
Mexico, 114, 156, 188, 317, 361; discredited economic reforms in, 368; drop in oil prices in, 320;

"effective suffrage" in, 318; electoral fairness in, 324; indigenous people of Chiapas, 367; judicial corruption in, 365; revenue-sharing schemes in, 257; silent integration with the United States, 321;1994
Michnik, Adam, 329
Middle East, 15
Military policy: civilian control of, 282–84
Mill, John Stuart, 86
Mills, James, 83–84
Minorities: representation of, 105
Misery of the Small Nations of Eastern Europe, The, 331
Modernization hypothesis, 34
Modernization theory, 24, 26
Moi, Daniel arap, 208
Moldova, 327
Monarchy: abolition of, 175
Mongolia, 20, 207
Mongolian People's Revolutionary Party, 207
"Montana Freemen," 133
Moore, Barrington, 329
Morganthau Memorial Lecture, 13
Moscow, terrorist bombings in, 334–35
Moser, Robert G., 191
Mozambique, 201
Muller, Edward N., 170
Musharraf, Pervez, 357
Muttahida Qawmi Movement (Pakistan), 357

NAFTA, 313, 320
Nakasone, Yasuhiro, 293
Namibia, 201
Nanyang, 30
Nationalism in China and Japan, 30; World War II and, 32
National Renovation party (Chile), 250
NATO, 332

Nehru, Jawaharlal, 106
Nemtsov, Boris, 341
New Zealand, 359; demands for
    electoral reform in, 302
Niblock, Tim, 44, 46
Nicaragua, 115, 201, 254–55, 313
Niger, 356
Nigeria, 179, 181, 356; 1983
    military coup in, 355; 1993
    election in, 356; crises of
    governance in, 364; discredited
    economic reforms in, 368;
    judicial corruption in, 365;
    minority peoples in, 367; need
    for conflict mediation in, 367;
    regional and ethnic divisions in,
    364
Nonviolence, 20
Norway, 192
NTV (Russian TV network), 335

O'Donnell, Guillermo, 146, 153,
    155, 156, 169, 193, 197
OECD, 328
Oil crisis: of 1973–74, 292; of
    1979–80, 292
Olson, Mancur, 170
ORT (Russian TV network), 341
Ottoman Empire, 106
Ownership diversity, 100
Oxford English Dictionary, 106

Paine, Thomas, 82
Pakistan, 13, 181; 1999 military
    coup in, 356; corruption in, 358;
    crises of governance in, 364;
    drug smuggling from, 358; rates
    of illiteracy in, 358; Shi'ite
    Muslims in, 357; Sunni Muslims
    in, 357; terrorist training and
    financing in, 356; unemployment
    in, 358
Panama, 115, 145
Paraguay, 114, 156, 195; lack of
    constitutional democracy in, 319

Park, Chung Hee, 349
Parsons, Talcott, 25
Partial regimes, 161
Particularism, 119–24
Party loyalty, 301–2
Party systems: East European, 185;
    institutionalized, 185; Latin
    American, 185
Pastrana, Andrés, 314
Pérez, Carlos Andrés, 255
Perón, Isabel, 246
Perón, Juan, 188
Peru, 114, 115, 187, 192, 195, 196,
    197, 239, 255, 356, 361;
    electoral volatility in, 189; lack of
    constitution democracy in, 319;
    pork-barrel spending in, 257
Philippines, 24, 25, 27, 181, 359
Pinochet, Augusto, 137, 246, 343
Poland, 143, 145, 159, 191, 195,
    327, 328, 362, 363; 1990
    presidential election, 193;
    economic reform in, 329
Polis, 103, 107
Polish-Lithuanian Commonwealth,
    106
Political alienation: Harris Poll of,
    296
Political conflict: resolving, 95
"Political identities," 157
Political development: sequence of,
    106
Political parties: electoral volatility
    and, 190; societal roots in, 190
Political society: definition of, 96
The Politics of Democratic
    Consolidation: Southern Europe
    in Comparative Perspective, 131
Pol Pot, 232
Polyarchies, institutionalized, 117–
    20, 146; Latin American, 146;
    Southern European, 146
Polyarchy, 113–18, 167; definition
    of, 115
Portugal, 102, 131, 141, 185, 191,

195
Prague Spring, 329
PRI (Mexico), 188, 317
Pridham, Geoffrey, 133
Primakov, Yevgeny, 338
Privatization, 107
Proportional representation, 105,
    220
Przeworski, Adam, 7, 178, 219
Puhle, Hans-Jürgen, 140
Putin, Vladimir, 333
Putnam, Robert, 363

Qur'an, 40

Radio Liberty, 344
Rahman, Fazur, 42, 47
Reagan, Ronald, 293
Rechstaat (State of law), 98
Red Brigades (Italy), 133
Reform Act of 1867 (United
    Kingdom), 85
Renan, Ernest, 38
Republica Serbska, 212
Riker, William H., 217–18, 219
Romania, 328, 332, 363; economic
    reform in, 329
Rose, Richard, 191, 194
Rousseau, Jean Jacques, 172
Rule of law, 96, 97; creation of,
    366–67; Muslims and, 48
Russia, 171, 191, 196, 327, 332;
    1992 coup in, 172; 2000 election
    in, 333; bandit capitalism in, 231;
    Chechens in, 367; democracy in,
    345; discredited economic
    reforms in, 368; judicial
    corruption in, 365; need for
    conflict mediation in, 367
Saladin, Sultan, 15
Sandinista government, 254
Santillana, 42
Sarney, José, 247
Sartori, Giovanni, 160, 200
Saudi Arabia, 361

"Savage capitalism," 318
Schattschneider, E.E., 300
Schmitter. Philippe C., 158–59
Schneider, Ben, 153
Schumpeter, Joseph, 300
Second Treatise of Government, 80
Secularism: Muslims and, 39–40
Sen, Amyarta, 233
Shari'a, 42–45
Sharif, Nawaz, 356
Shevardnadze, Eduard, 338–39
Shugart, Matthew, 174
Shura, 44
Sierra Leone, 356
Sindh Province (Pakistan): political
    violence in, 357
Singapore, 6, 7, 23, 27, 29, 31, 33,
    361; GNP of, 360
Skach, Cindy, 174
Slovakia, 332, 363; party
    identification in, 191, 195
Slovenia, 143, 145, 363
Smith, Adam, 100–1
Smith, Wilfred Cantwell, 39
Social Science Research Council,
    131
Societies, Asian, 33; rights of the,
    19
Sol, Armando Calderón, 252
Solidarity (Poland), 329
Somalia, 8
South Africa, 20, 201, 205, 362;
    Constitution of, 268;
    Independent Electoral
    Commission of, 208; tainted
    federalism in, 367
South Korea, 7, 9, 13, 24, 25, 33,
    143, 168, 181, 340, 362
Southern Europe, 145; new
    democracies in, 359
Southeast Asia, 24
Soviet Union, 8; crises of
    governance in former, 364;
    demise of federalism in, 331;
    former, 350; former republics of,

Soviet Union *(cont'd)*
22, 104; nostalgia for, 340;
"putting-together" federalism in,
219; support for democracy in
former, 363
Spain, 131, 133, 141, 142, 145,
185, 191, 195, 247; 1981 coup
attempt in, 142; constitution of,
218; "holding-together"
federalism in, 218; as
multinational democracy, 216;
socialists in, 248
Sri Lanka, 216, 362
Stalin, Joseph, 331
START II, 343
State bureaucracy: use of in
postcommunist Europe, 100
"State-nations," 106
Statism: Word War II and, 32
Stepan, Alfred, 156, 174
Stephen, James Fitzjames, 85
Suharto, 349
Suriname, 181
Sweden, 192; declining political
confidence in, 304; partisanship
in, 302; Riksdag (parliament),
297
Switzerland, 219, 225; as
multinational democracy, 216; as
state-nation, 106

Tagore, Rabindranath, 12
Taha, Mohamed Mahmoud, 47
Taiwan, 20, 27, 168, 349, 350, 362
Talbi, Mohamed, 48
Tamil Nadu (Indian state), 11
Tanzania: 1994 local elections in,
208
Thailand, 9, 13; 1991 military coup
in, 355
Thatcher, Margaret, 293
Third wave, 149. See also
Democracies; Democratization
Tiananmen Square, 31
Tibet, 20

Tito, Josip Broz, 329
Titov, Konstantin, 341
Tocqueville, Alexis de, 34, 227
Togoland, 201
Touraine, Alain, 48
Trilateral Commission, 295
Trilateral countries, competitiveness
in, 293; governments of, 292;
political skepticism in, 303
Trinidad and Tobago, 313
Trust index, 195
Tue, Wei-ming, 28
Turkey: group-specific rights in,
228; judicial corruption in, 365;
Kurds in, 368; need for conflict
mediation in, 367; regional and
ethnic division in, 364; tainted
federalism in, 367
Tyminski, Stanisław, 192

Uganda, 181; 1994 elections in, 200
Ukraine, 327; judicial corruption in,
365
UNECLAC (UN Economic
Commission for Latin America
and the Caribbean), 246, 252,
313
Union of Right Forces (SPS,
Russia), 341
United Kingdom, 228–29
United Nations, 86–87
United States, 26, 27, 33, 219, 359;
Constitution of, 225, 268;
democratic surge in, 291;
Department of State, 355;
elections in, 190; electoral
volatility in, 189; federal system
in, 220; group-specific rights in,
217; partisanship in, 302;
political confidence in, 304;
political disenchantment in, 296;
as state-nation, 106; symmetrical
federalism in, 217, 227; upper
house representation in, 20
Unity bloc (Russia), 339

Universal Declaration of Human
    Rights, 86
Uruguay, 69, 115, 143, 145, 169,
    187, 191, 195, 315
Upanishads, 11

Valenzuela, J. Samuel, 156
"Velvet divorce," 104
Venezuela, 115, 187, 195, 255, 362;
    floods in, 320; inadequate
    constitutional democracy in, 319;
    oil prices in, 320; presidential
    impeachment in, 256
Vietnam, 27, 361
Villalobos, Joaquin, 252
Vinaya, 19

Watanuki, Joji, 291, 304, 308
Wealth of Nations, 101
Weber, Max, 331–32
Weberian states, 102
Western Europe: parliamentary
    system in, 181
White, Stephen, 194
World Bank, 170, 239
World Values Survey, 304
World War II: Austria, Germany,
    and Italy after, 198

Yabloko party (Russia), 338, 341
Yajnvalkya, 11
Yavlinsky, Grigory, 338, 340
Yeltsin, Boris, 114, 192, 334
Yugoslavia, 107, 328, 331, 332,
    343, 350; demise of federalism
    in the former, 331; wars in the
    former, 332

Zakaria, Fareed, 78–79, 88
Zambia, 356
Zamora, Ruben, 252
Zedillo, Ernesto, 257
Zhirinovsky, Vladimir, 340, 341
Zyuganov, Gennady, 337, 340